# Grenada
## Carriacou • Petite Martinique

the Bradt Travel Guide

**Paul Crask**

edition

www.bradtguides.com

Bradt Travel Guides Ltd, UK
The Globe Pequot Press Inc, USA

D0789656

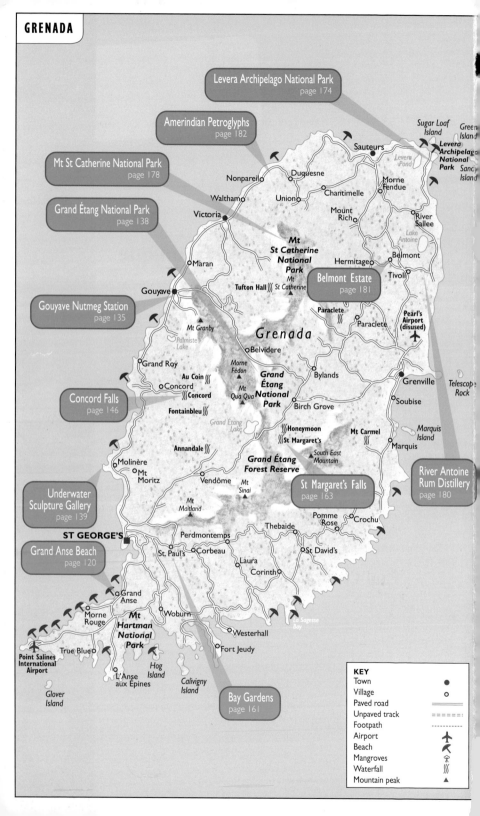

# GRENADA

**Levera Archipelago National Park**
page 174

**Amerindian Petroglyphs**
page 182

**Mt St Catherine National Park**
page 178

**Grand Étang National Park**
page 138

**Gouyave Nutmeg Station**
page 135

**Concord Falls**
page 146

**Underwater Sculpture Gallery**
page 139

**Grand Anse Beach**
page 120

**Belmont Estate**
page 181

**River Antoine Rum Distillery**
page 180

**St Margaret's Falls**
page 163

**Bay Gardens**
page 161

Sugar Loaf Island
Green Island
Levera Archipelago National Park
Sancy Island
Levera Pond
Sauteurs
Morne Fendue
River Sallee
Lake Antoine
Duquesne
Nonpareil
Waltham
Union
Chantimelle
Victoria
Mount Rich
Belmont
Hermitage
Tivoli
Maran
**Mt St Catherine National Park**
Tufton Hall
Mt St Catherine
Gouyave
Paraclete
Pearl's Airport (disused)
Paraclete
Mt Granby
Palmiste Lake
*Grenada*
Belvidere
Grand Roy
Morne Fédon
Bylands
Grenville
Telescope Rock
Au Coin
Concord
Concord
Mt Qua Qua
**Grand Étang National Park**
Birch Grove
Soubise
Fontainbleu
Grand Étang Lake
Annandale
Honeymoon
St Margaret's
Mt Carmel
Marquis Island
Molinère
**Grand Étang Forest Reserve**
Marquis
Mt Moritz
Vendôme
Mt Sinai
South East Mountain
Mt Maitland
Pomme Rose
Crochu
**ST GEORGE'S**
Perdmontemps
Thebaide
St Paul's
Corbeau
St David's
Laura
Corinth
Grand Anse
Woburn
**Mt Hartman National Park**
Morne Rouge
La Sagesse Bay
Point Salines International Airport
True Blue
Hog Island
Westerhall
Fort Jeudy
Glover Island
L'Anse aux Epines
Calivigny Island

| KEY | |
|---|---|
| Town | ● |
| Village | ○ |
| Paved road | |
| Unpaved track | ====== |
| Footpath | ------ |
| Airport | ✈ |
| Beach | |
| Mangroves | ♈ |
| Waterfall | ⅀ |
| Mountain peak | ▲ |

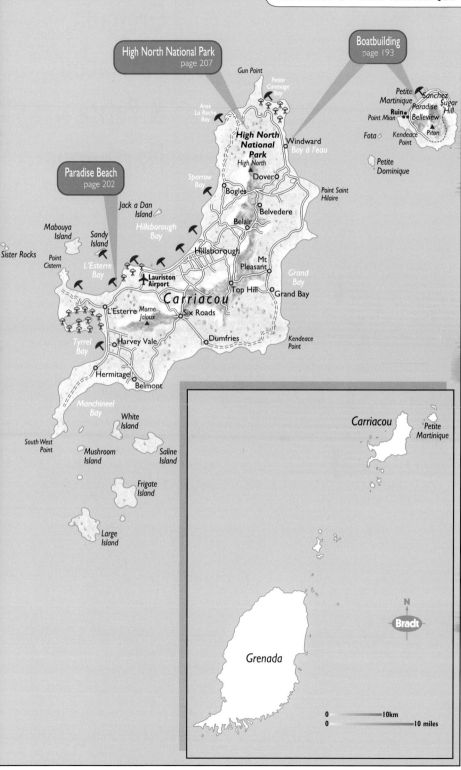

**CARRIACOU & PETITE MARTINIQUE**

High North National Park
page 207

Boatbuilding
page 193

Paradise Beach
page 202

Gun Point

Petite Carenage Bay

Petite Martinique
Sanchez
Paradise
Sugar Hill
Point Mion
Ruin
Belleview
Fota
Kendeace Point
Piton

Anse La Roche Bay

High North National Park
High North

Windward
Bay à l'eau

Petite Dominique

Sparrow Bay

Dover

Bogles

Point Saint Hilaire

Belvedere

Belair

Jack a Dan Island

Hillsborough Bay

Hillsborough

Mabouya Island

Sandy Island

Mt Pleasant

Sister Rocks

Point Cistern

L'Esterre Bay

Lauriston Airport

Carriacou

Grand Bay

Top Hill

Grand Bay

L'Esterre

Morne Jaloux

Six Roads

Tyrrel Bay

Dumfries

Kendeace Point

Harvey Vale

Hermitage

Belmont

Manchineel Bay

White Island

South West Point

Mushroom Island

Saline Island

Frigate Island

Large Island

Carriacou

Petite Martinique

Grenada

N

Bradt

0 ——— 10km
0 ——— 10 miles

# Grenada, Carriacou & Petite Martinique

**Underwater reefs, wrecks and sculptures**
*Vicissitudes* at the Underwater Sculpture Gallery (JT) page 139

**Cultural heritage and festivals**
Sailing festivals and workboat regattas attract enthusiasts from all over the world
(GBT) page 83

**Beautiful beaches and bays**
Paradise Beach, Carriacou – a stunning oasis of powder-white sand and turquoise seas
(CS) page 202

**Tropical forests, mountains and waterfalls**
St Margaret's Falls, Grand Étang Forest Reserve
(CS) page 163

**Spice, cocoa and rum production**
Nutmeg and mace, separated by hand and ready for processing
(CS) page 14

*above*  The Carenage at St George's — a picturesque natural harbour and one of Grenada's most photographed locations (CS) page 100

*left*  Grenville Anglican Church, one of many beautiful stone churches found throughout the islands (CS) page 155

*below*  St George's market in the heart of Bay Town — buy fruits, vegetables, souvenirs and spices here (CS) page 98

*above*    Bel Air Plantation — just one example of the colourful gardens, pretty cottages and traditional board houses that make for enchanting places to get away from it all (CS) page 153

*right*    Petite Martinique traditional board house and small cemetery (CS) page 214

*below*    Hillsborough, Carriacou's main town, with its pretty bay, beaches and outlying islands from the viewpoint at Mt Royal (CS) page 200

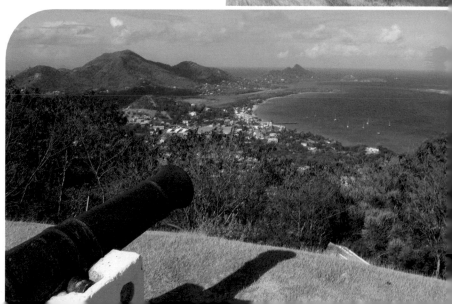

| | |
|---|---|
| *top left* | Organically grown cocoa (*Theobroma cacao*) |
| *& right* | is used by the Grenada Chocolate Company to produce delicious chocolate (CS) page 14 |
| *above left* | Nutmegs (*Myristica fragrans*) are one of the spice island's key exports (CS) page 14 |
| *above right* | The River Antoine Rum Distillery uses processes that date back to the 18th century (CG/ena) page 180 |
| *below left* | Boatbuilding on Carriacou and Petite Martinique is a traditional industry (PC) page 193 |
| *below right* | Local fishermen selling their catch in St George's Carenage (CS) page 100 |

# AUTHOR

Paul Crask was born in England in 1965. He grew up in Lancashire and Yorkshire and graduated from Leeds University in 1988. He also studied in the former East Germany, lived for a year in the former West Germany, and worked as a teacher for two years in the Yamaguchi prefecture in Japan. In 1991 he returned to the UK and embarked on a career in information technology. Shortly after returning from his journeys, Paul met Celia who introduced him to her place of birth, Dominica. They travelled to this beautiful island every year to visit Celia's family before finally dropping out for good and emigrating there in 2005.

Paul's lifestyle change means he now earns a living as a freelance writer, hiking guide, scuba-diving instructor and underwater videographer. Paul has a passion for exploring and learning about the natural environment, cultural heritage and the lives of those who eke a living out of land and water. He is the author of *Dominica*, published by Bradt Travel Guides in 2007. He is also writer and researcher for *Dominica Food & Drink* magazine, and has written features for regional publications and websites. *Grenada, Carriacou & Petite Martinique* is his second Bradt guidebook.

For more information about Paul and his work go to www.paulcrask.com.

## AUTHOR'S STORY

After writing about my adopted home, Dominica, I was very keen to write another Bradt guide. The experience had been really enjoyable and I loved the fact that Bradt had supported me in not only covering the major sites and natural attractions, but also in exploring, learning about and trying to highlight the less well known and the hard to find. I also respect and support Bradt's attitude to positive tourism. We had talked about a number of possibilities for a new guide, but for me the tri-island state of Grenada was by far the most captivating. Several months later, when I was watching Big Drum dancing at a village maroon festival on Carriacou, listening to the stories of nutmeg farmers who had suffered at the hands of Hurricane Ivan, and climbing through dense bush to the summit of Fédon's Camp, I knew I had made the right decision.

But that is the essence of writing for Bradt. I came back from that mountain covered in mud and scratches – but also with a huge grin on my face. The same goes for the trips I made to so many other interesting places and meeting new people. When I am researching a Bradt guide, I feel like I am encouraging travellers to get out and explore the places that lie beyond the organised tours, to meet locals and maybe even help them out.

And I love the unexpected. I had heard of some waterfalls beyond the remote village of Paraclete and bumped into a couple of young guys who said they would take me. When I returned a few days later for the hike, they had invited all their friends along who also wanted to see the falls. So off I set, with a band of machete-wielding lads, chopping bush, sliding through mud and discovering new places together. If life can be full of experiences like this, then I just want more of it.

## PUBLISHER'S FOREWORD
*Adrian Phillips*

The first Bradt travel guide was written in 1974 by George and Hilary Bradt on a river barge floating down a tributary of the Amazon. In the 1980s and 1990s the focus shifted away from hiking to broader-based guides covering new destinations – usually the first to be published about these places. In the 21st century Bradt continues to publish such ground-breaking guides, as well as others to established holiday destinations, incorporating in-depth information on culture and natural history with the nuts and bolts of where to stay and what to see.

Bradt authors support responsible travel, and provide advice not only on minimum impact but also on how to give something back through local charities. In this way a true synergy is achieved between the traveller and local communities.

\* \* \*

What I love about Paul Crask's guidebooks is that they reveal a textured side to the Caribbean that you rarely find in other writing about the place. We've all read travel magazines pronouncing the best resorts and the newest honeymoon spots. But in this book Paul reveals where to find Grenada's most haunting shipwrecks, where to learn about the making of rum and chocolate, and how to avoid mischievous spirits. There are white-sand beaches, of course, but somehow I can't imagine Paul spending all his time sunbathing when there are rainforest-covered mountains to explore ...

**First published January 2009**
Bradt Travel Guides Ltd
23 High Street, Chalfont St Peter, Bucks SL9 9QE, England
www.bradtguides.com

Published in the USA by The Globe Pequot Press Inc, 246 Goose Lane,
PO Box 480, Guilford, Connecticut 06475-0480

Text copyright © 2009 Paul Crask

Maps copyright © 2009 Bradt Travel Guides Ltd

Photographs © 2009 Individual photographers

ISBN-13: 978 1 84162 274 3

British Library Cataloguing in Publication Data
A catalogue record for this book is available from the British Library

**Photographs** Paul Crask (PC), Jason de Caires Taylor (JT), ena: CaféMoka Gallery (CG/ena) & Theodore U Ferguson (TF/ena), Ethan Gordon (EG), Grenada Board of Tourism (GBT), Anthony Jeremiah (AJ), Celia Sorhaindo (CS)
*Front cover* St George's harbour, Grenada (Travelshots/Alamy)
*Title page* Big Drum Dance drummers (GBT), Grand Anse Beach (CS), Nutmeg (CS)
*Back cover* Big Drum Dance dancer (GBT), Underwater Sculpture Gallery (JT)

**Maps** Terence Crump and Dave Priestley

Typeset from the author's disc by Dorchester Typesetting Group
Printed and bound in Malta by Gutenberg Press

# Acknowledgements

My thanks to the following people for their help and support: Lisette Davis, Lennox Thomas, Rebecca Sawyer, Michael Ward, Evelyn and Michael Vogel, Alister 'Archie' Bain, Lucille Sylvester, Phil Saye, Jason de Caires Taylor, Lawrence Lambert, Philip Nash, Roxanne Russell, Jennifer Johann. Thanks also to all the lovely people I met in Grenada, Carriacou and Petite Martinique who made work on this book both an adventure and a pleasure.

A 'big up' to my fabulous hiking guides: Justin A Modeste (aka Gurry), Dwane Thomas, Reean Gibson, Kirby Thomas and Abijah Abraham. Respect.

Thanks for the photography and love always to my beautiful wife, Celia.

## CONTRIBUTORS

Written contributions from Neil Winsborrow, Lucille Sylvester, Phil Saye.

## DEDICATION

To my fantastic brother, John Crask, and to my wonderful parents, Diane and Roger Crask. You are the best.

## FEEDBACK REQUEST

Obviously things change. Some of the hikes I have described in this book were still suffering the effects of Hurricane Ivan when I made them, but this may have improved by the time it goes to print. Perhaps a bar has closed or a new resort has sprung up where there was once a secluded beach. I will be back and forth to Grenada checking on these things but your feedback is always very welcome; email: e info@bradtguides.com. As with my Bradt Dominica guide, I will publish regular online updates that include anything I notice as well as those things you tell me about. You can find these updates on www.paulcrask.com as well as my contact details and links to other websites.

# Contents

## FIND IT QUICK

*Twenty of the most popular visitor attractions*

## LIST OF MAPS

## KEY TO SYMBOLS

N

Bradt

| | | | |
|---|---|---|---|
| ⬚⬚⬚ | Market | 🛈 | Tourist information |
| ═══ | Main road (regional) | † | Church/cathedral |
| ─── | Other road (regional) | ✚ | Hospital/clinic |
| ■ | Capital | ⊠ | Post office |
| ● | Town | 🝢 | Museum/gallery |
| ○ | Village | ✿ | Park/garden |
| ✈ | Airport (international) | ⊞ | Historic/important building |
| ✛ | Airstrip | ♜ | Historic castle/fortification |
| 🚌 | Bus station | ✓ | Beach |
| 🅿 | Car park | ⚑ | Monument/statue |
| ⚑ | Stadium | ∭ | Waterfall |
| △ | Marina | ❄ | Scenic viewpoint |
| | | ∴ | Historic site |
| | | ♧ | Mangroves |
| | | ▲ | Summit |

# Introduction

Self-proclaimed 'Isle of Spice', this tri-island nation is a place for sun worshippers, sailing enthusiasts, culture vultures, hikers, walkers and scuba divers. It has some amazing beaches, tranquil bays and sheltered coves, waterfalls, mountain trails, tropical gardens, coral reefs, shipwrecks and captivating sites of historical interest. You may be lucky enough to see a traditional Carriacou sloop being built and launched, experience a Big Drum Dance or Maroon Festival, or perhaps take part in one of Grenada's popular sailing festivals. All three islands have something to savour and visitors should try, if they can, to experience a little of them all.

To be honest, I was a bag of nerves when I agreed to take on a second Bradt travel guide. Writing my first book about Dominica had been an exciting challenge for me; it is my adopted home and I love every inch of the place. Writing about Grenada was an altogether different and formidable prospect. But the more I researched and explored, the more hooked I became on this extremely fascinating and truly beautiful place. As with research for *Dominica* in 2007, I have tried to travel to every nook and cranny, to be as inclusive and as representative as I possibly can, describing not only the popular visitor attractions but also the more remote places, the villages and the lives of ordinary people who eke a living from the land, and by highlighting the islands' natural history and cultural heritage at every opportunity. *Grenada, Carriacou & Petite Martinique* turned out to be an equally enjoyable project and I hope I have managed to do a decent job.

Although Grenada's spice and agricultural industry was severely impacted by Hurricane Ivan in 2004, it survives and is very slowly recovering thanks to the remarkable patience, hard work and inspirational resolve of farming communities whose livelihoods have depended upon it for generations. I encourage you to try to support these ordinary Grenadians as much as possible by taking tours of nutmeg stations and cocoa estates, by purchasing locally manufactured products such as nutmeg oils, syrups, spices, jams and organic chocolate, and by continuing to ask for Grenada spices and rums when you get back home.

Have a wonderful holiday.

# Part One

## GENERAL INFORMATION

**Location** Grenada 12°07'N, 61°40'W, Carriacou 12°29'N, 61°27'W, Petite Martinique 12°31'N, 61°23'W. The three islands can be found at the southernmost tip of the Windward Islands in the West Indies between St Vincent and The Grenadines and Trinidad and Tobago.

**Size** 344km$^2$ (tri-island state includes Grenada, Carriacou and Petite Martinique)

**Climate** Tropical: average daytime 25°C winter, 31°C summer

**Status** Parliamentary democracy within the Commonwealth of Nations

**Population** Approximately 90,000

**Capital** St George's

**Other main towns** Gouyave, Grenville, Sauteurs (Grenada), Hillsborough (Carriacou)

**Economy** Tourism and agriculture. GDP 2007: US$487million

**Language** English

**Main religions** Roman Catholic, Anglican

**Currency** East Caribbean dollar (EC$)

**Exchange rate** US$1 = EC$2.7 fixed, £1 = EC$3.9 variable, €1 = EC$3.3 variable

**Airports** Grenada: Point Salines International Airport. Carriacou: Lauriston Airport

**International dialling code** +1 473

**Time** GMT −4 hours

**Electricity supply** 220V, 50Hz (many hotels also offer a 110V supply)

**Marine VHF** Channel 16

**Flag** Four triangles of yellow (left and right) and green (top and bottom) form a rectangle against a red background with a line of three gold stars above and three below. At the centre is a red circle with a seventh gold star. On the left-hand green triangle is a nutmeg pod.

**National bird** Grenada dove (*Leptotila wellsi*)

**National flower** Bougainvillea (*Bougainvillea spectablis*)

**Public holidays** See page 61

# I

# Background Information

## GEOGRAPHY

Grenada is an independent tri-island nation that is located at the southern tip of the Windward Islands in the West Indies at 12°07'N and 61°40'W. To the north of Grenada is St Vincent and the Grenadines and to the south is Trinidad and Tobago from where it is just a short hop to Venezuela and the South American continent.

**Grenada** is the main island of the three and is approximately 34km long and 18km wide. The Atlantic Ocean is to the east and the Caribbean Sea is to the west. Located in the southwest of the island, on a natural harbour, is the nation's capital, St George's, which is also its major sea port. Grenada's interior consists of a mountainous terrain that is testament to its volcanic origin. High, narrow, forest-covered ridges create a vertiginous environment of sheer slopes and deep valleys that are home to small farming communities. Located in the north is Mt St Catherine, Grenada's tallest peak at an elevation of 840m. The island's magnificent coastline combines precipitous cliffs and a rugged volcanic environment with numerous sheltered bays and beautiful beaches of both powder white and rich volcanic black sand. The beaches and natural anchorages of Grenada's southwest peninsula attract the majority of the island's visitors with the 3km-long Grand Anse Beach one of its most popular.

**Carriacou** is the second largest of the three islands and is located approximately 37km north of Grenada at 12°29'N and 61°27'W. It is approximately 11km long, 5km wide and covers an area of 34km². Carriacou's main town is Hillsborough which is located on the west coast of the island. Carriacou has a fairly hilly interior that is predominantly covered in farmlands and dry scrub forest. Its two highest points are High North at 291m and Morne Jaloux in the south at an elevation of 290m. The island's exposed eastern coastline faces the wind and weather from the Atlantic and consists of a rocky shoreline with both black- and white-sand beaches. The more leeward-facing coastlines to the west of the island have a number of sheltered bays, natural anchorages, turquoise seas and picture-postcard white-sand beaches.

**Petite Martinique** is located approximately 5km to the northeast of Carriacou at 12°31'N and 61°23'W. This diminutive island has an area of just 2km² and largely consists of a single conical peak, called Piton, which rises to 225m. The island's residents live predominantly around its western shoreline with the remainder of it uninhabited, save for sheep, cattle, mules and goats. Petite Martinique's closest neighbour is Petit St Vincent (PSV) which is just a short boat ride to the northwest, and the southernmost point of the St Vincent Grenadines.

The Grenadines are a chain of more than 125 islands and islets that are located at 12°30'N and 61°30'W belonging to both Grenada and St Vincent. The **Grenada Grenadines** meet the St Vincent Grenadines at a partition between Petit St Vincent and Petite Martinique. Carriacou, Petite Martinique, Île de Ronde (commonly known as Ronde Island) and around 30 islets and rocky pinnacles form Grenada's dependencies and therefore part of the state of Grenada.

3

## CLIMATE

Grenada, Carriacou and Petite Martinique have a tropical climate with average daytime temperatures ranging from around 25°C in January and February, which are the coolest months, to 31°C in July and August. Grenada is usually at its wettest between the months of July and December when the rains arrive with the Atlantic trade winds. Average rainfall is around 250cm with most of it falling on the windward east coasts and the mountainous interior of Grenada. There can be frequent showers and some heavy, prolonged bouts of rainfall throughout this period, especially at higher elevations. July to November is also the time when the West Indies becomes vulnerable to tropical storms and hurricanes that originate on the west coast of Africa.

The driest and sunniest months tend to be from January to June but visitors to Grenada should always anticipate showers and be prepared for excursions into the interior to occasionally be wet and almost always humid. Throughout the islands and especially along the sheltered leeward coasts, it is usually very hot and sunny at this time of the year. Higher elevations as well as the windward-facing coastlines usually benefit from a cooling breeze which helps to make the tropical climate a little more comfortable.

Hurricanes that have the potential to impact Grenada tend to develop from tropical depressions in the Atlantic Ocean near the Cape Verde Islands. The season for hurricanes and tropical storms usually begins in July and lasts until November, with August and September being the months when the risk is usually greatest. Though it is situated to the south of most hurricanes' tracks, Grenada was impacted in 1955 (Hurricane Janet), 1999 (Hurricane Lenny), 2004 (Hurricane Ivan) and 2005 (Hurricane Emily). Although Hurricane Janet was devastating, Hurricane Ivan is generally considered to have been the worst hurricane to hit Grenada.

## A BRIEF HISTORY

**EARLY SETTLERS** The first people to arrive in Grenada would have been Amerindian adventurers from South America somewhere between 5000BC and 3000BC. Very little is known about these people as their lineage has long since died out, although we can assume they were hunter-gatherers who lived off plants, fish and shellfish, and used stones for basic hand-held tools. Some historians refer to these first people as **Ortoiroid people** based on archaeological findings at Ortoire in Trinidad, which lies very close to the continental mainland. A common misconception is that they were Ciboneys. The Ciboney were indeed an ancient people but they are believed to have settled in the area around present-day Cuba, in a different age. Archaeological finds suggest the Ortoiroid people gradually moved northwards through the Lesser Antilles island chain and reached as far as the island of Puerto Rico.

Sometime between 1000BC and 500BC, a new group of people made their way northwards from the Amazon Basin. These people are often referred to as **Arawaks**, a term derived from a family of languages spoken by Amerindian tribes of that region. These Arawakan-speaking people travelled from the Orinoco region of South America and, as they established themselves in both the Lesser and Greater Antilles, they developed their own identity, culture and variations in language over the next 2,000 years or so.

In the Greater Antilles, the dominant group of Amerindians were the **Taino** who settled in Cuba, Jamaica, the Bahamas, Puerto Rico, the Virgin Islands and Antigua. Their counterparts in the Windward Islands were the **Igneri** who, it is believed, occupied Guadeloupe, Dominica, Martinique, St Lucia, St Vincent and Grenada.

The Igneri would have lived in thatched huts made from wood and woven leaves and would have slept in traditional hammocks. It is thought they lived in relatively small communities with a single headman, or chief, who was in charge of affairs and who also provided guidance. They hunted with spears, bows and arrows, and carved canoes from single tree trunks for fishing. These boats provided them with a vital lifeline. In addition to fishing, their canoes were also a means of transportation between islands, enabling them to trade with other migratory groups, including the Taino of the north. The Igneri were also farmers. They cultivated cassava, yam, maize, sweet potato, calabash, paw-paw, cotton and annatto. They were potters too, creating very ornately fashioned ceramics, and they worshipped nature spirits which were often represented by three-cornered *zemi* stones. In relative peace and harmony with each other, their neighbours and with nature, the Igneri are believed to have lived in this region until around AD1200.

Around this time, another group of people from the South American mainland, called the **Kalinago**, had begun to make forays, in their own very impressive dugout canoes, to the Greater and Lesser Antilles island chain. Over time, they too began to establish settlements, gradually displacing the Igneri as they did so. They were said to be a more warfaring people whose chiefs were selected on their virtues as brave fighting men. Records indicate that the men of the village all lived together in a large central house which was called a *carbet*, and the women and children lived in surrounding family huts. The Kalinago were also skilful fishermen, basket weavers and excellent boat makers. According to Father Raymond Breton, a Dominican priest who lived with the Kalinago of Dominica for many years, the name they gave to the island that we now call Grenada was **Camàhogne**. This name is recorded in Father Breton's famous *Dictionnaire Français–Cariabe* and, although some scholars believe it translates to 'those people', its meaning is really not at all clear.

The Kalinago probably completely displaced the Igneri in Grenada somewhere between AD1000 and AD1300 and from this point onwards, the Igneri seem to have disappeared. The Kalinago traded with the Taino people of the Greater Antilles but, it seems, more often fought with them. However, it was not from Kalinago raids that the Taino faced their greatest threat. This was to come from an entirely different people altogether.

**NEW ARRIVALS** On his third voyage to the region in 1498, Christopher Columbus sighted Grenada and named it **La Concepción** in honour of the Virgin Mary. It is said he may actually have named it Assumption – no-one can be sure, as he is said to have sighted what are now Grenada and Tobago from a distance and named them both at the same time. However, history has accepted that it was Tobago he

5

named Assumption and La Concepción was the name he gave to the island we now call Grenada. But it didn't end there. In 1499, the Italian explorer Amerigo Vespucci travelled through the region with the Spanish explorer Alonso de Ojeda and mapmaker Juan de la Cosa. Vespucci is reported to have renamed the island **Mayo**, which is how it appeared on maps for around the next 20 years. In the 1520s the Spanish named the islands to the north of Mayo as Los Granadillos (Little Granadas), presumably after the mainland Spanish town. Shortly after this, Mayo disappeared from Spanish maps and an island called **Granada** took its place. Although it was deemed the property of the King of Spain, there are no records to suggest the Spanish ever landed or settled on the island.

The Kalinago were referred to as **Caribs** by the European explorers of the time. Today they are also referred to as 'Island Caribs' in an effort by western scholars to distinguish them from the 'Caribs' of mainland South America. The reason for this distinction is that it is thought the Caribs who settled in the Greater and Lesser Antilles developed a cultural identity of their own. The name *Carib* finds its roots in some rather dubious and very questionable assumptions of 15th-century European explorers. Described by the Europeans as a warfaring people, the Kalinago, it is said, would capture brides, kill menfolk and take a limb from the body of a victim as a prize. This trophy was taken back to their village as proof of victory and a symbol of bravery and manhood. As part of the celebration ritual, it was noted that a warrior may take a mouthful of his victim's flesh, chew it and spit it out in a display of ferocity and malice. The Europeans also recorded that the Kalinago preserved the bones of their ancestors within their houses in the belief that the spirits of their forefathers were protecting them. These two aspects of Kalinago culture were interpreted as cannibalism – a word that itself finds its roots in the names used by both the Igneri and Taino, and then subsequently by the Europeans, for the Kalinago people. In Columbus's journal of 1492 he records that the people he encountered were frightened of those of *caniba* or *canima*, actually seeming to refer to the name of a place rather than the name of a people. From there the word took on several variations including *caribi*, *caribe*, *carib* and, in Spanish text, *canibal*. Throughout this book I shall refer to these people as Kalinago, which was the name they gave themselves.

Granada, as it was then called, was left undisturbed by Europeans until 1609 when a group of British merchants landed there and tried to establish a settlement which they called Megrin Town, located in the present-day parish of St David. Finding themselves under constant attack and harassment by the island's Kalinago, they ultimately abandoned their venture and sailed back to London the very same year. Thirty years later a group of Frenchmen tried their luck as fishermen but were also forcibly removed.

In 1650, under the leadership of Monsieur Du Parquet, then Governor of Martinique, another group of French settlers arrived in a different area of the island. They landed on the spit of land known today as the Ballast Ground on the western side of the Lagoon in St George's, and were met by the Kalinago chief, Kaierouanne. Du Parquet offered the chief gifts and then set about establishing a settlement which, very significantly, included a barricade and a fort with mounted cannons. It was named **Fort Louis** after the reigning French monarch. The settlers meant business and, in a very short period of time, they felled trees and began cultivating a large tobacco plantation. Following its introduction to Europe, tobacco was a much sought-after product and there was a great deal of money to be made from it. After a period of only eight months, the settlers harvested their first crop and Du Parquet returned to Martinique naming a Monsieur Le Compte as the island's new governor.

Realising their European visitors were in fact here to stay, the disgruntled Kalinago mounted a number of isolated attacks on individuals though they resisted the temptation to attack the fortification itself. In response, Le Compte attempted an attack on a large Kalinago village but he failed and many Frenchmen were killed. Du Parquet then decided to send 300 soldiers as reinforcements to Le Compte from Martinique, instructing the governor to drive the Kalinago out of the island completely. Whilst the French were reinforcing their numbers, so too were the Kalinago, welcoming brothers-in-arms from the islands of Dominica and St Vincent.

In 1652, the French learned of a planned attack on Fort Louis and, when it occurred, they launched a devastating counter, killing many Kalinago and forcing them into retreat. Some Kalinago escaped over the mountains to the east of the island, while others fled to the north. It is recorded that around 40 Kalinago reached a rocky peninsula in the very north of the island and, realising their situation completely hopeless, threw themselves from the cliffs, choosing certain death in favour of capture and humiliation. This is the area that is known today as Leapers' Hill or Carib's Leap and is located in the northern village of Sauteurs (which is in fact French for 'leapers').

This battle proved to be a defining moment for the Kalinago. Though a number remained, predominantly in the less accessible east, their fight for survival was essentially over. They managed to organise themselves into small bands and launched sporadic guerrilla-style attacks, instilling fear and panic into French settlements. Governor Le Compte moved to quell this threat once and for all with a push of 150 soldiers over the mountains to the east. The soldiers killed every Kalinago man, woman and child they encountered and they burned their villages to the ground. By the end of the campaign, the Kalinago were almost entirely wiped out. A few survived but eventually they too disappeared. For the next 100 years, **La Grenade** became a colony of the French Crown.

During French rule La Grenade was divided into six parishes: Basseterre (now St George), Gouyave (St John), Grand Pauvre (St Mark), Sauteurs (St Patrick), Megrin (St David) and Marquis (St Andrew). Churches were constructed and the main town was moved north from Fort Louis to its current location and was renamed **Fort Royal** after a fortification built by French engineer Monsieur de Caillus in 1706. Plantations were established by the French throughout the island and west African slaves were brought to work them.

**CONFLICT AND REBELLION** On 10 February 1763 the island of La Grenade was ceded to the British under the Treaty of Paris. The British renamed it **Grenada** and set about thoroughly anglicising everything the French had established. Fort Royal was renamed **St George's** and its main fortification was renamed Fort George. The French owners of around 80 sugar and 200 coffee plantations, which were the new cash crops of the time, found themselves under British colonial rule and it was not long before Anglo-French conflict started to surface. Protestant British planters began plotting against their Catholic French counterparts, attempting to coerce them into subscribing to the Test Act which was, in essence, a rejection of their religion. During this period of British rule the island's economy thrived. In the year 1772, there were over 300 plantations in total, of which around 140 were run by French settlers and 170 by British planters. There was a total of 125 sugar estates and Grenada had become the largest coffee and cocoa producer in the British West Indies.

In 1776, war broke out between Britain and France once again, this time over the latter's assistance to the British colonies in America and their attempt at independence. In 1779, under the command of the Count d'Estang from Martinique, the French recaptured Grenada from the British with a force of 25 ships and 6,500 soldiers. Over the next four years of French rule, the island was

## SLAVERY IN GRENADA

It is estimated that around 20 million people were taken from west Africa in ships to work as slaves in the Americas. Records indicate that British-controlled islands of the West Indies received approximately two million slaves and the French-controlled islands some 1.5 million slaves from the mid 17th century up to the abolition of the slave trade in the early 1800s. In Grenada the years between 1735 and 1780 witnessed the highest number of slave arrivals – a time when planters were reaping the financial benefits of a highly lucrative sugar trade. In the 30 years between 1750 and 1780 the slave population of Grenada jumped from around 10,000 to approximately 35,000, the highest that slave numbers would reach until emancipation in 1838.

It was an entirely miserable and unforgivably inhumane existence. From the moment of capture in west Africa, they were crammed like sardines into ships for the Atlantic crossing. *En route*, many died and many others killed themselves. For those who made it to the other side, unfortunately the tragedy was only just unfolding.

governed in an equally despotic manner, this time with a focus on suppressing the British population of planters and their families. On 3 September 1783, Grenada was once again ceded to the British, on this occasion under the Treaty of Versailles. The French planters felt the wrath of the British after living for four years under an oppressive regime, particularly by ultra-Protestant leaders such as Governor Ninian Home. Many French residents found it unbearable and left the island, taking their slaves with them. Catholic churches were seized and transferred to the Protestants, and marriages, baptisms and burials were considered illegal unless they were celebrated in Anglican churches. A further act was passed which stated that French Catholics were required to submit to the Test Act before they could hold any form of political office. Similar legislation also effectively excluded French Catholics from holding public office and from voting in elections.

With such rising levels of discrimination and dissatisfaction, everything inevitably came to a head. In 1795 a free, black, estate owner from Martinique named Julien Fédon, together with hundreds of other free, black, French ex-slaves and French planters, staged a rebellion that was supported by French commanders in Guadeloupe. The **Fédon Rebellion** lasted from March 1795 to June 1796. Inspired by the French Revolution, Fédon led a bloody and destructive island-wide revolt against British rule, liberating slaves, ransacking estates and killing British planters. At the height of the rebellion Fédon controlled most of the island but he was unable to drive home his superiority by taking the capital, St George's. It was this failing that eventually allowed the British to regroup and strengthen their numbers until they were successful in quelling the insurgency and either killing or capturing the rebels. During the rebellion Fédon infamously executed 43 prisoners at his headquarters at the Belvidere Estate, including Ninian Home. No-one knows what became of Julien Fédon after he was routed from his mountain stronghold, though many believe he drowned trying to escape to Trinidad. The rebellion brought ruin to Grenada's economy. It is estimated to have destroyed property to the tune of £2.5million and brought about the death of some 7,000 slaves. See box, *Fédon's rebellion*, *Chapter 6*, page 136 for more information.

**EMANCIPATION AND INDEPENDENCE** Following the Treaty of Versailles the French threat disappeared and, despite Fédon's rebellion, the island's plantation system recovered and continued to prosper under British rule. In 1833, however, things started to change. Together with years of resistance from the victims themselves, the British anti-slavery movement finally succeeded in forcing the British Parliament to end slavery in its colonies. The **Imperial Act of Emancipation** was passed in 1833, abolishing slavery and the slave trade on 1 August 1834. There was a great deal of resistance to this Act, in particular from the plantation and estate owners who relied on enforced labour for their businesses and for their personal wealth. Although it is recorded that almost 24,000 slaves were freed in Grenada on 31 July 1834, their liberation was unfortunately far from realised. In order to appease colonial plantocracy, the British Parliament agreed to set up a system called **compulsory apprenticeship** which required liberated slaves to continue working for their former masters for a designated period of time. This meant that field slaves were bound to work for six years and other slaves up to four years, without pay. In return for their labour, the apprenticed workforce would be given food rations and granted time to tend and sell produce from their own kitchen gardens. It was hardly liberation. It was a system that was doomed to failure, however. Many estate and plantation owners simply used it as a means to further exploit their workforce. Apprentices protested bravely against great odds and in an environment of very real physical danger. By 1838, four years after the Emancipation Act had been passed, the apprenticeship system was abolished formally through legislation. On 31 July that year Grenada's slaves were finally free.

Because they no longer enjoyed the fruits of an enslaved workforce, many estates and plantations simply failed and were ultimately abandoned. Freed slaves built houses and established smallholdings around former estate lands, creating the rural communities and villages that exist today. The estates that continued to operate switched production from sugar to cocoa during the mid 19th century and then to nutmeg during the 1900s. In Carriacou, corn and pigeon peas became the main crops following the collapse of the sugar industry.

In order to compensate for the refusal of many former slaves to continue working on the surviving estates following the abolition of apprenticeship, Grenada introduced **indentured immigration** programmes which involved importing a cheap labour force from west African nations, India, Malta and Madeira. The scheme was largely a failure with the majority of early immigrants migrating to Trinidad. It is recorded that in the latter half of the 19th century just over 3,200 immigrants arrived from India and over half of them remained. They settled in communities both in the interior and in the east of the island and they gradually became absorbed into the emerging post-emancipation Grenadian culture and society. The Indo-Grenadian population that still lives in Grenada is relatively small yet very influential. There have been and still are a number of extremely successful Indo-Grenadian families, businesses and entrepreneurs.

Following a succession of failed attempts at federating a number of islands belonging to the British colonies in the West Indies during the mid 20th century, the British government announced on 3 March 1967 that Grenada would be granted self-rule under a system of **associated statehood** through the 1967 West Indies Act. **Eric Gairy**, leader of the Grenada United Labour Party (GULP) became Grenada's premier and his extremely controversial leadership sparked a period of unrest and political conflict that is still hotly debated today. One point that everyone agrees on, however, is that Gairy was absolutely determined to be rid of associated statehood which he considered a 'farce' and he sought nothing less than complete independence from Britain. Despite strong opposition to his policies and his questionable regime, mounting civil unrest, and incidents of violence and brutality that infamously took place on 'Bloody Sunday' (18 November 1973) and 'Bloody Monday' (21 January 1974), the British government granted full **independence** to the state of Grenada on 7 February 1974. Some commentators suggest it was almost as if Britain was finally relieved to wash its hands of what had become an economic and political burden.

**REVOLUTION AND INTERVENTION** The Gairy regime had been accused by its opponents of financial irregularities, brutality and unconstitutional power-mongering prior to and following independence. Though he had begun his political life as the voice of ordinary Grenadians, it seemed Gairy had become an authoritarian figure who has been described by some respected commentators as nothing short of a dictator. Disenfranchised from ordinary people, in particular the young, growing opposition to his right-wing leadership manifested itself in the organisation of strikes, riots and public protests, and ultimately in the creation of a socialist opposition party calling itself the **New Jewel Movement**. Formed in March 1973 by the amalgamation of two opposition groups, the Movement for Assemblies of the People (MAP) and the Joint Endeavour for Welfare, Education and Liberation (JEWEL), the New Jewel Movement (NJM) was led by the charismatic **Maurice Bishop**. In November 1973, Bishop had been one of six NJM members who were brutally beaten, allegedly by members of Gairy's secret police, at a meeting in Grenville. Known as 'Bloody Sunday' this inhumane act was one that would return to haunt Grenada's premier in the years to come. The NJM's manifesto 'Power to the People' voiced a left-wing ideology that demanded a fundamental change to the nation's governance, and was influenced by contemporary movements such as Castro's Cuban Revolution. The party appealed to the young, the trade unions, and those who had become disillusioned with the Gairy administration.

On 13 March 1979, Gairy's GULP government was overthrown in an armed *coup d'état*. The constitution was suspended and 63 People's Laws were implemented by the newly established **People's Revolutionary Government** (PRG). The PRG was a non-elected government that administered the country through a Central Committee. Maurice Bishop became prime minister and his comrade Bernard Coard became deputy prime minister. The new regime received financial and political support from Cuba and the former Soviet Union and under People's Law No 7, the PRG created the **People's Revolutionary Army** (PRA). From 1979 Cuba began supplying the PRA with arms and ammunition. Grenada thus became a one-party, military state pursuing a socialist programme that promised one day to develop a revised and more appropriate 'people's constitution'.

The period that followed is one that still generates strong emotions in Grenada, with few agreeing on the rights and the wrongs that were committed, and fewer still able to forgive and to forget. Economic pressures mounted on the PRG regime and deep ideological conflict took hold within the Central Committee itself. It was also a time of brutality and oppression. Despite the nation's deeply entrenched religious beliefs, the Church became a target of the PRG. It is said priests were spied upon and church meetings monitored for 'counter-revolutionary activities'. It is also claimed that there were a series of human rights abuses including the tortures, murders and executions of innocents during the PRG's rule. A power struggle emerged within the Central Committee between Bernard Coard and Maurice Bishop which ultimately culminated in the house arrest of Bishop on Wednesday, 12 October 1983. Ideological disagreements became extremely bitter with little hope for a positive outcome to the conflict and the revolution was in danger of collapsing.

On 19 October 1983, known later as **Bloody Wednesday**, a mass demonstration of thousands of Grenadians released Bishop from his captors and then escorted him to Fort George (at the time renamed Fort Rupert in memory of Bishop's father who was murdered in 1974), which was the military headquarters of the PRG. Bernard Coard and his supporters appeared to have a choice of either risking possible incarceration themselves due to mounting support for Bishop, or by taking a course of action that would deal with the threat once and for all. The outcome of these deliberations was an armed assault by the PRA on the fort and on the people within it. Some of Bishop's supporters tried to escape by throwing themselves over the fort's 20m-high walls, while others faced the bullets. Bishop and a core of his supporters were captured and taken to the fort's upper courtyard. Once there, they were lined up against a wall and executed. Their bodies are said to have been taken to the site of Fédon's Camp where they were burned and never recovered. The PRA announced the formation of a **Revolutionary Military Council** that would govern the country until further notice.

The left-wing ideologies of Castro's Cuba and Bishop's Grenada had certainly made some leaders in the region very uncomfortable. And so it was that the events of Bloody Wednesday gave the Reagan administration in the US sufficient reason, they felt, for an intervention which would remove Grenada's Cuban-backed military regime and restore a more 'Western' democracy. With the support of some, though by no means all, Caribbean countries, **Operation Urgent Fury** was implemented. On the morning of 25 October 1983, just six days after Bloody Wednesday, 1,900 US troops, together with a force of over 300 soldiers from six Caribbean countries, collectively referred to as the Caribbean Multinational Force, landed in Grenada and engaged in armed conflict with Cuban and Grenadian PRA militia. By 31 October, the combined forces had secured the island and, on 2 November, Carriacou and Petite Martinique were taken without conflict. The US-led intervention drew a great deal of international criticism, with the British Parliament condemning the invasion of one of its Commonwealth nation members as illegal. Following the operation, those who were accused of being responsible for the acts of Bloody Wednesday were tried and, after initially being sentenced to death, were imprisoned for life. This trial, sentencing and subsequent incarceration was and still is the subject of much debate, including questions over fair trials and human rights. For those who were involved on both sides, their families, friends and supporters, the events and outcomes of 1983 remain extremely emotional and sensitive subjects.

An interim **Advisory Council** was set up after the intervention with the mandate of restoring the country's constitution and preparing it for free elections which were held a year later on 3 December 1984. Herbert Blaize of the New National Party (NNP) became Prime Minister of Grenada for the next five years. The NNP and the National Democratic Congress (NDC) became Grenada's two main political parties and have governed the country in turn up to the present day. The longest-serving prime minister was Keith Mitchell of the NNP who led Grenada from 1995 to 2008. Tillman Thomas of the NDC became prime minister on 9 July 2008. In 1996, his notoriety somewhat forgotten in light of subsequent events, Eric Gairy was celebrated as Grenada's 'Father of the Nation' during the country's independence celebrations. He died the same year and, in 2008, he was declared Grenada's first National Hero.

**HURRICANE IVAN** Hurricane Ivan struck Grenada a near-fatal blow on 7 September 2004. By the time it hit, Ivan had strengthened to a category three hurricane and it ravaged the island with sustained 193km/h winds for over eight hours. Until that fateful day, it had been Hurricane Janet that most Grenadians remembered and considered the worst storm to ever hit the island. Janet had blasted northern Grenada and Carriacou with winds of up to 260km/h, destroying everything in its path and leaving 120 people dead in its wake. The nation's agricultural economy was severely impacted by Janet and many structures were destroyed, including the already weakening St George's harbour jetty and buildings.

The eye of Hurricane Ivan passed approximately 10km south of Point Salines and thoroughly ransacked the island. It either completely levelled or damaged around 90% of residences and other buildings, leaving countless Grenadians homeless. It ravaged the island's forests and farmlands, destroying the majority of the nation's crops, including nutmeg, and it crippled the island's infrastructure. Schools, churches, hospitals, roads, water and electricity supplies, homes, hotels, businesses, farms and orchards were left in complete tatters. Immediately after the hurricane there followed some very frightening days of lawlessness with widespread looting and violence. The Grenadian people were in a state of immeasurable shock and altogether fearful for their very existence.

The world came to Grenada's assistance in the days, weeks and months following Ivan. A programme of donor and loan aid commenced and plans were initiated to reconstruct schools and hospitals, to clear and replant crops, and to repair and rebuild homes. The estimated cost of Ivan's fury was put at around US$1billion and it was clearly going to take a long time to completely recover. The island's tourism industry which was beginning to thrive, together with nutmeg and cocoa crops, suffered an unmitigated setback.Before Ivan, Grenada was the world's second-largest producer of nutmegs after Indonesia. With only 10% of nutmeg trees still standing, and a period of seven to ten years for a seedling to reach maturity, it is no wonder that very many livelihoods were in serious jeopardy.

After picking themselves up from the rubble and the despair, Grenadians would be forgiven for feeling entirely desperate when just one year later, Emily passed over their island as a category one hurricane. Though nowhere near as devastating as Ivan, Emily caused an estimated US$100million worth of damage to the island as well as immeasurable psychological harm to its people.

Today Grenada is still in the process of recovering. The tourism industry has received boosts from global investors, real estate speculators and entrepreneurs and is now the island's primary source of revenue. The agriculture industry has not yet recovered and, though new nutmegs were planted, it appears highly unlikely that this industry will ever thrive as it once did. Visitors to Grenada will witness some of Ivan's legacy when travelling around the island. Many buildings, such as the Anglican church and the Roman Catholic cathedral in St George's, are still awaiting repair, skeletons of abandoned domestic residences can still be seen in many villages, and tours of nutmeg stations tell their own sad tale of the storm's impact on this once significant spice crop.

## GOVERNMENT AND POLITICS

Grenada is a parliamentary democracy within the Commonwealth of Nations, an association of 53 independent sovereign states with Queen Elizabeth II as its head. The queen is represented in Grenada by a governor general who is appointed as head of parliament on the advice of Grenada's prime minister.

The country's political and legal systems closely mirror those of the United Kingdom. Parliament consists of two chambers, the House of Representatives and the Senate. There are 15 members of the House of Representatives who represent single-seat constituencies in Grenada, Carriacou and Petite Martinique. They are elected by democratic vote for a period of up to five years. The Senate has 13 members who are appointed by the ruling government (10) and by the leader of the opposition (3). The prime minister is head of government which represents the country's executive branch. Grenada's legislative power resides within parliament.

Grenada has seven administrative divisions, which consist of dependencies and parishes. They are Carriacou and Petite Martinique, St George, St David, St Andrew, St Patrick, St Mark and St John.

Grenada has two major political parties: the New National Party (NNP) and the National Democratic Congress (NDC). Minor parties include the Grenada United Labour Party (GULP), which is Grenada's oldest political party, and the Maurice Bishop Patriotic Movement (MBPM) which was founded by survivors of the Bloody Wednesday coup.

**LAW** Grenada's legal system is based on English common law. It upholds freedom of speech and freedom of religion, and it prohibits discrimination based on race, gender, place of origin, colour and creed. Grenada's law is enforced by the Royal Grenada Police Force (RGPF), a paramilitary Special Services Unit (SSU) and the Grenada Coast Guard.

## ECONOMY

Grenada is a member of CARIFORUM (Caribbean Forum of African, Caribbean and Pacific States), CARICOM (Caribbean Community and Common Market) and the OECS (Organisation of Eastern Caribbean States). Together with other OECS members, Grenada is committed to the free movement of goods, services and labour across participating countries within the region.

Prior to Hurricane Ivan, Grenada's main sources of revenue were agriculture and tourism. Following Ivan, the New National Party (NNP) government actively pursued the development of an investment-led economy, encouraging large-scale project development and growth within the island's tourism sector. Agriculture, though still considered important, has benefited less and has thus far failed to materially recover from the effects of the 2004 and 2005 hurricanes. In 2007, Grenada's GDP was US$487million which represented growth at just over 7%.

Grenada has one of the highest unemployment rates in the Caribbean, particularly among the young living in rural areas of the island. According to the International Fund for Agricultural Development (IFAD), a specialist unit of the United Nations, over 30% of Grenadians are considered 'poor' with over 10% considered 'extremely poor'. In 2006, the International Monetary Fund (IMF) approved a three-year loan arrangement of around US$18million under its Poverty Reduction and Growth Facility programme. Grenada was ranked 82 out of 177 countries listed in the UN Human Development Index of 2007. In the same year, Grenada's average per capita annual income was recorded at a mere US$4,600.

Of particular concern to both the nation and institutions such as the IMF and World Bank is Grenada's growing national debt which, at the time of writing, amounts to some US$493million. The IMF has suggested that the country's debt to GDP ratio is significant cause for concern and that there is a pressing need to control expenditures and work within more prudent budgetary frameworks. The organisation supports the introduction of a value added tax (VAT) system and has urged debt reduction as a fiscal priority.

**AGRICULTURE** Grenada is affectionately known as the **Spice Island of the Caribbean** and, wherever you travel, you will see vendors selling spices, you will encounter numerous references to spice and, at some point or other, you will probably find yourself on a spice tour. Grenada's spice heritage is succeeding in bridging the divide between agriculture and tourism, creating a new **agro-tourism** (sometimes written as 'agri-tourism') product that now constitutes a small part of the country's economic development and provides a potential area of wealth generation for some of the island's rural people.

**Cocoa** Cocoa was grown alongside sugar in the 18th and 19th centuries as a secondary crop and, from the 1880s, following the decline of the sugar industry, it became the mainstay of Grenada's economy. Native to the Amazon region of South America, the **cacao** tree (*Theobroma cacao*) is believed to have been introduced to Grenada in the late 17th century where it was cultivated on the elevated hillsides of the island's interior. It is a small evergreen tree that grows to between 4m and 8m in height and produces ovoid pods up to 30cm long. Within each pod there are between 20 and 50 seeds, commonly called beans, that are embedded in a thick white pulp. Each seed contains up to 50% fat which is commonly referred to as 'cocoa butter'.

Though yields are possible after three years, cocoa trees usually bear their fruit in their fourth or fifth year. Once ripe, the cocoa is harvested and the mix of pulp and beans removed from their pods. The pods are discarded and the bean and pulp mixture is stored in a large bin or container where it undergoes a natural fermentation process, removing the beans' bitterness and enriching their flavour. The pulp can reach temperatures of up to 50°C during the fermentation process. After several days naturally fermenting, the beans are removed and dried. This is done by spreading the beans on large trays and leaving them out in the tropical sunshine, turning them at regular intervals. Cocoa drying sheds, known as *boucans*, contain numerous drying trays that can be rolled out or retracted under cover along purpose-built steel rails. Turning the beans was traditionally undertaken by a method called 'walking the beans' where estate workers, usually women, would walk through the trays of beans, turning them with their bare feet. After drying, the beans are graded and packed in large sacks ready for consumption and export.

At the turn of the 20th century Grenada was producing as much as 4,500 tonnes of cocoa at the industry's peak. In 1955, Hurricane Janet uprooted many mature cocoa trees, causing a significant decline. Younger trees were planted and, though cocoa production increased, it never regained pre-war levels and when Hurricane Ivan struck in 2004, the industry was dealt another shattering blow. Today Grenada still produces cocoa for export as well as for domestic consumption, and cocoa grown at the Belmont Estate in St Andrew is used for the production of organic chocolate by the **Grenada Chocolate Company** (see page 181 for more information).

**Nutmegs** It is said that nutmegs were first planted as an experiment on the Belvidere Estate in 1843 from seeds brought from the **Banda Islands** of Indonesia by a man called Frank Gurney. It is believed commercial planting of nutmegs began in the 1850s on the Bellevue and Capitol estates in the parish of St Andrew. Until the 19th century, the Banda Islands were the only place in the world where this particular species of nutmeg tree could be found.

Nut-Med is a pain-relieving spray and cream that is made from a combination of nutmeg oil and plant extracts. Nutmeg has been used for centuries to improve health and relieve muscle pain through its natural analgesic properties, and is a key ingredient in several mainstream pharmaceutical products. Created by Dr Denis Noel, a man whose family have been associated with the nutmeg industry for years, Nut-Med is a real Grenadian success story. Those who have used it swear by it, and his company, Noelville Ltd, is going from strength to strength. Nut-Med is available from pharmacies island-wide. You can also find it for sale at the Gouyave Nutmeg Station. For more information go to www.nut-med.com.

The nutmeg (*Myristica fragrans*) is an evergreen tree that grows well in the elevated hillsides of Grenada's interior. The nutmeg is the actual seed of the tree and grows inside a tough shell which in turn resides within a roundish yellow pod. Surrounding the nutmeg shell is a lacy, reddish coating known as **mace**. Nutmegs have a wide variety of applications. Most commonly, when ground into a fine powder, nutmegs are used as a food and drink flavouring, notably in desserts, puddings, potato dishes and soups. Nutmegs also produce an essential oil that is used in the cosmetic and pharmaceutical industries and is an ingredient in some perfumes, toothpastes and cough syrups. It is also used in medicinal massage and pain-relieving oils and sprays. The nutmeg pod that surrounds the seed is used to make delicious jams and jellies, and the brittle shells that are removed to expose the nutmeg seed are recycled as a very effective garden mulch or path covering. Mace is also used in cooking and is especially well known as a natural meat preservative.

In the 1880s, following the decline of the sugar industry and the subsequent search for new economic crops, which included cocoa, Grenada began exporting nutmegs and mace for the first time. Production increased and by 1910 Grenada was responsible for 14% of world nutmeg exports. By the 1990s Grenada was exporting around 23% of the world's nutmegs, and was the second-largest producer in the world behind Indonesia.

In 1955, the devastation wreaked by Hurricane Janet culled Grenada's nutmeg production by around 80% and it was not until the mid 1970s, around 20 years later, that pre-Janet levels were regained. In 2004, Hurricane Ivan destroyed 90% of Grenada's nutmeg crop as well as around EC$11million of nutmegs that were sitting in stock. Numerous livelihoods were either entirely lost or at the very least put on long-term hold. Many receiving stations around the island were closed and of the three main operating plants (or 'pools') at Gouyave, Victoria and Grenville, it would only be the one at Gouyave which would continue processing the surviving crop. Based on the experiences of Hurricane Janet, and despite efforts to plant faster-growing species, it is the view of most experts that it will take two decades for Grenada's nutmeg industry to recover. Whether it will ever recover to pre-Ivan levels is the subject of much debate with some in the industry disillusioned by what they perceive as a lack of adequate support from their government. A further factor that will inevitably influence the recovery of the nutmeg industry is the younger generation's apparent lack of interest in pursuing careers in agriculture. Many see it as high-risk, hard, unattractive and unrewarding work compared with the trappings of alternative, more 'fashionable' lifestyles. With an ageing farming population and a reluctance of younger people to get involved, the outlook for the industry is far from bright.

**Cinnamon** (*Cinnamonum verum*) An evergreen tree that grows to around 15m in height, cinnamon is native to parts of Asia and the Indian subcontinent. The tree is pruned, or coppiced, every two years to produce a number of new branches which are harvested for the inner skin of their bark. The bark is removed from the branch and left to dry. The thin inner bark is removed from the outer bark which is discarded. This inner bark curls up into cinnamon sticks or 'quills' which are then prepared for sale either whole or by grinding into a powder. Cinnamon is commonly used as a spice to flavour desserts and beverages.

**Clove** (*Syzygium aromaticum*) An evergreen tree, clove produces aromatic flower buds that are dried and used as a spice in cooking. Cloves are also said to have medicinal uses and their essential oil is frequently applied as a herbal painkiller, particularly for toothache. It is also said to be an effective remedy for upset stomachs. Grenada is a minor clove producer with over 80% of the world's output coming from Indonesia.

**Turmeric** (*Curcuma longa*) A member of the ginger family, turmeric is a perennial plant that is native to south Asia. It is cultivated for its rhizome, or underground stem, which is boiled, dried and then ground into an orange-yellow powder that is commonly used as a spice in curry dishes.

**Allspice** (*Pimenta dioica*) Allspice is a tree similar in appearance to bay laurel. Its small, unripe fruit is harvested and dried in the sun before either being ground or sold whole as a spice. Also known as pimento, allspice has a variety of culinary applications that vary around the world. In the Caribbean, in particular Jamaica, it is used as a key ingredient of jerk seasoning. Though it is not harvested in huge quantities, allspice is an important part of Grenada's spice-island make-up.

**Bananas** (*Musa*) Bananas are grown all around Grenada, from plantations in the island's interior to the vegetable gardens of resorts in the south. The crop is no longer a significant export, however, and is largely consumed by the domestic market, in particular the hotel industry. In the face of world trade practices and large-scale food production, small Caribbean islands just cannot compete. In Grenada's case, the natural disasters of recent years have simply added to the mix of what many perceive as insurmountable hurdles. Though some islands' banana producers are now successfully fighting back thanks to the assistance of the Fairtrade Foundation, many of Grenada's large-scale banana farmers have left the industry. Visitors to Grenada will still see plenty of banana plants growing alongside rural roads, hiking trails and dotted around the island's interior, but these plantations are relatively small-scale in comparison with the past. Visitors will also come across **plantain** and **bluggo**, varieties of banana that are usually cooked before eating and are a traditional staple in Caribbean cuisine.

**Corn** (*Zea mays*) **and pigeon peas** (*Cajanus cajan*) Both are very commonly grown in Carriacou, though you will also find them on the main island, Grenada. They are usually inter-cropped, rotated and farmed together. Again, they are primarily grown on subsistence farms for local consumption and are staples of the Grenadian diet. Pigeon peas are usually eaten in pea soup and rice and peas, and corn is most commonly used in very traditional dishes such as *conkie* and *cou-cou*.

**FISHERIES** Many Grenadians make their living in the fishing industry which, like agriculture, is becoming inextricably intertwined with the growing tourism industry. Grenadian fishermen can make a manageable living selling their catch to the island's restaurants and hotels as well as to luxury island resorts located in the St Vincent Grenadines where prices are said to be very high indeed. Though a controlled, seasonal catch, the tourism industry's insatiable desire for fresh lobster is where many fishermen are able to make some money. Other more lucrative catches include queen conch (*Strombus gigas*), commonly known as lambie, and sea turtles, in particular the hawksbill (*Dermochelys coriacea*), which are only protected between the months of May to September.

Fishing practices include long-line fishing, hand-lining and the use of seine nets. The most common fish caught and consumed include yellow-fin tuna (*Thunnus albacares*), black-fin tuna (*Thunnus altantivus*) and blue marlin (*Makaira nigrican*). A very popular catch is dorado, or *mahi-mahi* (*Coryphaena hippurus*) which is locally, and somewhat confusingly, known as 'dolphin'.

Visitors to Grenada will see very many colourful wooden fishing boats along the shoreline all around the three islands as well as a number of larger long-liners tied up in St George's Carenage. If you are lucky, you may get to see locals helping to haul in seine nets near villages such as Gouyave, Duquesne, or in the bays of the southeast.

**TOURISM** The tourism industry has become the Grenadian government's primary focus in recent times, usurping agriculture and the spice business as the tri-island state's main source of earned overseas income. Grenada has an international airport, constructed in 1985, assisting the island develop this industry which, despite setbacks from natural disasters, continues to recover and surpass pre-2004 levels. Prior to 2004 there were almost 400,000 visitors to Grenada, with around 250,000 arriving on cruise ships. Of those who stayed over in hotels, around 27% travelled from North America and 21% from the UK. Grenada's white sandy beaches and beautifully secluded bays have given it immense pulling power when it comes to attracting sun worshippers, sailing enthusiasts and those looking for a period of escape and luxury. The southwest peninsula in particular, thanks to the famous Grand Anse Beach, is now a burgeoning community of shops, hotels, resorts, restaurants, marinas and foreign-owned high-end domestic residences. Annual sailing regattas in Grenada and Carriacou are a huge draw to yachtspeople from all over the world and, with numerous wrecks, including the *Bianca C*, lying at recreational diving depths Grenada is justifiably trying to establish itself as the 'wreck-diving capital of the Caribbean'.

The decline of the agricultural industry, primarily through natural disaster and lack of reinvestment, means that those living in rural areas are also very dependent on the arrival of the peak tourist season and cruise-ship visitors. Though by no means matching the levels of prosperity once earned through pure agriculture itself, agro-tourism attractions such as the Belmont cocoa estate, the Gouyave and Grenville nutmeg stations, Gouyave's Fish Friday, the Bay Gardens and Laura Herb & Spice Gardens are providing some communities with a vital source of income in very hard times. Visitors to Grenada should be encouraged to travel beyond the beaches and also try to support those living in less affluent, rural Grenada.

The resurgence of the tourism industry has also attracted the conceptual design and, in some cases, the actual initiation of a number of overseas-funded investment projects. These include the substantial marina developments of Port Louis in St George's Lagoon, and also at Prickly Bay, luxury residential community developments such as Grand Harbour and Pointe Marquis, and further high-end holiday resorts such as Bacolet Bay. Controversy surrounds some project developments, such as those planned and in construction at Levera and Mt Hartman, as they are both located in or near to designated national parks, the latter being home to the endangered Grenada dove. Critics of government support for an investment-led recovery suggest that this strategy will ultimately lead to land prices becoming too high for Grenadians to ever be able to afford and that jobs in construction and tourism are both short term as well as condemn ordinary Grenadians to a lifetime of menial ancillary work such as cleaning and serving. The International Monetary Fund (IMF) has welcomed efforts to develop Grenada's economy through tourism, services and investment, but has also expressed concern over what will happen when construction on the current programme of projects is completed. Time will tell.

## PEOPLE

Grenadians are lovely people. They are approachable and very friendly. Indeed if you spend your holiday holed-up in a resort, never giving yourself the opportunity to interact with local people, it is safe to say you will most certainly have missed out.

Many Grenadians have a tough life and are relatively poor by Western standards, living in conditions that contrast starkly with the numerous luxury residences of the southern peninsulas on the main island. In spite of hardship and a history of conflict, setbacks and rebellion, Grenadians are predominantly a quiet and reserved people who are very polite and genuinely warm towards visitors. As the revolution and incidents of 1983 are still in recent memory and, at the time of writing, those found guilty remain incarcerated, visitors should be a little wary of the subject. Strong feelings and emotions can surface from time to time so please be sensitive.

If you plan on visiting Carriacou and Petite Martinique (which you absolutely should) you may notice a difference between these islanders and those on Grenada. Also extremely friendly and hardworking, they are a very independent people with a strong sense of identity with their island home, with their cultural heritage and with their historical roots, which – you may be surprised to learn – are as diverse as Africa and Scotland.

### CUTLASS AND MACHETE

Sailors and pirates of the Caribbean in the 17th and 18th centuries would carry a cutlass as their main weapon. It was a short sabre with a broad curved blade and was especially effective in close combat on ship and shore, as well as for cutting rope and wood. On land it was also occasionally used as an agricultural tool, especially for cutting through rainforest or even for harvesting sugarcane.

Also used both as a weapon and an agricultural tool was the machete. Very similar in shape and length to a cutlass, the machete also has a broad blade with a very thin, sharp cutting edge. It is however much less elegant in design than the cutlass, and is sometimes referred to as the 'poor man's sword'. Variations of the machete exist in many countries. The *parang*, *golok* and *bolo* are very similar long knives used in Malaysia, Indonesia and the Philippines; in Nepal it is the *kukri* and in China the *dao*.

In Grenada today the machete is commonly used as an agricultural tool and most households will possess at least one. Commonly referred to as a cutlass, it is in fact a basic machete, rather than its upmarket relative. Visitors to Grenada may see both men and women walking along the roadside carrying a machete. This should not cause alarm, although it almost certainly will at first. The machete is an agricultural tool and is used by Grenadians for cutting overgrown bush, pruning trees, weeding and for getting the refreshing water out of a young coconut.

**POPULATION** The population of Grenada is estimated to be approximately 90,000 with roughly a third of the nation's people living in or around the capital St George's. With an average age of 22, Grenada has an increasingly young population due to high fertility rates and economic migration.

**ETHNICITY** The majority of Grenadians (approximately 80%) are descendants of slaves brought to the island by both the French and the British from west Africa. There are also a small number of people (around 5%) of East Indian origin who are descendants of the indentured workforce that was introduced following the abolition of slavery during the mid 19th century.

## LANGUAGE

The official language of Grenada is English, which is spoken throughout the island. French Patois (also called French Creole, Kwéyòl, Patwa or Patois) is still spoken in some communities, such as L'Esterre in Carriacou for example, though it is becoming very rare.

The English spoken by Grenadians can occasionally be heavily accented and illustrated with colourful expressions that have their origins in both French and English Creole. These dialects were born during slavery and combined the grammar and syntax of their masters' languages with those of their native Africa. Some 'Grenadianisms' are also influenced by expressions and words that reflect the East Indian origins of the island's former indentured workforce. It may take a little time to tune in to the accent if you are not accustomed to it.

Listen out for some of the following words and expressions that add a distinct linguistic spice to the English spoken on all three islands:

| | |
|---|---|
| *Wa gwan/W'ap'nin?* | What's going on/happening? (usually a greeting) |
| *One time* | All at once |
| *Oh shrimps man!* | Oh goodness! |
| *He went out to come back* | He'll be back soon |
| *She swallow a breadfruit* | She's pregnant |
| *Saraca* | Feast (usually related to a ceremony) |

## RELIGION

Despite the dominance of the British influence in colonial times, the majority of Grenadians (approximately 53%) follow the Roman Catholic faith. It is thought that the British Protestant plantocracy behaved so badly towards the slave population that, once liberated and allowed to worship in churches, the freed slave population rejected their former masters' faith in an act of defiance and became Roman Catholics instead. Approximately 14% of Grenadians are practising Anglicans. A number of other Christian denominations are present in Grenada including Methodists, Pentecostals, Seventh-Day Adventists, Baptists and Jehovah's Witnesses. Minority faiths include Islam, Baha'i, Rastafarianism and Scientology.

## EDUCATION

Grenada's educational system is based to a large extent on the British system. Education is free and compulsory for children between the ages of five and 16. Primary education in Grenada lasts for seven years and secondary education for five years.

Grenada's further education institutions include the T A Marryshow Community College, which is located near the Lagoon in the capital, St George's. Students wishing to pursue degree courses travel abroad to study and are usually reliant on scholarships or bursaries to pay for their tuition. In True Blue there is a large, private US further education institution called the St George's University Medical School which was founded in 1977. The school provides medical training for students from overseas countries, in the main from the US.

## CULTURE

Although they inhabited the islands for longer than any of their successors, the cultural influences of the original Amerindian settlers have sadly been lost. Grenada's cultural heritage is largely the result of African, French, British and also, to a certain extent, East Indian and Latin American influences. African tribal traditions including music, dance, dress and belief systems merged with the culture of the island's French settlers, and then later on with those of the British plantocracy. Unlike some Caribbean nations whose culture continued to be strongly influenced by the proximity of islands that were governed by France, Grenada's **French Creole** began to wane once the country became a British Crown Colony. Nevertheless, despite the dominance of the British and the Anglican and Roman Catholic churches, French influence still managed to survive in the form of dress, language and also in many of Grenada's place names. Stronger still were the residual influences of the liberated population's African heritage, which can still be enjoyed today in the form of music, dance, festivals, belief systems and cooking. East Indian cultural influences originally stem from the island's indentured labour force of the mid 19th century and more recently from the neighbouring island of Trinidad. This tends to manifest itself primarily in local cuisine and also in music.

**MUSIC AND DANCE** Traditional music and dance finds its roots deep within the island's history. From the slaves of west Africa, the influences of their European masters, and the more contemporary sway of neighbouring islands such as Trinidad and Tobago, Grenada's musical instruments, songs, music and dance have evolved as heady concoctions of past and present that are still used, performed and enjoyed by many today.

Central to most traditional music and dance festivals, especially in Carriacou, is usually the goatskin drum, or *la peau cabrit*, providing the celebration with an unmistakable rhythm of Africa that harks back to the Akan tribes of the former Gold Coast and the Igbo and Mandingo of Nigeria. Interestingly, the lyric of many traditional songs is sung in French Creole, creating what is often a haunting yet ebullient fusion of cultures. Grenada's most celebrated music and dance expression is the **Big Drum Dance** which is performed in Carriacou. Big Drum is also occasionally known as the African Nation Dance and is a central feature of many festivals and ceremonies in Carriacou, such as maroons, boat launchings, weddings and so on. It consists of three drums, the *cot* and two *bula*, plus an assortment of simple percussion accompaniments such as the *shak-shak* and the *old hoe*. Many types of dancing accompany the drumming, which is led by the cot, all of which combine African and Creole influences. Singing is traditionally in Creole, and its lyric usually tells of a time of slavery and a longing for a return to the homeland of Africa (see page 196).

The *bélé*, or *belair*, is a Creole dance of African origin. Again, the drum is the centrepiece of the dance which traditionally reflects a courtship between a man and a woman. The dancers move in turn towards the drum and, by the time the dance reaches its conclusion, the drum is beating ever louder and the man and woman are dancing together with quick steps and vigorous body movements that symbolise their union.

The *quadrille* is a more formal square dance that has its origins in the French court of the 19th century. The style is aristocratic, graceful and elegant, with four couples dancing together and usually accompanied by a four-instrument ensemble.

Couples dancing the *quadrille*, the *bélé* and Big Drum are likely to have worn colourful outfits that were in stark contrast to the drab uniforms they were forced to wear when they were in servitude. These outfits may have included white chemises, flowing skirts and a colourful material known as *madras*. This material is an East Indian cotton that was made by the Kalabari people in the vicinity of Chennai (formerly Madras, India) and still known by them as *injiri*. Though it became an essential part of traditional French Creole wear, it was originally traded by Portuguese merchants in west Africa where it was worn by the Igbo of southern Nigeria. After arriving in the West Indies as slaves, the Igbo are thought to have continued to wear *madras* whenever they could, especially on Sundays or feast days. Although Grenada's French Creole heritage is not as strong today as it is on other islands, dancers continue to wear brightly coloured skirts and chemises, adding to the ancestral spirit of Africa that prevails throughout the nation's music and dance festivals.

*Parang* is a traditional form of Latin American music that probably arrived in Grenada from Trinidad where it is also very common today. A *parang* music ensemble usually consists of string instruments, drum and percussion who accompany a singer. The lyric is either impromptu or rehearsed, and its theme reflects a story, perhaps a scandal, a rumour or a critique of something or someone from the local community. In Carriacou, *parang* festivals usually take place at Christmas time and can be lively, raucous affairs, depending on the subject, the humour and the skill of the lyric.

*Calypso* is very similar to *parang* in that its lyric usually comprises a social commentary of some kind. This music form evolved as part of the preparations for carnival (see below) and was traditionally performed by women who sang short, cutting ballads that ridiculed members of the plantocracy, administrators or overseers, and in particular perpetrators of bad deeds. Today *calypso* songs are much longer and usually performed in competitions at carnival time. The lyric still contains at least a hint of irony or some kind of political comment.

Grenada's popular music scene finds its roots in *calypso* and the popularity of **steel pan** music during the 1960s. Strongly influenced by neighbouring islands, in particular Trinidad and Tobago, music forms such as **soca** became very prominent from the 1980s. *Soca* is essentially a fusion of *calypso* and Trinidad's Indian music, sometimes called *chutney* music. Other contemporary music influences from neighbouring islands include **zouk** and **bouyon** which have emerged as popular music genres in Guadeloupe, Dominica and Martinique and, of course, **reggae** and **dancehall** music from Jamaica.

**FESTIVALS** Grenada celebrates a number of festivals that have a very interesting blend of traditional influences. The **Maroon Festival** is in reality a series of festivals rather than one event (though from time to time, a larger festival is arranged). Celebrated in Carriacou, maroon festivals find their roots in Africa and in the emergent communities of liberated African slaves who provided each other with assistance, celebrated bountiful harvests and prayed for newly planted crops. Essential components of a village 'maroon' are good-humoured people, lots of great food and usually a Big Drum Dance (see page 195 for more information).

**Carnival** is traditionally celebrated on the Monday and Tuesday before Ash Wednesday. This is still the case in Carriacou, though the Grenada Carnival is now celebrated in August (so that it does not take place at the same time as the Trinidad Carnival). The **Spice Mas** has its origins in the masquerade balls of the French court, though it was liberated African slaves who added rhythm, vibrancy, colour and a strong sense of rebellion.

Contemporary carnival is a mix of both the traditional and the modern. Booming amplifiers on flatbed trucks mix with vivacious costumes and colourful traditional figures such as the *jab-jabs*, *wild Indians*, *shortknees*, *moko jumbies* and *tamboo-bamboo* bands, as well as the *paywo* or *Shakespeare mas* of Carriacou. (For more information on Grenada's carnivals go to www.spicemasgrenada.com; see also *Chapter 2, Public holidays and events*, page 61.)

**ART AND SCULPTURE** Grenada has some very talented homegrown and resident artists and sculptors. Perhaps one of the nation's most celebrated artists is **Canute Caliste**, from L'Esterre in Carriacou. Born in 1914, Canute Caliste became a revered Carriacouan artist and musician who was known for his simple style of painting, capturing the everyday life and vivid natural beauty of his island home. He worked mainly with acrylics on hardboard and canvas and, it is said, he could 'knock-out' 20 paintings a day when the mood caught him. Mermaids appeared as a motif in many of his works, reflecting an experience he claimed to have had as a child when a mermaid appeared to him in a vision, telling him that if he followed the Bible he could achieve anything. When he was not painting, Canute Caliste was a boatbuilder and *quadrille* dance musician, playing both guitar and fiddle. Caliste's paintings have been exhibited in North America and Europe. Visitors to Grenada can view some of his artwork at the Yellow Poui Gallery in St George's, and reproductions can be found at the Grenada National Museum in St George's and the Carriacou Museum in Hillsborough. *The Mermaid Wakes* was a book published in 1989 showcasing many of his works. Canute Caliste died in 2005.

**Susan Mains** is a self-taught artist from the US who is also a citizen and resident of Grenada. Susan works in both acrylic and oil on canvas and her works depict beautiful, colourful images of Caribbean life, landscapes and people. Her subjects include traditional boatbuilding and launching, farming, coastal and countryside scenes, portraits and tropical flora. In Grenada her artwork is on display at a number of hotels including the Flamboyant and Mount Cinnamon at the western tip of Grand Anse Beach. You will also find them both on display and for sale at the Art & Soul shop in the Spiceland Mall, also in Grand Anse. For more information go to www.susanmains.com.

**Asher Mains** is a young Grenadian artist who produces beautiful acrylic images of people, often Afro-Caribbean musicians, with one of his favourite subjects being Bob Marley. His work is inspiring and can also be found on display at some of Grenada's hotels, including the True Blue Bay Resort. You can also purchase his work from Art & Soul in the Spiceland Mall, Grand Anse. For more information go to www.ashermains.com.

**Elinus Cato** was born in St Patrick in 1933 and rose to prominence as a very popular painter. His works of town and rural Grenadian life depict bright and colourful scenes and one such piece, *People at Work*, was presented to Queen Elizabeth II when she visited the island in 1985. Some of Cato's work can be seen at the Yellow Poui Gallery in St George's.

**Jackie Miller** is a celebrated Grenadian artist, producing paintings and drawings in a variety of media including watercolour, acrylic and charcoal. Miller's works can also be found on display at the Yellow Poui Gallery in St George's.

**Oliver Benoit** is a Grenadian-born artist who began as a still-life and landscape painter. His more contemporary pieces are beautiful abstracts of colour, depth and texture that aim to perplex and stimulate perspective and perception. For more information go to www.artingrenada.com/oliver-benoit-artist/oliver-benoit.html.

Although seeking out artwork in Grenada is quite tricky, a great place to begin is at the **Yellow Poui Gallery** in St George's. The gallery was set up by Jim Rudin and his wife in 1968 and it exhibits and sells paintings, sculptures and carvings by artists either from, working in or inspired by the Caribbean. You could also seek out **Art Grenada** upstairs in the Grand Anse shopping mall. In addition to those mentioned above, visitors should look out for artists and sculptors such as **Trish Bethany**, **Frankie Francis**, **Michael Paryag**, **Joseph Rome**, **Joseph Browne**, **Rene Froehlich**, **Ivan Godfrey** and **Stanley Coutain**, to name just a few.

**LITERATURE** Grenada has produced no real literary giants, although many of its more contemporary writers, poets and playwrights are definitely worth seeking out. **Merle Collins** has published poetry and short-story collections such as *Because the Dawn Breaks* and *Rain Darling*, as well as novels such as *Angel* and *The Colour of Forgetting*. **Jacob Ross** is a Grenadian-born writer who has published acclaimed short-story collections such as *Song For Simone* and *A Way to Catch the Dust*. Children's writer **Verna Allette Wilkins** has written a number of charming and popular books such as *Dave and the Tooth Fairy*, *Toyin Fay* and *Kim's Magic Tree*. **Joan Anim-Addo** is a Grenadian poet and publisher of *Haunted by History*, a collection of poems that explore history and its effect on individuals. She is also the author of works that study African–Caribbean women's writing, such as *Touching the Body* and *Framing the Word*. **Jean Buffong**'s novels *Under the Silk Cotton Tree*, *Jump Up and Kiss Me* and *Snowflakes in the Sun* are colourful portrayals of Grenadian life from the perspectives of young and old. **Claude J Douglas** has published interesting books about the history and development of Grenada such as *When the Village was an Extended Family in Grenada* and *The Battle for Grenada's Black Gold* which is a fascinating study of the island's turbulent nutmeg industry. Anyone interested in Grenada's history should definitely own a copy of *Grenada: Island of Conflict* by historian and former prime minister, **George Brizan** (see *Appendix 3*, page 225).

**FOLKLORE** Grenada's folkloric heritage originates in the fascinating myths, legends, spirit tales and rites of west African tribal traditions. For many Grenadians this lore still goes beyond mere superstition and is inextricably bound with the island's more contemporary practices and belief systems.

*Obeah*, a kind of magic or witchcraft, is still practised by some Grenadians, though it is rare. It is a combination of superstition, medicine and divination whose rituals included the sacrifice of animals and the use of symbols or amulets to call upon or quell evil spirits. Traditionally an obeahman or obeahwoman would be hired to help you with advice, protection, potions or spells in your efforts to satisfy a particular ambition or desire.

The *soucouyant* is a night spirit of west African origin who sheds her skin and flies through the forest in the form of a ball of fire. She is continuously on the lookout for innocents and for the blood of people and animals. In order to catch a *soucouyant* you must find her skin after she has shed it (usually she hides it in a mortar or beneath a stone) and then rub it with salt before she can put it on and transform herself back into a human being. Alternatively you can place a bowl of peas or grain next to her skin which she must count before transforming herself again. The *ligarou* is a male version of the *soucouyant* and is equally unpleasant. **La Diablesse** (or 'Lajabless') is a beautiful woman who walks through the forest by the light of the moon and lures unsuspecting men deeper and deeper into the woods until they are lost. Once there, she reveals herself as a she-devil who causes her victims either to go mad or to die. In some variations of the myth she wears a large hat to hide her skeletal face, or she walks in long grass to disguise both the appearance and sound of her cloven hooves. **Mama Glo** is a female spirit of lakes and rivers who may take the form of a beautiful young woman or a mermaid. It is said that she will command you to perform menial tasks such as scratching her back or collecting leaves. If you ignore or disobey her she becomes extremely angry and may strangle or drown you. Mama Glo is worshipped by believers of Shango (see page 176).

Staying indoors, not walking in the forest, avoiding water and hiding beneath your covers does not necessarily guarantee your safety, however. A *jumbie* (or *jombie*) is the spirit of a dead person who brings you bad luck or ill health if it discovers you sleeping, and **Mama Maladie** is the angry spirit of a woman who has died in childbirth and who walks back and forth between her grave and her former home. She may also linger, waiting for unsuspecting mothers to open their doors and let her inside. You will know she is in your home because you will hear the voice of a crying child, and with it comes a plague of disease. It is said that cursing the spirit in French Creole may help to make her disappear. The *baccoo* is a temperamental spirit who lives in a bottle, rather similar to a genie, and who can bring both wealth and happiness as well as financial ruin and even death. Usually a *baccoo* is viewed as simply an unattractive, mischievous spirit who may be returned to its bottle by beating a drum. So if you return to find your hotel room a mess, it may not be that room service forgot you; it could be that someone has sent a *baccoo* to cause you trouble. Better go buy a drum.

# NATURAL HISTORY

**HABITATS** Though all three islands of the state of Grenada are relatively small, they contain a variety of natural habitats with a surprising diversity of vegetation and wildlife. The impact of the 2004 and 2005 hurricanes is very visible, particularly in the high mountain elevations and along windward-facing slopes. These areas were exposed to the full force of the storms and there was considerable damage to tall, mature trees as well as vulnerable, shallow-rooted vegetation. The condition of these interior habitats today is one of flux and they are in the process of sorting themselves out. Vegetation that is accustomed to a dark, shady and very wet rainforest environment that is created by the tall, lush canopies of magnificently tall and mature trees such as the gommier or gum tree (*Dacryodes excelsa*) or the karapit (*Amanoa caribea*), also known as *bois rouge*, now find themselves exposed to sunlight, wind and a much drier habitat than they like because many of the tall trees fell in the storms. Some of these habitats may require a long period of time to re-establish themselves.

The highest mountain peaks, pinnacles and ridges of Grenada's interior will often be hidden by a blanket of cloud. The rain-laden weather that arrives with the prevailing winds across the Atlantic Ocean tends to reach the island's eastern shoreline and then sit over the high elevations of the interior. These areas can therefore be quite cold and wet for much of the year and their vegetation reflects this moist and exposed environment. Habitats of this type are usually referred to as **elfin woodland** or cloudforest and tend to consist of low-growing species of trees such as *Clusia*, a selection of ferns, mountain palms (*Prestoea montana*), moss and grasses such as *Scleria*, or razor grass. Visitors to Grenada's elevated interior will certainly encounter elfin woodland habitats at the summit of peaks such as Mt St Catherine, which is the island's tallest mountain, and Morne Fédon (Fédon's Camp).

Located just below elfin woodland is a habitat usually referred to as **montane forest**, sometimes also called montane thicket. The vegetation found here is similar to that of the rainforest though its growth tends to be a little more stunted. Below the montane thicket is the **rainforest**. It is here that some of the largest and most impressive trees are found. They include the gommier, or gum tree (*Dacryodes excelsa*), the maruba (*Simarouba amara*), mahogany (*Swietenia mahogani*) and the small- and large-leaf santai (*Sloanea caribaea* and *Sloanea truncata*). A species of Caribbean pine (*Pinos caribaea*) can also be found in the Grand Étang region. This tree was introduced to Grenada in an effort to reduce the country's need for wood imports. The rainforest habitat is also where you will encounter a wide variety of ferns and epiphytes such as bromeliads and orchids.

Grenada's extensive **coastal woodland**, also known as dry scrub woodland, is a dry forest habitat that reflects an environment that receives much less rainfall than in the interior. Carriacou and Petite Martinique are predominantly dry scrub woodland environments where trees are usually semi-deciduous, shedding some of their leaves during the dry season to conserve moisture and survive. Trees found in this habitat include the white cedar (*Tabebuia heterophylla*), the campeche or dogwood (*Haematoxylum campechianum*), acacia (*Acacia*), black sage (*Cordia curassavica*) and the blackthorn (*Pisonia aculeata*). Along the fringes of sandy beaches you will encounter torchwood (*Jacquinia armillaris*), sea grape (*Coccoloba uvifera*), sea almond (*Terminalia catappa*), the poisonous manchineel (*Hippomane mancinella*) and, of course, the prolific coconut palm.

Grenada and Carriacou have a number of inland and coastal **mangrove forests** and **swamps**. Here you will find black mangrove (*Avicennia germinans*), red mangrove (*Rhizophora mangle*) and, around the margins of the Grand Étang Lake, the arum lily (*Montrichardia arborescens*).

See page 28 for information on the islands' marine environment.

## FLORA

**Flowers** Grenada has a very rich variety of flowers and flowering trees. As well as flowers growing in the wild, there are several ornamental gardens for visitors to enjoy. In 2006, Grenada's exhibit 'Beautiful Grenada' was awarded a Silver Gilt at the Chelsea Flower Show and then Gold in 2007 for 'Island in the Sun'.

The **national flower** of Grenada, Carriacou and Petite Martinique is the **bougainvillea** (*Bougainvillea spectablis*) which grows all over the islands and is often found in the carefully tended gardens of many homes. Visitors to Grenada will very commonly see many other varieties of colourful flowers and plants including gingers, heliconias, bromeliads, orchids, crotons, hibiscus, euphorbias, begonia and ixoras. Endemic to Grenada is the *bois agouti* (*Maytenus grenadensis*), a tree with simple leaves and small white flowers. Also endemic to Grenada are *Rhytidophyllum caribaeum*, a small shrub with cream or orange flowers, *Lonchocarpus broadwayi* and *Cyathea elliotii*.

**Fruits and vegetables** In addition to its wonderful spices, Grenada's farmers grow a wide variety of interesting and delicious fruits and vegetables. Most Grenadian families own a piece of land that enables them to plant produce for themselves where they tend to grow traditional subsistence crops such as yams, calalou, sweet potatoes and pigeon peas. Vegetable crops such as beans, carrots, cabbage, potatoes and peas are also common. Banana plantations are small though quite widespread. In addition to the bananas that most visitors recognise, Grenadians also cultivate plantain and bluggo as well as harvesting unripe bananas, known as 'green bananas' or 'figs', which are used in soups, stews and the national dish, 'oil down'. In addition to pigeon peas, corn is a traditional crop which is still commonly cultivated in dry areas. Fruits that can be found growing in the wild as well as in managed farms include mango, grapefruit, lime, pawpaw (also known as papaya), guava, passionfruit, sapodilla, pineapple, watermelon and breadfruit.

## FAUNA

**Birds** Grenada's forests, coastal woodlands, bays, estuaries, rugged coastlines and floral gardens combine to create habitats for birds of all kinds. Grenada's **national bird** is the **Grenada dove** (*Leptotila wellsi*). It is thought to be endemic to Grenada and is becoming very rare. The dove has been observed mainly in the southwest of Grenada within the Mt Hartman National Park and Clarke's Court Bay areas. It has also been recorded around Perseverance, Beauséjour, Black Bay and Halifax Harbour. Little is known about the dove though its numbers are believed to be small. Also considered endemic to Grenada is the endangered **hook-billed kite** (*Chrondrohierax uncinatus*), one of the smallest species of hawks and also observed in the dry scrubland of the southwest.

Grenada has three nesting species of hummingbird. The rufous-breasted hermit (*Glaucis hirsuta*), also known as the hairy hermit, is thought to be endemic to Grenada and Trinidad and Tobago. It has a brown-coloured head, a bronze and green upper body, and a rufous underbelly. It prefers the habitat of the elevated rainforest, making a feast of heliconia and ginger lilies, but is rarely encountered. More common is the emerald-throated hummingbird (*Sericotes holosericus chlorolaemus*), also known as the green-throated carib. Its very distinct colouration includes a covering of shimmering emerald and a vivid, violet-blue breast. This hummingbird can be observed all around Grenada. The third hummingbird is the Antillean-crested hummingbird (*Orthorhyncus cristatus*), also known locally as the *colibri*, a name thought to have Amerindian origins. Said to be the smallest bird found in the islands, it is brightly coloured with an emerald green and blue crest, and can be observed throughout Grenada.

Bird enthusiasts should also look out for the magnificent frigatebird (*Fregata magnificens*), which can be observed circling and diving along inshore waters, along with boobies, terns, herons and egrets. Woodland and mangrove birds that can be seen and heard in Grenada include the unmistakable bananaquit (*Coereba flaveola*), the loggerhead flycatcher (*Myiarchus nugator*), the southern mockingbird (*Minus gilvus antillarum*), the smooth-billed ani (*Crotophaga ani*) and the mangrove cuckoo (*Coccyzus minor grenadensis*). Birds of prey include the barn owl (*Tyto alba*), also known as the jumbie bird because it is thought to contain evil spirits, the osprey (*Pandian haliaetus*) which is rarely seen, and the broad-winged hawk (*Buteo platypterus*), also known as the chicken hawk, which is more commonly sighted.

**Mammals** The **mona monkey** (*Ceropithecus mona*) is also known as the macaque and was probably brought from west Africa to Grenada by slave traders in the 18th century. The population is thought to have developed from very small numbers though studies have suggested it is healthy and lives off fruits, leaves and insects in Grenada's mountainous, forested interior. Though hurricanes have devastated its habitat in recent years, it is thought to survive well and in relatively high numbers.

The **mongoose** (*Herpestes auropunctatus*) was introduced to Grenada in the late 19th century in an attempt to control rodents in sugarcane plantations. Its impact on pests is thought to have been extremely negligible and it was soon considered a pest itself. In the second half of the 20th century it was discovered that the mongoose carried the rabies virus and an island-wide vaccination and eradication programme commenced. Though rabies may still exist in the mongoose population it is no longer considered a serious problem. Visitors to Grenada should nevertheless avoid contact with this animal if it is encountered (see page 43 for advice on rabies).

The **nine-banded long-nosed armadillo** (*Dasypus novemcinctus hoplites*) is a small mammal with a bony, armour-like shell. It was probably introduced by the island's original settlers and is known locally by its Amerindian name, *tatu*. Though it is classified as rare, it is sadly considered a game animal. The forests of Grand Étang provide its habitat where it lives on insects, small animals, vegetables and decaying flesh. Interesting facts about this particular species of armadillo are that it produces four identical offspring, it can inflate its intestine, making it buoyant enough to float or swim across rivers, and, if swimming is an unattractive proposition, it can hold its breath long enough to be able to walk across riverbeds instead.

**Manicou** is the name given to two species of opossum found in Grenada. They are Robinson's mouse opossum (*Marmosa robinsoni*) and the large opossum (*Didelphis marsupialis insularis*). The mouse opossum lives in Grenada's interior, feeding on fruits and insects and is considered rare. The large opossum is hunted for its meat and is also rare.

Eleven species of bat have been recorded in Grenada. With the exception of the greater fishing bat, all feed on insects. All of the bat species hunt at night and are most commonly sighted in forest habitats.

## Reptiles and amphibians

There are thought to be around ten species of lizard found in the tri-island state. The most common is the **green lizard** (*Anolis aenus*), also known locally as the *zandoli*, which grows to around 20cm in length and has the ability to change colour according to its environment. The male green lizard has a distinctive colourful throat fan that it uses in courtship and also as a territorial warning. Slightly larger than the green lizard, and also quite commonly observed, is the **tree lizard** (*Anolis richardi*) which is either green or brown and has a distinctive crest running the length of its head and neck. The **ground lizard** (*Ameiva ameiva*), also known as the *zagada*, does not climb trees and prefers to live in dry undergrowth or to sit stock-still, sunning itself on a rock. The male is usually a bluish colour and the female brown with lighter stripes along her flanks. The largest lizard found in Grenada is the very colourful **green iguana** (*Iguana iguana*) that has been known to grow as large as 1.5m in length. It is herbivorous and usually lives in trees where it feeds on leaves and flowers. The iguana is considered a threatened species in Grenada due to loss of habitat and illegal hunting.

Four snake species are recorded as still living in Grenada although exact numbers are unknown. The largest snake is the **tree boa** (*Corallus enydris*), also known locally as the *serpent*. As its name suggests, it is usually found living in trees where it feeds on lizards, rodents and birds. The **cribo** (*Clelia clelia*) is a large snake that has its home in the forest, often close to water, and is said to have the appearance of a large eel. It is thought to be endemic and extremely rare. The two other snakes found in Grenada are the **grass snake** (*Mastigodryas bruesi*) and the **blind worm snake** (*Typhlops tasmicris*). An encounter with a snake should be considered fortunate as they are rarely observed. None of Grenada's snakes are venomous, though the cribo is rumoured to have a bad temper if it is annoyed. So don't call it an eel.

The **red-legged tortoise** (*Geochelone carbonaria*), or *morocoy*, is rare because it was hunted for its meat and shell. Once considered practically extinct, captive animals were reintroduced to the environment to supplement native populations that had managed to survive. It is thought that the *morocoy* still lives in the High North National Park in Carriacou as well as on Frigate Island.

The **giant toad** (*Bufo marinus*), or *crapaud*, is the only toad found in Grenada. Also known as the giant cane toad, this large amphibian was introduced in the early 19th century in an attempt to control pests in the sugarcane fields of the island's estates and plantations. It is a rather ugly beast that uses a milky secretion called bufotalin as a defence measure. Following the decline of the estates, the *crapaud* now finds its home by water in forested areas of the island and is rarely sighted. In addition to the cane toad, Grenada has three species of frog that include **Garman's woodland frog** (*Leptodactylus validus*), which is found in the forest and is quite rare. The two remaining species are responsible for the chorus of sound that you hear at night-time if you are staying near woodland areas, especially during the rainy season. They are **Johnstone's whistling frog** (*Eleutherodactylus johnstonei*) and the **highland piping frog** (*Eleutherodactylus urichi*). Both are tiny, nocturnal and feed on small insects.

**MARINE ENVIRONMENT** Along the rugged windward coastlines of Grenada, Carriacou and Petite Martinique, powerful seas roll in from the Atlantic Ocean, crashing against impenetrable rocky volcanic outcrops and cliffs, and stretches of isolated black- and white-sand beaches. In these areas the marine environment is wild and unforgiving with strong currents, formidable surges and tall plumes of white spray. In the southeast of the main island, Grenada, a coastal landscape of sheltered harbours and deep horseshoe-shaped bays combine with inshore reefs to provide peaceful havens from the might of the open ocean. Here you will also find a number of secluded beaches and protected anchorages for sailing boats and fishermen.

In the channels of the Grenada Grenadines the waters are deep, clear and unpredictable. Strong currents rip around barren rocky outcrops, tall pinnacles and uninhabited islets, forming a unique underwater environment where Caribbean Sea and Atlantic Ocean merge. The unpredictable currents carry nutrient-rich waters that attract huge shoals of fish and large pelagics. The active submarine volcano of Kick-Em-Jenny, located off the north coast of Grenada, adds a certain aquatic spice to this challenging environment.

Along the leeward coastlines of the three islands the difference is stark. The calm seas of the Caribbean lap gently against tall cliffs, rocky peninsulas, secluded bays and picture-postcard, powder-white sandy beaches. As well as idyllic escapes for beach lovers and sun worshippers, the calmer Caribbean Sea offers a marine environment that is safe to explore. Its waters contain an exuberance of aquatic life that includes whales and dolphins, sharks, turtles, colourful fish and coral reefs. Also within these more sheltered waters, you will encounter shipwrecks and underwater sculptures that have become artificial reefs and home to a wide variety of interesting marine creatures.

**Coral reefs** Grenada's reef topography includes long, undulating ledges and steep drop-offs. From sandy shorelines, reefs along leeward coastlines tend to develop in deeper waters and usually contain quite a high degree of turbidity. The reefs and waters in the channels and around the islets and pinnacles of more exposed waters tend to be much clearer and have a far more dramatic marine topography. Here, shallow reefs quickly end in breathtaking drop-offs and deep blue water. Grenada's marine environment is a healthy one and its reefs contain an interesting mixture of hard and soft corals, sponges and gorgonians. Stony coral varieties include finger coral, sheet coral and large brain coral. Gorgonians are widespread, particularly along the reefs of Grenada's southwest, and include sea fans and sea whips.

**Fish** Large numbers of fish live in and around Grenada's reef systems and migratory pelagics and predators are also common visitors. Shoals of Napoleon and Creole wrasse patrol expansive reef systems where shelter and food are available to a wide variety of other brightly coloured fish, including damselfish, angelfish and butterflyfish. Within the nooks and crannies of the reef system itself live both green and spotted varieties of moray eel together with lobster, crab and octopus. Parrotfish, cowfish, trunkfish and trumpetfish add further interest to the reef environment.

It is common to see nurse sharks resting on the sand between reef formations or beneath the natural shelters provided by hard corals. Reef sharks are also common visitors, especially in and around some of the deeper wrecks and reef systems of the Atlantic channels. Stingrays and large eagle rays are frequently sighted along Grenada's reefs together with patrolling barracuda, predatory jacks and mackerel.

**Whales and dolphins** Around 15 species of whale have been recorded in Grenada's waters, many of which are regular sightings between the months of December to April, though some can be seen all year round. They include humpback whales (*Megaptera novaengliae*), sperm whales (*Physeter macrocephallus*), Bryde's whales (*Balaenoptera brydei*) and pilot whales (*Globicephala melaena*).

Large pods of dolphin are frequently encountered offshore and include spinner dolphins (*Stenella longirostris*), bottlenose dolphins (*Tursiops truncatus*), Fraser's dolphins (*Lagenodelphis hosei*) and common dolphins (*Delphinus delphis*).

**Other marine creatures** From March to October each year, along the coasts of Grenada, in particular the beaches of the Levera Archipelago National Park and High North National Park, giant **leatherback turtles** (*Dermochelys coriacea*) return to lay their clusters of eggs. The giant leatherback is the largest of all living sea turtles and is a protected species. The **hawksbill turtle** (*Eretmochelys imbriocota*) is the most common species of turtle sighted in Grenada's waters along with the **green turtle** (*Chelonia mydas*). The **loggerhead turtle** (*Caretta caretta*) is also observed, though more rarely. Other interesting creatures that can be found in Grenada's diverse marine environment include **echinoderms** such as the sea cucumber, long-spined sea urchins, crinoids and sea eggs.

For additional information see *Protected seascapes*, page 31.

## CONSERVATION

In an effort to protect areas of both natural and cultural significance, the government of Grenada came up with a national park and forestry management system. As part of the plan, selected areas and landmarks were aligned to management and conservation categories that included national parks, natural landmarks, cultural landmarks, and protected seascapes. Some conservationists would argue that the work seemed to stop there as many of these protected areas are somewhat neglected and others are the subject of controversial hotel resort and golf course development projects. At the time of writing there is no charging framework for most of these protected areas and so little funding appears to be available for ploughing back into their management and upkeep. Visitors will find that some trails can be overgrown, sometimes blocked by fallen trees or landslides, signage can be poor and, in the case of protected seascapes, there are currently no permanent moorings or enforced rules preventing boats dropping anchors and damaging reef systems. In their defence, presumably due to the reinvestment and work efforts that have been needed since recent hurricanes, Grenada's conservation and park systems have simply fallen down the list of priorities for the country's government. Hopefully they will make it back up there again soon.

**FOREST RESERVES** As part of the country's forestry management policy, Grenada has a number of forest reserves. Designating areas as forest reserves means that both land and timber resources, important water catchments and the prevention of soil erosion can be properly managed and protected. Grenada's forest reserves include the **Mt St Catherine Forest Reserve**, the **Grand Étang Forest Reserve** and, in Carriacou, the **Belair Forest Reserve**.

**NATIONAL PARKS** Grenada's national parks take conservation one step further. Within the boundaries of the park, all of the flora and fauna is protected year-round.

To the northwest of the Grand Étang Forest Reserve is the 1,000ha **Grand Étang National Park**. The park is located in the central mountain range in the middle of Grenada and covers several high peaks including Mt Granby, Mt Qua Qua and Morne Fédon. Also within the park is the Grand Étang crater lake and the three Concord waterfalls: Concord, Au Coin and Fontainbleu. In Grenada's northern interior, to the west of the Mt St Catherine Forest Reserve, is the 580ha **Mt St Catherine National Park**. The park encompasses Grenada's highest peak, Mt St Catherine, at 840m. Along Grenada's northeastern coastline is the 182ha **Levera Archipelago National Park**. Located within this park are the 259m-high Levera Hill, Levera Pond, Levera Bay, Sugar Loaf Island, Green Island and Sandy Island. The park contains marine reef systems, giant leatherback turtle nesting sites and a bird sanctuary. The **Mt Hartman National Park** in Grenada's southwest contains a bird sanctuary and provides one of the main habitats for the endangered Grenada dove. The 276ha **Nigh North National Park** is located in the north of Carriacou. It encompasses deciduous forest, mangrove forest, the 291m High North Peak, the L'Appelle bird sanctuary, turtle nesting sites, Anse La Roche Beach and Petite Carenage Beach.

**NATURAL LANDMARKS** Designating a natural landmark means that the area should be protected and developed as a natural attraction for Grenadians and for visitors. In some cases, these landmarks are located on private property which means that the government commits to work with the landowner to facilitate access to and provide visitor facilities for these areas. Designated natural landmarks include Lake Antoine, Concord waterfalls, River Sallee hot springs, Annandale Waterfall, Marquis Island, Hog Island, Quarantine Point and Mt Carmel Waterfall.

**CULTURAL LANDMARKS** In a similar vein to natural landmarks, cultural landmarks have been identified as sites of historic significance that should be preserved and developed with government assistance as attractions for Grenadians as well as for visitors. Designated cultural landmarks include the River Antoine Rum Distillery, the Westerhall Rum Distillery, Carib's Leap (Leaper's Hill), Mt Rich Amerindian petroglyphs, Marquis village, Fort George and Fort Frederick. In Carriacou they include the Dover ruins, the La Pointe ruins and Belair Estate. See also *Culture*, page 20.

**PROTECTED SEASCAPES** Protected seascapes include those stretches of coastline, beaches, mangrove forests and swamps, oyster beds and coral reefs that are considered to be of significant natural interest and should therefore become the subject of conservation efforts. Designated protected seascapes include Molinère Reef, North East Seascape (Bathway Beach to Telescope Rock), Southern Seascape (the peninsulas of Grenada's southwest) and La Sagesse Bay. In Carriacou they include Tyrell Bay, L'Esterre Bay (including Mabouya Island and Sandy Island), Sabazan, White Island and Saline Island.

Some of Grenada's dive and watersports operators would like Molinère Reef to step up from a protected seascape to become part of a fully managed and protected marine reserve. This seascape includes the unique Underwater Sculpture Gallery (see page 139).

See also *Marine environment*, page 28.

**ORGANISATIONS** Organisations involved with the management and conservation of Grenada's wildlife and natural environment include the following:

**KIDO Ecological Research Station** Carriacou ✎ 473 443 7936; e kido-ywf@spiceisle.com; www.kido-projects.com. A non-profit NGO that aims to preserve natural resources & ecosystems, promote sustainable development & provide environmental education. It is involved in a number of conservation efforts that include sea turtle protection, monitoring, rescuing & rehabilitating wildlife, & facilitating educational & research programmes especially for young people.

**Ministry of Agriculture, Lands, Forestry, Fisheries, Public Utilities & Energy** ✎ 473 440 2708; e agriculture@gov.gd. Government ministry with divisions responsible for the management of forests & national parks.

**Ocean Spirits** e info@oceanspirits.org; www.oceanspirits.org. A NGO focused primarily on the protection of Grenada's marine turtles. Research, school trips & volunteer programmes are also part of the project.

See also *Chapter 2, Giving something back*, page 65.

# Belair Garden Cottage

peaceful, private
Caribbean style cottage
with a magnificent view

www.belairgardencottage.com
belaircottage@spiceisle.com
(473) 443-6221

Rebecca Sawyer &
Michael Ward

## Belair, Carriacou, Grenada

# The Flamboyant Hotel & Villas
GRENADA

Enjoy... Be comfortable... Be pampered & rejuvenate...
Wine & dine... Have fun... Scuba Dive... Relax...
Weddings, Honeymoons & Special occasions.

The Flamboyant Hotel & Villas.
P.O. Box 214, Grand Anse, St. George's Grenada, WEST INDIES

Reservations.
Tel: 473 444 4247 / Fax: 473 444 1234
Email: flambo@spiceisle.com / www.flamboyant.com

# 2

# Practical Information

Whether you are travelling with friends, a young family, or perhaps arriving by sailing boat, Grenada, Carriacou and Petite Martinique are certainly fun and interesting places to visit. The tri-island state caters for a diverse range of interests and activities. You can hike to waterfalls, explore rainforest-covered mountains, see how rum and chocolate are made, experience cultural activities and events like boat-launching or drumming, scuba dive evocative shipwrecks and wonderful reef systems, learn about Grenada's long tradition of spice cultivation, or simply chill out and enjoy the tranquil waters and powder-white sands of some of the Caribbean's most beautiful beaches.

## WHEN TO VISIT

Without doubt the busiest time of the year is during the cruise-ship season, which begins in November and runs for around six months to the end of April. Grenada's hotels, restaurants, tour operators and taxi drivers gear themselves up for this period as it is when their revenue-earning potential is at its highest. It means that at this time there will be more people on the beaches (though the latter are never really busy), on the roads and at natural and cultural sites of interest. It is a very lively time, full of excitement, colour and activity, when the islands' populations experience a short-term explosion with visitors from the UK, US, Canada and Europe who are escaping the cold weather back home. The weather in Grenada at this time of the year is usually very good, though the months of November and December can be a little unpredictable as the seasons make the transition from wet to dry. From January onwards the clouds become fewer, the sea temperatures begin to rise and the sun shines. By the time it gets to April and May, Grenada can be very steamy indeed. If you are planning on venturing into the interior you should be aware that elevated mountain habitats tend to attract cloud and can be wetter and considerably cooler than elsewhere. In these areas you should always come prepared for the occasional shower.

There seems to be a regatta or a festival taking place at most times of the year in Grenada. Sailing enthusiasts from all around the world are drawn to the Grenada Sailing Festival in January, the Round-Island Regatta at Easter, the Carriacou Regatta during the Independence period in August, and the Carriacou Sailing Series in November. During these times marinas and anchorages may be crowded as well as hotels and restaurants. Carriacou's carnival festivities begin as early as January and reach their peak on the Monday and Tuesday before Ash Wednesday. Grenada's carnival takes place in August. During carnival it is common for Grenadians living abroad to return home for the party and therefore flights and hotels can become booked up fairly quickly. Carnival is a great time to visit the islands, with around-the-clock festivities, street parades, traditional 'jump-up' and carnival queen and calypso competitions.

If you enjoy walking and hiking, then April, May and June are especially good months to visit. The cruise-ship season has usually wound down by this time, so popular sites are far less crowded, and skies are usually very clear, making mountain climbing especially rewarding with fine panoramic views across the islands. Scuba diving is good all year round though perhaps the best months are also during the dry season when run-off and rains do not affect visibility quite as much.

The Atlantic hurricane season starts in July and usually ends in November, though it tends to peak in the months of August and September which are usually quiet months for visitors. Hurricanes form on the west coast of Africa or in mid-Atlantic and make their way westwards towards the Caribbean and the Gulf of Mexico. Whether tropical depressions become tropical storms and then develop into hurricanes is down to a combination of sea temperature and wind shear. In some years these conditions are more favourable for development than others. Despite two recent pummellings, Grenada actually lies to the south of the most common tracks and hurricanes usually pass to the north of the islands.

Also see *Public holidays and events*, page 61.

## HIGHLIGHTS AND SUGGESTED ITINERARIES

**HIGHLIGHTS** Grenada, Carriacou and Petite Martinique offer a lot of diversity and so there will always be something that suits your particular taste, budget and range of interests.

**Accommodation highlights** Grenada's southwest peninsula is stuffed full of hotels, resorts and self-catering accommodation. For those with deep pockets and a taste for luxury then the **Spice Island Beach Resort** (see page 112) on Grand Anse Beach is one of the country's best. In a similar vein, **Mount Cinnamon** (see page 113), **Laluna** (see page 113), **La Source** (see page 113) and the **Calabash** (see page 112) at L'Anse Aux Épines are all excellent alternatives. If you are interested in self-catering then you have equally luxurious options such as the unique **Mount Hartman Bay Estate** (see page 115) or **Maca Bana Villas** (see- page 115). If you are on a more moderate budget and want to be right on Grand Anse Beach then you could also consider the **Grenada Grand Beach Resort** (see page 113), the **Coyaba Beach Resort** (see page 113), the **Flamboyant Hotel and Villas** (see page 114) and the **Blue Horizons Garden Resort** (see page 116) which has beautiful gardens and offers excellent self-catering accommodation. For a full list of accommodation options in the southwest, see page 112.

There are some great places to stay along the more peaceful and secluded bays and anchorages of the southeast. **La Sagesse Nature Centre** (see page 152) and **Cabier Ocean Lodge** (see page 153) are very noteworthy hotel options and will appeal to nature lovers, and **Bel Air Plantation** (see page 153) and **Petit Bacay Villa Hotel** (see page 153) are excellent for self-caterers. On the west coast, **Blue Bay Lodge** (see page 130) offers very affordable accommodation with a personal touch, and is ideally located for exploring the Gouyave region. If you are arriving by sailing boat and would like a little land-based luxury after your trip, then you could do a lot worse than the **True Blue Bay Resort** (see page 113) and the new facilities that are being developed at **Le Phare Bleu** (see page 123) on the south coast, both of which offer anchorages, berths, marine services, restaurants and accommodation.

There are far more places to stay on Carriacou than you might expect, particularly if you enjoy self-catering. Carriacou and Petite Martinique should definitely be part of your travels to Grenada and staying on Carriacou for at least two or three days is highly recommended. The **Caribbee Country House** (see page 198) and the **KIDO Ecological Research Station** (see page 199) offer fine options for nature lovers. **Villa Sankofa** (see page 198) is one of several luxurious options on the popular Craigston Estate, and the **Belair Garden Cottage** (see page 199) is a wonderfully secluded and comfortable place to stay in the heart of the island.

**Sightseeing highlights** Whatever your interest, most holidays to Grenada will inevitably include time spent enjoying sand and surf. Grenada's signature beach is the 3km-long **Grand Anse Beach** (see page 120) located on the southwest peninsula. Bordered by a number of resort hotels it is popular and beautiful, though rarely crowded. It is also worthwhile looking a little further afield. **Morne Rouge Beach** (see page 120) is gorgeous, calm and serene, making it perfect for families with small children. **Magazine Beach** (see page 121) is definitely worth visiting, especially on Sundays when you can also enjoy live music and a barbecue at the fabulous **Aquarium Restaurant** (see page 117). The infrequently visited **Dr Groom's Beach** (see page 121) is also very pretty and rounding off your day in the sun with dinner at the **Beach House Restaurant and Bar** (see page 118) is highly recommended. **Anse La Roche** (see page 208) and **Petit Carenage** (see page 209) on Carriacou are secluded and beautiful, but perhaps the very best of all, also on Carriacou, is the stunning **Paradise Beach** (see page 202).

All around the three islands there are some lovely bays, islets and secluded anchorages. Along the southeast coast of Grenada a trip to **La Sagesse Bay** (see page 156) is an absolute must, but you should also try to make it to **Cabier Beach** (see page 157), **Great Bacolet Bay** (see page 157), **Westerhall Bay** (see page 156) and **Prickly Bay** (see page 122) if possible. Islets definitely worth exploring and snorkelling include **Sandy Island** (see page 207) and **White Island** (see page 207) located just off Carriacou.

Mainland Grenada has four national parks. The **Grand Étang National Park** (see page 138) is the most accessible and frequently visited of the four. Located in the centre of Grenada, it encompasses several forest-covered mountains including Mt Qua Qua and Morne Fédon as well as the **Grand Étang Lake** (see page 143) and several waterfalls. If you are interested in doing some low- to moderate-level hiking then this is a good place to start. Though the Grand Étang Lake is also part of a cruise-ship shore excursion, few people tend to venture beyond the visitor centre. A hike up the **Mt Qua Qua** trail (see page 144), even if you do not go all the way, is definitely worth the extra effort. Many tour operators offer trips to the **Concord waterfalls** (see page 146), though they rarely go beyond the first one which is by the roadside. It is really worth hiking at least to the second one – it is fun, the falls are pretty and the pool is a nice place to cool off. Though an extremely tough hike, the climb to **Fédon's Camp** (see page 145) is not only exhilarating, it is also steeped in myth and history. You definitely need a knowledgeable guide for this one, however. Try to visit the **St Margaret's Falls** (also known as the Seven Sisters Falls, see page 163) if you can. It is a moderate hike of around an hour each way with two small, but very accessible cascading waterfalls and pools. It is very scenic and well worth the walk. For the adventurous, try the short but tricky detour from St Margaret's Falls up to the **Honeymoon Falls** (see page 164).

The **Mt St Catherine National Park** (see page 178) is where you will find Grenada's highest peak, Mt St Catherine, which is 840m at its summit. The mountains and steep forest-covered ridges of this park are very dramatic and for those looking for something more challenging, a hike to the top of **Mt St Catherine** (see page 186) or a trek to the waterfalls at **Paraclete** (see page 187)

2

and **Tufton Hall** (see page 184) is tremendous fun. Again, a knowledgeable guide is essential.

The **Levera Archipelago National Park** (see page 174) is located on Grenada's northeastern coastline and offers beautiful beaches, three pretty offshore islands, marine reef systems, a bird sanctuary and giant leatherback turtle nesting sites. The infrequently visited **Mt Hartman National Park** (see page 122) in Grenada's southwest is the habitat of the endangered **Grenada dove**. Both Levera and Mt Hartman are an absolute must for birdwatchers.

On the island of Carriacou there is the **High North National Park** (see page 190). It is a wonderful place for walking and has a variety of natural habitats including deciduous forest, mangrove forest, a bird sanctuary, turtle nesting sites and two breathtaking beaches at Anse La Roche and Petit Carenage.

The **Molinère Protected Seascape** (see page 132) on the west coast of Grenada is home to a reef formation that is suitable for both snorkelling and scuba diving. The reef is alive with hard and soft corals, sponges and of course lots of very colourful reef fish. Also located within the nooks and crannies of this reef system is the unique **Underwater Sculpture Gallery** (see page 139), which you should definitely try to see. Those interested in scuba diving should include a few outings in both Grenada and Carriacou if possible, where there are some interesting wrecks lying in recreational-dive depths. There are wreck sites for all levels of ability, including the famous *Bianca C* (see page 76) for the more seasoned divers. It is for good reason that Grenada is gaining the reputation of 'wreck-diving capital of the Caribbean'.

The **River Antoine Rum Distillery** (see page 180) still uses the same machinery and methods to squeeze and ferment cane juice that it did a couple of hundred years ago. It is a fascinating spectacle. At the **Belmont Estate** (see page 181) and the **Dougaldston Estate** (see page 141) visitors can see how cocoa is fermented, dried and processed ready for chocolate production and export. You can even try and buy some of Grenada's very own organic chocolate if you like. In the towns of **Gouyave** (see page 142) and **Grenville** (see page 160) the nutmeg stations are a revelation and should not be missed. Though ravaged by recent storms, the island's nutmeg industry still manages to survive and visitors to these **nutmeg 'pools'** are not only offered a fascinating insight into the workings of the 'isle of spice', they are also helping communities that have fallen on somewhat hard times. Also in Gouyave, and certainly not to be missed, is **Fish Friday** (see *Chapter 6*, page 141), a weekly event where the town comes alive with people, music, drink and fantastic fish and lobster dishes.

A visit to Carriacou should be on everyone's agenda, preferably two or three days at least. Carriacou and Petite Martinique have a long tradition of **boatbuilding** (see page 193) and visitors to the shorelines of Windward or Sanchez will usually see evidence of construction work in progress. If you are lucky, your trip may coincide with a boat-launching, which is tremendous fun and is still carried out in the time-honoured manner. Carriacou is also famous for its tradition of **Big Drum Dance** (see page 194) and **Maroon** (see page 195) festivals, and it is certainly worth trying to find out in advance if any village maroons are taking place during your visit. These festivals are very special indeed.

Sailing enthusiasts no doubt have the numerous **sailing regattas** (see page 83) and festivals of Grenada and Carriacou firmly etched in their diaries already. These events draw people from all over the world and are great fun for visitors, locals as well as the wider Caribbean community.

## SUGGESTED ITINERARIES

Many people arrive at Grenada's hotels and resorts content to take in the sun and the surf, laze by a pool, sample a few rum cocktails and eat some delicious food for the entire duration of their stay. If you are on holiday with the aim of simply catching some rays, recharging batteries and doing nothing much at all, then fair enough, Grenada will certainly allow you to do that in comfort, luxury and style. But if you can prise yourself out of your sunlounger and away from the pool, you may just enjoy one or two other aspects of this very interesting and beautiful tri-island nation.

Most hotels and resorts have travel desks that are affiliated with established tour operators who offer organised excursions to some of Grenada's main attractions. Grenada, Carriacou and Petite Martinique are also great destinations for more independent travellers. Whatever your particular penchant, here are a few suggestions of how you may want to plan seven days.

**I'd like to be spoiled silly and spend most of my holiday horizontal** Spend four days relaxing at the resorts and on the beaches of the southwest. Consider an all-inclusive stay at La Source on Pink Gin Beach, or treat yourself to some luxury at the Spice Island Beach Resort on Grand Anse Beach. Take a day out on a charter boat and enjoy a barbecue or traditional 'oil-down' on a secluded beach or island. Take a bus tour to the River Antoine Rum Distillery, the Belmont Estate, the Gouyave Nutmeg Pool and then end up at Gouyave's Fish Friday.

**I'd like plenty of sand and surf plus a few easily accessible sites of natural and cultural interest** Spend about three days chilling out on the beaches of the southwest peninsula (Grand Anse Beach, Morne Rouge Beach, Magazine Beach). One day visiting the Annandale Falls, the Grand Étang National Park (Grand Étang Lake and viewpoints), the Concord Falls (first fall). One day visiting the Dougaldston Estate, the Gouyave Nutmeg Pool, the Belmont Estate and the River Antoine Rum Distillery. One day visiting Carriacou on the Osprey ferry. Spend it on Paradise Beach and perhaps charter a water taxi to Sandy Island for some snorkelling. Spend a day in St George's and include a trip up to Fort Frederick and perhaps also to the Bay Gardens.

**I'd like some beaches, a bit of exertion, and a few sites of natural and cultural interest** Spend two days in the southwest peninsula on the beach, perhaps doing some snorkelling or ocean kayaking. One day hiking to the Concord waterfalls, visiting the Dougaldston Estate, the Gouyave Nutmeg Pool and Fish Friday. One day visiting Carib's Leap in Sauteurs, the Levera Archipelago National Park, the Belmont Estate, Lake Antoine and the River Antoine Rum Distillery. One day visiting Carriacou by Osprey ferry and spending time on Paradise Beach where you could charter a water taxi to Sandy Island. One day visiting the Annandale Falls, the Grand Étang National Park (take a look around the Grand Étang Lake and walk up to the viewpoints), and then have a look around St George's. One day in the southeast (take a look at the Mt Carmel Waterfall, La Sagesse Bay, Great Bacolet Bay and Prickly Bay).

**I'd like some moderate hiking, a few beaches and some sites of natural and cultural interest** One day hiking to the Concord waterfalls and visiting the Dougaldston Estate, the Gouyave Nutmeg Pool and Fish Friday. One day visiting Carib's Leap at Sauteurs, the Levera Archipelago National Park, the Belmont Estate, Lake Antoine, and the River Antoine Rum Distillery. Spend two full days in Carriacou (walk to Paradise Beach from Hillsborough and take a boat to Sandy Island to do some snorkelling. On the second day walk through the High North National Park via Anse La Roche and Petit Carenage from Bogles to Windward). One day hiking to the summit of Mt Qua Qua, then to the St Margaret's Falls and the Honeymoon Falls. One day exploring the southeast (walk to Cabier Beach, La

Sagesse Bay, visit the Bay Gardens and perhaps the Mt Hartman National Park). One day in the southwest looking around St George's and spending some time relaxing on Grand Anse Beach and Magazine Beach.

## I'd like some serious hiking and adventure with a splash of beach and culture

Spend one day hiking to the three Concord waterfalls, Palmiste Dig and Black Bay, and then visit the Dougaldston Estate, the Gouyave Nutmeg Pool and Fish Friday. One day visiting Carib's Leap in Sauteurs, the Levera Archipelago National Park, the Belmont Estate, Lake Antoine and the River Antoine Rum Distillery. Spend three days in Carriacou (walk to Paradise Beach from Hillsborough and take a boat to Sandy Island and White Island to do some snorkelling; walk through the High North National Park via Anse La Roche and Petit Carenage from Bogles to Windward; and walk right around Petite Martinique). One day hiking to the summit of Mt Qua Qua, then to the St Margaret's Falls and the Honeymoon Falls. One day walking the beaches and peninsulas of the south (try Cabier Beach, La Sagesse, Point Jeudy, L'Anse Aux Épines, Magazine Beach and Grand Anse Beach).

## TOUR OPERATORS

A number of international tour operators offer flight and accommodation packages to Grenada, though very few include Carriacou and Petite Martinique. These operators tend to offer accommodation in the large resort hotels of Grenada's southwest peninsula, especially around the very popular Grand Anse Beach. Here is a selection of the travel operators offering flight, accommodation and all-inclusive packages to Grenada:

### UK

**Dial A Flight** ↘ 0870 366 2183; www.dialaflight.com
**Just Grenada** ↘ 01373 814214;
www.justgrenada.co.uk
**Kuoni** ↘ 01306 747002; www.kuoni.co.uk

**The Holiday Place** ↘ 020 7644 7061;
www.theholidayplace.co.uk
**Trailfinders** ↘ 0845 054 6060; www.trailfinders.com
**Virgin Holidays** ↘ 0871 222 5825;
www.virginholidays.co.uk

### US AND CANADA

**Air Jamaica Vacations** ↘ +1 800 LOVEBIRD or +1 800 568 3247; www.airjamaicavacations.com
**Classic Vacations** ↘ +1 800 635 1333;
www.classicvacations.com

**Expedia Vacations** ↘ +1 800 551 2534;
www.expedia.com
**Responsible Travel** www.responsibletravel.com

Details of local tour operators are listed in *Chapter 3*, under specific activity headings, ie: *Birdwatching operators and guides*, page 67; *Boat charters and day-cruising operators*, page 68; *Bus-tour operators*, page 69; *Cycling and mountain-biking operators*, page 70; *Garden, farm and food tour operators*, page 72; *Kayaking operators*, page 72; *Off-roading and jeep-tour operators*, page 73; *River-tubing operators*, page 73; *Carriacou scuba-diving and snorkelling operators*, page 77; *Grenada scuba-diving and snorkelling operators*, page 79; *Sport-fishing operators*, page 71; *Turtle-watching operators*, page 79; *Walking/hiking operators and guides*, page 82; and *Whale- and dolphin-watching operators*, page 83.

(Also see *Wedding operators and services*, page 40; *Car-hire firms*, page 54 and *Scooter-hire company/operator*, page 56).

## ℹ️ TOURIST OFFICES

The **Grenada Board of Tourism** head office (*PO Box 293, St George's, Grenada;* ☏ *473 440 2279/2001;* f *473 440 6637;* e *gbt@spiceisle.com; www.grenadagrenadines.com*) is located just off Wharf Road on the southeastern tip of the Carenage in St George's, next to the Grenada Taxi Association office. It has plenty of printed literature (though check publication dates) and staff who are happy to assist with general information as well as help arrange guided tours.

In **Carriacou** the Grenada Board of Tourism has an office on Main Street, Hillsborough (☏ *473 443 7948;* f *473 443 6127;* e *carrgbt@spiceisle.com*). Worldwide offices are as follows:

**Canada** 439 University Av Suite 920, Toronto, Ontario M5G 1Y8; ☏ +1 416 595 1339; f +1 416 595 8278

**Germany** Schenkendorfstrasse 1, 65187 Wiesbaden; ☏ +44 0611 267 6720; f +44 0611 267 6760; e grenada@discover-fra.com

**UK** 11 Blade's Court, 121 Deodar Rd, London SW15 2NU; ☏ 020 8877 4516; f 020 8874 4219; e grenada@representationplus.co.uk

**US** PO Box 1668, Lake Worth, FL 33460; ☏ +1 561 588 8176, toll free ☏ +1 1 800 927 9554; f +561 588 7267; e cnoel@grenadagrenadines.com

## RED TAPE

**ENTRY REQUIREMENTS** All visitors to Grenada must be able to present a valid passport and a return or an onward ticket. British and US citizens may present two documents proving their citizenship, one of which must have photographic identification. Examples of this include a driving licence and a birth certificate. Visitors from the UK, US, Canada, Commonwealth countries, EU countries, Japan and South Korea do not need a visa.

**DEPARTURE TAXES** Airport passenger charges for travellers departing the state of Grenada from either **Point Salines International Airport** in Grenada or **Lauriston Airport** in Carriacou are EC$25 (US$10) for persons aged five to 12 years, EC$50 (US$20) for persons aged 13 years and over. Children under five years of age are exempt from departure tax. There are departure tax payment booths located in the departures hall next to the check-in desks. Pay your departure tax after you have checked in and before you go through immigration to the departure gates. Passengers flying to Grenada from Lauriston Airport in Carriacou are required to pay EC$10 departure tax.

Visitors entering Grenada by air but leaving by boat must pay an embarkation tax of EC$1 per person to the immigration office at the time of departure.

**MARRIAGE REQUIREMENTS** For couples interested in tying the knot in Grenada there are a number of operators offering wedding services. To be sure you have met the country's legal requirements, please refer to the following list:

- You must be resident on the island for at least three working days (excluding weekends) before you may apply for a licence.
- Your application for a marriage licence is made at the Prime Minister's Office after the requisite stamp duty and marriage licence fees have been paid. (Though this sounds quite daunting, it actually only takes about two days and is something your wedding planning service will do for you.)
- Documents you must have with you when you marry in Grenada are: valid passports; birth certificates; proof of a decree absolute, if either party is divorced; proof of single status (this is usually in the form of a letter from a lawyer or clergyman stating that neither of you has previously been married); proof of a name change, if relevant; a death certificate, if either of you have been widowed; evidence of parental consent if either of you is under 21 years of age.

*Lucille Sylvester of Grenada Wedding*

Everyone knows destination weddings usually cost less than traditional weddings, but does everyone know just how easy it is to indulge in this affordable luxury? Formerly such exotic ceremonies were reserved for ultra-rich celebrity types, but now they are accessible and desirable to couples looking to add an exotic twist to their day as well as a relaxed atmosphere. The bride and groom also get to enjoy an unforgettable honeymoon, and provide the perfect excuse for a Caribbean vacation for the lucky guests who join them.

A wedding-moon, as it is now known, is certainly special in Grenada. You can choose the setting of a beach wedding, where tying the knot on a sun-kissed beach with swaying palm trees bearing witness is a perfect choice. But this is just one option. Maybe your ideal wedding is in a breathtaking tropical garden overflowing with beautiful flowers such as gardenias, 'jump up and kiss me', anthuriums and our national flower, bougainvillea, with more colours of bloom than there are days of the year! Some couples may choose to make a stylish splash as they declare their love against the backdrop of one of the islands' cascading waterfalls. Or how about a plantation house, bursting with natural character and romance? Nothing is too much trouble when it comes to pleasing a destination wedding couple in Grenada, where the warmth of the people is as hot as the sunshine!

**Wedding operators and services** Here is a small selection of wedding planners and hotels offering wedding services:

**Cabier Ocean Lodge** ✆ 473 444 6013; e info@cabier.com; www.cabier.com
**Caribbean Horizons** ✆ 473 444 1550; e macford@spiceisle.com; www.caribbeanhorizons.com
**Flamboyant Hotel & Villas** ✆ 473 444 4247; e flambo@spiceisle.com; www.flamboyant.com

**Grenada Wedding** ✆ 473 443 3866; e wedding@spiceisle.com; www.grenadawedding.com
**True Blue Bay Resort** ✆ 473 443 8783; e wedding@truebluebay.com; www.truebluebay.com

## Ⓔ CONSULATES AND EMBASSIES

**British High Commission** ✆ 473 440 3536
**Chinese Embassy** ✆ 473 439 6227
**Cuban Embassy** ✆ 473 444 1884
**French Consulate** ✆ 473 440 6349
**German Consulate** ✆ 473 440 7260 or 473 409 7260
**Guyanese Consulate** ✆ 473 440 3152

**Jamaican Consulate** ✆ 473 444 5210
**Netherlands Consulate** ✆ 473 440 3459
**Spanish Consulate** ✆ 473 440 2087
**Swedish Consulate** ✆ 473 440 3578
**US Embassy** ✆ 473 444 1173
**Venezuelan Embassy** ✆ 473 440 1721

## GETTING THERE AND AWAY

✈ **BY AIR** Grenada's **Point Salines International Airport** services flights to and from the United Kingdom, the United States, Canada and the Caribbean. The airport is located in the southwest of Grenada and is very close to the large resorts and beaches of Grand Anse.

### Flights from the United Kingdom

**Air Jamaica** Reservations toll free ✆ 0208 570 7999; www.airjamaica.com. Flights to Grenada from London via Jamaica.

**British Airways** Reservations ✆ 0844 493 0787 or 0844 493 0759; www.britishairways.com. Flights & holidays to Grenada from London.

**Caribbean Airlines** Reservations ☎ 0870 774 7336; www.caribbean-airlines.com. Flights from London to Barbados & Trinidad with same-day connections to Grenada with LIAT Airlines.

**Virgin Atlantic** Reservations ☎ 0870 380 2007; www.virgin-atlantic.com. Flights & holidays from London to Grenada.

## Flights from the United States and Canada

**Air Canada** Reservations toll free ☎ +1 888 247 2262. Direct flights to Grenada from Toronto.

**Air Jamaica** Reservations toll free ☎ +1 800 523 5585; www.airjamaica.com. Flights from Toronto & a number of US cities to Grenada via Jamaica.

**American Airlines** Reservations toll free ☎ +1 800 433 7300; www.aa.com. Flights from US cities to San Juan, Puerto Rico, with connecting American Eagle flights to Grenada. Daily direct flights from Miami.

**Caribbean Airlines** Reservations toll free ☎ +1 800 920 4225; www.caribbean-airlines.com. Flights from New York, Miami & Toronto to Barbados & Trinidad with connections to Grenada with LIAT airlines.

## Inter-island flight services and connections

**LIAT** Reservations toll free ☎ +1 800 888 844; e reservations@liatairline.com; www.liatairline.com. With destinations throughout the Caribbean, LIAT flies to Grenada's Point Salines International Airport usually from Antigua, Barbados & Trinidad & Tobago.

**St Vincent Grenada Air (SVG Air)** Reservations toll free ☎ +1 800 744 7285, Grenada ☎ 473 444 3549, Carriacou ☎ 473 443 8519; f 473 444 2898; e info@svgair.com. Based in St Vincent operating charter flights throughout the Caribbean. SVG also has daily domestic charter flights between Grenada & Carriacou.

**Checked-baggage allowances** The standard allowance for checked baggage is two pieces together totalling no more than 23kg. Check with your airline prior to travelling for up-to-date travel information on baggage allowances and restricted cabin items.

**Point Salines International Airport** Grenada's Point Salines International Airport is located on the southwest peninsula of the island, some 11km from the capital St George's and 5km from the popular resorts of Grand Anse. The airport is simple to navigate and has a small number of air-conditioned restaurants, cafés, bars and souvenir shops. The information desk is located between the departures and arrivals halls next to the flight information screens. You will find taxis and limousine buses directly opposite the exit near the clearly marked passenger pick-up area. There is also an ATM located here.

Taxi drivers work to fixed tariffs for journeys from the airport. For an idea of taxi fares from Point Salines International Airport, it costs EC$50 to St George's, EC$40 to Grand Anse, EC$35 to True Blue, EC$40 to L'Anse Aux Épines, EC$110 to Gouyave and EC$150 to Sauteurs (the furthest point from the airport at 45km). A minimum fare of EC$25 is charged for short distances. An additional charge of EC$5 per person is levied when passenger numbers exceed four persons per taxi. You should also expect it to cost a little more on public holidays.

Once outside the airport, the road to the right leads away from the southwest peninsula to the capital. The airport car park is also located a short walk to the right on the opposite side of the road. Opposite the car park you will see a memorial to the soldiers who lost their lives during the US military intervention of 1983. Dedicated by US president Ronald Reagan in 1986, the concrete arches and epitaphs cite dedications and thanks to the soldiers of 'Operation Urgent Fury'. For more information on the US military intervention of 1983, see page 11.

Follow the road to a traffic island. To the right is True Blue and straight ahead is the main road heading north. The main road north to St George's widens and passes an industrial estate before reaching a second traffic island. To the right is the road to the east (Grenville, La Sagesse, Westerhall, L'Anse Aux Épines), and the road to the left leads to St George's, Grand Anse and the west coast.

## BY SEA
### Ferry

**Osprey Lines Ltd** ➤ 473 440 8126;
e ospreylines@gmail.com; www.ospreylines.com. Operates a daily high-speed ferry service between Grenada, Carriacou & Petite Martinique. The journey between Grenada & Carriacou takes around 90mins. It is a further 30mins to Petite Martinique.

**Cruise ship** Grenada is visited by several cruise lines. The cruise-ship terminal is located in the capital, St George's, where two ships are able to put in at the same time. Additional ships either berth at the port or in St George's Harbour where passengers are transported by tender to the cruise-ship terminal. Cruise prices vary according to time of year and cabin type, and schedules are also subject to change. When booking cruises, you have the option of booking shore excursions in advance. If you are interested in what people have to say about the various cruise options to Grenada, then it may be helpful to take a look at www.cruisecritic.com. Here are the details of a selection of cruise-ship lines that visit Grenada:

**Aida** www.aide.de. A cruise ship for German-speakers that departs from the Dominican Republic.
**Celebrity Cruises** www.celebritycruises.com. Luxury cruise ships departing from San Juan, Puerto Rico.
**Cunard** www.cunard.com. Caribbean cruises on the *Queen Mary II* departing from New York, incorporating Grenada.
**Holland America** www.hollandamerica.com. Southern Caribbean cruises calling at Grenada depart from New York & Fort Lauderdale.
**Norwegian** www.ncl.com. Caribbean cruises calling at Grenada depart from New York.
**Ocean Village** www.oceanvillageholidays.co.uk. Casual Caribbean cruises aimed at holidaymakers from the UK depart from Barbados.

**P&O Cruises** www.pocruises.com. Caribbean cruises calling at Grenada depart from Southampton & Barbados.
**Princess Cruises** www.princess.com. Caribbean cruises calling at Grenada depart from Fort Lauderdale.
**Sea Cloud Cruises** www.seacloud.com. Cruises aboard luxury modern windjammers calling at Grenada depart from Barbados.
**Silversea Cruises** www.silversea.com. Caribbean & transatlantic cruises calling at Grenada depart from European, Caribbean & US ports.
**Windjammer Barefoot Cruises** www.windjammer.com. Windjammer have a wide selection of cruises that depart from many Caribbean ports, including Grenada.
**Windstar Cruises** www.windstarcruises.com. Caribbean cruises calling at Grenada depart from Barbados.

**Private yacht or cruiser** Visitors to Grenada, Carriacou and Petite Martinique arriving by private or charter vessel should notify authorities within two hours of arrival at one of the designated ports of entry. The captain of the vessel must also prepare the requisite customs and immigration paperwork. (See page 85 for more information on entry, exit and clearance procedures as well as details of marinas and anchorages.)

Clearance is provided at the following ports of entry:

**Grenada Marine** Grenada; ➤ 473 443 1065
**Grenada Yacht Club** Grenada; ➤ 473 440 3270
**Grenville** Grenada; ➤ 473 438 7678

**Hillsborough** Carriacou; ➤ 473 443 8399
**Le Phare Bleu** Grenada; ➤ 473 444 2400
**Prickly Bay Marina** Grenada; ➤ 473 444 4509

**BEFORE YOU GO** There are no immunisation requirements for visitors to Grenada unless you are arriving from infected areas. Grenada does not have malaria and the water is usually safe to drink. It is recommended that standard vaccinations such as tetanus, diphtheria and polio, which comes as an all-in-one vaccine (Revaxis), are up to date and travellers may also wish to consider protecting themselves from hepatitis A. **Rabies** is endemic in Grenada but is only usually a problem for those staying for extended periods or working with animals. It may be present in any warm-blooded mammal and is spread through the transfer of saliva from a bite, a scratch or a lick over broken skin. If you fit into either of the above categories you should get pre-exposure rabies vaccine which consists of three doses given over a minimum of 21 days. Whether or not you have had the vaccine you should scrub the wound with soap and running water, apply an antiseptic and get yourself to medical help as soon as possible. Visitors requiring health care in Grenada are required to pay upfront for treatment. Medical insurance is usually a good idea, particularly if you will be participating in activities such as hiking or scuba diving.

**INSECT BITES** Although there is no risk of malaria in Grenada, **mosquito** bites can still spoil your trip, particularly if you react badly to them. It is definitely worth bringing insect repellent containing DEET and ensuring you apply it between dusk and dawn, when most attacks occur. Though it is difficult, try to remember that scratching your mosquito bites can result in open wounds and infections, especially in Grenada's tropical climate. Anti-itch remedies containing ammonia work well where your repellent may have failed. Most hotels will have either mosquito screens or bed nets if mosquitoes are a problem.

During the day you are usually fairly safe from mosquitoes unless walking in dark, damp areas of forest or beside mangrove swamps. Long, loose clothes are a very good idea in this kind of environment. You can even purchase clothes that are impregnated with an anti-mosquito formula. **Dengue fever** occurs from time to time in the region and is caused by a day-biting mosquito (*Aedes aegypti*). Dengue is very rarely fatal, though it can cause a week or two of acute unpleasantness including high fever, severe headache, joint and muscle pains.

**Sand flies** (sometimes called biting midges or no-see-ums) are members of the subfamily Phlebotominae and are tiny blood-sucking insects. They are attracted to warm-blooded animals and can be a nuisance on some beaches and in areas of mangrove. The small bites of the female can irritate and become inflamed if you rub or itch them. Sand flies are often roused by digging up the damp sand in which the female may lay her eggs. Insect repellent containing DEET helps to deter them.

**Biting ants** can catch the unaware by unpleasant surprise. This is usually the result of either standing and pausing on a nest accidentally or by brushing against or holding onto branches or foliage where ants are going about their business. Take care where you put your feet and hands and, if you have placed clothes or shoes on the ground, give them a good shake before putting them back on again.

**Chiggers** (*Trombicula alfreddugesi*) are the parasitic larvae of the harvest mite that move to the tips of leaves, grasses and bushes waiting to catch a ride with a passing host. Once there, they find a relatively protected spot, often in the waistband of pants or skirts, where they pierce the skin and suck up tissue. Lovely. An extremely irritating rash appears, caused by an allergic reaction to the salivary secretions of the larvae which drop off the skin once they have been fed. The rash can develop into severe welts, swelling and even a fever depending on the sensitivity of the victim. Scratching obviously makes it worse. Insect repellents containing DEET are effective against chiggers. Chiggers do not feed straight away and may move around the body for hours before doing so. It is therefore very worth while having a hot, soapy bath or shower as soon as you can after being exposed to dense bush.

**HARMFUL PLANTS** The **manchineel** (*Hippomane mancinella*) is native to the Caribbean and Central America. Its name is derived from the Spanish word *manzanilla*, meaning 'little apple' in reference to the similarity of this tree and its fruit to those of an apple tree. The full Spanish name, however, is *manzanilla de la muerte*, meaning 'little apple of death'. It is a very poisonous tree and it is very common along beaches and coastlines in the Caribbean. Growing to around 15m high, the manchineel provides natural shade from the hot sun and it helps to prevent sand and soil from erosion by the sea. Unfortunately, it contains toxins which, in wet or damp weather, can cause severe skin irritation or worse, if you stand beneath one and allow drops from the tree to fall on you. Eating its fruit can be fatal, so please do not mistake it for an apple. Usually there are signs warning visitors about the potential hazards of the manchineel. So long as it is dry and you do not touch the tree or its leaves, then you should be fine using it as a shade from the sun. If it rains, run like the clappers.

The **stinging** or **devil's nettle** (*Laportea aestuans*) has broad leaves with tiny hairs on the leaf. Touching the plant and its leaves causes inflammation and itching of the skin. The **stinging vine** (*Tragia volubilis*) has small leaves that have a similar effect. Both plants are known locally as *zouti*.

**Cow-itch** (*Mucuna pruriens*), also known as *pwa-gaté*, is a plant that grows in dense bush and is very difficult to spot. The plant has pods which, when dry and brown, are covered with tiny hairs that become extremely irritating if they come in contact with the skin.

**PRICKLY HEAT** A very itchy red skin rash known as *miliaria*, or prickly heat, is caused by sweating a lot in humid weather conditions. In high levels of humidity, particularly in Grenada's forest interior, this can be a problem for visitors who are not used to such conditions. Dead skin cells and bacteria block sweat glands and the skin becomes inflamed. Air conditioning, cold showers, calamine lotion or, in severe cases, steroid creams can bring some relief. Aloe also helps. People suffering from prickly heat should try to avoid exerting themselves for a couple of days in order to reduce sweating and give their skin a chance to recover.

**DEHYDRATION, HEAT EXHAUSTION AND HEATSTROKE** A combination of high temperatures, humidity, exertion and a lack of fluids will inevitably result in dehydration, heat exhaustion and possibly even heatstroke. It is incredibly easy to become dehydrated in a tropical climate and most people do not even realise that their irritability, weariness, headaches and dizziness are actually due to a lack of water. Travellers to tropical climates frequently underestimate the volume of water they should consume to remain hydrated and healthy. It is said that exertion in the tropics requires replenishment of around three litres a day. When out walking take as much water as you can comfortably carry – at least one to two litres per person. Drink plenty of water before hiking and try to drink at regular intervals, regardless of whether you actually feel thirsty or not. Beer and carbonated soft drinks are no substitute for water when it comes to rehydrating your body.

Heat exhaustion occurs when the body's cooling system hits overdrive. Profuse sweating, pale clammy skin, fast shallow breathing, nausea, headaches, rapid weak pulse and stomach cramps are all signs of heat exhaustion. It is important to counter heat exhaustion as quickly as possible by trying to cool your body down by finding shade, taking a dip in a river or pool, drinking plenty of water and relaxing.

Heatstroke can be fatal. This occurs when the body's cooling system has collapsed completely. Skin becomes hot and red, breathing slows and confusion and dizziness can ultimately lead to unconsciousness. Cooling the body down as quickly and as effectively as possible is absolutely essential and you should seek immediate medical assistance.

**SUN DAMAGE** In a very short period of time the hot Caribbean sun will redden and burn your skin. Try to stay in the shade for most of the day and, when exposed to the sun, wear a hat and protect fair skin and eyes and apply a high-factor sunscreen. Sun reflecting on the water can be especially damaging if you are exposed to it for too long without adequate protection. If your skin is not used to a tropical climate, limit direct exposure as much as possible. Wearing a T-shirt to protect your back when snorkelling is a good idea. If you must sunbathe, try to limit your daily session to 20–30 minutes. Sunburn is not only harmful to your skin, it is very painful and can ruin your holiday. Light-coloured, loose shirts, long-sleeved shirts, skirts and trousers made from cotton are among the best precautions.

**SCUBA-DIVING INJURIES** Certified scuba divers should always dive conservatively and within recreational dive limits. Do not dive beyond your training and avoid alcohol and strenuous activities before dives. Diving in Grenada is mostly easy, though some wrecks are in deep water and islets such as Île de Ronde involve strong currents and are for experienced divers only. Be sure to dive with a reputable operation, stay with your buddy or the dive master, maintain good buoyancy and always check depth and no decompression limits.

Decompression sickness can be avoided by ensuring you always dive conservative profiles, ascend slowly, looking and listening for boat traffic, and making safety stops at 5m. Signs and symptoms of decompression sickness include tingling or numbness in extremities, aching joints, rashes, headaches, dizziness and nausea. Request 100% pure oxygen and seek medical assistance. Decompression sickness can be fatal and, whilst the most severe symptoms become apparent within the first two hours of surfacing, problems can emerge up to 24 hours after diving. Allow dive crew to help and advise you as they are trained in dive emergencies.

Grenada does not have its own recompression chamber. Should a diver require emergency recompression treatment, he or she will be evacuated by a 30-minute low-level flight to either Trinidad or Barbados. It is always a sensible precaution to take out dive insurance to cover the cost of any evacuation and emergency recompression treatments that may be required.

St George's General Hospital ℡ 473 440 2051. Ambulance crews are trained in dealing with emergencies.

Divers Alert Network (DAN) Americas ℡ +1 919 684 2948 for information, ℡ +1 919 684 4326 for diving emergencies.

**AQUATIC-LIFE INJURIES** Whether scuba diving, snorkelling or just having fun in the sea, it is always possible to pick up an injury from aquatic life. Grenada's seas are safe, though there are reef sharks patrolling the formations and wrecks that lie in deeper waters. Most aquatic injuries tend to come from contact with sea urchins or small jellyfish. Sea urchins are bottom-dwellers, usually found around rocks in the shallows. They have sharp spines that can pierce the skin of a foot that stands on them or arms that brush against them. Typically the tips of the spines break off and embed themselves under the skin. This can be very painful and if not treated may cause an infection. It is prudent to seek medical assistance if you are unsure.

*Dr Jane Wilson-Howarth*

Long-haul air travel increases the risk of deep vein thrombosis. Although recent research has suggested that many of us develop clots when immobilised, most resolve without us ever having been aware of them. In certain susceptible individuals, though, large clots form and these can break away and lodge in the lungs. This is dangerous but happens in a tiny minority of passengers.

Studies have shown that flights of over five-and-a-half hours are significant, and that people who take lots of shorter flights over a short space of time form clots. People at highest risk are:

- Those who have had a clot before – unless they are now taking warfarin
- People over 80 years of age
- Anyone who has recently undergone a major operation or surgery for varicose veins
- Someone who has had a hip or knee replacement in the last three months
- Cancer sufferers
- Those who have ever had a stroke
- People with heart disease
- Those with a close blood relative who has had a clot

Those with a slightly increased risk:

- People over 40
- Women who are pregnant or have had a baby in the last couple of weeks
- People taking female hormones or other oestrogen therapy
- Heavy smokers
- Those who have very severe varicose veins
- The very obese
- People who are very tall (over 6ft/1.8m) or short (under 5ft/1.5m)

Contact with small jellyfish can result in a small but painful sting. Rubbing makes it worse. If possible remove any visible traces of tentacles with tweezers (not with your fingers, as the tentacles still retain their sting) and douse the affected area with white vinegar.

**SEXUALLY TRANSMITTED DISEASES** Unprotected sex is risky in any part of the world and Grenada is no exception. The official number of incidences of HIV infections is relatively low, but discrimination and the stigma attached to the disease may mean that reported cases do not necessarily reflect the true picture. Common sense, protection and caution is always the best advice.

**TRAVEL CLINICS AND HEALTH INFORMATION** A full list of current travel clinic websites worldwide is available from the International Society of Travel Medicine on www.istm.org. For other journey preparation information, consult www.tripprep.com. Information about various medications may be found on www.emedicine.com.

## UK

**Berkeley Travel Clinic** 32 Berkeley St, London W1J 8EL (near Green Park tube station); ☎ 020 7629 6233 **Cambridge Travel Clinic** 48a Mill Rd, Cambridge CB1 2AS; ☎ 01223 367362; e enquiries@

travelcliniccambridge.co.uk; www.travelcliniccambridge.co.uk; ⏰ 12.00–19.00, Tue–Fri, 10.00–16.00 Sat **Edinburgh Travel Clinic** Regional Infectious Diseases

A deep vein thrombosis (DVT) is a blood clot that forms in the deep leg veins. This is very different from irritating but harmless superficial phlebitis. DVT causes swelling and redness of one leg, usually with heat and pain in one calf and sometimes the thigh. A DVT is only dangerous if a clot breaks away and travels to the lungs (pulmonary embolus). Symptoms of a pulmonary embolus (PE) include chest pain that is worse on breathing in deeply, shortness of breath, and sometimes coughing up small amounts of blood. The symptoms commonly start three to ten days after a long flight. Anyone who thinks that they might have a DVT needs to see a doctor immediately who will arrange a scan. Warfarin tablets (to thin the blood) are then taken for at least six months.

**PREVENTION OF DVT** Several conditions make the problem more likely. Immobility is the key, and factors like reduced oxygen in cabin air and dehydration may also contribute. To reduce the risk of thrombosis on a long journey:

- Exercise before and after the flight
- Keep mobile before and during the flight; move around every couple of hours
- Drink plenty of water or juices during the flight
- Avoid taking sleeping pills and excessive tea, coffee and alcohol
- Perform exercises that mimic walking and tense the calf muscles
- Consider wearing flight socks or support stockings (see www.legshealth.com)
- Take a meal of oily fish (mackerel, trout, salmon, sardines, etc) in the 24 hours before departure to reduce blood clotability and thus DVT risk

If you think you are at increased risk of a clot, ask your doctor if it is safe to travel.

Unit, Ward 41 OPD, Western General Hospital, Crewe Rd South, Edinburgh EH4 2UX; ℡ 0131 537 2822; www.mvm.ed.ac.uk. Travel helpline (℡ 0906 589 0380) ⏰ 09.00–12.00 weekdays. Provides inoculations & advises on travel-related health risks.
**Fleet Street Travel Clinic** 29 Fleet St, London EC4Y 1AA; ℡ 020 7353 5678; www.fleetstreetclinic.com. Vaccinations, travel products & latest advice.
**Hospital for Tropical Diseases Travel Clinic** Mortimer Market Bldg, Capper St (off Tottenham Ct Rd), London WC1E 6AU; ℡ 020 7388 9600; www.thehtd.org. Offers consultations & advice, & is able to provide all necessary drugs & vaccines for travellers. Runs a healthline (℡ 0906 133 7733) for country-specific information & health hazards. Also stocks nets, water purification equipment & personal protection measures.
**Interhealth Worldwide** Partnership Hse, 157 Waterloo Rd, London SE1 8US; ℡ 020 7902 9000; www.interhealth.org.uk. Competitively priced, one-stop travel health service. All profits go to their

affiliated company, InterHealth, which provides health care for overseas workers on Christian projects.
**Liverpool School of Medicine** Pembroke Pl, Liverpool L3 5QA; ℡ 0151 708 9393; f 0151 705 3370; www.liv.ac.uk/lstm
**MASTA** (Medical Advisory Service for Travellers Abroad) Moorfield Rd, Yeadon, Leeds, West Yorks LS19 7BN; ℡ 0113 238 7500; www.masta-travel-health.com. Provides travel health advice & vaccinations. There are over 25 MASTA pre-travel clinics in Britain; call or check online for the nearest. Clinics also sell mosquito nets, medical kits, insect protection & travel hygiene products.
**NHS travel website** www.fitfortravel.scot.nhs.uk. Provides country-by-country advice on immunisation, plus details of recent developments, & a list of relevant health organisations.
**Nomad Travel Store/Clinic** 3–4 Wellington Terrace, Turnpike Lane, London N8 0PX; ℡ 020 8889 7014; travel-health line (office hours only) ℡ 0906 863 3414; e sales@nomadtravel.co.uk;

www.nomadtravel.co.uk. Also at 40 Bernard St, London WC1N 1LJ; ☎ 020 7833 4114; 52 Grosvenor Gardens, London SW1W 0AG; ☎ 020 7823 5823; & 43 Queens Rd, Bristol BS8 1QH; ☎ 0117 922 6567. For health advice, equipment such as mosquito nets & other anti-bug devices, & an excellent range of adventure travel gear. Clinics also in Bristol & Southhampton.

## Irish Republic
**Tropical Medical Bureau** Grafton Street Medical Centre, Grafton Bldgs, 34 Grafton St, Dublin 2; ☎ 1 671 9200; www.tmb.ie. A useful website specific to tropical destinations. Also check website for other bureaux locations throughout Ireland.

## USA
**Centers for Disease Control** 1600 Clifton Rd, Atlanta, GA 30333; ☎ 800 311 3435; travellers' health hotline (fax service) f 888 232 3299; www.cdc.gov/travel. The central source of travel information in the USA. The invaluable *Health Information for International Travel*, published annually, is available from the Division of Quarantine at this address.
**Connaught Laboratories** Pasteur Merieux Connaught, Route 611, PO Box 187, Swiftwater, PA 18370; ☎ 800 822 2463. They will send a free list of specialist tropical-medicine physicians in your state.

**IAMAT** (International Association for Medical Assistance to Travelers) 1623 Military Rd, 279, Niagara Falls, NY14304-1745; ☎ 716 754 4883; e info@iamat.org; www.iamat.org. A non-profit organisation that provides lists of English-speaking doctors abroad.
**International Medicine Center** 915 Gessner Rd, Suite 525, Houston, TX 77024; ☎ 713 550 2000; www.traveldoc.com

## Canada
**IAMAT** Suite 1, 1287 St Clair Av W, Toronto, Ontario M6E 1B8; ☎ 416 652 0137; www.iamat.org

**TMVC** Suite 314, 1030 W Georgia St, Vancouver BC V6E 2Y3; ☎ 1 888 288 8682; www.tmvc.com. Private clinic with several outlets in Canada.

## Australia, New Zealand, Singapore
**IAMAT** PO Box 5049, Christchurch 5, New Zealand; www.iamat.org
**TMVC** ☎ 1300 65 88 44; www.tmvc.com.au. Clinics in Australia, New Zealand & Singapore, inc:
*Auckland* Canterbury Arcade, 170 Queen St, Auckland; ☎ 9 373 3531

*Brisbane* 75a, Astor Terrace, Spring Hill, QLD 4000; ☎ 7 3815 6900
*Melbourne* 393 Little Bourke St, 2nd floor, Melbourne, VIC 3000; ☎ 3 9602 5788
*Sydney* Dymocks Bldg, 7th floor, 428 George St, Sydney, NSW 2000; ☎ 2 9221 7133

## South Africa and Namibia
**SAA-Netcare Travel Clinics** Sanlam Bldg, 19, Fredman Dr, Sandton, P Bag X34, Benmore, JHB, Gauteng, 2010; www.travelclinic.co.za. Clinics throughout South Africa.

**TMVC** NHC Health Centre, Cnr. Beyers Naude & Waugh Northcliff; PO Box 48499, Roosevelt Park, 2129 (postal address); ☎ 011 888 7488; www.tmvc.com.au. Consult website for details of other clinics in South Africa & Namibia.

## Switzerland
**IAMAT** 57 Chemin des Voirets, 1212 Grand Lancy, Geneva; www.iamat.org

# SAFETY

Grenada is a safe country for visitors and precautions you should take when visiting Grenada, Carriacou and Petite Martinique are no different from those you would take travelling anywhere else in the world. It is usually very safe to walk around, both by day and by night. Most people are very friendly and helpful. There are few reported incidents of visitors experiencing crime though you should apply common-sense precautions such as not flaunting wealth openly, dressing conservatively, and avoiding conflict. If approached by people asking for money, or offering you illegal drugs, politely decline and walk on. Do not lose your temper or decide to give a lecture. It is simply not worth it. If you are travelling to more remote places be sure to tell someone where you are going and do not take valuables along with you. If you do find yourself in a threatening situation your focus should be on getting through it peacefully and not on fighting back.

**Police** Emergencies ❭ 911

See also *Security and health* in *Chapter 4*, page 99.

# WOMEN TRAVELLERS

Inevitably as a visitor you will attract attention – whatever your gender. You are the subject of possible friendship, a link to the world beyond the confines of life on the islands, and a potential source of income. This attention should not, however, be misinterpreted as a threat. As mentioned, Grenada is a very safe place and women travelling alone need only take the same, common-sense precautions they would at home. Certainly women travellers are generally more vulnerable to theft or unwanted attention than men, but this should not prevent you from exploring and enjoying the freedom of these beautiful islands. The best advice as always is common sense. If you can, you should avoid going to remote places alone, both by day and by night, try to dress as conservatively as your taste in fashion will allow, and do not sunbathe topless. You could consider carrying a flashlight at night and trying to blend in as much as you can. Wearing similar clothing to local people is one way of doing this, as is not wearing ostentatious jewellery. If you do attract unwanted attention from amorous men, be as polite and good humoured as possible in the way you express your wish to be left alone. Try to extract yourself from the situation as quickly as you can, avoid conflict, resist becoming angry and do not try to humiliate or belittle those you feel are harassing you. Some recommend wearing dark sunglasses as this helps you avoid eye contact and may also enhance your confidence.

# DISABLED TRAVELLERS

Grenada is not especially disabled-traveller friendly. Many hotels do not make special provision for wheelchair access, some are located on steep slopes and have lots of steps, and public buses are predominantly the small minibus type. Nevertheless, with a little research and planning, it is certainly possible to work your way around these obstacles.

Several of the hotels along Grand Anse Beach have hotel rooms and self-catering facilities on ground-floor level, and access to the resorts themselves is flat and just a short distance from the main road (see pages 112–14). The Grenada Grand Beach Resort, the Coyaba Beach Resort and the Spice Island Beach Resort are three examples. The Calabash at L'Anse Aux Épines is also a good option. In terms of sightseeing, there are many private bus- and taxi-tour operators (see page 69 for a small selection) and your hotel may also be able to arrange something specific to your needs. In addition to driving tours, sites and attractions that are accessible by wheelchair include: River Antoine Rum Distillery (most parts), Belmont Estate (there is a slope, but the immediate area around the *boucan*, drying sheds and museum should be fine), Concord Waterfall (viewing the first waterfall), Annandale Waterfall (the path is flat and paved most of the way), Gouyave Fish Friday (though the streets are narrow and can be crowded). Boarding and disembarking the Osprey Ferry between Grenada, Carriacou and Petite Martinique is certainly not wheelchair friendly; indeed anyone with significant manoeuvrability challenges will probably find this very difficult.

## TRAVELLING WITH CHILDREN

Travelling with children is certainly not a problem in Grenada and most hotels and self-catering accommodations welcome families. Nice beaches with calm waters include Morne Rouge, L'Anse Aux Épines and Paradise Beach on Carriacou. The Grenada Grand Beach Resort is located on Grand Anse Beach and has excellent facilities for family holidays including a large 'fantasy pool', manmade waterfalls as well as a wide selection of adventure packages such as snorkelling, boating and kayaking. Children will enjoy the natural waterfalls at Concord and Annandale, both of which are easily accessible, and the Belmont Estate should provide lots of interest for cocoa and chocolate lovers. Other outdoor activities that are fun for families include river tubing (check minimum age limits with operators), turtle watching and hiking – the St Margaret's Falls (sometimes referred to as the Seven Sisters Falls) is a good pick and an adventure you are sure to talk about into the evening.

## WHAT TO TAKE

Grenada is only 12° from the Equator and it has a hot and humid climate. Carriacou and Petite Martinique can feel particularly hot and are considerably more exposed to the sun than mainland Grenada. You will need to take shorts, light skirts and tops, a hat and swimming costumes. For hiking, a pair of training shoes works fine. Some hikes involve mud, small river crossings or scrambles over rocks, so water shoes and sandals are good options. Footwear with soft soles is best for slippery conditions. It is always worth taking along a light rain jacket if you are planning on venturing away from the beach and the hotel. If you are staying in the interior, on the windward east coast or at a high elevation, it is worth taking a sweater too, as it can become cool in the evenings. Lightweight long pants are also good for the evenings when the mosquitoes are on the prowl. They are also useful for hiking on trails that have razor grass (usually encountered towards the summits of mountains). A long-sleeved shirt is also helpful in this circumstance.

A small backpack and waterproof bags are very handy for day trips, both on sea and on land. Take a small first-aid kit, plenty of sunscreen, after-sun and mosquito repellent.

If you are a photographer, it is always worth bringing sufficient digital storage media with you. If you are travelling to some of the nation's more remote corners, you should also consider bringing a small supply of batteries as you may find that those on offer in small convenience stores are occasionally past their expiry dates.

The supermarkets and pharmacies of Grand Anse and St George's have a good selection of toiletries and medicines, but if you are taking prescription drugs please ensure you have an adequate supply with you on your trip.

If you are planning on bringing electrical appliances with you, there should be little problem. The default electricity supply is 220V, 50Hz with UK-style three-pin plugs and sockets, but many hotels and self-catering accommodations have dual voltage systems so 110V circuits with two-pin plugs and sockets are also widely available. It is worth checking in advance to ascertain whether your accommodation offers the supply you need. With regard to electrical appliances, please remember that you are travelling to a tropical climate. Heat, exposure to direct sunlight and high levels of humidity may have a detrimental effect on sensitive equipment if it is not adequately protected.

## $ MONEY AND BUDGETING

**CURRENCY** Grenada's currency is the East Caribbean dollar (commonly written EC$ though officially XCD) and it has been fixed to the US dollar at a rate of US$1 = EC$2.7 since 1979. Notes come in denominations of EC$100, EC$50, EC$20, EC$10 and EC$5. Coins come in denominations of EC$1, and then 50, 25, 10, 5, 2 and 1 cents. In addition to Grenada's dependencies, the East Caribbean dollar is also the official currency of Anguilla, Antigua and Barbuda, Dominica, St Kitts and Nevis, St Lucia, Montserrat, and St Vincent. It is issued by the Eastern Caribbean Central Bank, which is based in St Kitts and Nevis.

US dollars are widely accepted throughout Grenada and visitors will usually be quoted prices in both EC and US dollars. If you pay for goods or services in US dollars, be prepared to receive any change you may expect in East Caribbean dollars. You will rarely receive your change in US dollars. Some of the larger hotels and restaurants also quote prices in, and accept, British pounds.

**Travellers' cheques** can be exchanged at the main banks and in most of the larger hotels. ATMs can be found in St George's, Grand Anse and also the larger villages across the island. You will also find ATMs on Carriacou. Most stores, hotels, restaurants and tour operators accept all major **credit cards** though some do not accept American Express. Market vendors, independent guides, taxi drivers, water taxis and ferries will expect to be paid in cash.

**BANKS** Banks are open 08.00–14.00 Monday to Thursday and 08.00–16.00 Friday. They are closed on Saturdays, Sundays and public holidays. You will find banks with ATMs in most of the following locations:

**Bank of Nova Scotia** ↘ 473 440 3274. Branches in St George's (Grenville St), Grand Anse, Grenville.
**Capital Bank International Ltd** ↘ 473 440 7399. Branches in St George's (Grenville St), Grand Anse, Victoria, Grenville, Sauteurs, Gouyave, Hillsborough (Carriacou), Petite Martinique.
**First Caribbean International Bank** ↘ 473 440 3232. Branches in St George's (Church St & Halifax St), Grand Anse, Grenville, Hillsborough (Carriacou).

**Grenada Cooperative Bank Ltd** ↘ 473 440 2111. Branches in St George's (Church St), Grand Anse (Spiceland Mall), Grenville, Sauteurs.
**Republic Bank (Grenada) Ltd** ↘ 473 444 2265. Branches in St George's (Melville St), Grand Anse, Grenville, Gouyave, Sauteurs, Hillsborough (Carriacou), Petite Martinique.

### MONEY TRANSFERS

**Moneygram** ↘ 473 440 2909. Branches in St George's (Carenage), Grand Anse, Sauteurs, Grenville, Gouyave.

**Western Union** ↘ 473 435 7903. Branches in St George's (Bruce St), Grand Anse, Grenville, Gouyave, Sauteurs, Hillsborough (Carriacou).

**BUDGETING** As Grenada's southwest peninsula is the hub of tourist activity, accommodation and dining, this region also tends to be a little more expensive than elsewhere. Nevertheless, Grenada offers a wide variety of options and,

2

whatever your particular taste and budget, you should easily find something that suits. Outlined below is a basic guide that describes a range of daily budgets for two people, including accommodation. It is meant to give you a general idea of how much your holiday may cost you, depending on your needs.

**Low budget – US$50–75 per day** You can get guesthouse or self-catering accommodation for as little as US$50 per night, even in the more touristy southwest peninsula. For dining, you should eat local, heading for the snackettes and local eateries that serve traditional Grenadian dishes. Here you can get a decent meal for between US$5 and 10. For around US$5, fish, vegetable or chicken roti is always a great filler if your stomach is beginning to rumble. To see the sights, avoid organised excursions and be independent. The bus system is excellent and great value for money.

**Medium budget – US$75–150 per day** For between US$75 and US$120 per night, your options are plentiful; there are some wonderful places to stay both on mainland Grenada as well as on Carriacou. You should still try to eat at local eateries whenever you can, though you can afford to have the occasional treat in one of the fancier international restaurants. Blend organised tours with independent travel and stick to buses. They are cheap, reliable and easy to use. A day at the beach is cheap and fun, though you will pay more for meals and drinks at beachside restaurants and bars.

**High budget – US$150–300** Many of Grenada's mid- to high-end hotels and self-catering villas charge between US$150 and US$200 per night in the peak season, based on double occupancy. This leaves you with between US$50 and US$100 per day to take an organised excursion, splash out on a nice meal, or rent a vehicle for a more independent holiday. The Osprey Ferry to Carriacou costs US$62 per person for a return ticket and the journey is definitely worth it. Consider getting value for money from your ticket by overnighting there rather than just going for a day.

**Luxury budget – US$300 plus** Grenada has some extremely luxurious hotels, resorts and private villas and the amount of money you can spend is rather limitless. If your budget allows it, you should certainly consider staying at the Spice Island Beach Resort, Maca Bana Villas, Laluna, Mount Cinnamon, or the lavish La Source where you can treat yourself to an all-inclusive and riotously self-indulgent pampering.

## GETTING AROUND

Getting around Grenada, Carriacou and Petite Martinique is relatively straightforward. The public transport system of buses is very good and inexpensive, taxis are freely available and there are a good number of very reputable car-hire firms.

**BY BUS** Grenada has an excellent bus system. It is very convenient, affordable and extremely reliable. The only real downside is that many buses tend to stop operating after around 19.00 most days.

The system is very straightforward. Almost all bus routes start and finish at the bus terminal on Melville Street near the Esplanade Mall and cruise-ship terminal. The terminal is very easy to find. It is a busy and very noisy place, yet deceptively well organised, with buses seeming to arrive and depart in droves. The buses themselves are the minibus variety and can be identified by the prefix H on their number plate as well as the route number and colour code on the front windscreen. Many drivers also have their own colourful slogans, nicknames or mottos plastered on both front and rear windows. Some bus drivers may be accompanied by a 'conductor' who makes appeals to potential passengers and collects money. Where there is no conductor simply pay the driver at the end of your trip. Catching a bus is great value for money and fares will rarely top EC$10 and in fact are usually much less. Here is a sample of typical adult bus fares: St George's to Grenville EC$6.50; St George's to La Sagesse EC$4; St George's to Grand Étang EC$5; St George's to Crochu EC$4.50; St George's to Gouyave EC$6; Grenville to Sauteurs EC$4.50.

There is an 'off-route' system that takes in the beaches, hotels and bays of the southwest peninsula that is a little more expensive. For example, the bus fare from St George's to La Source or the Aquarium restaurant is EC$15; to True Blue, L'Anse aux Épines and Point Salines International Airport the fare is EC$10.

In Carriacou, the buses used to follow a similar system with number 10 (red) and number 11 (yellow) plying routes to opposite sides of the island. This was not deemed to be a sustainable system by the bus drivers in Carriacou, who have now applied a far more flexible method. Buses look the same as on the main island and have the same H prefix on the number plate, but the number system has gone. Each driver is identified by his bus name or motif only. All routes are covered and you can usually wave down a bus very easily. Buses tend to congregate at the jetty in Hillsborough, or on Main Street near Ade's Dream. There are no buses on Petite Martinique.

**BY TAXI** Grenada's taxi drivers are licensed by the government and should prominently display their official credentials. Aside from fixed journeys from Point Salines International Airport, there are no specific rates set for private taxi hire and so it is down to the individual driver and a little negotiation. Many taxi drivers will also offer island tours, and again, fares are negotiable. If you have any complaints regarding your taxi services in Grenada, or if you would like more information, please contact the **Grenada Taxi Association** office (*473 440 6850*) which is located on Wharf Road on the southeastern tip of the Carenage in St George's.

**CAR HIRE** A number of car-hire companies operate in Grenada. The most common hire cars are small 4x4 vehicles, usually Suzuki Vitara or Escudo models. The Toyota Yaris is also a common car. Prices vary but are on average between US$40 and US$50 per day with discounted rates for longer periods. Collision damage waiver is usually an additional cost. Many hire companies offer free drop-off and pick-up at the airport and hotels. Check with them before committing. Also check the car over very carefully before signing your rental agreement. Look for scratches and bumps, test lights and brakes, examine tyre tread and make sure any bodywork defects are properly recorded. If the vehicle has poor tyre tread, request a replacement. If the car handles poorly when driven, return it and request a replacement straight away. Do not settle. Grenada has very steep roads, some along high cliffs. If you are exploring the interior, you may also have to drive along rough, perhaps muddy vehicle tracks. Be sure you are happy with your car before driving off in it.

The Grenada government also requires the purchase of a visitor's temporary driving licence. This costs EC$30 or US$12 for a one-month licence and is either obtained from the car-hire company itself or from a local police station. Your car-hire company will help you with this. In order to hire a car and purchase a visitor licence, you must be able to present either your domestic or international driving licence, so make sure you bring it on holiday with you or you will be taking the bus after all.

Here is a selection of car-hire companies. This list is by no means comprehensive.

On the windscreen of each bus you will see a number against a coloured background and a list of some of the places the bus will pass along the route. Each number and colour refers to a designated zone. Within each zone there may be slight variations to the routes. These names help you to understand which route the bus will take so check them to ensure your bus is going where you want to go. If in doubt, simply ask. The route designations are as follows, with the final destination (and therefore turnaround point) in italic:

**Zone 1/gold** St George's–Lagoon Road–Grand Anse–*Calliste*–Grand Anse–Lagoon Road–St George's

**Zone 1/gold** St George's–Belmont–Grand Anse–*Calliste*–Grand Anse–Belmont–St George's

**Zone 2/orange** St George's–Springs–Woodlands–*Woburn*–Woodlands–Springs–St George's

**Zone 2/orange** St George's–Calivigny–Westerhall–*Grenville*–Westerhall–Calivigny–St George's

**Zone 3/purple** St George's–Richmond Hill–Morne Jaloux–*Marian*–Morne Jaloux–Richmond Hill–St George's

**Zone 4/bright green** St George's–St Paul's–Perdmontemps–*Vincennes*–Perdmontemps–St Paul's–St George's

**Zone 4/bright green** St George's–Beaton–La Tante–*Pomme Rose*–La Tante–Beaton–St George's

**Zone 4/bright green** St George's–St Paul's–*Mardigras*–St Paul's–St George's

**Zone 4/bright green** St George's–St Paul's–*La Borie*–St Paul's–St George's

## Grenada

**Alexander's Car Care Centre & Rent A Car** St George's; ✆ 473 435 0131; e cralexander@spiceisle.com

**Archies Auto Rental** St George's; ✆ 473 439 0086; www.archierentals.com

**Azar's Auto Rentals** St George's; ✆ 473 439 2911; e rent@azarsrentals.com; www.azarsrentals.com

**C&J Auto Rental** St George's; ✆ 473 444 5108; e brockle9@hotmail.com

**Chris & Nicky Vehicle Rental** St George's; ✆ 473 443 2881; e chris_nicky@spiceisle.com

**Dabs Car Rentals** St George's; ✆ 473 444 4116; www.dabscarrentals.com

**Dollar Rent A Car** Point Salines International Airport; ✆ 473 444 4786; www.dollargrenada.com

**Gabriel's Rental & Taxi Service** Westerhall, St David's; ✆ 473 443 2304; www.gabrental.com

**Hestel Rentals Ltd** St George's; ✆ 473 407 4692; e hestelrental@hotmail.com

**Indigo Car Rentals Ltd** True Blue; ✆ 473 439 3300; www.indigocarsgrenada.com

**J&B Auto Rentals** St George's; ✆ 473 405 4889; www.jandbautorentals.com

**Nedd's Rentals** St George's; ✆ 473 440 5599; www.neddsrentals.com

**Reggie's Car Rental** St George's; ✆ 473 440 6374; www.reggierental.com

**Sanvics Jeep & Car Rentals Ltd** St George's; ✆ 473 444 4753; e sanvics@caribsurf.com

**C Thomas & Sons Car Rental** True Blue; ✆ 473 444 4384; www.spiceisle.com/ctscarent

**Wontee's Payless Car Rentals** Grenville; ✆ 473 442 6913; www.wonteesrentals.com

**Y&R Car Rentals** St George's; ✆ 473 444 4448; www.y-r.com

**Zone 5/yellow** St George's–Grand Roy–Gouyave–*Victoria*–Gouyave–Grand Roy–St George's

**Zone 5/yellow** St George's–Gouyave–Victoria–*Sauteurs*–Victoria–Gouyave–St George's

**Zone 5/yellow** St George's–Concord–Grand Roy–*Gouyave*–Grand Roy–Concord–St George's

**Zone 6/white** St George's–Grand Étang–Birch Grove–*Grenville*–Birch Grove–Grand Étang–St George's

**Zone 7/red** St George's–Annandale–New Hampshire–*Willis*–New Hampshire–Annandale–St George's

**Zone 7/red** St George's–Beaulieu–Boca–*Vendôme*–Boca–Beaulieu–St George's

**Zone 7/red** St George's–River Road–Tempe–*Mt Parnassus*–Tempe–River Road–St George's

**Zone 8/blue** St George's–Cherry Hill–Fontenoy–*Happy Hill*–Fontenoy–Cherry Hill–St George's

**Zone 8/blue** St George's–Cherry Hill–Fontenoy–*Mt Moritz*–Fontenoy–Cherry Hill–St George's

**Zone 8/blue** St George's–Happy Hill–Beausejour–*Brizan*–Beausejour–Happy Hill–St George's

**Zone 9/pink** Sauteurs–Rose Hill–Mt Rose–River Sallee–*Grenville*–River Sallee–Mt Rose–Rose Hill–Sauteurs

**Zone 9/pink** Sauteurs–Hermitage–Tivoli–*Grenville*–Tivoli–Hermitage–Sauteurs

## Carriacou

Ade's Dream Rentals ℡ 473 443 7317
Barba Auto Rental ℡ 473 443 7454
Franklyn's Rental ℡ 473 443 8496
John's Unique Rental ℡ 473 443 8346
Mark's Rental ℡ 473 443 8375

Martin & Wayne's Auto Rental ℡ 473 443 7221
Quality Jeep Rentals ℡ 473 407 2928
Sunkey's Auto Rentals ℡ 473 443 8382
Talk Back Rental ℡ 473 443 6721

**Driving in Grenada, Carriacou and Petite Martinique** Driving in Grenada, Carriacou and Petite Martinique is on the left. Roads are generally good, though they are occasionally narrow with sharp, blind corners and very steep precipices. Exercise caution and keep your speed low. If you are approaching a blind corner on a narrow road be sure to hit your horn to let anyone coming the other way know you are there. Do not be shy about it. Beeping horns is like a language in Grenada (you will have fun trying to figure it out) and it may prevent a nasty surprise. There are not too many pot-holes on Grenada's roads, but look out for them as they can cause punctures or worse if taken too hard or too quickly. During your stay there will inevitably be a vehicle (or several) right up against your rear bumper trying to pass. Usually this will be a bus. Let vehicles pass you rather than allow them to influence your speed, even if it means slowing down and pulling over. Do not race

2

nor be stubborn or macho about it. Keep it slow and relaxed, be alert for the unexpected, and leave your road rage at home. There is no point in letting a silly and irrelevant driving incident spoil your holiday.

**SCOOTER HIRE** For around US$35 per day you can rent a scooter to get you around. Not especially practical for long journeys or expeditions along rough vehicle tracks, but a scooter is a handy alternative to a car if your trips are short.

### Scooter-hire company/operator
**Sun Dance Enterprises** Le Marquis Complex, Grand Anse; ☎ 473 420 2508; e sundancegrenada@ hotmail.com. Scotter hire with deals on long-term rentals. Guided island scooter tours also available.

**WATER TAXI** An interesting, fun and fast (and sometimes quite wet) way to either explore or simply get from A to B is to take a water taxi. A ride on one of these colourfully painted wooden motorboats can cost as little as US$2 or as much as US$100; it all depends on where and how far you would like to go. During the cruise-ship season water taxis make frequent runs between the cruise-ship terminal and Grand Anse Beach. Simply follow the signs to the water taxis in the Esplanade shopping mall. Prices are usually on a per-person basis. They also operate from the Carenage in St George's. Water taxis are supposed to be licensed by the Grenada Port Authority and carry basic safety equipment such as life jackets.

Water taxis may also take you further afield to other beaches or to the islands off Grenada's southwest peninsula. Some of these trips may include a spot of fishing and a barbecue on the beach. They can be great fun. Many hotels can set you up with water taxis that they recommend. Alternatively you can simply look for one and negotiate. Very few actually advertise, however.

In Carriacou water taxis can take you to Sandy Island, White Island, Petite Martinique, or even further afield to places like the Tobago Cays, a beautiful 'desert island' and a location for the film *Pirates of the Caribbean*.

**HITCHING** Hitching a ride is common in Grenada and, if your budget is very tight, or if buses do not operate along your planned route, it is an inexpensive way to get around. You will often see people trying to get a ride, especially on Sundays and in the evenings when fewer buses operate. Hitching may involve long waits, of course, sometimes in heavy downpours, but together with travelling by bus, it is a nice way to meet local people and experience a part of their lives and their island that may not be possible in other circumstances.

## 🏠 ACCOMMODATION

The accommodation available in Grenada, Carriacou and Petite Martinique reflects the diversity of the country's visitors. For those seeking comfort and elegance, there are a number of excellent, award-winning luxury resorts and boutique hotels that offer extremely high-quality accommodation, dining and services. Many offer all-inclusive packages that include meals, excursions and a range of activities such as golf and watersports. If you are travelling in a little less luxury, mid-range hotels are numerous, conveniently located and usually of a very high standard. For the budget traveller, there are plenty of guesthouses and moderately priced hotels.

Grenada also has a wide range of self-catering accommodation from stylish, luxury villas, to beachside apartments, cottages and homes. There are currently no campsites on any of the three islands.

All accommodation charges are subject to a government tax of 8% and many establishments will also add their own 10% service charge. Before booking your accommodation, you may also want to check for any additional charges that you may have expected to be included. Some places charge for wireless internet use, for example.

Most of Grenada's accommodation is located on the southwest peninsula of the main island. If you plan on seeing and experiencing more of Grenada than the beautiful white-sand beach outside your room, you may wish to consider staying in two or three places during your holiday, including Carriacou which is well worth visiting for more than just a day.

**Note:** the accommodation listed in this guide is deliberately selective and by no means comprehensive. Price codes quoted are current at the time of writing and are based on double occupancy per room per night during the peak season, or roughly the equivalent for self-catering accommodation with weekly rates, unless stated otherwise. Please be aware that these price codes are meant as guides only and are subject to change, see box above for details.

## ✖ EATING AND DRINKING

Grenada's original settlers would probably have survived on a diet of seafood and animals such as the agouti that they brought with them in their canoes as they moved north along the Lesser Antillean island chain from the Amazon River Delta of South America. As time passed they would have cultivated crops such as sweet potatoes, yams and cassava from which they made a simple bread. European settlers brought bananas, breadfruit, mangoes, plantain, cocoa, sugar and spices, and their west African slaves would have combined all these ingredients to make simple one-pot soups or stews that were heavily seasoned and cooked over open fires.

Caribbean Creole is a culinary style that emerged from the heritage of islands whose histories reflect a past similar to the one described in *Chapter 1*, page 4. Those islands that continued to have a strong French influence after emancipation would have developed French Creole cuisine. Other islands, such as Grenada, where stronger influences came from indentured East Indian immigrants, Trinidad and Tobago, and the British plantocracy, would have taken a slightly different path and developed their own unique style of Caribbean cooking.

Today, traditional Grenadian cuisine still includes many of these ingredients and is often cooked outside, over an open fire, in a single pot. You will find very authentic, great tasting and very reasonably priced local dishes in many of the islands' smaller and sometimes more remote eateries and roadside snackettes. World-class international dining has become a by-product of Grenada's burgeoning tourism industry, with its luxury resorts, hotels and sailboat regattas. Visitors to the country will find a wonderful selection of restaurants offering various culinary styles and fine-dining experiences that suit all pockets and tastes, including, of course, traditional Grenadian.

**LOCAL DISHES** Grenada's national dish has to be **oil-down**. It is a simple, one-pot dish that is often cooked over an open fire or on a traditional coal pot. Typically its ingredients include a combination of provisions such as breadfruit, yams, tannia, green bananas and dasheen, flavoured with meat such as pork or beef, and then cooked in coconut milk and spices until the liquid boils right down to leave only an oily residue remaining. Both international and local restaurants offer oil-down occasionally on the menu, though it is usually eaten as a picnic or festival dish outdoors. Another very traditional dish with coconut as a key ingredient is *cou-cou*. This dish is thought to have its roots in west Africa and is made from cornmeal flour, seasonings and coconut milk. The ingredients are mixed in a large pot over a stove or open fire and continuously stirred, or 'turned', until the mixture thickens. It is often eaten with fish and in Carriacou, it is traditionally blended with pigeon peas.

**Calalou** is frequently used to describe dasheen, a ground provision whose young leaves are cooked as a vegetable similar to spinach, or alternatively as the basis of calalou soup, a very common Caribbean and Creole dish. Calalou soup is often served with crab and is a seasonal speciality. Land crabs are also used in the preparation of another favourite dish, **crab backs**. The crab's flesh is mixed with a combination of spices and seasonings and then stuffed back into the shell, sprinkled with breadcrumbs and baked in a hot oven.

Some of the exotic fresh fruits and vegetables you may encounter on your visit to Grenada:

**Ackee** Related to the lychee and toxic when immature or overripe, the ackee is commonly grown and eaten in Jamaica, often fried with salt fish.

**Bluggo** Related to the banana and plantain, usually cooked before it is eaten.

**Breadfruit** A large round fruit with white flesh that is sometimes fried in butter or served in a salad.

**Calalou/Dasheen** A small, starchy tuber, usually eaten like a potato. The leaves, known as calalou, are eaten like spinach or made into a soup.

**Carambola** Also called star fruit or 'five finger'; it is usually eaten as a fruit or blended as a juice.

**Christophene** A pear-like green-skinned squash, usually eaten boiled or fried as a vegetable.

**Golden apple (pomme-sité)** A very common fruit in Grenada, either eaten as a fruit, pickled when still green or, more commonly, blended to make a very refreshing juice.

**Green banana** Confusingly referred to as *figs*, but actually unripe bananas, usually boiled and eaten as a provision. They are a common ingredient in oil-down.

**Guava** The original Arawakan name for this scented fruit which is eaten raw, turned into jam or blended as a juice.

**Noni** A fruit with a very pungent odour when ripe (hence the name *vomit fruit* in some countries). Considered medicinal, it is either eaten as a fruit or blended as a drink.

**Okra** Long, crisp green pods, often used as a flavouring for stews and soups. Also eaten parboiled and fried.

**Passionfruit** A round yellow fruit with soft sweet pulp, usually blended for juice.

**Pawpaw** Also called papaya, with an elongated shape, yellow when ripe and eaten as a fruit. Green, unripe pawpaw is sometimes used in salads or pickles.

**Plantain** A type of banana that is either fried or boiled and eaten as a provision.

**Sapodilla** A round fruit with reddish brown skin, its fleshy pulp is often used to make custard or ice cream.

**Sorrell** A member of the hibiscus family, it is a plant with edible flowers which are usually brewed as a tea or blended for juice, traditionally at Christmas time.

**Soursop** A large green ovoid fruit with soft spines and tart, white flesh which is sweetened to make juice or ice cream. A sweet version (sweetsop) can be eaten as a fruit.

**Sweet potato** Not a yam, and not a potato. Actually belonging to the bindweed family, this elongated vegetable has a sweet flavour and is often boiled, roasted or mashed.

**Tamarind (Tambrand)** This tree has a segmented pod with a reddish brown shell. The inner pulp is very bitter and is mixed with sugar to make tamarind balls, a popular confectionery.

**Tannia** A small, starchy tuber, usually eaten like a potato.

**Yam** A large tuber which is boiled, fried or roasted as a provision. It is a common ingredient in oil-down.

Given Grenada's strong fishing heritage, seafood features prominently in local cuisine. **Lambie** is the queen conch (*Strombus gigas*) and has been eaten in Grenada ever since the first settlers landed there. It is a seasonal dish and is usually served stewed, fried or in a Creole sauce. The discarded, cleaned and polished conch shell is often sold in souvenir and gift shops and is also traditionally blown by fish vendors to let people know their catch is for sale. Conch is found in shallow waters with sandy beds and caught by free divers. According to conservationists, conch is the victim of over fishing throughout the Caribbean. **Titiwi** is a juvenile goby that is caught in nets at the mouths of rivers at certain times of the year. The fish are eaten whole, usually in a seasoned fritter, often known as a titiwi cake or titiwi ackra. Fish caught by local fishermen and also frequently used in local cuisine are tuna, bonito, marlin (known locally as *ocean gar*), flying fish, jacks, and dorado, also known by many as *mahi-mahi* or *dolphin fish*, and by locals simply as *dolphin*. Lobster is a seasonal catch and many restaurants will offer it on their menus. A great place to try out some lobster or delicious local fish dishes is at **Gouyave's Fish Friday** which is held every Friday evening from around 19.00 in the heart of the town (see page 141).

The influence of East India is evident in curried food, such as curried goat, as well as the very popular **roti**. The latter is a dish made of a flat bread that is stuffed with a mixture of curried vegetables, chicken or fish. It is an inexpensive and tasty dish that is very filling. Roti connoisseurs should note that quite a number of local eateries in Grenada may serve chicken rotis with bones. You may therefore wish to ask before you order.

Vegetarians should have few problems finding good food to eat in Grenada. As well as a number of vegetarian eateries, many restaurants will have vegetarian options on the menu. Rice and peas, fried plantain, roasted breadfruit, boiled or stewed provisions, grilled corn, pumpkin soup and calalou are all common local dishes.

## LOCAL DRINKS

**Non-alcoholic** Tap water is safe to drink on all three islands though most supermarkets, convenience stores and hotels will sell bottled water. Grenada's local product, available island-wide, is **Glenelg Natural Spring Water**. Expect to pay between EC$3 and EC$4 for a half-litre bottle. **Mauby** is the name of a drink that is made from the bark of the mauby tree (*Colubrina elliptica*). The bark is boiled with spices and sweetened with sugar to produce a concentrated syrup that is diluted with cold water. The drink is an acquired taste and can be a little bitter.

Freshly made **fruit juices** are widely available in Grenada and your choice is usually based on what is in season. There are also a number of excellent juice bars in St George's Esplanade Mall and the Spiceland Mall in Grand Anse that are really worth seeking out. Golden apple, mango, pineapple, guava, passionfruit, orange and grapefruit are all common juices and are very refreshing.

**Alcoholic** The signature drinks of the Caribbean are **rum** and **rum punch**, and Grenada is no exception. With three distilleries producing a range of high-quality rums, connoisseurs are quite spoiled for choice. **Clarke's Court Estate** produces a great range of rums and rum punches including the very popular Old Grog. **Westerhall Estate** also has a nice selection, including its fabled Jack Iron. The **River Antoine Estate** is an amazing place. One of the oldest working distilleries in the Caribbean, it is still using the same machinery and processes it did during the 18th century, as well as using sugarcane cultivated on its own estate. Its Rivers rums are also a very popular range (see page 180). **Carib** is Grenada's local lager beer and is brewed in the southwest, near Grand Anse.

Average price of a main course:

| | | |
|---|---|---|
| $$$ | **Fine dining** | Often more than EC$75$ |
| $$ | **Mid priced and casual** | Somewhere between EC$25 and EC$75 |
| $ | **Cheap as chips** | Less than or around EC$25 |

**EATING OUT** Grenada has a nice selection of dining options ranging from cheap-and-cheerful roadside snackettes to high-class restaurants offering haute international and Caribbean cuisine. Most snackettes and local eateries are very similarly priced as are the majority of restaurants. Instead of including sample dinner prices in this guide, I have used a simple code that you can use as a broad guide to eating out. Check menus to see if prices include government sales tax and service charge.

Most restaurants are open daily and you can usually just turn up. Some are very popular, however, and I recommend you either pass by or call in advance to avoid disappointment – where this is the case it's included in the listing. Save for roadside snackettes, you can expect to pay by major credit cards at most restaurants.

## PUBLIC HOLIDAYS AND EVENTS

| | |
|---|---|
| **January** | New Year's Day (1 January). Also taking place during this month are the Grenada Sailing Festival (see page 83) and the Spice Island Billfish Tournament (see page 71). |
| **February** | Independence Day (7 February). The Carriacou Carnival takes place on the Monday and Tuesday before Ash Wednesday. |
| **March** | In 2011, Ash Wednesday falls in March, so look out for the Carriacou Carnival during this month. |
| **April** | Good Friday and Easter Monday. Also taking place during Easter is the Grenada Round-the-Island Easter Regatta (see page 85). |
| **May** | Labour Day (1 May) and Whit Monday. |
| **June** | Corpus Christi and Whit Monday. Fisherman's Birthday is celebrated in Gouyave on 29 June (see page 134). |
| **July** | This month sees the build-up to Grenada's carnival celebrations. |
| **August** | Emancipation Day (4 August). This is also the month of the Grenada Carnival with Carnival Monday (J'Ouvert and Carnival Pageant) and Carnival Tuesday (Parade of Bands), both public holidays. Carnival celebrations also encompass the National Soca Monarch final and the Miss Spicy Grenada Queen Show. Also during this month, over the Emancipation weekend, is the Carriacou Regatta (see page 85). |
| **September** | Most people spend September recovering from carnival celebrations but, if you are still in the mood, you can check out the Grenada Culinary Fest. |
| **October** | Thanksgiving Day |
| **November** | The Carriacou Sailing Series take place during November (see page 85). |
| **December** | Christmas Day (25 December) and Boxing Day (26 December). Also taking place around Christmas time is the Carriacou Parang Festival. |

See also *When to visit*, page 33, and *Chapter 1, Festivals*, page 21.

When visiting new places it is always nice, and extremely worthwhile, to support small businesses, artisans and cottage industries through the purchase of original products that are made locally, often by hand. Here is a small selection of some of Grenada's excellent local products. Please buy!

**Amba Kaila** Excellent homemade jams, jellies, hot pepper sauce, essences and concentrates. Look out for the Amba Kaila craftshop in Constantine, just south of the turn-off to Annandale Waterfall.

**Arawak Islands** (*www.arawak-islands.com*) Perfumes, sweets, gifts, soaps, body oils, soaps, candles, balms and much more.

**Barguna Enterprises Ltd** Alcoholic wines flavoured with *bois bandé*, ginger, lemon grass, almond and spice (cinnamon). Try the Tibli Grog, known as the 'under the counter rum'. Also look out for Kay tea, Spice Isle herbal and fruit tea.

**Belinde Crafts** Very original handmade stuffed dolls. Look out for them in Grenada Essentials.

**Caribbean Naturals** Handmade soaps, candles, spices, jams and perfume. Available in a number of craft and souvenir shops.

**Chanse** A small producer from Gouyave making delicious passionfruit honey.

**De La Grenade Industries Ltd** (*www.delagrenade.com*) Award-winning nutmeg products containing no colours or artificial preservatives including De La Grenade liqueur, Morne Delice nutmeg jam and jelly, Morne Delice nutmeg syrup, De La Grenade guava jam and jelly, hot pepper sauce, pepper jelly, orange and grapefruit marmalade, seamoss, rum punch, mauby syrup.

**Fidel Productions** Excellent original T-shirts from Paradise Beach (L'Esterre), Carriacou. You will find Fidel products in various craft and souvenir stores in St George's and Grand Anse. Look out for a Fidel store opening in Port Louis Marina.

**Grenada Essentials** Community-based business that supports authentic crafts created by Grenada's craftspeople. The store (*Museum Bldg, Monckton St, St George's;* ☎ *473 435 5958; www.grenadaessentials.com*) contains pieces by artisans such as Shawnley Lewis (producing jewellery made from sea shells), Anita Blair (creator of original bracelets made from flamboyant tree seeds) and Margaret Lewis (basket weaver, painted wooden coasters). All profits from the business are ploughed into conservation projects such as turtle protection and reforestation.

**Moses** A range of essences for cakes and ice cream including pear, aniseed and vanilla. Produced in La Fortune, St Patrick's.

**Noelville Ltd** A Grenville-based company producing Nut-Med, Spice Island noni juice and Noel's lemon grass tea. Look out for their products in the Gouyave Nutmeg Pool. The Nut-Med painkilling spray and lotion are extremely popular and very effective after those long hikes!

**Spice Isle Plantations** Handmade soaps from St George's.

**Sugar & Spice** Grenada's local ice cream.

**Veronica's Visions** Original painted fabric designs from Concord. Look out for Spicewear and *jola* bags with a nutmeg theme, produced by Viv's Production Studio.

**White Cane Industries** Workshop for the blind and disabled located on the Carenage in St George's, near BB's Crabback restaurant, producing excellent white-cane basketware.

# 🛒 SHOPPING

The majority of shops in Grenada are located in the capital, St George's, and in the southwest peninsula around Grand Anse where there are three shopping malls. You should always be able to find what you are looking for here as most of the stores and pharmacies in St George's and Grand Anse are well stocked and diverse. This includes essentials such as baby foods, nappies and sanitary products as well as toiletries, medicines and prescription drugs. You will also find a number of shops selling crafts and souvenirs. In towns such as Gouyave, Grenville and Sauteurs you will find small supermarkets, chemists and convenience stores selling basic items.

Hillsborough is Carriacou's main town and is where you will find small supermarkets, convenience stores, pharmacies and a variety of other small shops and boutiques. Both St George's and Hillsborough have markets and street vendors selling fruits, vegetables and spices. They also have fish markets.

Shopping in Petite Martinique may be more of a challenge, though it does have a few small convenience stores selling groceries and other essential items.

**OPENING HOURS** Inevitably there are variations to the rule but, generally speaking, you should aim to do your shopping within the following opening hours: 08.00–16.00 Monday to Friday and 08.00–13.00 Saturday. Expect most shops to be closed on Sundays and Saturday afternoons. Exceptions include some shops in Grand Anse which may stay open later. Supermarkets also often stay open a little later. Shopping centres may open all day on Saturday as do most stores in Grenville. Spiceland Mall in Grand Anse is open on Sundays.

# 🎭 ARTS AND ENTERTAINMENT

**THEATRE** At the time of writing there is no permanent theatre located in any of the three islands, though there are productions from time to time that are performed by local drama groups. These tend to take place in sports halls, schools or community centres. To find out about them you have to check the newspapers, look for flyers and posters, listen to the radio or ask local people. One such drama group worth checking on is the Theatre of Unique Music & Dramatic Arts (✆ *473 420 2775 or 473 404 0343*).

**ART GALLERIES, MUSEUMS AND WORKSHOPS** If you are interested in seeking out both local and regional art and cultural exhibits then the following places are definitely worth a visit:

**Art Grenada** Grand Anse shopping mall, Grand Anse. Upper-floor art gallery with a selection of works by local artists.

**Body & Soul** Spiceland Mall, Grand Anse. Bookstore & gallery with a collection of works by Susan Main which are also for sale.

**Camàhogne Gallery** St Paul's, St George's. Excellent local woodcarvings on exhibit & for sale. Easy to find, right along the side of the main road.

**Carriacou Museum** Hillsborough, Carriacou. The museum contains a wonderful collection of Amerindian artefacts & ceramics from archaeological sites around the island. There are also informative exhibits of African heritage, European occupation & Carriacouan culture, illustrated by the Big Drum and Maroon festivals. (See page 195.)

**Grenada National Museum** Monckton St, St George's. The museum has a number of fascinating exhibits & displays including a collection of Amerindian & Yoruba artefacts, plus plantation machinery & tools as well as antique firearms & cannons. (See page 101.)

**Helvellyn Pottery Workshop & Learning Centre** Helvellyn, near Sauteurs. You can see pottery being made from local clay & you can also give it a try yourself. The pottery is jam-packed with beautiful pieces that are sold at various shops in Grenada as well as exported abroad. (See page 183.)

2

63

**Yellow Poui Art Gallery** Young St, St George's. A wonderful gallery of paintings, sculptures & carvings by artists from, working in, or inspired by the Caribbean.

## *C* MEDIA AND COMMUNICATIONS

**MEDIA** Grenada's national weekly newspapers include the *Grenada Advocate*, the *Spice Isle Review*, the *Grenada Informer*, and the *Grenadian Voice*. Look out for latest editions in stores island-wide on Fridays and Saturdays. In addition to local and regional news and information, cable television channels are predominantly American. Radio stations are a good source of information as well as a great way to find out about local events. Stations include the Grenada Broadcasting Network (GBN) broadcasting **Hott FM** (105.5FM) and **Klassic 535** (535AM); **Voice of Grenada** (95.7FM and 103.3FM); **CRFM** (89.5FM); **City Sound** (97.5FM); **WeeFM** (93.9FM) and Carriacou's own **Kayak 106 FM** (106FM).

✉ **POST** Grenada's postal service is called the Grenada Postal Corporation. The main office is located on the southern tip of the Carenage in St George's. You will also find small post offices and stations in most villages. The main post office in Carriacou is located in Hillsborough next to the jetty. Post office opening hours are 08.00–15.30 Monday to Friday. They are closed at weekends and on public holidays. A stamp for a postcard to either the UK or the US costs EC$1.

*C* **TELEPHONES** Grenada has a digital telecommunications system that is mainly provided by Cable & Wireless. There are pay and pre-paid card phones located around the island and most of Grenada's hotels provide facilities for international direct dialling. Calls are usually charged on a per-minute basis and are subject to a 10% government tax.

**International calls** The international dialling code for Grenada, Carriacou and Petite Martinique is +1 473 followed by a number consisting of seven digits. A sample of international direct-dialling codes from Grenada is as follows:

**Belgium** ➘ 011 + 32 + number
**Canada** ➘ 1 + area code + number
**Caribbean** ➘ 1 + area code + number
**People's Republic of China** ➘ 011 + 86 + number
**Cuba** ➘ 011 + 53 + number
**France** ➘ 011 + 33 + number
**Germany** ➘ 011 + 49 + number
**Guyana** ➘ 011 + 592 + number

**Netherlands** ➘ 011 + 31 + number
**Norway** ➘ 011 + 47 + number
**Spain** ➘ 011 + 34 + number
**Sweden** ➘ 011 + 46 + number
**UK** ➘ 011 + 44 + number
**US** ➘ 1 + area code + number
**Venezuela** ➘ 011 + 58 + number

**Mobile phones** Mobile-phone providers in Grenada include Digicel and Cable & Wireless. If you do not have a mobile phone and wish to have one during your stay, it is possible to purchase an inexpensive pay-as-you-go phone for as little as EC$60–70 from either of these providers. You will find both a Cable & Wireless and a Digicel store located near to the Esplanade shopping mall in the capital, St George's. A number of hotels either rent or loan out pay-as-you-go mobile phones to their guests.

● **INTERNET** Many hotels will provide either hard-wired or wireless internet access. Most offer free wireless services, though some charge by the day or half-day. Point Salines International Airport is also a wireless internet zone. There are a number of internet cafés located around Grenada as well as in Carriacou. Many are attached to bars and restaurants, and some can be found in computer stores.

## BUSINESS

Hours of business vary although most will begin around 08.00. On weekday mornings expect traffic to be busy in and around the capital St George's from 07.30 onwards. Some businesses seem to take a little longer to get warmed up in the mornings with their shutters making half-hearted efforts at opening any time between 08.00 and 10.00, though they eventually make it. Everything gets rather busy around the Esplanade shopping mall and the bus terminal in St George's when cruise ships are calling and also in the streets around St George's marketplace. Carriacou and Petite Martinique never really get busy although there is always a good deal of activity around the jetty when supply boats and the Osprey ferry arrive and depart.

Most businesses end their working day between 16.00 and 17.30. Again, expect heavy traffic in and around St George's at this time of day. A five-day week is standard though some businesses may also open for a short time on Saturday morning.

If you are dealing with government-related services you will need to be aware that processes and working practices may be very different from what you are accustomed to back home. It is not uncommon to have to make several trips between different offices or departments, and they may not always be located in the same building. Patience and a generous allocation of your time are essential ingredients for keeping your cool and making progress.

## CULTURAL ETIQUETTE

Though Grenada's population is becoming increasingly younger and many have either lived or have experienced life overseas, on the whole they are quite a reserved and religious people whose views on proper behaviour and sexuality are fairly conservative and usually reflect those of their Church. Homosexuality, for example, is considered by many to be immoral and offensive, and therefore overt displays of affection between same-sex couples are likely to draw unwelcome attention.

When walking around towns, villages, shops and malls, it would be considerate to ensure you are wearing a shirt. You should also dress appropriately when visiting churches, even if they are standing in ruins. Sunbathing topless is against the law and, although you may well encounter someone smoking marijuana, or you may even be offered it, remember it is also illegal. The best advice is simply to use common sense and try if you can to respect the views and perspectives of your hosts, whether you agree with them or not. Greet people with a handshake and a smile, just as you would back home, and when visiting people's homes do not be surprised if you leave with an armful of fruits or vegetables. Please accept them.

## GIVING SOMETHING BACK

Throughout this guide visitors to Grenada, Carriacou and Petite Martinique are encouraged to look out for and try to support local businesses, small bars and snackettes, farmers, artists, craftspeople and so on. Grenada also has many practical problems, particularly following two recent, very devastating hurricanes, that a number of NGOs and local groups of volunteers are trying to resolve or improve upon. Overseas charities and Grenadians living abroad are continually a great source of assistance to these organisations by sending materials and helping with fundraising. You, as a visitor to Grenada, can also help to make a difference, even if it is just in a small way, to someone somewhere who will appreciate it. It would therefore be nice to consider contacting one of these organisations before or during your visit and asking how you might be able to help.

You may also be interested in checking the following website before you travel, www.stuffyourrucksack.com, to see if there are any organisations registered who may benefit from a small item or two that you could bring with you (see box above). Also, at the end of your visit to Grenada, think about whether you could leave any of your clothes or children's books to a local charity instead of taking them back home. You may be surprised how small things like this are a big help to those who need them.

**Boaters for Books** www.boatersforbooks.org. A sailing fraternity network aimed at helping to improve literacy in the Caribbean by collecting & distributing books to young people at ports of call throughout the islands.

**Carriacou Children's Medical Trust** Carriacou; ☎ 473 443 6424; contact: Sue Fretwell. Raising money for children who need medical care in Carriacou.

**Carriacou Children's Education Fund** Carriacou; e boatmillie@aol.com; contact: Melodye Pompas. Raising money for children's education, school uniforms, books, etc in Carriacou.

**Foundation for Carriacou & PM Development** Carriacou; ☎ 473 443 7334; contact: Rhonda McLawrence. Raising money for children's education, scholarships & seasonal events in Carriacou.

**Grenada Sailing Association** ☎ 473 415 2022. Offering young Grenadians sailing instruction & practical training.

**Grenada Society for the Prevention of Cruelty to Animals** St George's, Grenada & Hillsborough, Carriacou; ☎ 473 440 4874; www.grenadaspca.org

**Queen Elizabeth Home For Children** ☎ 473 440 2327. Collecting & distributing toys & clothes for children, especially at Christmas time.

**JJ Robinson Trust** www.jjrtrust.com. Provides financial assistance for further education for those who are unable to afford it. Also provides financial support for the School for Pregnant & Adolescent Mothers.

# 3

# Activities and Special Interests

There are very many ways to enjoy the culture and the natural environment of Grenada, Carriacou and Petite Martinique. Visitors to the islands will find a diverse choice of activities that suit many interests, ages and abilities. Established operators offer everything from yacht charters to bus tours, scuba diving to river tubing – there is a lot to do. Culture vultures may be interested in experiencing some of Grenada's fascinating and colourful traditions and heritage sites, and those with green fingers may fancy a stroll through some of the country's beautiful tropical gardens. Whatever you decide to make of your trip to Grenada, whether travelling independently or with the assistance of tour operators and guides, whether looking for activity and adventure, or relaxation, massage and cocktails, you are sure to have an enjoyable trip.

## BIRDWATCHING

Birdwatching is an undeveloped activity in Grenada with relatively few operators offering speciality birdwatching outings. If you are travelling independently and are interested in knowing where to go then the following places should definitely be on your list: Mt Hartman National Park, La Sagesse, Levera Archipelago National Park, Lake Antoine, High North National Park (Carriacou), Grand Étang Lake and National Park, and Palmiste Lake.

**BIRDWATCHING OPERATORS AND GUIDES** The following operators offer birdwatching excursions:

**Caribbean Horizons** ℡ 473 444 1555; e info@caribbeanhorizons.com; www.caribbeanhorizons.com
**Eco Guide Expeditions** ℡ 473 416 0191 or 473

533 7767; e tonydove200@yahoo.com. Birdwatching tours with Anthony 'Jerry' Jeremiah. **Henry's Safari Tours** ℡ 473 444 5313; e safari@caribsurf.com; www.henrysafari.com

## BOAT CHARTERS AND DAY CRUISING

Several operators offer half- and full-day motor or sailing boat excursions around Grenada. Half- and full-day boat trips usually cost anywhere between US$50 and US$150 depending on the duration and distance of the trip. Check operators for prices, availability and minimum passenger quotas. Many of them offer trips along the west coast from Point Salines up to Molinère Point and the Molinère Protected Seascape. The southwest peninsula and around to Hog and Calivigny islands are also popular cruise and sailing destinations. All-day sailing trips will take you up the west and then north coasts to Sandy Island. Some operators offer a full circumnavigation of Grenada.

These are some of the bird species you may observe in Grenada, Carriacou and Petite Martinique:

Antillean-crested hummingbird (*Orthorhyncus cristatus*)
Bananaquit (*Coereba flaveola*)
Bare-eyed thrush (*Turdus nudigrenis*)
Barn owl (*Tyto alba*)
Barn swallow (*Hirundo rustica*)
Blue-faced grassquit/black-faced grassquit (*Tiaris bicolor*)
Broad-winged hawk/chicken-hawk (*Buteo platypterus*)
Carib grackle/blackbird (*Quiscalus lugubris*)
Cattle egret (*Bubulcus ibis*)
Emerald-throated hummingbird/green-throated Carib (*Sericotes holosericus chlorolaemus*)
Glossy cowbird/corn bird (*Molothrus bonariensis*)
Grenada dove (*Leptotila wellsi*)
Ground dove (*Columbina passerina*)
Grey kingbird (*Tyrannus dominicensis*)
House wren/rock bird (*Troglodytes aedon*)
Hook-billed kite (*Chrondrohierax uncinatus*)
Lesser Antillean bullfinch (*Loxigilla noctis*)
Loggerhead flycatcher (*Myiarchus nugator*)
Magnificent frigatebird (*Fregata magnificens*)
Mangrove cuckoo (*Coccyzus minor grenadensis*)
Osprey (*Pandian haliaetus*)
Rufous-breasted hermit hummingbird (*Glaucis hirsuta*)
Smooth-billed ani (*Crotophaga ani*)
Southern mockingbird (*Minus gilvus antillarum*)
Yellow-bellied elaenia (*Elaenia flavogaster*)
Zenaida dove (*Zenaida auriculata*)

Operators usually have a minimum passenger quota for their trips so please remember to check this when making enquiries or bookings. Excursions frequently include snorkelling-equipment hire, refreshments and, if sailing all day, a packed lunch or a beach cook-up of some kind. Remember to take sun protection with you – in the form of lotion, a hat, or a long-sleeved shirt. It is extremely easy to get sunburned aboard a boat. Drink lots of water and try to limit your exposure to direct sunlight. Wearing a T-shirt is always a good idea when snorkelling to protect your back and shoulders from those harmful rays. Operators offering motorised and sailing adventures include the following:

## BOAT CHARTERS AND DAY-CRUISING OPERATORS

**Carib CATS** ✆ 473 444 3222; e helvellynhouse@ spiceisle.com. All-inclusive & very popular sailing excursions aboard *Wizard*, a 20m sailing catamaran that has been custom built for day charters. A southern full-day cruise lasts around 7hrs & departs from Grand Anse Beach. It sails around the southwest peninsula & includes a BBQ picnic & snorkelling. The 4hr snorkel cruise incorporates the reefs of the west coast. The sunset cruise is a 2hr relaxing meander along the pretty west coast. The northern cruise heads up to the islands off the Levera Archipelago National Park, near Sauteurs. The

trip includes snorkelling & a beach BBQ. Dinner & party cruises also available.

**Catch the Spirit** ✆ 473 444 4753; e sanvics@ caribsurf.com. A 10m twin-engine pirogue offering customisable, private half- or full-day trips. Great for snorkelling, fishing, cruising or sunbathing.

**First Impressions** ✆ 473 440 3678; e starwindsailing@spiceisle.com; www.catamaranchartering.com. Full-day catamaran sailing tours around the island. A 7hr sailing trip takes you along the west & north coasts to Sandy Island, & an 8hr trip takes you all the way around the island. A cruise around the southwest peninsula & Calivigny Island takes around 7hrs. Other tours & private charter options are also available. Call or email for prices & schedules.

**Footloose Caribbean Yacht Charters** ⟍ 473 440 7949; e footloose@spiceisle.com; www.grenadasailing.com. Day charters for private groups. Sail from St George's to Sandy Island or Île de Ronde or around the southwest peninsula to Calivigny & Hog islands. Prices include drinks, lunch & snorkelling-equipment hire. Both trips require a min of 4 persons.

**Grenada Seafaris** ⟍ 473 405 7800; e seafarisales@hotmail.com; www.grenadaseafaris.com. Short, fast & fun rides along the west coast in a custom-made, high-speed 'safari boat'. 1 or 2hr tours take you to the Carenage & the beaches & coves of the west coast. Exhilarating. Pick-up & drop-off on Grand Anse Beach. Private charters also available. A Seafari trip may not be for those with back problems, disabilities or who are pregnant. Call for advice.

**Horizon Yacht Charters** ⟍ 473 439 1000; e horizonyachts@spiceisle.com; www.horizonyachtcharters.com. Bareboat or crewed, fully equipped yacht charters from Grenada & around the Grenadines. Yacht handling & chartering briefings, advice on provisioning & land-based accommodation & excursions.

**Mostly Harmless** Carriacou; ⟍ 473 443 7984; e goldhill@spiceisle.com; www.carriacoucottages.com. Snorkel trips, half- & full-day cruises on the *Mostly Harmless*, a 9m modified motor launch. Call or email for prices.

**Native Spirit** ⟍ 473 420 1080 or 473 415 1080;

e dive_adrian@hotmail.com. Half- & full-day tours aboard the motor launch *June*. With pick-up from Grand Anse Beach, the half-day trip takes you around the Carenage & along the west coast. Snorkelling is at Turtle Head Reef & Flamingo Bay. The full-day trip heads up the west coast from Grand Anse Beach for snorkelling at Turtle Head Reef, past the fishing village of Gouyave, up to Sauteurs, & then across for lunch on Sandy Island in the Levera Archipelago National Park. Open bar, lunch & snorkelling equipment rental included.

**Shadowfax Banana Boat Tours** ⟍ 473 437 3737; e shadowfax@spiceisle.com; www.bananaboattoursgrenada.com. Half- & full-day sailing in the catamaran *Shadowfax*. The 4hr Snorkelling Cruise takes you from St George's Harbour along the west coast to snorkel the reefs of the Molinère Protected Seascape. The 6hr Champagne & Lobster Cruise takes you around the southwest peninsula where you will snorkel & have a champagne & lobster lunch on the beach of Hog Island; fish broth, chicken & vegetarian dishes also available if requested in advance. An 8hr sailing trip takes you on a complete circumnavigation of Grenada with a stop-off at Sandy Island for swimming, sunbathing & snorkelling; lunch is included or how about a 2hr Sunset Cruise with champagne?

**Sunsation Tours** ⟍ 473 444 1594; e qkspice@spiceisle.com; www.grenadasunsation.com. Day sailing around Carriacou, Petit St Vincent & Petite Martinique on the 40ft (13m) yacht *Cinderella*. Lunch & snorkelling. Flight from Grenada to Carriacou also arranged. Contact for prices.

# BUS TOURS

A very popular and leisurely way to enjoy a taste of Grenada is to take organised bus tours. There are many options available, run either by the larger operators or by numerous independent taxi drivers. Most tend to encompass Grenada's more easily accessible attractions and prices are usually based on the tour's duration rather than the number of people on the bus. If you are arriving in Carriacou on the Osprey ferry you will be offered private taxi tours of the island as soon as you emerge from the jetty in Hillsborough. Buses and private taxis are standard minibuses, some are very modern with air conditioning, others are a little more battle-weary. If you have not organised your bus excursion with a tour operator, be sure to check that your driver is a licensed bus or taxi operator before you discuss a tour, part with any cash or step onboard.

**BUS-TOUR OPERATORS** Here is a small selection of operators offering bus tours. There are very many to choose from and your hotel may also make recommendations:

**Caribbean Horizons** ➘ 473 444 1550 or 473 444 1555; e info@caribbeanhorizons.com; www.caribbeanhorizons.com. Offers a number of standard half- & full-day island tours incorporating many of Grenada's natural & cultural sites of interest.

**Henry's Safari Tours** ➘ 473 444 5313; e safari@caribsurf.com; www.henrysafari.com. Offers a very wide selection of half- & full-day tours to many of Grenada's natural & heritage sites.

**Joe's Tours & Taxi** ➘ 473 417 5710; e joestours@spiceisle.com; www.joestours.com. Joe offers a number of half- & full-day tours around Grenada on his AC tour bus.

**Kennedy Tours** ➘ 473 444 1074; e kennedytours@caribsurf.com; www.kennedytours.com. Kennedy is an English- & Spanish-speaking guide who offers half- & full-day AC bus tours around Grenada.

**Mandoo Tours** ➘ 473 440 1428; e mandoo@grenadatours.com; www.grenadatours.com. Mandoo is an award-winning operator offering a wide selection of half- & full-day tour options around Grenada.

**Robert Taxi & Tours Company** ➘ 473 443 7271. Carriacou operator offering a range of tours around the island.

**Sunsation Tours** ➘ 473 444 1594 or 473 439 4447; e qkspice@caribsurf.com; www.grenadasunsation.com. Half- & full-day tours incorporating many of Grenada's main attractions. There is also an option to design your own tour.

## CYCLING AND MOUNTAIN BIKING

A nice way to explore some of Grenada's villages and country tracks is to hire a bike or take a guided cycling tour. Bike rentals are usually around US$20 per day with discounts available for weekly rentals. Some operators have age limits so check before booking. Grenada's roads are good and some of the vehicle tracks and coastal pathways make for a fun and interesting way to spend a few hours. Carriacou is a great place for road cycling and mountain biking. It is always worth checking with your hotel to see if they can recommend anyone who rents bicycles.

### CYCLING AND MOUNTAIN-BIKING OPERATORS

**A & E Tours** ➘ 473 435 1444; e aandetours@caribsurf.com; www.grenadaguide.com/aetours. Mountain-bike hire & guided tours available. The Adventure Biking Tour takes around 3hrs & takes you from St George's down to the south coast to explore Mt Hartman National Park, Fort Jeudy & Calivigny.

**Trailblazers** ➘ 473 444 5337; e trailblazers@grenadajeeptours.com; www.grenadajeeptours.com. Offers bike hire & guided tours. Rentals come with a complimentary route sheet that includes several on- & off-road options. All mountain bikes have front suspension shocks & hire includes safety helmets & security locks. Guided bike tours include a personal guide to help you explore.

**Wild Track Cycles** Carriacou; ➘ 473 443 6472; e wildtrackcycles@grenadines.net. Half-day, full-day or weekly mountain-bike hire, delivered to your hotel.

## FISHING

Fishing enthusiasts travelling to Grenada can choose between a sedate coastal trip with a little fishing followed by a beach barbecue, or a full- or half-day charter excursion for some serious sport fishing. If the former is your preference, check with the charter-boat operators listed on page 67 or ask your hotel if they can recommend water taxis or fishermen. For sport-fishing charters, see the list opposite. Half-day sport fishing usually costs between US$400 and US$500 with full-day charters around US$700-800.

Grenada's west coast waters deepen to around 1,000m after a short 20–30-minute boat ride. Charter operators tend to fish along this contour and then deeper at the 2,000m mark which is around one hour from the dock. Anglers can expect

## SPICE ISLAND BILLFISH TOURNAMENT

The Spice Island Billfish Tournament has been running since 1964 and attracts sport fishermen from all around the region. It takes place in January at the height of the billfish season and is a modified tag-and-release tournament. This means that the participants are encouraged to tag and release the majority of billfish they catch, and only land the ones they believe are large enough to win the tournament. The three-day event takes place at the Grenada Yacht Club. Entry fee is US$150 per angler. The prize for the angler breaking the current blue marlin record will win a prize of EC$30,000.

to catch an assortment of large pelagics including yellowfin tuna, blue marlin, white marlin, sailfish, dorado and wahoo. A billfish tag-and-release system is the norm and therefore most fish of this kind return to the water.

**TAG AND RELEASE** Sport-fishing operators employ the tag-and-release policy advocated by the Billfish Foundation when catching billfish during their fishing trips. Billfish include Atlantic blue marlin, sailfish, white marlin and short- and long-bill spearfish. Tag and release means that when caught, the fish are not brought into the boat, nor are they brought back to shore. Instead, once alongside the boat, the billfish are tagged and an estimate of the weight of the fish is made by the crew based on its size and length. The fish is then fully revived, ensuring oxygenated water is flushed through its gills and it is strong enough to be released. Whilst it is being resuscitated, all hooks are carefully removed.

The Billfish Foundation's tag-and-release programme provides scientists and fishery managers worldwide with data on billfish migration patterns, age and growth rates, feeding and spawning grounds, stock structure and numbers. Sport-fishing operators around the world are encouraged to participate in tag-and-release sport fishing by joining the Billfish Foundation and stocking their fishing boats with official tagging supplies. As part of a conservation effort started by fishermen themselves, the Billfish Foundation has succeeded in bringing about successful regulations and petitions regarding endangered species and long-line fishing. For more information go to www.billfish.org.

### SPORT-FISHING OPERATORS

**Grenada Sportfishing** ℡ 473 418 5508 or 473 443 4343; e molliedalby@hotmail.com; www.grenadasportfishing.com. Prize-winning skipper, Badger, offers half- & full-day fishing trips aboard his 2006 Luhrs 38 Convertible, comfortably accommodating up to 6 anglers. Fully equipped with top-brand tackle, fighting chair & galley. Billfish tag-&-release policy employed. Half day. Prices include transport to & from your accommodation & onboard refreshments.

**Reel Affair** ℡ 473 435 4521. Sport fishing aboard *Reel Affair II*, a Bertram 38 Convertible, skippered by Howard A Otway. Fully equipped with top-brand tackle, this charter operates billfish tag & release. Half- & full-day fishing trips available for up to 6

anglers. Call for prices.

**True Blue Sportfishing** ℡ 473 444 2048 or 473 407 4688; e grclifford@spiceisle.com; www.yesaye.com. Skipper Gary Clifford offers full- & half-day fishing trips aboard his 1988 Innovator *Yes Aye*. Fully equipped with top-brand tackle & fighting chair. Billfish tag-&-release policy employed.

**Wayward Wind** ℡ 473 439 7929 or 473 538 9821; e stewart@grenadafishing.com; www.grenadafishing.com. Captain Stewart offers full- & half-day sport fishing on his fully equipped Bertram 31 with top-quality fishing tackle & fighting chair. A billfish tag-&-release policy is in operation.

# GARDENS, FARMS AND FOOD

Grenada's climate and volcanic soil provide the perfect growing environment for a wide variety of vegetables, tropical plants, flowers and flowering trees. The island is also home to beautiful private gardens and accomplished gardening enthusiasts, some of whom have won awards at London's prestigious Chelsea Flower Show.

**GARDEN, FARM AND COOKING TOUR OPERATORS** Grenada has several operators who offer speciality tours that encompass private gardens, farms or cooking some of Grenada's favourite dishes.

**Bay Gardens** St Paul's, St George's; ✆ 473 435 4544 or 473 404 6266; e thebaygardens@aol.com; www.baygardensgrenada.com. Located near the village of St Paul's this beautiful tropical garden is certainly worth a visit. Entrance fee EC$5 or US$2 pp, includes an excellent guided tour. (See page 161 for more information on visiting the Bay Gardens.)
**Caribbean Horizons** ✆ 473 444 1550 or 473 444 1555; e info@caribbeanhorizons.com; www.caribbeanhorizons.com. Designed by a member of Grenada's 2002 gold-medal-winning team at the Chelsea Flower Show, this 3–4hr tour incorporates many of Grenada's private gardens & nurseries. Caribbean Horizons also has a very unique 'beekeeper' tour where you can spend time with some of Grenada's honey-makers.
**Creative Caribbean** ✆ 473 536 5234; e info@creativecaribbean.net; www.creativecaribbean.net. Imaginative Grenada

experience that takes you on a trip through farms, learning about & gathering all the fresh ingredients you need for a delicious oil-down which is prepared for you on the beach over an open fire. Fishing & BBQ on the beach also offered. Call or email for prices & details.
**Laura Herb & Spice Garden** Laura, St David's; ✆ 473 443 2604; e minorspices@spiceisle.com. A guided walk around the gardens of this spice-production business, learning about Grenada's natural spices, what they look like, how they smell & what they are used for. Tours cost EC$5 pp & last around 30mins.
**Sunsation Tours** ✆ 473 444 1594 or 473 439 4447; e qkspice@caribsurf.com; www.grenadasunsation.com. A leisurely visit to 2 private gardens that have featured on UK TV. Standard-tour prices start at US$50 per tour (not pp) & include entrance fees.

# GOLF

At the time of writing, Grenada has just one golf course, though there have been rumours of a second being planned. The **Grenada Golf Course & Country Club** (✆ *473 444 4128*) is located to the northeast of Grand Anse Beach. It is a nine-hole golf course with nice views of both the Caribbean Sea and the Atlantic Ocean. Club hire, instruction and caddy service are available. The clubhouse has a restaurant and bar. Green fees are US$16 for nine holes and US$23 for 18 holes. A number of resort hotels at Grand Anse offer complimentary golf club membership as part of their hotel rates.

# KAYAKING

Kayak hire and guided kayak tours are available both in Carriacou and on Grenada's southwest peninsula. Kayaking is usually undertaken in very sheltered waters, in coves, bays and around coastal mangroves. It is great fun, not too challenging, and suitable for adults and supervised children.

**KAYAKING OPERATORS** In addition to the following specialist kayak operators, check also with the dive shops on Grand Anse Beach, at True Blue, L'Anse Aux Épines and in Carriacou (see *Grenada scuba-diving and snorkelling operators* on page 77 for more details).

**S & S Kayaking** ☏ 473 449 9237; e snskayaking@caribsurf.com; www.grenadaexplorer.com/kayaking. A very original 90min clear-bottomed kayaking tour around the Molinère Protected Seascape. Kayakers of all ages can experience the beautiful reefs, marine life & Underwater Sculpture Gallery without having to snorkel or scuba dive. Price includes a complimentary drink at the Sunset View Restaurant. **Spice Kayaking & Eco Tours** ☏ 473 439 4942; e info@spicekayaking.com; www.spicekayaking.com. Guided mangrove & eco tours in kayaks & pedal boats on Grenada's south coast around Clarke's Court Bay & Hog & Calivigny islands. Exploring the mangroves & reefs of this beautiful sheltered bay is great fun with half- & full-day tours available. A sunset tour from Grand Anse to St George's Harbour or Morne Rouge Bay is a pleasant way to end your day.

## OFF-ROADING AND JEEP TOURS

A nice way to experience some of Grenada's interior without too much exertion is to take a tour in a vehicle that is equipped for either off-roading or taking on some of the island's steeper mountain routes. These tours may involve short forest hikes or bathing in rivers or pools – so come prepared.

### OFF-ROADING AND JEEP-TOUR OPERATORS

**Adventure Jeep Tours** ☏ 473 444 5337; e info@grenadajeeptours.com; www.grenadajeeptours.com. Operating modified all-terrain jeeps with open sides for views. Full-day tours include forest & plantation ride, waterfall, hot spa & local food. Price includes hotel pick-up & drop-off, lunch & site entrance fees.

## RIVER TUBING

Grenada's Great River is the island's longest, finding its source deep within the Grand Étang Forest Reserve and meeting the Atlantic Ocean at the expansive Great River Bay to the north of Grenville. The Great River is a beautiful, fast-flowing river, and is home to one of Grenada's more recent pastimes of river tubing. Taking place on the Balthazar Estate to the west of Grenville and near the community of Bylands, river tubing is a fun activity. The river journey lasts around 90 minutes and takes you on a spin and a whirl downriver, riding the currents and passing picturesque tropical vegetation. A safety briefing and demonstration is provided along with all the equipment you will need – a buoyancy jacket and an inflatable tube – before you set off, accompanied by guides who are there to provide assistance and security. Popular with day visitors arriving on cruise ships, river tubing is certainly a different way to explore and enjoy Grenada's natural environment. Travellers with back, neck or heart conditions should seek advice before river tubing. Also check with operators for minimum age restrictions if you are planning on river tubing with your children. Prices are around US$45 per person.

### RIVER-TUBING OPERATORS

**Adventure River Tubing** ☏ 473 444 5337; e info@grenadajeeptours.com; www.grenadajeeptours.com. Offering 3 scheduled departure times of 09.00, 11.30 & 14.00 & requiring reservations, there is a min group size of 10 & a max of 40 per tour.

**Fun Sun Grenada** ☏ 473 439 3925 or 473 404 8005; e funsun@spiceisle.com. 3hr 'River Rush' river-tubing tour. Call or email for prices & schedules.

**SCUBA DIVING** Grenada is the self-proclaimed 'wreck-diving capital of the Caribbean'. There are numerous wreck sites within recreational dive limits, including the largest wreck in the Caribbean, the *Bianca C*. Conditions along the many inshore reefs of both Grenada and Carriacou are usually quite easy. There are lots of marine creatures, colourful reef fish, hard and soft corals, as well as interesting underwater topography including drop-offs and flat reefs. On some sites you can also expect to see larger creatures such as eagle rays and sharks. Visibility is usually good though it can vary according to weather conditions and prevailing currents which can create turbidity by stirring up the sandy sea bed. All scuba diving must be undertaken via one of Grenada's dive centres and is usually from a boat.

A combination of calm conditions and excellent dive-resort facilities make Grenada and Carriacou ideal places to learn to scuba dive or to do an accompanied try-dive. Most dive centres have instructors offering recreational and speciality dive courses as well as first-time dive experiences for those interested in seeing what scuba diving is like.

Divers must remember to bring their certification card. Few operators will ask to see log books though you should take them if you are planning on some wreck or advanced diving. If it has been a while since your last dive trip, do the sensible thing and take a short refresher in the pool or off the beach with an instructor before backward rolling off the side of a dive boat. It will make your dive safer and also much more enjoyable. Two-tank boat dives are usually around US$95.

No marine life may be hunted or taken whilst scuba diving in Grenada. This includes coral, sponges and shellfish. Please restrict yourself to observation of aquatic life only.

**SNORKELLING** Most dive operators also offer snorkelling trips to inshore reefs. A popular destination is the Molinère Protected Seascape which is home to the **Underwater Sculpture Gallery** (see page 139), **Flamingo Bay** and **Molinère Reef** itself. Longer excursions on charter-boat cruises from mainland Grenada usually also include snorkelling and take you to **Hog Island** in the south or **Sandy Island** in the north. Snorkelling trips are great fun for all the family and a nice way to enjoy the sights of underwater Grenada. Visibility in the shallows is usually good and surface conditions calm. Snorkellers can expect to see a wide variety of colourful marine fish as well as corals and sponges. On Carriacou dive operators and water taxis offer snorkelling trips to **White Island** and **Sandy Island**. Accomplished snorkellers may also wish to take a look at the reef system just off **Anse La Roche Beach**.

**GRENADA DIVE SITES** So far all the explored and named reefs are located around the southwest peninsula. This area is home to a number of wrecks as well as some very nice reef formations. Naturally, as the southwest is an area of heavy tourism and resorts, this is also where most of the dive shops are located. The remainder of the west coast has yet to be extensively explored and made accessible by Grenada's dive centres. Here is a broad selection of the most popular dive site in the southwest. You will encounter others and some with slightly different names. This is because dive centres have favourites (they sometimes name new sites themselves or areas of reef they like to dive) and also because site names have not been standardised. There are presently no permanent moorings for Grenada's dive sites. This is primarily a funding issue and something the **Grenada Scuba Diving Association** (*www.grenadascubadivingassociation.com*) is trying to address, together with improving the status, protection and rules of the Molinère Protected Seascape.

**Flamingo Bay** (depth 6–28m) is a frequently visited and highly rated dive site. Located within the Molinère Protected Seascape, it is a reef and wall dive with plenty to see and, because it is shallow, it is also visited by snorkellers. Dive encounters include large shoals of small reef fish such as chromis and Creole wrasse, sea fans, whips, sponges and elkhorn coral. Look out for seahorses, lobster, moray, grouper and rays. **Happy Valley** (depth 6–28m) is a popular and pretty reef and wall dive located within the Molinère Protected Seascape close to the shore. It has an abundance of marine life, including large shoals of reef fishes, anemone, black coral and lots of sea whips along the wall itself. Look out for a coral-encrusted admiralty anchor. **Dragon Bay** (depth 6–28m) is also located within the Molinère Protected Seascape. It is a reef dive that begins in the shallows and gradually descends before reaching a wall. It has some interesting volcanic topography including deep fissures in the rock. There are lots of colourful reef fish, green morays, grouper and angelfish. **Molinère Reef** (depth 6–28m) is a large expanse of reef with hard and soft corals, colourful fish, sea plumes and sea rods. It is located within the Molinère Protected Seascape and is also popular with snorkellers. At its northern edge is the **Underwater Sculpture Gallery** (see page 139). Just beyond Molinère Reef is the wreck of the *Buccaneer* (depth 22m). It is an 18m steel schooner with an open hull that experienced wreck divers can enter and explore. Look out for giant grouper, octopus and garden eels. **Grand Mal** (depth 19–25m) is a deep dive along a wall to the north of St George's Harbour. Usually a drift dive, this one is also for more experienced divers.

Directly east of St George's Harbour is the shallow wreck of the *Veronica* (depth 6–12m). This is a nice site for those who have never done wreck diving before as well as for complete beginners. A 40m cargo vessel, it has a deck with machinery including an anchor windlass and crane. The hold is open and empty and home to a wide variety of interesting marine creatures. To the southeast of the *Veronica* is the top of **Boss Reef** (depth 6–24m). This is a long stretch of reef that extends southwards with hard and soft corals, patrolling barracuda and some large green morays. This reef formation includes sites known as **Valleys**, **Japanese Gardens**, **Middle Boss** and **Lower Boss**. Also part of this reef system is **Northern Exposure** (depth 10–23m), a pretty reef with lots to see including brain corals and the occasional passing hawksbill turtle. *Shakem* (depth 30m) is the wreck of a 50m cargo ship that was transporting bags of cement to the port at St George's in 2001. Overloaded and listing from the moving, heavy cargo, the boat sank within sight of the harbour and landed on the bottom completely upright. It is now an interesting site for experienced divers and, though a relatively new artificial reef, it is already home to a variety of marine life. *Unity Courier* (depth 12m) is a dive over three sections of the sunken *Unity Courier* that went down in the Carenage in 1991. The vessel was cut up into four sections with three of them placed off Quarantine Point (the site is sometimes called 'Three Wrecks'). The ship's two boilers lay side by side nearby. It is an interesting dive with soft corals, reef fish and sometimes stingrays. **Quarter Wreck** (depth 8–20m) is – yes, you guessed it – the remaining quarter, in fact the stern section, of the *Unity Courier*. Its propeller, engine room, deck and pilot house combine well with a pretty reef and wall to make a great dive.

The *Bianca C* (depth 28–40m) is the Caribbean's largest diveable shipwreck. Nicknamed 'the Titanic of the Caribbean', this wreck is an awe-inspiring dive. At 200m long and sitting upright, the *Bianca C* is considered by some diving magazines to be one of the top-ten wreck sites in the world. Owing to its depth and location it attracts large pelagics. Interesting features include the swimming pool, the promenade staircase and the huge funnel. This is a site experienced divers will want to visit again and again. The **Rhum Runner** (depth 30m) is the wreck of a charter catamaran that was used as a tourist and party vessel (you may have seen the *Rhum Runner II* taking tourists to Morne Rouge Beach – now you know). The wreck is explored first on this dive and then you move to more shallow waters over a pretty reef that is teeming with colourful and interesting marine life. **Whibble Reef** (depth 15–30m) is a great reef dive with beautiful hard and soft corals and lots of fish life including shoals of jacks, passing pelagics and large barracuda. You may see nurse sharks and hawksbill turtles on this dive. **Purple Rain** (depth 6–25m) is so named because of the large shoals of Creole wrasse that divers often encounter over this beautiful reef. Usually a drift dive, this site is one of the prettiest in the southwest, with giant barrel sponges, lots of reef fish, barracuda, rays and turtles. **Kahonee** (depth 6–15m) is a shallow coral garden with a wealth of life and activity. Divers regularly see lobsters, spotted morays and nurse sharks. The deeper edges of this dive site are sometimes also known as **Black Wall**, which descends to around 30m. **Windmill Shallows** (depth 18–40m) is a narrow coral-encrusted ridge and wall that plummets into the abyss on the extremities of Grenada's inshore reef system. It is a stunning reef and, because of the depth, attracts large passing pelagics. Usually there are currents on this drift dive.

On Grenada's south coast dive conditions are usually more challenging. There can be rougher surface chop and there are often fairly strong currents. These sites are suitable for experienced or advanced divers only. They include the **San Juan** (depth 22–31m), the wreck of a 35m-long cargo ship lying upright and regularly attracting reef sharks, nurse sharks and eagle rays. The **Hema 1** (depth 30m) is the wreck of a freighter that sank in 2005 in rough Atlantic sea conditions on its way from Grenada to Trinidad. It is prone to strong currents but advanced divers can enjoy the wreck with lots of nurse sharks, who seem to have made it their home, as well as patrolling reef sharks and eagle rays. *King Mitch* (depth 28–34m) is the wreck of a World War II minesweeper that sank 5km from the southern coast of Grenada. Because of its location it is an advanced dive, often with rough surface conditions and strong currents. Shark sightings are virtually guaranteed. **Shark Reef** (depth 10–20m) is located off Glover Island on the south coast. Atlantic surface swells and strong currents make it a site for experienced divers only. The large rocks, hard corals, overhangs and deep water conditions attract nurse sharks, eagle rays, lobster, crabs and the occasional grouper.

### Grenada scuba-diving and snorkelling operators

**Aquanauts Grenada** True Blue Bay Resort, L'Anse Aux Épines & Grand Anse Beach; ✆ 473 444 1126; e aquanauts@spiceisle.com; www.snorkelgrenada.com. PADI Gold Palm resort. Operates 3 fully equipped dive boats & offers PADI dive courses. Equipment hire, retail shop, enriched air (Nitrox) & underwater scooters available.

**Devotion 2 Ocean** Rex Grenadian Resort, Point Salines; ✆ 473 444 3483; www.devotion2ocean.com. PADI Gold Palm IDC offering a range of PADI recreational- & professional-level scuba courses as well as daily boat diving.

**Dive Grenada** Flamboyant Hotel, Grand Anse; ✆ 473 444 1092; e info@divegrenada.com; www.divegrenada.com. PADI dive centre offering PADI courses & daily boat diving. Equipment hire available.

**Eco Dive & Trek** Coyaba Beach Resort, Grand Anse; ✆ 473 444 7777; e dive@ecodiveandtrek.com; www.ecodiveandtrek.com. A PADI 5-star resort offering dive courses, daily boat diving, watersports & hiking. Enriched air (Nitrox) & equipment hire are available.

**Native Spirit Scuba** Grenadian Grand Beach Resort, Grand Anse Beach; ✆ 473 439 7013; e info@nativespiritscuba.com; www.nativespiritscuba.com. Grenadian-owned & operated PADI dive centre offering PADI dive training & daily boat diving. Equipment hire available.

**Scubatech** Calabash Hotel, L'Anse Aux Épines; ✆ 473 439 4346; www.scubatech-grenada.com. PADI dive centre located on the south coast at Prickly Bay, offering PADI courses & daily boat diving. Equipment hire available.

**Wind Dancer (Peter Hughes Diving Inc)** True Blue Bay Resort, True Blue; ✆ 473 444 1126; e peter@aquanautsgrenada.com; www.peterhughes.com. Live-aboard diving around Grenada, Carriacou & the Grenadines. Prices US$1,600–1,800 for 7 nights on board the *Wind Dancer*. Includes all meals & beverages & up to 5 dives per day. Excludes port & fuel surcharges.

**NORTHERN ISLETS DIVE SITES** Advanced divers may be interested in a day excursion to the sites around the isolated dependences that are located between the islands of Grenada and Carriacou. There are dive sites at **Île de Ronde**, **Three Sisters**, **Frigate Rock**, **Diamond Rock** and **Bird Rock**. Conditions can be difficult on these sites with surface swell, surge and very strong currents. Reef formations are pristine and sightings of large pelagics are common. There are also some interesting cave formations at the Sisters dive sites. Advanced divers should definitely try to make these sites part of their trip.

**CARRIACOU DIVE SITES** Fondly known as the 'land of reefs', Carriacou offers excellent scuba diving and snorkelling. The reef formations are pristine and there is an abundance of hard and soft corals, sponges and colourful marine fishes. Nurse sharks, barracudas and turtles are common sightings. There is no standardisation when it comes to dive-site names and none are marked by moorings. Operators have their own names, favourite sites and ways of diving them. Nevertheless, here is a selection.

Around the diminutive **Mabouya Island** to the west of Carriacou, there are interesting reef formations and wreck sites. Many of the reef sites suit less experienced divers though they can have a little current. Sites around this island include **Mabouya North**, a spectacular wall dive to 20m which is suitable for

*Phil Saye of Dive Grenada*

I have dived all around the world but my first trip to Grenada in 2001 was the beginning of a love affair. I was instantly enchanted by the experience. The reefs are beautiful, healthy, and enjoy a rich diversity of marine life. And with well over 30 dive sites we are truly spoilt for choice.

My favourite reef dive is a gentle drift out over Wibble Reef. Just ten minutes' boat trip from Grand Anse Beach, the ride offers views of the southwest coast and a chance to catch up on a bit of sunshine and the latest cricket scores with my boat captain. We typically drop onto the reef at a depth of 15m and allow ourselves to drift westwards with the current. The reef is festooned with soft corals and enormous barrel sponges and we swim through showers of Creole wrasse. It's a good location for pelagic life. Out of the blue we are often joined by a majestic spotted eagle ray as well as barracuda and hunting horse-eye jacks.

Grenada has rightly earned the reputation of 'wreck-diving capital of the Caribbean'. By far its most famous is the *Bianca C*, but my personal favourite is the *Hema 1*. This freighter came to grief off the Atlantic coast and now rests on the sea bed in 30m, several miles offshore. A trip to this site, approximately 25 minutes by boat, creates a palpable level of excitement on board. It is an advanced dive. We drop a descent line and make a swift negative descent to beat the current and find the wreck below. This is guaranteed to get the adrenalin flowing and it continues to pump as we are greeted by squadrons of spotted eagle rays. At the sea bed, around the hull and foremast, we find large nurse sharks, reef sharks and lobsters. An old barnacled hawksbill turtle frequents the forward hold and often joins us for photographs. Sadly we are limited by bottom time and always return to the surface craving more.

Grenada has so much to offer divers of all abilities and, in sharing a couple of my favourite sites, I hope I have given you a taste of the diversity of diving here.

most divers; **World of Dreams** (depth 8–20m), a sloping reef with plenty of giant soft corals and the occasional stingray; and **Sharkey's Hideaway** (depth 8–20m), a reef formation descending steeply to undulating rock formations that hide sleeping nurse sharks. **Mabouya South**, also known as **Twin Tugs**, is a wreck site at a depth of around 25m. The *Westsider* is a 1960s tugboat that worked the waters of the Caribbean before being deliberately sunk off Mabouya Island as an artificial reef. *Boris*, another tug, was also sunk as an artificial reef near to the *Westsider* in September 2007. Though they are young as dive sites, many interesting marine creatures are moving in, making them fun and interesting dives for more experienced scuba divers.

**Sandy Island**, also to the west of Carriacou, has a long reef starting at around 7m that plummets into deeper water at 20m, making for a nice wall dive that is suitable for both inexperienced as well as more advanced divers. This reef is usually explored as two dives and site names include **Sandy Island North**, **Sandy Island South** and **Western Adventure**. The other site often visited off this island is **Sandy Island Lighthouse** (depth 7–22m), which is a steeply sloping reef that is also suitable for all levels of diving ability. Look out for crabs, lobsters and moray eels as well as an abundance of reef fish including snapper and angelfish.

To the north of Sandy Island there is a small island called **Jack A Dan**. This easy reef dive (depth 7–20m), also known as **Millennium 2000**, is popular with beginners as it has little current. It starts in the sandy shallows, follows a nice reef with beautiful coral formations, and always has lots of interesting creatures to see including shrimps, lobster, moray eels, stingray and even the occasional passing eagle ray.

At Sister Rocks to the west of Mabouya Island and Carriacou there are a number of interesting sites that suit the more adventurous, experienced scuba diver. Reef and wall dives tend to have strong currents but are blessed with a wide variety of marine creatures, colourful reef fish, hard and soft corals, tube and barrel sponges, patrolling barracuda, nurse and reef sharks. **Barracuda Point** (depth 9–23m) is one such superb wall dive and **Sister Rocks** (depth 9–35m), sometimes also called **Deep Blue**, is usually a drift dive because of the strong current, where you may encounter huge schools of jacks as well as barracuda and sharks.

To the south of Carriacou is **Frigate Island** where there is a challenging dive called **Chinatown** (depth 8–23m), sometimes also called **Chinese Pagodas**. Strong currents in the convergence of the Caribbean Sea and the Atlantic Ocean mean this dive is definitely one for advanced scuba divers only. Usually explored as a drift dive, this sloping reef has some dramatic hard coral formations as well as barracuda, sharks and the occasional eagle ray.

Two-tank boat dives are usually around US$95.

## Carriacou scuba-diving and snorkelling operators

**Arawak Divers** ✆ 473 443 6906; e arawakdivers@spiceisle.com; www.arawak.de. Located at Tyrrel Bay, this English- & German-speaking PADI dive centre offers training & daily boat diving. Equipment hire available.

**Carriacou Silver Diving** ✆ 473 443 7882; e scubamax@spiceisle.com; www.scubamax.com. English- & German-speaking PADI Gold Palm IDC centre offering recreational & professional dive training & daily boat diving. Equipment hire available.

**Lumbadive** ✆ 473 443 8566; e lumbadive@lumbadive.com; www.lumbadive.com. English- & French-speaking Beuchat dive centre located in Tyrell Bay offering PADI training courses & daily boat diving. Equipment hire available.

# TURTLE-WATCHING

From March to October each year giant leatherback turtles (*Dermochelys coriacea*), the largest of all living sea turtles, return to Grenada's beaches. Some of Grenada's tour operators, plus specialist conservation and research groups, offer evening expeditions to observe these wonderful creatures.

## TURTLE-WATCHING OPERATORS

**Caribbean Horizons** ✆ 473 444 1555; e info@caribbeanhorizons.com; www.caribbeanhorizons.com. Turtle-watching trips to the Levera Archipelago National Park.

**KIDO Ecological Research Station** Carriacou; ✆ 473 443 7936; e kido-ywf@spiceisle.com; www.kido-projects.com. NGO that aims to preserve natural resources & ecosystems. Turtle-watching trips offered. Contact for details.

**Ocean Spirits** e info@oceanspirits.org; www.oceanspirits.org. NGO focused primarily on the protection of Grenada's marine turtles. Turtle-watching trips offered. Contact for details.

# WALKING AND HIKING

Grenada is beautiful and the very best way to appreciate it fully is to get off the bus or out of the car and take a walk. There are walks and hikes for everyone, whatever your ability, time constraints or interest. For the adventurous there are mountain and river hikes, and for those more sedate ramblers there are coast, lakeside and village walks. Grenada's interior has a network of trails running between the Grand Étang Lake, Mt Qua Qua, Fédon's Camp and the three waterfalls that make up the Concord falls. These hikes were always for the more adventurous, but since

3

Hurricane Ivan they have become even more difficult. Fallen trees and landslides have seriously impacted some routes and hikers should not attempt them without a guide. At the time of writing, this is particularly the case with Fédon's Camp and the trails from Fédon's Camp and Mt Qua Qua to Concord. The trail from Grand Étang Lake to the summit of Mt Qua Qua is clear but very exposed owing to high-elevation deforestation caused by the hurricane. The hikes to the summit of Mt St Catherine and to the Paraclete Falls were difficult even before the hurricane and you should always seek a guide for these particular challenges.

Very few trails currently have markers along the route or at the trailhead itself. Where there is a clear path this is not a problem but when paths fork, cross rivers or pass through open clearings, it is easy to become lost. This book describes most trails in detail though it will also recommend a guide if the trail is difficult, hard to follow or simply disappears in places. Do not forget that things change. A bamboo thicket that marks a trailhead or a turning today may well be scaffolding on another new luxury resort development project tomorrow.

In addition to the established forest, waterfall and mountain hikes, I have added a few of my own. These routes are easy to follow and usually involve walking along paved tracks, coastal paths or beaches. They are my attempts to add some variety to the range of walking options on this island to include villages, coast and beaches, and places of history and cultural heritage.

**DEGREES OF DIFFICULTY AND DURATION** For each of the hikes described in this book there is an associated degree of difficulty. The grading system I have used does not relate to any official or published grading standards. It is based on personal experience of these hikes and their relative difficulty to each other and the many hikes I have made in other places. It is simply meant as a broad indication to assist selection and planning. Naturally, what may be difficult for one person may be less so for another. Nevertheless, as the ratings are relative and also quite conservative, once one hike is completed, you will have a better understanding when selecting a hike for your next outing. The ratings used (in the *Walks and hikes* sections of *chapters 5–9*) are as follows: **Easy (grade 1)** is for a hike that is relatively flat with no climbing or river crossings. **Easy/medium (grade 2)** is for a hike that is fairly flat but which may have a short series of steps, mild slopes or perhaps shallow stream crossings. **Medium (grade 3)** is for a hike that has moderate ups and downs, and may involve some short, easy rock scrambles or shallow river crossings. **Medium/difficult (grade 4)** is for a hike that has some steep climbs, or tricky sections such as boulders or river crossings. **Difficult (grade 5)** is for a tough hike with steep slopes, rock scrambles, river crossings or climbs. Additionally, for each of the hikes described there is an associated duration. This is the time it takes on average, at a steady walking pace, to complete the hike. Clearly people walk at differing rates. The numbers quoted are again on the conservative side.

**THE BENEFIT OF HIRING A GUIDE** Knowledgeable trail guides know which way to go when routes are not clear, they have often received specialised training, and they can provide interesting information about the history of the trail, the area, and the flora and fauna that you may encounter along the way. Hiring a guide also provides a valuable source of income to local people and, by extension, their villages. In the rural communities of Grenada where farming has suffered immensely following recent hurricanes, this kind of income is very welcome. By increasing the demand for guides, visitors are also potentially creating career and employment opportunities for young Grenadians who may otherwise have little to look forward to. And no matter how detailed the guidebook, there is absolutely no substitute for local knowledge, anecdotes, and the reassurance a good guide can provide when a trail is new, daunting or difficult.

For each one of the walks and hikes described, there is advice on whether a guide is required or not. Where a guide is *recommended* it means that hiring a guide will enhance the walk by providing information, local knowledge and help with the route itself. Where a guide is *highly recommended* it means that in addition to basic enhancement of your hiking experience, a guide will provide useful assistance where the trail may become unclear, for example across or around landslides and temporary trail diversions. Where a guide is *essential* it means that at some point during the trail, or perhaps for most of it, the trail is either unmarked, disappears entirely, or there may be areas of risk. As already mentioned, at the time of writing, some of Grenada's more difficult interior hikes have been impacted by Hurricane Ivan and have not yet been cleared. It is very important that you assess these hikes properly before taking them on and that you have a guide you can rely on to both take you to your destination and bring you back again in one piece.

'Extreme hikers' who are interested in exploring some of the lesser-known trails of 'hidden' Grenada may find it difficult to find guides or operators who have sufficient knowledge of these routes. Many registered guides and tour operators specialise in mainstream hiking trails only. In this case some hotels or tour operators may be able to put you in contact with local people. Simply turning up in a remote location and asking for a guide who can take you on an extreme hike should be avoided if possible, though in some cases it may be the only way. Try to hire someone with a good reputation or who has been recommended, and always let someone else know where you are going.

**BEING PREPARED** The degree of preparedness will naturally depend on the difficulty and duration of the trail. It is essential to make sure your time of departure is early enough to make it back before nightfall. Always plan to return by 17.00 at the latest as at some times of the year it is dark by 18.00. There is little light pollution in Grenada so when it is dark, it is really dark.

Take plenty of water with you, at least a one-litre bottle each, and more if you can carry it. It is very easy to dehydrate in the humidity of the forest or in the heat of the sun's rays. Some areas of Grenada are blessed with mountain springs with clean, fast-flowing water. If you encounter one, it is an excellent place for a refill if your water supplies are running low. Drink at regular intervals and do not wait until your mouth is dry or you feel thirsty. Dehydration can give you a headache, make you grumpy and affect your judgement.

Wear sensible footwear such as walking shoes, trainers or strong sandals. A soft-soled shoe is better than a tough plastic one for river crossings and wet rocks and boulders. Flip-flops are not a good idea, neither is walking barefoot.

Walking in Grenada's forest and up its mountains can mean getting wet and dirty. Sometimes very wet and dirty, especially in the rainy season, so leave your designer gear at the hotel or on the boat. A towel and a change of clothes either to take along or to leave in a vehicle is a sensible idea. If taking a change of clothes with you, put them in a waterproof or plastic bag. As trails can sometimes pass through areas of razor grass, it is also worth taking along a small first-aid kit with antiseptic ointment or cream for any cuts or scratches that may be picked up along the way. Informing your hotel or guesthouse of your planned hike plus an expected return time is also a wise idea. Many hotels offer rental pay-as-you-go mobile phones. Get one – they are usually inexpensive and may come in very handy.

**WHEN NOT TO GO** Generally speaking it is not a good idea to go to waterfalls or attempt to cross rivers if there has been heavy rain, or if heavy rain is expected, as flash flooding could occur. Many of Grenada's mountain hikes pass along very narrow and steep ridges. These dirt trails become very hazardous in heavy rain and high winds can contribute to unstable footing that may cause you problems. Exercise common sense and a reasonable degree of caution when deciding where to go in inclement weather. If local people warn against a hike because of heavy rainfall, high winds or swollen rivers, then take their advice and do not go. See also *When to visit* in *Chapter 2*, page 33.

**WALKING/HIKING OPERATORS AND GUIDES** Many of Grenada's tour operators are generalists and make a great percentage of their annual income during the cruise-ship season when they run bus and taxi excursions to heritage sites and easily accessible natural attractions. There are few operators who specialise just in hiking, primarily because the demand for it is lower than that for more general tours. The following operators have hiking in their portfolio of services and, if they cannot help you themselves, they may be able to put you in touch with a local guide who can:

**A & E Tours** ℄ 473 435 1444; e aandetours@caribsurf.com; www.grenadaguide.com/aetours. Bus tours & guided hiking to Concord, Seven Sisters, Grand Étang.

**Caribbean Horizons** ℄ 473 444 1555; e info@caribbeanhorizons.com; www.caribbeanhorizons.com. Wide variety of generic & special-interest tours offered, including regular & advanced hiking.

**Dave Tours** ℄ 473 444 1596; e davetours@caribsurf.com; www.spiceisle.com/davetours. Specialising in AC bus tours to popular attractions around the island, but also offers some of the easier hiking options.

**Grenada Eco Dive & Trek** Coyaba Beach Resort; ℄ 473 444 7777; e dive@ecodiveandtrek.com; www.ecodiveandtrek.com. Dive & hiking operator based at the Coyaba Beach Resort on Grand Anse

Beach offering a range of hiking from easy to more advanced trails.

**Henry's Safari Tours** ℄ 473 444 5313; e safari@caribsurf.com; www.henrysafari.com. Offers a variety of generic & speciality tours with a range of hiking options, from the easy to the more difficult trails.

**Hike Grenada** ℄ 473 437 0997; e info@bluebaylodge.net; www.bluebaylodge.net & www.hikegrenada.com. A special week or two of hiking each year in Apr or May accompanied by guest hikers.

**K & J Tours** ℄ 473 440 4227; e kjtours@grenadaexplorer.com; www.grenadaguide.com/kjtours. Half- & full-day bus-tour operator offering a selection of hikes to suit you. Contact for more details.

**Kennedy Tours** ℄ 473 444 1074;

## HASHING

*Neil Winsborrow (www.grenadaexplorer.com)*

One of the nicest ways to see Grenada, especially the roads not widely travelled, is to go on a hash. Hashing is walking or running along a trail set by a hare (the unlucky individual tasked with setting the hash). The trail will usually take you through the countryside, along side roads and trails, through rivers and streams and along valleys and hills. It is the perfect way to see the hidden heart of the island, and carrying a camera is a must, as the views are unbelievable! One of the rules of the hash is that it must start and end at a rum shop. This is because hashers tend to develop a significant thirst, especially for the national beverage, beer, and there is usually food available at the end – barbecue, oil-down, etc. Hashers have been described as a 'bunch of drinkers with a running problem'. All joking aside, hashers are a bunch of friendly people who get together every second Saturday to walk, hike or run (you can travel at your own pace, as it is not a race) a trail set by one of them. The only requirement is that you show up for the hash. It is free to participate, and you meet some amazing people. To find out where the latest hash will be, all you need do is visit www.grenadahash.com.

e kennedytours@caribsurf.com;
www.kennedytours.com. Offering a selection of
AC island bus tours as well as hiking. Options
include the easy to the more advanced hiking
trails.
**Mandoo Tour & Taxi Service** 473 440 1428;
e mandoo@grenadatours.com;
www.grenadatours.com. Specialising in AC bus tours
to major attractions as well as a range of hikes,
mostly along the more accessible routes.
**Pete's Mystique Tours** 473 440 1671;
e pmistictors@spiceisle.com;
www.mystiquetours.com. Island-wide bus tours to

major attractions plus guided hiking on some of
the easier trails.
**Sunsation Tours** 473 444 1594;
e qkspice@spiceisle.com; www.grenadasunsation.com.
English-, German- & French-speaking operator with
a range of tours including some of the island's
gentler hikes.
**Telfor Hiking Tours** 473 442 6200. Telfor Bedeau
is a national treasure when it comes to hiking. At
over 70 years of age, he has been hiking Grenada
for most of his life & few could claim to know
the mountains, waterfalls & trails better than him.

## WHALE- AND DOLPHIN-WATCHING

The first thing you should know about a whale-and-dolphin trip (or 'safari' as it is sometimes known) is that it never guarantees sightings. It could simply turn into a pleasant boat ride. Nevertheless, the chances are good, with success rates claimed to be above 90%. And if you do encounter whales, it will be an experience you are unlikely to forget for quite some time. Certain times of the year are better than others. Usually sightings are more common between December and April though some species are observed all year round. A good tip is to ask about recent sightings before you book. You may be fortunate to encounter humpback whales (*Megaptera novaengliae*), sperm whales (*Physeter macrocephallus*), Bryde's whales (*Balaenoptera brydei*) and pilot whales (*Globicephala melaena*). Usually if whales are scarce, or if they have been spooked by predators, the boat captain is able to locate pods of dolphin somewhere along the coast. Dolphin sightings include spinner dolphins (*Stenella longirostris*), bottlenose dolphins (*Tursiops truncatus*), Fraser's dolphins (*Lagenodelphis hosei*) and common dolphins (*Delphinus delphis*).

### WHALE- AND DOLPHIN-WATCHING OPERATORS

**First Impressions** 473 440 3678;
e starwindsailing@spiceisle.com;
www.catamaranchartering.com. Offering a 4hr whale
& dolphin excursion aboard a purpose-built whale
catamaran for up to 35 passengers – power along

the northwest coast of Grenada in search of a
wide variety of whales & dolphins. Though sightings
are never guaranteed, First Impressions claims a
97% success rate. Call for prices.

## YACHTING

The waters around Grenada and the Grenadines offer some of the very best sailing in the Caribbean. Whether you are travelling to Grenada on your own boat or looking to charter one when you arrive, there are a number of options and services to choose from. Grenada has plenty of beautiful sheltered bays and anchorages, well-appointed marinas, marine servicing and repair facilities, as well as professional charter operators. World-class marina developments are underway at Port Louis in the Lagoon south of St George's, at Le Phare Bleu Marina in Petite Calivigny Bay, and also at Prickly Bay in L'Anse Aux Épines on Grenada's south coast.

**GRENADA'S SAILING REGATTAS** The **Grenada Sailing Festival** (*www.grenadasailingfestival.com*) is a five-day regatta that takes place towards the end of January each year and attracts yachting enthusiasts from all over the world. At an assortment of venues, including Port Louis Marina, La Source, Grand Anse Beach

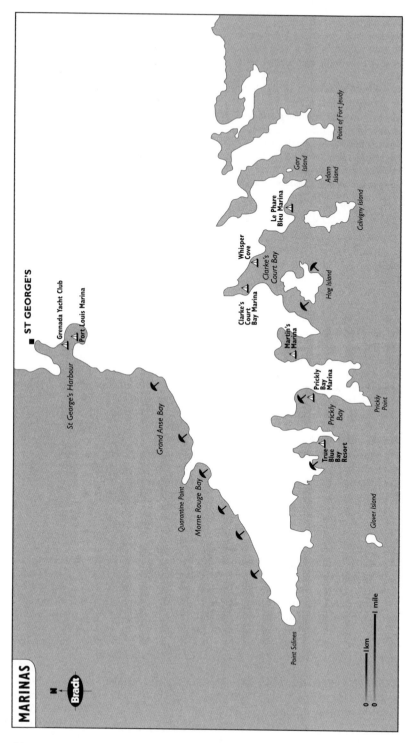

## MARINAS

**ST GEORGE'S**

Grenada Yacht Club

Port Louis Marina

St George's Harbour

Grand Anse Bay

Quarantine Point

Morne Rouge Bay

Point Salines

Glover Island

True Blue Bay Resort

Prickly Bay

Prickly Bay Marina

Prickly Point

Martin's Marina

Clarke's Court Bay Marina

Clarke's Court Bay

Whisper Cove

Le Phare Bleu Marina

Gary Island

Adam Island

Calivigny Island

Point of Fort Jeudy

Hog Island

N

Bradt

0    1km
0    1 mile

and True Blue Bay Resort and Marina, this event-filled festival includes yacht racing, live music entertainment, a workboat regatta, a swimming gala, kayak racing, and of course lots of delicious food and drink.

The **Grenada Round-the-Island Easter Regatta** (*www.aroundgrenada.com*) is also a five-day sailing event that includes wining and dining, children's events and a round-the-island yacht race. The race runs clockwise around Grenada and covers a distance of around 45 nautical miles. There are three classes – racing class, cruising class and multi-hull class – and a prize is awarded to the winner of each. With the first event taking place back in 1969, this regatta is considered the forerunner of around-the-island races in the Caribbean. The race disappeared from the racing calendar in 1991 but was recently resurrected by a new generation of Grenada's enthusiastic yachting fraternity.

The **Carriacou Sailing Series** (*www.ttsailing.org* or *www.grenadayachtclub.com*) is a four-day festival that takes place in Tyrell Bay, Carriacou, usually around the month of November. There are a number of organised beach- and water-based activities for families and sailing enthusiasts. There are five classes of yacht racing: racing with spinnaker, cruiser racing with or without spinnaker, cruising, J24 and multi-hull. The **Carriacou Regatta** (*www.carriacouregatta.com*) started in 1965 and is held over the Emancipation weekend every year. It is hugely popular and has become one of the largest sailing events in the region. The festival hosts a wide variety of sporting and cultural events as well as competitions and family activities. The events feature yacht, sloop, long open boat and traditional workboat races, the last forming the centrepiece of the festival with 12 classes of traditionally built workboat races that feature participants from around the region. Dates for the regatta are 26 July–3 August 2009, 25 July–2 August 2010, 24 July–1 August 2011 and 29 July–6 August 2012.

**CLEARANCE PROCEDURES** Grenada and Carriacou use the American standard (IALA B) **buoyage system**, thus red buoys should be to the starboard side when approaching from the sea. Private vessels entering the waters of Grenada, Carriacou and Petite Martinique can clear both boat and crew at a designated port of entry and anchor with a Q Flag and courtesy flag of Grenada clearly visible from the starboard spreader of the main mast. Official **ports of entry** are: Grenville (☏ *473 438 7678*), Grenada Marine (☏ *473 443 1065*), Grenada Yacht Club (☏ *473 440 3270*), Hillsborough, Carriacou (☏ *473 443 8399*), Le Phare Bleu (☏ *473 444 2400*) and Prickly Bay Marina (☏ *473 444 4509*).

The captain must notify authorities within two hours of arrival at one of these designated ports. It is also expected that the captain deals with all clearance procedures on behalf of passengers and crew. This includes preparing the following paperwork: five copies of the combined 'Customs/Immigration/Ports Authority Clearance Form' which is in six parts and includes vessel details plus crew and passenger lists, immigration cards for passengers and crew, ship's stores and health declaration, port clearance from the last port of call, passports of passengers and crew. Generally speaking, most customs and immigration offices are open 08.00–16.00. Entry charges are as follows: yacht length not exceeding 40ft EC$50; yacht length 40–60ft EC$75; yacht length 60–80ft EC$100; yacht length exceeding 80ft EC$150. Additionally there is a cruise levy of EC$8.10 per person arriving on the vessel.

**Anchoring** is not permitted in the Carenage or Grand Anse Bay area in Grenada or near the oyster bed at Harvey Vale in Carriacou. Anchoring is also not permitted within 200m of any beach in Grenada, Carriacou or Petite Martinique.

**Departing** vessels should clear customs and immigration within normal working hours but may leave up to 24 hours thereafter. There are no exit fees for yachts, their passengers and crew.

## MARINAS

**Carriacou Yacht Club** Tyrell Bay, Carriacou; ☎ 473 443 6292; VHF 16; e carriyacht@spiceisle.com. Facilities include wireless internet, accommodation, restaurant, mini-market, ice & water, showers & dinghy dock.

**Clarke's Court Bay Marina** Clarke's Court Bay, Woburn; ☎ 473 439 2593; VHF 16 & 74; e office@clarkescourtbaymarina.com; www.clarkescourtbaymarina.com; ⏰ 06.00–18.00 (office). Finger slip & swing moorings available. Facilities include water & electricity, laundry, showers, wireless internet access, bar & restaurant, 24hr security.

**Grenada Yacht Club** Lagoon, St George's; ☎ 473 440 6826; VHF 16 call sign GYC; e gyc@spiceisle.com; www.grenadayachtclub.com; ⏰ 08.00–17.00 (office). Founded in 1954, the GYC has a newly renovated dock & is located at the Lagoon to the south of St George's. The marina offers high-class facilities including docking for 44 yachts, customs & immigration, water & electricity, garbage disposal, fuel, laundry, showers & ice, bar & restaurant, 24hr security, wireless internet service.

**Le Phare Bleu Marina** Petite Calivigny Bay; ☎ 473 444 2400; e office@lepharebleu.com; www.lepharebleu.com. Located in the beautiful Petite Calivigny Bay, Le Phare Bleu offers 65 berths for vessels up to 30m, customs & immigration, water & electricity, fuel, laundry, ice, mini-mart, wireless internet access, pool, restaurants & bar & fine dining on a lighthouse boat. Current developments include swimming pool & onsite resort.

**Martin's Marina** L'Anse Aux Épines; ☎ 473 444 4449; VHF 16 & 71; e martinsmarina@caribsurf.com. 53-slip concrete marina, 42 stern-to slips, 11 alongside slips & 32 swing moorings.

Services include fuel, storage, dockage, showers, garbage, bar, wireless internet access, cottage rental, 24hr security.

**Port Louis Marina** Lagoon, St George's; ☎ 473 439 0000; e info@portlouisgrenada.com; www.portlouisgrenada.com. At the time of writing, this state-of-the-art marina is under construction. When completed it will have 275 slips for vessels up to 75m in length. There will be resort accommodation, restaurants, bars & shops. Facilities will also include electricity, fuel, wireless internet, laundry & probably very much more besides.

**Prickly Bay Marina** Prickly Bay, L'Anse Aux Épines; e sales@pricklybay.com; www.pricklybay.com. State-of-the-art marina & luxury waterside houses, apts & boutique hotel. Further investment & development is ongoing at the time of writing. The contemporary, award-winning architectural design resembles super-yachts & the marina will accommodate yachts up to 42m. Facilities include electricity, fuel, restaurant & bar, mini-market, laundry, wireless internet.

**True Blue Bay Marina** True Blue; ☎ 473 443 8783; e info@truebluebay.com; www.truebluebay.com. Located at the True Blue Bay Resort & close to Spice Island Marine for chandlery & haul-out services. There are 18 slips for boats up to 10m. Facilities include hotel, bar, restaurant, fuel, electricity, ice, showers, wireless internet, swimming pool, gift shop.

**Whisper Cove Marina** Clarke's Court Bay; ☎ 473 444 5296; e luke@whispercovemarina.com; www.whispercovemarina.com. 6 slips for boats up to 20m. Facilities include restaurant & bar, electricity, laundry & wireless internet.

## MARINE, HAUL-OUT AND BOATYARD SERVICES

**Grenada Marine** St David's Harbour, Corinth; ☎ 473 443 1667; e info@grenadamarine.com; www.grenadamarine.com

**Spice Island Marine** Services Prickly Bay; ☎ 473 444 4342; VHF 16; e simsco@spiceisle.com; www.spiceislandmarine.com

**Tyrell Bay Haul-Out** Tyrell Bay, Carriacou; ☎ 473 443 6940; VHF 16; e tbyh@usa.net

# CRUISE-SHIP VISITS

Grenada welcomes around 300,000 cruise-ship visitors a year, usually between the months of November and May. During this period the island gets a little busier, a little more colourful and certainly more international. Most cruise ships put in for a single day and very few stay overnight. This means that passengers have just a single day to sample and experience a little of what Grenada has to offer. Because of time constraints, very few will have the opportunity to explore Carriacou and Petite Martinique.

Cruise-ship travellers can book shore excursions through the cruise-line operators themselves. If you do this you will pay more for your excursions than you would if you arranged them independently. You are essentially paying a premium for having everything organised for you, and sometimes this can be quite high. Cruise-ship visitors also have the choice of planning land excursions independently with Grenada's tour operators, usually via email or the internet. You may find that some operators who have contracts with cruise-ship lines may be reluctant to accommodate you as an independent traveller. The third option is simply to turn up and just figure it out from there. Whatever you do, do take the opportunity to get off the boat, stretch your legs and experience a little of Grenada. Your dollars, pounds and euros provide an essential source of income to local people and many Grenadians are almost entirely dependent on the cruise-ship season for most of their annual income.

**PLANNING AHEAD** Cruise-ship visitors intent on experiencing as much as possible should plan ahead and figure out exactly how they would like to maximise their Grenada experience. Most of the cruise-ship lines have very good internet sites that contain destination information as well as detailed descriptions of their land excursions. You also have the opportunity to book and pay for them online or by phone. It is worth checking your cruise-ship itinerary to see what day of the week you arrive. If it is a Sunday, you should expect many stores to be closed and fewer tour operators or guides waiting for business at the cruise-ship terminal. If this is the case, you should seriously consider arranging something in advance. Planning ahead also relieves the stress and possible hassle of stepping into the unknown when you disembark, and your day will be much more relaxed and enjoyable.

**ARRIVAL** Cruise ships calling at Grenada will usually put in at the cruise-ship terminal in St George's. The terminal caters for two ships at a time. If there are several ships arriving on the same day, some may have to tender their passengers ashore, usually by lifeboat. If this happens to you, you will still be taken to the very same cruise-ship terminal. On rare occasions some cruise ships put in at Grenada's port, which is located between the Carenage and the Lagoon. Before leaving the ship, you will be told what time you must return.

If you arrive at the main cruise-ship terminal, once you pass through security and the turnstiles, you will find yourself inside the Esplanade shopping mall. This is located in Bay Town, at the heart of St George's. As soon as you are in the shopping mall you will see a large gathering of tour operators, taxi drivers and vendors, all vying for your attention. If you have booked a shore excursion with your cruise-ship line in advance, simply look for a sign with the name of your tour. If you have booked something independently, look for a sign with either your guide's or operator's name, or perhaps your own. If you have booked nothing in advance, there is a booth in the open area in front of the turnstiles where you can purchase a variety of island bus tours. When you exit the Esplanade shopping mall, you will encounter more local people offering to take you on tours. Some will not be licensed operators. This does not necessarily mean they are no good; it simply means they have had no formal training. Most will simply want to show you around St George's for a few dollars. You should certainly not get into a vehicle with a 'taxi driver' or 'guide' who cannot show you his or her official licence and photo ID.

**WHAT TO BRING ASHORE** Bring ashore a small bag, waterproof if possible, a towel, swimming costume, camera and cash. US dollars, pounds and euros are accepted just about everywhere. Try to bring small notes if you can because your change will usually be given to you in EC dollars. Bring a hat, sunglasses, sunscreen, a lightweight waterproof and perhaps a change of shorts, skirt or T-shirt. Wear trainers or good sandals. Flip-flops are not very practical either in town or in the rainforest. Leave jewellery and your favourite designer gear behind, and wear the sort of light clothes and shorts that will not cause distress if spoiled. If you will be scuba diving, bring proof of certification (your 'C card'). Bring a sense of fun, an open mind and, of course, make sure you bring this guidebook.

**TIPPING YOUR GUIDE** It is nice to tip your guide if you have had good service and an enjoyable time. Some guides will simply expect a tip regardless, however. You should bear in mind that cruise-ship visitors provide desperately needed income to islanders who may struggle to make a living once the season is over. You do not have to tip heavily and you may be surprised at how little some of your guides actually expect. It is all relative and a matter of perspective. US$5–10 may seem like very little to you, but in Grenada a few tips like that can go a very long way.

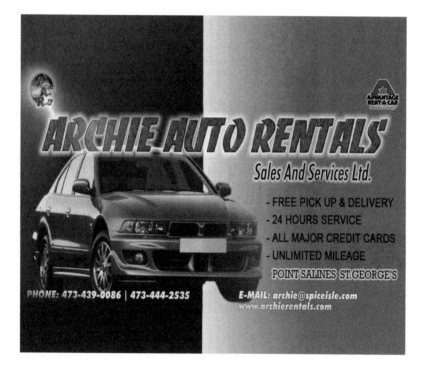

# Part Two

## THE GUIDE

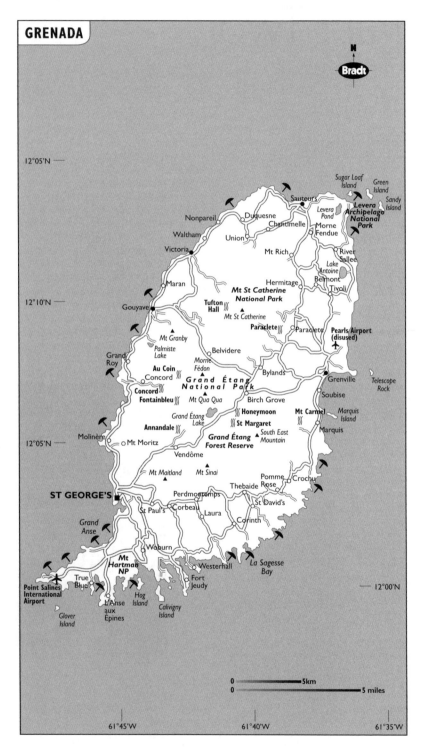

# GRENADA

**Bradt**

12°05'N

Sugar Loaf Island
Green Island
Sauteurs
Levera Archipelago National Park
Sandy Island
Nonpareil
Duquesne
Chantimelle
Levera Pond
Waltham
Union
Morne Fendue
Victoria
Mt Rich
River Sallee
Lake Antoine
Hermitage
Belmont
Tivoli
Maran
Mt St Catherine National Park
Gouyave
Tufton Hall
Mt St Catherine
Paraclete
Paraclete
Pearls Airport (disused)
Mt Granby
Palmiste Lake
Belvidere
Grand Roy
Au Coin
Concord
Morne Fédon
Bylands
Grenville
Telescope Rock
Concord
Fontainbleu
Grand Étang National Park
Mt Qua Qua
Birch Grove
Soubise
Grand Étang Lake
Honeymoon
Mt Carmel
Marquis Island
Annandale
St Margaret
South East Mountain
Marquis
Molinère
Mt Moritz
Grand Étang Forest Reserve
Vendôme
Mt Maitland
Mt Sinai
Pomme Rose
Crochu
St George's
Perdmontemps
Thebaide
St Paul's
Corbeau
Laura
St David's
Grand Anse
Corinth
Woburn
Mt Hartman NP
Westerhall
La Sagesse Bay
Point Salines International Airport
True Blue
Fort Jeudy
L'Anse aux Épines
Hog Island
Calivigny Island
Glover Island

12°10'N

12°05'N

12°00'N

0        5km
0        5 miles

61°45'W        61°40'W        61°35'W

# 4

# St George's

Most travel guides, magazines and directories tend to describe Grenada's capital, St George's, as one of the prettiest towns in the Caribbean. Whether travellers agree with this sentiment or not, few would dispute that it is certainly very pleasing on the eye. Built around a large natural harbour, the town's white and pastel-coloured houses, stone churches, terracotta tile and galvanised roofs fill the hillsides with an exuberance of colour as they rise up from the water's edge. Add to this the surrounding blue sea, luxury sailing boats at anchor, cruise ships and a verdant backdrop of mountains and lush tropical forest and it is easy to see why most people reach for their cameras when they see this capital for the first time.

Located in the southwest of mainland Grenada at 12°02'N and 61°48'W, St George's is the capital, administrative centre and major seaport of this tri-island state. The town is constructed around St George's Harbour, a natural haven that is said to have been carved by a particularly fortuitous burst of volcanic energy. There are two significant areas of the harbour: the Carenage which is on the northeast side and close to the main town; and the Lagoon, which is on the southeast side and is the home of the island's main port, a large marina development and an anchorage. To the north of the capital there is St George's Bay and several residential areas including Sans Souci and Tempe. To the east of the capital there are the high hillside areas of Mt Helicon and Richmond Hill. To the south of St George's there are the residential settlements of Paddock, Springs and Belmont. To the south of Belmont is Grand Anse and the southwest peninsula.

The capital still bears the scars of Hurricane Ivan. Sadly a number of buildings stand in ruin or disrepair, either abandoned or in the process of attempting to raise enough funds for renovation, restoration or, in some cases, a complete rebuild. Despite this, it is a lively place, full of interest, beauty and history. Visitors should be prepared for the hills of the town which are sometimes very steep, but which add character and always offer captivating views and scenes of vibrancy and life. Visitors to St George's are regular and numerous, thanks to the proximity of the international airport and the cruise-ship berth on the northwest side of town, so Grenadians are very used to seeing their capital even further crowded by an influx of international travellers. They are friendly, welcoming and more than happy to help you out with directions or offer you the chance to purchase their wares. Be sure to engage with the people of this pretty island capital, take your time to walk around and explore, and you will find your visit to St George's very pleasurable and extremely memorable.

## A BRIEF HISTORY

Though Columbus sighted and claimed Grenada in 1498 it was not until the mid 17th century that the first Europeans settled on the island. Governor of Martinique, Du Parquet, purchased Grenada, Martinique and St Lucia from the

Company of the Islands of America in 1650 for 1,660 livres. Of course, all of this was unknown and probably quite inconsequential to the Kalinago who had been living on Grenada for at least the previous 300 years. Upon landing on what is today known as the Ballast Ground to the west of the Lagoon, Du Parquet and his comrades were greeted by Kalinago chief Kaierouanne. Historians disagree on what happened next. Du Parquet offered the chief gifts – either as an appeasement according to some, or a land purchase according to others. Some also believe the gifts were in exchange for assistance in warding off the British. Regardless of which of these versions is the truth, all agree that Du Parquet spent the next year erecting housing, a church, and fortifications.

There was once a sandbar running across the mouth of today's Lagoon (known by the French as Étang d'Eau Salée, meaning 'saltwater lake'), joining the Ballast Ground with the area known today as 'The Spout' to the south of the port in the vicinity of Tanteen. The French crossed the sandbar and began clearing the Tanteen area of its trees to start work on a large tobacco plantation. The settlement was named St Louis after the reigning French monarch, Louis XIV. It was also referred to as Port St Louis and, more commonly, **Port Louis**. Realising their visitors were here to stay, the Kalinago mounted a series of isolated attacks but were eventually driven back by French soldiers, ultimately resulting in their near-total extermination on the island (see page 5).

Unfortunately the location of the settlement of Port Louis had one or two problems. The first was malaria. The settlers soon discovered that the brackish, stagnant waters of the Étang d'Eau Salée, then shallow and landlocked by the sandbar, was a perfect breeding ground for mosquitoes. The second problem was flooding. Tidal surges and storms meant that the relatively low and flat ground upon which Port Louis was built was frequently vulnerable to a rather unwelcome deluge. As the Kalinago had been routed, it seemed an opportune time for the settlers to pack up and move to a more comfortable place. This was to be the higher ground to the north of today's Carenage (then called simply 'Le Port'). By 1710 Port Louis was left to the whims of nature and the new settlement was named **Ville du Fort Royal**. Fort Royal was the name given to a fortification that had been constructed earlier, in around 1667, on the western end of today's Carenage. The fort was enlarged in the 1700s after the abandonment of Port Louis.

On 10 February 1763, the island was ceded to the British under the Treaty of Paris. The British renamed Ville du Fort Royal **St George's Town** (later shortened to St George's) after the country's monarch, King George III, and the fort was also renamed Fort George.

In 1776, war broke out between England and France again and in 1779, under the command of the Count d'Estang from Martinique, French forces recaptured Grenada. The French seizure of the island had been relatively easy and it was with this in mind that their first task was to improve its military fortifications. Unfortunately for the French, their occupation only lasted until 1783 when Grenada was once again ceded to Britain, this time under the Treaty of Versailles. The British continued what the French had started and soon St George's was a very fortified capital indeed. In addition to Fort George and the redoubts at Hospital Hill, the approaches to the north and the east of town were overseen by the four forts of Richmond Hill. Ironically all the forts became quite redundant immediately upon their completion. The Treaty of Versailles marked the final defeat of the French and the beginning of a period of British rule that lasted for around the next 200 years.

The town of St George's began to grow as the island's capital. The mangroves and swamps around the Tanteen area were cleared and drained. Mosquitoes were driven out firstly through the introduction of guppies (*Lebistes reticulatus*), small fish that are native to South America and which feed on mosquito larvae; the second method was the less environmentally friendly use of the chemical DDT in the 1950s. The Tanteen area was ultimately reclaimed by burning and burying the capital's refuse there. In the 1960s the sandbar across the Lagoon was cut and the 1980s saw dredging efforts aimed at widening the entrance and deepening the water for use as an anchorage. Residential houses and businesses expanded northwards to the Queen's Park area along St George's Bay, eastwards into the hills, down to the Carenage and around and beyond the Lagoon to the south.

The area known as The Spout, between the Lagoon and the Carenage, where French settlers first moored their sailing vessels, became the island's main port. Following a huge regeneration project in 2000 costing some US$11million, the port was extended and updated to accommodate large container ships. In the same year, the Esplanade on the western shore of the main town was also levelled and redevelopment began to create a large jetty and terminal facility that would accommodate cruise ships. This work was completed in 2004.

From the floods and disease of the first settlement of Port Louis, the capital has witnessed its fair share of setbacks and disasters. In 1771, a fire that began in a French bakery burned all through the night. Because the town's houses and buildings were constructed almost entirely of wood, by the next day virtually everything had been reduced to ashes. In 1774, another fire, this time one that was suspected of being started deliberately, destroyed much of the town once again. In May 1792, despite the imposition of building standards and regulations that required materials to include stone, brick and tile, a fire that began aboard a ship laden with rum destroyed much of the Carenage. In 1885, the Bonfire Act prohibited the lighting of bonfires in the town during the traditional 5 November Guy Fawkes Day celebrations. When 100 citizens were given the status of special constables to help enforce this law, opponents began rioting which, somewhat ironically, resulted in small fires breaking out around the town. Further fires in 1920, 1925, 1952, 1975, 1979, 2000 and 2002 all threatened to cause more damage to the town than eventually transpired. In 1955, Hurricane Janet caused widespread devastation to the island which included severe damage to St George's and the sinking of the wooden harbour buildings. In 2004, Hurricane Ivan, the worst storm in Grenada's history, either damaged or totally destroyed the majority of buildings in the capital. Some of this damage is still evident today.

## GETTING THERE

**BY TAXI** From Point Salines International Airport it costs EC$50 to St George's. An additional charge of EC$5 per person is levied when passenger numbers exceed four persons per taxi. The journey takes around 15 minutes.

St George's GETTING THERE

4

**BY BUS** Public buses are the most common mode of transportation in and out of the capital. All buses to and from St George's start and finish their journeys at the bus terminal on Melville Street near the cruise-ship terminal and the Esplanade Mall. Here are the buses that travel to and from the capital. (See *Getting around* in *Chapter 2*, page 52, for more about Grenada's bus system.)

**Zone 1/gold** Lagoon Road–Grand Anse–Calliste
**Zone 1/gold** Belmont–Grand Anse–Calliste
**Zone 2/orange** Springs–Woodlands–Woburn
**Zone 2/orange** Calivigny–Westerhall–Grenville
**Zone 3/purple** Richmond Hill–Morne Jaloux–Marian
**Zone 4/bright green** St Paul's–Perdmontemps–Vincennes
**Zone 4/bright green** Beaton–La Tante–Pomme Rose
**Zone 4/bright green** St Paul's–Mardigras
**Zone 4/bright green** St Paul's–La Borie
**Zone 5/yellow** Grand Roy–Gouyave–Victoria
**Zone 5/yellow** Gouyave–Victoria–Sauteurs
**Zone 5/yellow** Concord–Grand Roy–Gouyave
**Zone 6/white** Grand Étang–Birch Grove–Grenville
**Zone 7/red** Annandale–New Hampshire–Willis
**Zone 7/red** Beaulieu–Boca–Vendôme
**Zone 7/red** River Road–Tempe–Mt Parnassus
**Zone 8/blue** Cherry Hill–Fontenoy–Happy Hill
**Zone 8/blue** Cherry Hill–Fontenoy–Mt Moritz
**Zone 8/blue** Happy Hill–Beausejour–Brizan

**BY FERRY** Osprey Lines (*www.ospreylines.com*) operates a high-speed ferry service between St George's, Carriacou and Petite Martinique. In St George's, the ferry arrives and departs from the jetty opposite the fire station on the Carenage. The journey between Carriacou and St George's takes about 90 minutes. The ferry departs from St George's at 09.00 Monday–Saturday and 08.00 Sunday, and at 17.30 Monday–Friday and Sunday. From Carriacou the ferry leaves for St George's at 06.00 Monday–Saturday, and 15.30 daily. The prices are EC$160 or US$62 for an adult return and EC$80 or US$31 for an adult one-way ticket. For children aged between five and 12, the price is EC$100 or US$38 for a return, and EC$50 or US$19 for a one-way ticket. For children under five years the prices are EC$20 or US$8 for a return and EC$10 or US$4 for a one-way ticket. The ferry does not usually operate on Christmas Day, Boxing Day, New Year's Day or Good Friday.

## BY HIRE CAR
**From south to north** If you are driving from Grand Anse and heading into town or up the west coast towards the north then here is how to do it. Assuming you are on Lagoon Road driving north around the Lagoon, stick to the left at the roundabout near the Botanical Gardens and follow the road past the port. After the Tanteen recreation ground stay left at the next roundabout and follow the water. You should find yourself curving to the right and then onto the Carenage.

Follow the Carenage right around to the other side. Look out for the public library because the road that runs to the right of it, Monckton Street, is the one you need to take. When you reach a fork at the top, go left and you should find yourself at the entrance to the Sendall Tunnel. Drive through the tunnel and just follow the road as it emerges onto Bruce Street, past the Esplanade Mall, the bus terminal and the fish market, keeping the sea to your left. Soon you will find yourself arriving at the junction with the national stadium. The road to the right goes to the east and the Annandale Falls, the road straight ahead follows the west coast to Gouyave and eventually Sauteurs.

**From north to south** Assuming you are driving south from Gouyave and heading towards Grand Anse or the airport, or are just planning on a trip to St George's, here's how. At the junction with the national stadium, take the road on the right (left goes east). Follow the road until you reach the outskirts of the capital. You will see the fish market and the bus terminal on your right, and the Sendall Tunnel ahead of you. If you want to park in town then there is a car park above the bus terminal (alternatively, you can park around the far side of the Carenage near the fire station). If you are heading south, carry on, and before you reach the Esplanade Mall you must look out for a left turn up Granby Street towards Market Square. At the first junction on Granby Street you will see you are on the southwestern corner of the market. Turn right along Halifax Street and follow the road uphill. At the top of the hill you will be at a four-way junction. Go straight ahead, over the brow and down Young Street. Be careful on the brow as you are momentarily blind to what is ahead of you. You will see the Carenage in front of you but do not drive all the way down as part of the Carenage is one-way only. The last street on the left just before the Carenage is Scott Street. Take a left up there and follow it all the way to a traffic light junction. The road to the right should be H A Blaize Street. This is the one you should take. A short distance along H A Blaize Street you will see a road on the right called Hughes Street. Go down it towards the Carenage again and then turn left. Follow the Carenage and then around towards the port. At the roundabout take the road to the right past the port and the Tanteen recreation ground until you reach the Lagoon. Keep to the left around the Lagoon and you will be south of St George's on the road to Grand Anse and Point Salines International Airport. Just follow the signs.

## GETTING AROUND

**Driving** in St George's will be a challenge the first couple of times but after that you should find it is actually quite straightforward. The things that will throw curveballs at you as you sit wide-eyed and white-knuckled on your first attempt will be the rather poorly signposted one-way system, some very narrow and steep streets, lots of pedestrians who seem hell-bent on throwing themselves in front of your vehicle, somewhat small and hard-to-see traffic lights, and, if you are not accustomed to it, driving on the left.

Without doubt the best and most practical way to explore today's St George's is **on foot**. It is a fairly compact town and nothing is really very far, though please be warned, there are some very steep hills! Most roads have properly paved footpaths though around the market you may be forced to walk on the road itself so please be careful and aware of traffic. Finding your way around is fairly straightforward. St George's is built on a hill that climbs up and inland away from the sea. The hill has a ridge that essentially splits the main part of town into two halves: on one side of the slope is the main shopping and market area (known as Bay Town); on the other side of the slope is the Carenage. South of the Carenage, the road runs through Tanteen, past the port and around the Lagoon.

See also *Getting around* in *Chapter 2*, page 52.

## TOURIST INFORMATION

**Grenada Board of Tourism** Burns Point, southern tip of the Carenage towards Tanteen, between the port authority buildings & customs house; ℡ 473 443 7948; e gbt@spiceisle.com; www.grenadagrenadines.com; ☉ 08.00–16.00 Mon–Fri. This is a useful place to pick up brochures, leaflets, maps & other resources. The staff can also help to organise tours for you.

# 🏠 WHERE TO STAY

## UPPER-RANGE HOTELS

🏠 **Mi Hacienda Boutique Hotel** Belmont, between St George's & Grand Anse; ☎/f 473 439 2799; e mihacienda@sunnygrenada.com. Boutique hotel, restaurant & bar with sea views. Standard & superior rooms & SC apts. $$$

🏠 **The Lodge** (2 rooms) Richmond Hill; ☎/f 473 440 2330; e thelodge@spiceisle.com; www.thelodgegrenada.com. Luxury vegan escape, located high on the ridge of Richmond Hill with spectacular views of the interior & the coast. Each room has a double 4-poster bed, en-suite bathroom & private veranda. Bedrooms & laundry are cleaned with vegan products. To offset carbon footprints, a tree is planted for every guest who stays at the lodge. Fruits & vegetables are grown on site. The vegan restaurant serves b/fast, lunch & dinner. Price inc b/fast & airport transfers. Min stay 5 days. $$$

## MID-RANGE AND BUDGET HOTELS AND GUESTHOUSES

🏠 **Deyna's City Inn** (12 rooms) Melville St, near the cruise-ship terminal & Fort George; ☎ 473 435 7007; f 473 440 5431; e cityinn@spiceisle.com; www.deynascityinn.com. Rooms are stylishly decorated with en-suite bathroom, AC, TV, phone. Maid & laundry service, mobile-phone hire available. High-class & popular Spices Restaurant & Bar offers gourmet Creole dining. Continental b/fast inc. Long-term rentals also available. $$

🏠 **Town & Country Guest House** Belmont; ☎ 473 444 4516; e gracecharles@hotmail.com. Attractive guest hotel with sgl, dbl & trpl room accommodation. $

🏠 **Tropicana Inn** (20 rooms) Lagoon Rd; ☎ 473 440 1586; f 473 440 9797; e tropicanainn@spiceisle.com; www.tropicanainn.com. Business-style hotel located opposite the Lagoon, each room has double bed, en-suite bathroom, AC, TV, phone. Internet access available. Popular restaurant & bar serves Caribbean & Chinese cuisines. Conference room available. $

🏠 **St Ann's Guest House** Paddock; ☎ 473 440 2717; e info@stannsguesthouse.com. Family-run guesthouse located in Paddock, to the east of the Lagoon & within easy walking distance of the capital. $

## SELF-CATERING APARTMENTS AND COTTAGES

🏠 **Pelican Apartments** (4 apts) Belmont; ☎ 473 440 1121; f 473 409 0178; e augumar@spiceisle.com; www.grenadaexplorer.com/pelican. Located close to the Lagoon & within easy walking distance of the Carenage & the capital. Each self-catering apt has 2 bedrooms, bathroom, living area, kitchen, ceiling fans, TV & phone. Verandas have great views of the Lagoon & St George's beyond. Weekly $$

🏠 **Mind & Body Apartments** (2 apts) Above the Carenage; ☎ 473 439 9343; e info@mbtgrenada.com; www.mbtgrenada.com. Self-catering accommodation. Each apt has 2 bedrooms, 2 bathrooms, AC, kitchen, internet. $

🏠 **Lexus Inn** (18 apts) Belmont; ☎ 473 444 4780; f 473 444 4779; e lexus@spiceisle.com. Pleasant, clean & with beautiful ocean views, the Lexus Inn is located on the main highway in Belmont, halfway between St George's & the beaches of Grand Anse. 1- & 2-bedroom fully furnished & equipped self-catering apts with private balconies & sea views. $

🏠 **Lazy Lagoon** (6 cabins) Grand Anse; ☎ 473 443 5209; e lazylagoon@caribsurf.com; www.grenadaexplorer.com/lazylagoon. Basic wooden cabins overlooking the Lagoon. En-suite bathroom, kitchenette, balcony. Lazy Lagoon Bar located nearby. $

# ✖ WHERE TO EAT AND DRINK

St George's has a nice selection of local and international dining options, most of which are very similarly priced. For an explanation of the price codes used below, please see page 57. Most restaurants are open daily (except Sundays) and you can usually just turn up. Where this is not the case, I have commented.

## LOCAL AND INTERNATIONAL

✘ **Victory Bar & Grill** Port Louis, Lagoon Rd; ☏ 473 435 7263; ⏱ daily. Local & international dining in the new Port Louis Marina development. $$

✘ **BB's Crabback Caribbean Restaurant** Carenage; ☏ 473 435 7058. Eatery popular with visitors & locals. Good-value Caribbean food & drink. $$

✘ **The Nutmeg** Carenage; ☏ 473 440 2539; ⏱ Tue–Sun. Local & international dishes, bar & nice views of the Carenage. Popular with locals & visitors. Steaks, chicken, seafood, burgers, local juices & more. Dinner reservations recommended. $$

✘ **Ocean Grill Restaurant & Bar** Carenage; ☏ 473 440 9747. Waterfront restaurant located on the Carenage. Local & international lunches & dinners. $$

✘ **Patrick's** Lagoon Rd; ☏ 473 440 0364. Unique restaurant featuring a fixed-price menu of 20 mouth-watering local dishes to try. Great host. Arrive hungry, leave very full. Call ahead. $$

✘ **Spices Restaurant & Bar** 1st Floor, Deyna's City Inn, Melville St; ☏ 473 435 7007. Wide selection of delicious Creole & international dishes at this very popular downtown restaurant. Wed night 'Spice Isle Rocks' serves traditional oil-down, calalou, *cou-cou* & more. $$

## ITALIAN

✘ **Mona Lisa Restaurant** Belmont; ☏ 473 439 6555; ⏱ Mon–Sat. Located just off the main road between St George's & Grand Anse, the Mona Lisa claims to be the most authentic Italian restaurant

## VEGETARIAN/VEGAN

✘ **The Lodge** Richmond Hill; ☏ 473 440 2330. Vegan restaurant serving b/fast, lunch & dinner. Spectacular views. Dinner reservations advised. $$

## FAST FOOD

✘ **KFC** Granby St. $

✘ **Mario's Pizza/Pizza King** Esplanade Mall, Melville St. $

## FRUIT JUICE AND COFFEE

⛾ **Flavours** Esplanade Mall, Melville St. Fresh local fruit juices. $

⛾ **Rituals** Esplanade Mall, Melville St. Coffee shop, cakes, hot panini. $

⛾ **The Juice shop with no name** Esplanade Mall,

✘ **Tropicana Inn Restaurant & Bar** Lagoon Rd; ☏ 473 440 1586; ✉ tropicanainn@caribsurf.com; www.tropicanainn.com. Good selection of very reasonably priced Caribbean & Chinese dishes. Take-away also available. $$

✘ **Lexus Café & Restaurant** Belmont; ☏ 473 439 7213; ⏱ daily. Located on the main road between St George's & Grand Anse, serving a combination of Italian & traditional Creole dishes. Everything from pizza to calalou. Nice sea views. $$

⛾ **B's Hot Spot Roti Shop** Carenage; ☏ 473 440 6438. Great rotis. $

⛾ **Carenage Café** Carenage; ☏ 473 440 8701. Local food & fruit juices. $

✘ **Creole Shack Sports Bar & Grill** Carenage; ☏ 473 435 7422. Very popular & affordable eatery with great local food. $

✘ **Deyna's Tasty Food** Melville St; ☏ 473 440 6795. Very popular eatery opposite the bus terminal serving delicious local dishes as well as sandwiches, burgers, etc. $

✘ **Marvellous Marva's Place** Grenville St; ☏ 473 435 3184. Located above the bustling marketplace serving a wide selection of reasonably priced local food & drinks. $

✘ **Soca Kitchen** Grenada Craft Centre, south of the Carenage. Local lunches & fresh fruit juice. $

on the island. Wide selection of dishes available, & all pasta is handmade. Dinner reservations recommended. $$

✘ **Melissan's Vegetarian Delight** Wharf Rd, Carenage; ☏ 473 449 1314. Wholewheat rotis & a wide selection of soya & vegetable dishes, plus fresh juices. $

✘ **Subway** Esplanade Mall, Melville St. $

Melville St. Very popular juice shop selling a wide range of fresh local fruit juices. Look out for the crowds & the painted murals on the walls & ceilings. $

## BARS AND NIGHTLIFE

☆ **Karma Nightclub, Bar & Grill** Carenage; ☏ 473 435 CLUB (2582); www.karmavip.com. Fashionable nightclub with dance floor, lightshows, plasma screens, bars, booths & live music stage.

☆ **Odds & Ends Music Café** Lucas St; ☏ 473 440 9410; ⏲ 08.00–23.00 Tue–Sat. Live music entertainment including jazz from 20.00 most nights. AC café bar, no cover charge.

## SHOPPING

St George's has lots of small shops and boutiques selling everything from household items to clothes, food and drink. Larger supermarkets tend to be located outside the capital closer to Grand Anse, though there is one on the Carenage. The Esplanade Mall, near the bus and cruise-ship terminals, has a selection of souvenir and duty-free shops, fast-food restaurants and juice bars. Outside the mall there is a small vendors' market with stalls also selling crafts and souvenirs. St George's market tends to be fuller and busier on Fridays and Saturdays though there will usually be stalls open on other weekdays too. Most shops in Grenada close on Sundays.

In terms of payment, shops will usually accept US dollars and some will also accept British pounds and euros. The reason more shops accept US dollars over British pounds is that the exchange rate for the EC dollar and the US dollar is fixed (EC$2.7 = US$1) whereas for the pound the rate is variable, and therefore more difficult to figure out accurately. Boutiques and souvenir shops will usually accept major credit cards.

### SUPERMARKETS
**The Food Fair** Carenage. Wide selection of local & imported foods, beverages & household items.

### CRAFT, DUTY-FREE AND SOUVENIR SHOPS
**Angel Fish** Esplanade Mall, Melville St. T-shirts, artwork, jewellery.

**Art Fabrik** Young St. Hand-painted batiks, fashion, jewellery & gifts.

**Caribbean Naturals** Grenada Craft Centre, south of the Carenage. Handmade soaps, candles, spices, jams & perfume.

**Classique** Grenada Craft Centre, south of the Carenage. Ceramics & pottery.

**Colombian Emeralds International** Esplanade Mall, Melville St. Jewellery.

**Duty Free Caribbean** Esplanade Mall, Melville St. Fragrances, cosmetics, alcohol, tobacco.

**Fig Leaf** Esplanade Mall, Melville St. T-shirts, cards, general souvenirs.

**Ganzee** Esplanade Mall, Melville St. T-shirts, spices, chocolate, general souvenirs.

**New Dimension** Esplanade Mall, Melville St. Souvenirs, gifts & spices.

**Spice Isle Plantations** Grenada Craft Centre, south of the Carenage. Handmade soaps & bath products.

**Taffy's Tavern** Esplanade Mall, Melville St. Wood carvings & masks.

**The Gift Shop** Off Wharf Rd on the southeastern corner of the Carenage near the Grenada Port Authority building, selling a selection of gifts and souvenirs.

**Tikal** Young St. Local & international arts & crafts shop.

**Vineyard** Esplanade Mall, Melville St. General souvenirs, spices, rums.

**White Cane Industries** Carenage. Handmade crafts created by the visually impaired & disabled. Located between the Ocean Grill Restaurant & BB's Crabback Caribbean Restaurant.

**Yellow Poui** Young St. Art gallery with original paintings & sculptures by over 80 local & international artists.

**BANKS AND MONEY TRANSFERS** Banks are open 08.00–14.00 Monday to Thursday and 08.00–16.00 Friday. They are closed on Saturdays, Sundays and public holidays. Most banks have ATMs.

$ **Capital Bank International** Grenville St

$ **First Caribbean International Bank** Church St

$ **Grenada Cooperative Bank Ltd** Church St

$ **Republic Bank Ltd** Halifax St

There are Moneygram and Western Union offices located on the Carenage.

**SECURITY AND HEALTH** Grenada is a very safe place, the vast majority of its people are kind and friendly and really the only precautions you need to take are the same ones you would back home. St George's, especially around the Esplanade Mall and the Carenage, will attract people trying to make a living selling souvenir items, or offering guide services, because those places are where the majority of tourists are and therefore where they are more likely to earn a few dollars. There is no malice in it and you should not feel threatened, nor on the verge of being robbed. Try to relax, be friendly to the local people and enjoy where you are.

**Begging** From time to time you may be approached by people asking you for money, but it is rare. If it does happen, it is usually in the form of a very polite request asking for a dollar or two for food and drink. The most common place for this is around the Carenage, and in particular near to the jetty where the Osprey ferry arrives and departs. Whether you decide to give or not is up to you, but always be polite, regardless of how persistent people might be.

**Police** You will see plenty of police officers walking the beat and directing traffic in and around St George's, especially during the cruise-ship season. They will be happy to help you with directions if you find yourself a little lost. The emergency telephone number for police assistance is ☎ 911, and the police headquarters is located at Fort George.

**Hospitals and pharmacies** There are quite a few pharmacies in St George's, including a large one in the Esplanade Mall. The General Hospital is located on the south side of Fort George.

✚ **St George's General Hospital** ☎ 473 440 2051

See also the *Health* and *Safety* sections in *Chapter 2*, pages 43 and 49.

## COMMUNICATIONS

**Post office** Grenada's postal service is called the **Grenada Postal Corporation**. The main office is located at Burns Point, on the southern tip of the Carenage in St George's, near to the port. You have to go around behind the customs building to get there. There is also a small post office located on Bruce Street, opposite the Esplanade Mall. A stamp for a postcard to either the UK or the US costs around EC$1.

**Internet** You can check your email at a number of locations including some restaurants and computer stores. Most hotels and guesthouses offer either hard-wired or wireless high-speed internet service, sometimes for a small charge.

🅔 **Comp-Data Electronics** St John's St, St George's

🅔 **Internet Plaza** Esplanade Mall, St George's

4

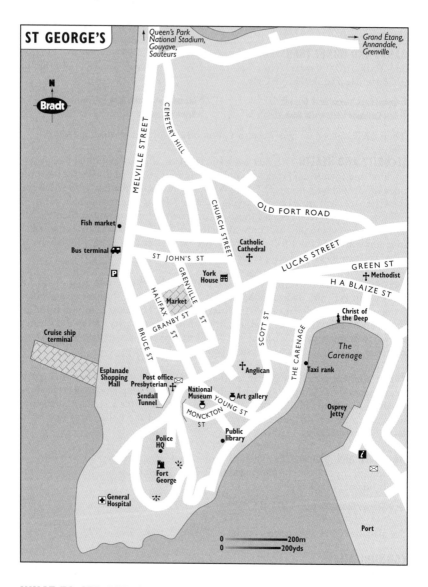

**ST GEORGE'S**

Queen's Park National Stadium, Gouyave, Sauteurs

Grand Étang, Annandale, Grenville

Bradt

MELVILLE STREET

CEMETERY HILL

CHURCH STREET

OLD FORT ROAD

LUCAS STREET

GREEN ST

Fish market

Bus terminal

ST JOHN'S ST

Catholic Cathedral

Methodist

H A BLAIZE ST

GRENVILLE ST

York House

Market

HALIFAX ST

GRANBY ST

BRUCE ST

SCOTT ST

THE CARENAGE

Christ of the Deep

The Carenage

Cruise ship terminal

Anglican

Taxi rank

Esplanade Shopping Mall

Post office

Presbyterian

Sendall Tunnel

National Museum

Art gallery

YOUNG ST

MONCKTON ST

Osprey Jetty

Police HQ

Public library

Fort George

General Hospital

*i*

Port

0 ——— 200m
0 ——— 200yds

## WHAT TO SEE AND DO

**THE CARENAGE** The Carenage is probably the most recognised and photographed part of St George's, perhaps even of Grenada itself. Acknowledged for its outstanding natural beauty as well as its classic Caribbean Georgian architecture, a slow meander around the Carenage is a treat for any visitor.

Said to be a partially filled submerged volcanic crater, the Carenage takes its name from the French *carénage* meaning careenage, a place where ships are repaired and cleaned. This name reflects the history of this natural harbour, once known simply as the port, where French and subsequently British ships, sloops and schooners put in for supplies and repairs. Though the port has now moved to the Tanteen area, the Carenage is still used by vessels of all kinds including long-liners, water taxis and boats transporting both people and supplies to and from the islands of Carriacou and Petite Martinique.

At the southern tip of the Carenage towards Tanteen, in an area known as Burns Point, there are the port authority buildings and customs house. Between these buildings you will find the offices of the **Grenada Board of Tourism** (see *Tourist information*, page 95), and from here there is a footpath that goes all the way around the Carenage. Opposite the capital's fire station is the departure and arrival jetty for the Osprey Line's **Grenada ferry service** between the main island, Carriacou and Petite Martinique (see *By ferry*, page 94, for schedule and fares).

Looking across the still water of the Carenage you can see Fort George on the far left together with St George's General Hospital and the renovated Caribbean Georgian buildings of the financial district further to the right. The hill of 'Carenage Town' or 'Over Town' is plain to see with its brightly painted houses, warehouses and offices. On the top of the ridge is the ruined Roman Catholic cathedral and beyond it, down the other side of the hill, the bustling shops and market stalls of the Bay Town district. The green hill that rises to the right of the cathedral on the northern side of the Carenage is known as the Observatory area of town.

Continuing around the Carenage the road passes a number of businesses and some small local eateries such as **Melissan's Vegetarian Delight** and the **Carenage Café**. On the northern shore of the Carenage, now facing out to the open waters of St George's Harbour, you will see some traditional English telephone boxes. Around this area of the Carenage you will often see brightly painted fishing boats tied up and selling fresh fish to passers-by. Also along this shore, near a set of covered benches called Pedestrian Plaza, is the **Statue of Christ of the Deep**, presented by the people of Genoa, Italy, to the residents of St George's for their assistance in saving the passengers of the *Bianca C* when it caught fire in the harbour in 1961.

Continuing around the Carenage there are a number of eateries serving good local food such as **B's Hot Spot Roti Shop** and the **Creole Shack**, a very popular lunchtime restaurant. Also along the western side of the Carenage is **The Nutmeg** restaurant which is popular with visitors and locals alike. Opposite The Nutmeg is a taxi stand. From this side of the Carenage it is possible to see all the way across St George's Harbour and beyond to Grand Anse Beach. The last stretch of the Carenage passes the renovated buildings of the financial district to two further restaurants, the very popular **BB's Crabback Caribbean Restaurant** and the ideally situated **Ocean Grill Restaurant & Bar**. If you are in this area please be sure to visit **White Cane Industries** where crafts are handmade and sold by the disabled and visually impaired.

Between the Georgian buildings along the western edge of the Carenage is the **Grenada Public Library**. The original library was founded in 1846 and was located in a building shared by the Supreme Court registry and the General Post Office. Following reorganisation and expansion it was moved to its current site in 1892. The library also houses the national archives.

To the right of the library is the junction of the Carenage with Monckton Street. Located on the corner of Monckton Street and Young Street is the **Grenada National Museum** (↘ *473 440 3725;* **e** *grenadamuseum@caribsurf.com;* ⊕ *09.00–16.30 Mon–Fri, 10.00–13.00 Sat, closed Sun; adults EC$5 pp, children EC$1 pp*). The museum is relatively new, established as recently as 1976 in an attempt by a group of private citizens to preserve and promote the island's cultural heritage. This group of individuals went on to form the Grenada Historical Society. The museum is located in one of the oldest buildings in Grenada, a former French army barracks that was constructed in 1704 as part of the original settlement of Fort Royal. The building was home to the town's gaol between 1763 and 1904 and later

The statue of Christ of the Deep that stands on the side of the Carenage in St George's is a replica of the original which lies underwater off San Fruttuoso Bay, Genoa, Italy. The original 1954 work, *Il Cristo Degli Abissi*, by Guido Galletti was recast and presented as a gift from the people of Genoa, via the Costa Shipping Line, to the people of Grenada. The statue is made of bronze and is around 2.8m in height. It is a figure of Jesus Christ with arms outstretched in a gesture of blessing to mariners leaving port.

The inscription on the statue reads:

To the people of Grenada in grateful remembrance of the fraternal Christian hospitality shown to passengers and crew of the Italian liner Bianca C, destroyed by fire in this harbour on October 22 1961. Dedicated by the Costa Line of Genoa, Italy.

Just before it was about to set sail for Europe, the Italian luxury liner, *Bianca C*, caught fire in St George's Harbour. With over 300 passengers and 200 crew members on board, the ship was evacuated with only one death and eight casualties. The surviving passengers were housed by the people of St George's until they managed to leave the island several days later. The ship did not sink, but its burned-out hulk was obstructing the entrance to the harbour, so a decision was taken to move it. Whilst it was being moved it sank 2.4km off Quarantine Point (see box, *Bianca C: 'The Titanic of the Caribbean'*, in *Chapter 3*, page 76).

The original idea was to have the statue facing out to sea, overlooking the wreck of the *Bianca C*. After much wrangling and disagreement, it was originally placed on the eastern entrance to the Carenage. In 1989, it was moved to its current position, though no longer in sight of the *Bianca C*'s final resting place.

became used as a warehouse and hotel. The museum has a number of permanent collections as well as alternating displays and exhibitions by local schoolchildren. A visit starts with an introduction to the island's indigenous people, the Amerindians and specifically the Kalinago. There are fine examples of ceramics and also Yoruba artefacts. The European occupancy of Grenada is represented by a collection of plantation machinery and tools as well as examples of firearms and cannons. There are also interesting displays of the history of conflict on the island from the battles between the French and the British to the Fédon Rebellion and the more recent revolution and US intervention. Whether you find yourself exploring St George's for just a day or for longer, the Grenada National Museum is well worth a visit.

Next to the museum on Monckton Street is **Grenada Essentials**, a shop that showcases and sells authentic arts and crafts made by talented Grenadians. All profits from the business are ploughed into conservation projects such as turtle protection and reforestation, so please drop in. Next to Monckton Street is Young Street which also has a number of arts and crafts stores including **Art Fabrik**, **Tikal** and **Yellow Poui**, all of them worth a visit. And if you are looking for a bottle of cold water and a snack, check out **D Roti Shop**, also on Young Street.

**FORT GEORGE** Fort George is located on Fort George Point at the northern entrance to St George's Harbour. Its initial construction was started by the French in 1667 when they first settled on the island. It was then called Fort Royal. When the French moved from their original settlement at Port Louis up to the new town of Ville du Fort Royal in the early 1700s, the fort was redesigned, enlarged and strengthened. In 1763, when Grenada was ceded to the British under the Treaty of Paris, the garrison was expanded further to include military barracks and was renamed Fort George. Following the Treaty of Versailles in 1783, the need for fortification became less and less. Between 1854 and 1979 Fort George was used as the headquarters of the Grenada Police Force.

In 1979, Fort George became the headquarters of the People's Revolutionary Army and was renamed Fort Rupert in honour of the father of then prime minister, Maurice Bishop. On 19 October 1983, Maurice Bishop, together with 24 supporters, was executed by the People's Revolutionary Army, leading to the US military intervention in Grenada just six days later (see *Revolution and Intervention* in *Chapter 1*, page 10).

Today Fort George is once again home to the headquarters of the Grenada Police Force and the site of some of the original military barracks is now the location of the Grenada General Hospital. Some of the administrative buildings within the fort have suffered the effects of both time and hurricane, and paint rather a sad picture. Though it is the police headquarters, the fort is open to the public and is best accessed from either the steps running up to the fort from the Esplanade on Bruce Street or directly up Grand Étang Road from the junction with Young Street. Whichever route you choose, be prepared for an uphill climb. At the time of writing there is no entrance fee.

Up the steps and through the narrow arched entrance to the fort you find yourself in the internal compound that witnessed the execution of Maurice Bishop and his supporters. On the wall you will see a plaque that was erected in 1993 in memory of those who were killed. To the right of this plaque is the way up to the top of the fort. Along the west wall you will see around five cannons symbolically pointing out to sea. At the top of the south wall, from a small grassy area you can enjoy great views of St George's Harbour and beyond. Lower down, near the entrance to the fort, opposite the police headquarters buildings, there is a walkway and viewing platform. From here there are good views of the capital and the Carenage.

**BAY TOWN** Bay Town, in reference to St George's Bay, is the name given to the northwestern half of St George's. To get from the Carenage to Bay Town, or vice versa, there are two options: climb and then descend the steep ridge that runs along the centre of town, or pass through the **Sendall Tunnel**. Named after a former governor, this 100m-long tunnel was constructed in 1895 to provide more direct and easier access to each of the two sides of St George's. It is located between Bruce Street near the Esplanade in Bay Town, and Monckton Street near the Carenage. It is a narrow tunnel, just 4m high and is a one-way street for vehicles travelling from south to north, in other words from the Carenage to Bay Town. People also walk through this tunnel, usually hugging one side in single file. Take care when doing this and be sure to pass your fellow pedestrians when no vehicles are approaching.

On the northwestern end of the Sendall Tunnel is Bruce Street and the bustling Melville Street. Here you will find the **Esplanade Mall**. Outside the mall, particularly on cruise-ship days, you may encounter entertainment, street vendors and a number of guides offering tours. Inside the mall you will find a selection of eateries, mainly fast food, a coffee shop, a couple of great juice bars and lots of souvenir and gift shops. Also within the Esplanade Mall, at the very far end, is the entrance and exit for the **cruise-ship terminal**.

Melville Street has a number of small snackettes and local eateries such as the very popular **Deyna's Tasty Food**. Melville Street is also where you will find the **St George's Bus Terminal** which is the hub of the island's bus system. Naturally this is a very busy and noisy place. Despite the crowds, the apparent confusion and the hubbub, the bus system is actually very straightforward and well organised. Once you know the number of the zone you are travelling to, just find the next bus in line with that number. All of the buses about to depart line up in number order. Conductors usually stand outside the bus trying to get it filled so the driver can depart. You can always double-check with the driver about the bus route, fare and destination. (For more information on Grenada's buses see pages 54 and 55). Above the bus terminal is a car park for those who have hired vehicles.

Further along Melville Street is the **fish market** where you can buy a wide variety of locally caught fish and seafood. Opposite the fish market you will see a number of small barbers' shops, bars and vendors selling fruits and vegetables. Melville Street continues northwards to Queen's Park where it becomes the main road along the west coast to Gouyave and to Sauteurs in the north.

From opposite the Esplanade Mall on Melville Street, there are two roads that head into the heart of Bay Town. They are Granby Street and Hillsborough Street. These two streets contain a number of general stores and boutiques. At the intersection with Halifax Street, at the very centre of the Bay Town district, is **Market Square**. When the French settlers moved from Port Louis to the new town of Ville du Fort Royal in the early 1700s, they set out this square as a parade ground and assembly point for their military. During the British occupation of the island it was used as a public square where political meetings and public executions would take place. This is where the captured insurgents of the Fédon Rebellion (see pages 136 and 137) were executed and also where a cage and gibbet were located for the incarceration, punishment and torture of escaped slaves. In the late 1700s the square was also used for Sunday markets where slaves would gather and meet on their rest day to socialise and enjoy the food they had grown and cooked.

Today Market Square is a very noisy and busy place, particularly on Friday and Saturday mornings which are the capital's main market days. It is surrounded on all four sides by roads, and visitors have to compete for space with each other, with street vendors, with stallholders and with vehicles to enjoy the lively atmosphere, the produce and the general vibes of the market. The colourful stalls are crammed very close together and sometimes it seems there can be no way through. It is almost as if they were just dropped haphazardly from the skies, with no order and little organisation. Nevertheless, with a great deal of patience, an open mind and a sense of fun and adventure, visitors should throw themselves wholeheartedly into the hullabaloo and enjoy the market to its fullest. The vendors are friendly and happy to explain their produce, show you their spices and even tell you how to cook an oil-down if you ask nicely enough. Look out for fresh fruits and vegetables as well as a wide selection of seasonings and spices. You will also see people selling clothes, accessories, music CDs, DVDs and natural oils. If you get there early enough you may also see young fishermen selling bundles of live crabs. If you decide you would like to take photographs of market vendors, it is always polite to ask first.

If you can find it, you may come across a **cenotaph** in the market square. There have been a number of odd location choices for a memorial to honour Grenada's fighting men, starting with the Esplanade in the 1960s. Prime Minister Gairy had it removed from this spot in 1968 and placed it where the Wallace Fountain used to stand in Market Square. The market and the monument became a bit of a mess, however, and it became less and less practical to have a cenotaph in a location that was more and more infrequently used for public gatherings. In 1994, a new cenotaph was placed in the Botanical Gardens near the ministerial offices between the Tanteen and Paddock areas of town. This is now the place where wreaths are laid each year on Armistice Day.

Surrounding the market, Granby Street, Halifax Street, Hillsborough Street and Grenville Street are crammed with a variety of stores, boutiques, roadside snackettes and great local eateries such as **Marvellous Marva's Place**. The whole area, especially the northern end of Halifax Street, has the feeling of a bazaar. It is quite an infectious, though perhaps a somewhat intimidating, place to visitors who are not accustomed to this kind of brouhaha.

St John's Street runs from Melville Street, opposite the bus terminal, across the ends of Halifax and Grenville streets and then steeply uphill where it meets Church Street. Granby Street becomes Market Hill which heads steeply upwards to also join with Church Street. Along the top of Church Street is **York House**, once the home of the Houses of Parliament. Built in the late 18th century, York House was originally a residential home. From the early 1800s, following the death of its original French owner, the building, one of the largest in the town at that time, was used as a home for both Parliament and Supreme Court. It also hosted state functions, banquets, exhibitions and concerts. Unfortunately York House suffered a great deal of damage during Hurricane Ivan, including the complete loss of its roof, forcing it to be abandoned until funds are allocated to its reparation. Hopefully this fine building will not stand abandoned and broken for too much longer. It is one of very few pre-colonial British buildings left standing in Grenada and is therefore very much part of the island's cultural heritage.

**CHURCHES** At the top of Church Street, very close to York House, is the **Roman Catholic Cathedral of the Immaculate Conception**. A small church known as St James' Chapel stood on this site in around 1804 when a decision was taken to replace it with something larger. As was common across the Caribbean at this time, the emancipation of slaves meant that they were allowed to worship freely in church. As the churches had only ever been built to house a limited number of worshippers from the white plantocracy, this sudden influx meant that many were too small. Records indicate that churches, particularly the Roman Catholic ones, were either enlarged or reconstructed during the 19th century. Most liberated slaves took to the Roman Catholic rather than the Anglican Church, either through the influence of French masters or in open rejection of the Church of their former British masters. Thus the numbers attending Anglican churches declined and the Roman Catholic churches began to thrive.

A confusion of dates upsets the exact story of the development of the capital's Roman Catholic cathedral. As with most cathedral constructions it is fair to assume that bits were added to the original over time. Parts of the tower are said to be the oldest surviving components of the church, dating as far back as 1818 and the life-size crucifix was believed to have been added in 1876. The cathedral was completed some time around 1884. Unfortunately much of the cathedral was destroyed during Hurricane Ivan in 2004. Visitors today will still see the tower, the walls and the frames of the arched windows, but it is a very sad reflection of its former glory. There is no roof, the windows on the windward side are all gone and the interior is succumbing to the elements. A campaign is ongoing towards raising funds for its restoration, but for the time being, the church has had to move to temporary accommodation across the street. For more information on the cathedral, fundraising and reconstruction plans, go to www.stgdiocese.org.

Further down Church Street in the direction of the Carenage there is the **St George's Anglican Church**. Located next to the St George's Anglican School, this church too has suffered the trauma of Hurricane Ivan. Also reduced to a shell, there is no roof, many windows have gone and the interior is exposed to rain. The bell tower remains however, and still chimes the hour. Reconstruction of the

This walk should take between two and three hours depending on your pace. Take lots of water and be prepared for steps and hills.

Start in front of the **Esplanade Mall** on Bruce Street near the Sendall Tunnel. With your back to the mall, walk right towards the tunnel. On the right-hand side of the tunnel entrance you will see steps climbing up the side of the hill. Walk all the way to the top where you will meet a tarmac road and the entrance to **Fort George**. Explore the fort or take a look at the town from the viewing platform which you will find up the steps opposite the police headquarters.

From Fort George walk down the narrow Grand Étang Road past St Andrew's Presbyterian Kirk and traffic lights to the four-way junction at the top of the ridge. Be careful of traffic on Grand Étang Road as well as at the junction itself. Turn right here and walk down Young Street. Along this street you will pass several craft shops and art galleries such as **Tikal**, **Art Fabrik** and **Yellow Poui**, all of which are worth investigating. Continue all the way down Young Street to the end. You should now be at the **Carenage**. Before heading to the left for a walk around the Carenage, take a short diversion to the right to see the **public library** building. Stroll around the Carenage at your leisure, past a number of very nice local bars and eateries. When you reach the cargo and tour boats in the corner of the Carenage, continue around the water's edge until you reach the **Christ of the Deep statue**. From here, carry on walking around the Carenage to the traditional red telephone boxes. Now look across the road for a street running off the Carenage, called Hughes Street. It is next to the large white and blue Cable & Wireless building. Walk up Hughes Street to the top where you should turn left. You are now on H A Blaize Street. Walk along this street until you reach **St George's Methodist Church**. Now look for some steps going up Chapel Alley next to the church. Go up these steps and then turn left on

Anglican church is underway and hopefully it will soon be restored to its former glory.

In 1690, French settlers erected the town's first church on this site – the St James' Roman Catholic Church. During British occupancy in 1784 it was confiscated and transformed into an Anglican church. An earthquake in 1825 destroyed it and it had to be rebuilt. Inside the church, along its walls were a number of marble plaques, some of which remain. A fascinating snapshot of history, these plaques commemorate those who were held captive and who were later executed on the orders of Julien Fédon during the insurrection of 1795–96 (see pages 136 and 137). One such plaque states that it is sacred to the memory of Ninian Home, former governor and one of 47 people who were executed by the rebel leader. It goes on to name the others, describing them as:

> Proprietors and inhabitants of this colony, all of whom were taken prisoners on 3rd March 1795, by an execrable banditti, composed principally of white new-adopted subjects of this island, and their free colour'd defendants, who stimulated by the insidious arts of French Republicans, lost all sense of duty to their sovereign, and mindful of the advantages they had long enjoy'd by participating in the blessings of the British Constitution, open'd on that day those destructive scenes which nearly desolated the whole country; And on 8th April following, completed the measure of their iniquity, by barbarously murdering (in the Rebel Camp at Mount Quaqua) the above innocent victims to their diabolical and uprovoked cruelty.

A partially restored and covered section of the Anglican church is still used for services.

Lucas Street. You should be next to the Wesley Hall and opposite the Swedish Consulate.

Continue along Lucas Street past some stone arches on your left and a box from where police officers direct traffic during the rush-hour periods. You will come to a junction with Church Street where you should turn right. You will pass **York House** and then arrive at the ruined **Roman Catholic cathedral**. Take a look inside.

From the cathedral you will see St John's Street heading steeply downhill. Follow it to the junction with Grenville Street where you should turn left. Walk along Grenville Street to **Market Square**. Take a look around the market and then return to the same spot. Now walk past Market Square to the next road junction and turn left up Market Hill. This will take you back to the four-way junction with Lucas Street and Church Street. Turn right down the lower part of Church Street. On your left you will see a very pretty, privately owned period house, then the Anglican school followed by the ruins of **St George's Anglican Church**. Take a look inside.

From the church, follow the road as it curves to the left and look out for cobbled steps going downhill on the right. Walk down these steps until you emerge at the bottom. You are back on Young Street. A little to the right is Monckton Street and the **Grenada National Museum**. The museum is really worth visiting as is the **Grenada Essentials** shop which showcases and sells authentic Grenadian crafts for income that is ploughed into conservation projects.

Walk down to the end of Monckton Street and then turn right. You should be at the entrance to the **Sendall Tunnel**. With care and due attention to traffic, which will be travelling in the same direction as you, walk through the tunnel in single file on the left-hand side. You will emerge at Bruce Street and the Esplanade Mall where you began your walk.

Located close to Fort George is **St Andrew's Presbyterian Kirk**, which is known locally as the Scots' Kirk. Now sadly in a state of ruin following Hurricane Ivan, this church is testament to the relatively high population of Scots who arrived in Grenada, Carriacou and Petite Martinique amongst the first British settlers. The influence of these people is still very evident throughout all three islands in the form of place names, family names and the traditions of boatbuilding in Carriacou and Petite Martinique. The beautiful Gothic church with its prominent bell tower was constructed in 1831 with the assistance of Freemasons. Today it is unfortunately too dangerous to enter.

**ST GEORGE'S ENVIRONS** If you continue along Melville Street and follow the coastal road beyond the bus terminal and the fish market you will eventually arrive at the St John's River and the Queen's Park **National Stadium** (number 5 or 7 bus from town). Queen's Park was designated a 'place of recreation' by the Grenada government in 1887 and it became the home of cricket and then horse racing. The space was also used for parades, various other sports events, festivals, music concerts, political rallies and carnival celebrations. In 1997, the original pavilion was demolished to make way for a national sports facility. The project was completed in the year 2000 at an estimated cost of over US$20million. In 2004, Hurricane Ivan destroyed everything. A year later, in 2005, the People's Republic of China began work on a US$30million reconstruction project with the aim of completing a cricket stadium that would host matches for the 2007 Cricket World Cup. The new National Stadium was completed in time and has a seating capacity of around 15,000.

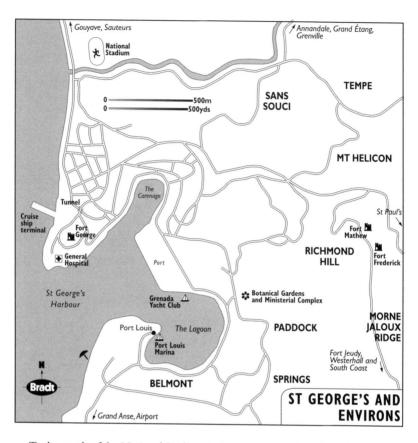

To the south of the National Stadium is the cemetery and up above it, **Hospital Hill**. The name comes from the French *Morne L'Hôpital*, where the settlement's first hospital was located in the 1730s. The British constructed a set of three gun batteries in this position in the 1760s and it proved to be their main, though ultimately losing, defensive line during the successful French invasion of 1779. This conflict wrought considerable damage to the original fortifications and, once the Richmond Hill forts had been built, the batteries of Hospital Hill were abandoned. Today these sites remain neglected and are overgrown with weeds.

South of the Carenage is the port and an area called Tanteen. Tucked into a corner, very close to the port and almost at the back of the customs house and the Grenada Board of Tourism office, is the **St George's Postal Corporation**. Opposite the busy entrance to the port is the Tanteen Recreational Ground which is used for local sports events. Behind the playing field is the Marryshow Community College and a short distance to the south of it, the **Botanical Gardens**. The gardens began life as a botanical station, constructed in 1887 as a facility to aid in the development of the islands' agriculture. They provided the island's farmers and agriculturalists with research, experimentation and education facilities, as well as a nursery for plant propagation. After many years, interest in and use of the station declined and the area became a garden showcasing some of the islands' tropical flowers, plants and trees. In 1968, a small zoo was opened at the rear of the gardens. In the 1980s both the zoo and the gardens entered a period of neglect. The zoo was closed and in its place new government ministry offices were constructed. Unfortunately this building work encroached upon much of the flora, thereby reducing the gardens to a very small park. In 1994, a new cenotaph was placed here commemorating those Grenadians who died in conflict. The gardens also house a small bandstand.

A short distance from the Botanical Gardens and the playing field is the **Lagoon**. Once landlocked and full of rather stagnant, brackish water that, together with the mangroves of Tanteen, served as an ideal breeding ground for mosquitoes, the Lagoon was dredged and opened up in the 1980s and '90s to create a quite beautiful anchorage. The Lagoon is home to the **Grenada Yacht Club**, which was founded in 1954, and the new **Port Louis Marina** development (*www.portlouisgrenada.com*). The total investment in this waterfront village and marina project is expected to end up being around US$500million. Located on the site of the first French settlement (the malaria has long since departed), the Port Louis Marina will also include the renovation of a former luxury hotel, the Islander (once also known as the Santa Maria and location of the 1957 Hollywood film *Island in the Sun*). There will also be boutique hotels, retail outlets, duty-free stores, luxury holiday and private apartments, town houses, restaurants and bars, tropical gardens, spa facilities, gym, tennis courts, pool and beach. It will also be a fully equipped, state-of-the-art marina with berths for regular vessels as well as super-yachts.

**RICHMOND HILL AND FORT FREDERICK** To the east of St George's, high above the town, are the two remaining forts of **Richmond Hill**. Originally there were four of them: Fort Frederick, Fort Mathew, Fort Lucas and Fort Adolphus. Only Frederick and Mathew are recognisable and accessible today, with Fort Frederick, the main fort, an interesting visitor attraction. The fortifications along the ridge of Richmond Hill go back to 1778 when the British built defences there. With the aim of defending St George's from an attack from the east, the forts face inland and look out across the interior towards Mt Parnassus, Mt Maitland and beyond. During the French invasion of 1779, these defences were easily overrun and it was for this reason that, once in power, the French set about strengthening them. But it was not until the British returned that the forts were finally completed. By then the Anglo-French wars were over.

**Fort Frederick** is definitely worth visiting (*top of Richmond Hill, to the east of St George's; US$2; number 3 bus from town*); it is an impressive fortification and has been well preserved and maintained. From the highest points of the fort there are super views for miles around. You can see St George's, the southwest peninsula and Grand Anse, the south coast and Fort Jeudy, and the high mountains of the interior both to the east as well as to the Grand Étang Forest Reserve in the north.

Wayward Wind berthed at the Grenada Yacht Club

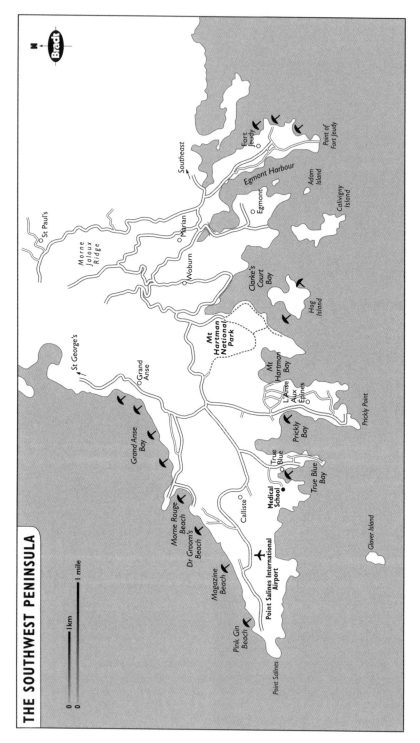

THE SOUTHWEST PENINSULA

# 5

# The Southwest Peninsula

Grenada's southwest peninsula is like no other place in the tri-island state. It is so different, in fact, that once you travel beyond it, you feel like you have crossed a border into a different country entirely. It is home to the majority of Grenada's hotels, resorts, apartments and villas, restaurants, tour operations, marinas and anchorages, luxury residential homes and gated communities. Its proximity to the capital, St George's, and also to the Point Salines International Airport, together with its stunning powder white-sand beaches, turquoise seas and beautifully natural and tranquil bays, all combine to provide Grenada with an almost entirely self-contained tourist industry.

This region is for travellers who are looking to simply relax on a beach, take in some sun, enjoy the sea, and live and dine in a little luxury. Indeed, Grand Anse Beach, one of the Caribbean's most famous stretches of sand, is sometimes all that some visitors to Grenada may ever actually see.

This chapter will start by explaining how to get to the southwest peninsula, it will list a selection of places to stay, eat and drink, and places to go shopping for practical items as well as souvenirs. After that, it will explore the southwest peninsula in detail, discovering its beaches, bays and anchorages, taking in the Mt Hartman National Park on a journey around the south coast to the east. Finally, the chapter will take a look at some of the things there are to do in this region, as well as describe walking and hiking options.

## GETTING THERE

If you are arriving at Point Salines International Airport, check whether your hotel or resort is going to meet you with a free shuttle service. Many do. If you are travelling by taxi then expect to pay in the region of EC$40 to Grand Anse and L'Anse Aux Épines, and EC$35 to True Blue. If you are driving a hire car from the airport, simply follow the main highway for around five minutes until you reach the first roundabout. True Blue is to your right. Continue straight ahead for Grand Anse and L'Anse Aux Épines. After a long stretch of road past an industrial estate you come to a second roundabout. L'Anse Aux Épines is the road to the right, and then right again at the very next junction. Grand Anse is left at the roundabout and then left again at the next. Grand Anse, True Blue and L'Anse Aux Épines are all signposted so you will not have too much difficulty.

If you are staying at La Source or Maca Bana Villas, instead of heading towards St George's and Grand Anse, follow the airport road in the opposite direction, past the staff car park and around a couple of sharp bends to a narrow road that runs towards the very end of the southwest peninsula. Your accommodation is located along this road on the right-hand side.

If you are travelling to the southwest peninsula from the bays, marinas or anchorages of the southeast, simply follow the signs to St George's until you reach

Grand Anse. At the traffic island near Camàhogne Park, the first left will take you towards True Blue and Point Salines International Airport, the second left goes to Grand Anse and the region's hotels and beaches, and right will take you to the capital, St George's.

## GETTING AROUND

If you have a hire car you will have little trouble finding your way around the southwest peninsula as Grand Anse, L'Anse Aux Épines and Point Salines International Airport are all very well signposted. A number 1 bus from St George's will get you to Grand Anse and as far south as Calliste. A number 2 bus will get you to Grand Anse from the southeast. Once in Grand Anse there is an 'off-route' system that takes in the beaches, hotels and bays of the southwest peninsula. The bus fares here are a little more expensive than elsewhere on the island (see pages 54 and 55 for more on Grenada's bus system).

## ⌂ WHERE TO STAY

The southwest peninsula has the largest selection of hotels, resorts, apartments and villas that you will find anywhere in Grenada. Most places accept major credit cards and many offer a wide variety of packages that may include meals, tours, use of watersports equipment, and even golf course membership. Before you finalise any booking, check whether the price quoted to you includes taxes and service charges and, if you are likely to want to use internet and Wi-Fi services, be aware that some hotels charge extra for this.

The accommodation listed below is deliberately selective and by no means comprehensive. Price codes quoted are current at the time of writing and are based on double occupancy per room per night during the peak season, or roughly the equivalent for self-catering accommodation with weekly rates. Please be aware that these price codes are meant as broad guides only and are subject to change, see page 75

### UPPER-RANGE BOUTIQUE HOTELS AND LUXURY RESORTS

⌂ **Spice Island Beach Resort** (64 rooms) Grand Anse; ☏ 473 444 4258; e reservations@spiceislandbeachresort.com; www.spiceislandbeachresort.com. Stunning luxury hotel accommodation located on Grand Anse Beach. Light, airy & immaculately designed, the hotel has a selection of suites, all of which have balcony or patio, AC, flat-screen TV, DVD, minibar, phone & en-suite bathroom facilities. The Oleander, Ocean & Garden suites have living rooms & are situated in tropical gardens. The Sea Grape Beach suites are right on the beach & have private patio garden & hammock. The Anthurium Pool suites have a private entrance, garden & personal plunge pool. The Luxury Almond Pool suites have a private swimming pool, outdoor dining terrace & sea views. The Royal Collection Pool suites have a private swimming pool & cedar wood sauna. The Cinnamon & Saffron Beach suites are located on the beach & have living room, dining room, wet bar, master bedroom with floating canopy bed, 2 bathrooms, private gardens & hammocks. The hotel is home to Oliver's Restaurant for fine Creole & international dining. Spa treatment & recreational activities available. 2 people sharing for a minimum of 7 nights: price inc b/fast, lunch, afternoon tea, dinner, beverages, golf club membership, tennis court use, non-powered watersports facilities (kayaks, Hobie Cats, etc). $$$$$

⌂ **Calabash Hotel & Villas** (30 suites, 2 luxury villas) L'Anse Aux Épines; ☏ 473 444 4334; f 473 444 5050; e calabash@calabashhotel.com; www.calabashhotel.com. Beautiful & luxurious hotel comprising 30 elegantly furnished suites located in 3ha of tropical gardens with pool, secluded beach & bay frontage. Rhodes' Restaurant offers fine dining & the beachside deck bar serves refreshing drinks. Each suite has en-suite bathroom with shower & whirlpool bath, AC, CD, TV, DVD, minibar, private patio or balcony. A maid serves b/fast for you each morning. The Thornycroft Suite has a private pool. Luxury villas, the Swallow & Hummingbird, are located on the exclusive Amber Belair development, a secluded peninsula to the west of the Calabash & L'Anse Aux Épines. Both have 3 en-suite bedrooms, kitchen, AC, living room, TV, swimming pool, housekeeper & cook. B/fast inc. $$$$$.

🏠 **Laluna** (16 cottages) Morne Rouge; ☎ 473 439 0001, US toll free ☎ 866 4 LALUNA; f 473 439 0600; e info@laluna.com; www.laluna.com. Exclusive, luxury accommodation in thoughtfully designed 1- & 2-bedroom cottages. Each cottage has 4-poster Balinese king-size bed, en-suite bathroom, AC, TV, CD player, day bed, ceiling fan, phone, wireless internet access, private deck & plunge pool. All cottages have open views with access to the secluded white-sand Portici Beach. Swimming pool, restaurant serving fine Italian cuisine, lounge & cocktail bar. Massage, yoga & spa treatments are also available. $$$$$

🏠 **La Source** (100 rooms) Pink Gin Beach; ☎ 473 444 2556; f 473 444 2561; e lasource@theamazingholiday.com; www.theamazingholiday.com. Extremely private, high-class resort located on the powder-white sands of Pink Gin Beach. All-inclusive packages focus on relaxation, rejuvenation & luxury. Gourmet food, wellness, massage, golf, watersports & scuba diving all feature in a complete experience for those who wish to get away from it all. All rooms have AC, ceiling fan, king-size or twin beds, en-suite bathroom, balcony or terrace. Price inc all food, drinks, services & activities. $$$$$

## MEDIUM-RANGE HOTELS AND RESORTS

🏠 **Grenadian (Rex Resorts)** (212 rooms) Magazine Beach; ☎ 473 444 3333; f 473 444 1111; e grenrex@spiceisle.com; www.rexcaribbean.com. Large resort located on Magazine Beach. A wide selection of room options include hillside, beachfront, ocean view & deluxe suites. All rooms have AC, TV, en-suite bathroom, fridge, balcony or patio. The resort has 3 restaurants, 2 bars & a lounge. Activities include watersports, scuba diving, tennis, fishing & windsurfing. Prices are not published though are available on request. Check website for links to booking accommodation or contact your local travel agent.

🏠 **True Blue Bay Resort** (38 rooms, villas & suites) True Blue; ☎ 473 443 8783, US toll free ☎ 888 883 2482; f 473 444 5929; e mail@truebluebay.com; www.truebluebay.com. Imaginatively designed resort hotel with a selection of tastefully decorated en-suite rooms, suites & villas. True Blue Restaurant & Dodgy Dock Restaurant & Lounge Bar offer both formal &

🏠 **Mount Cinnamon** (21 suites & villas) Grand Anse; ☎ 473 439 9900; f 473 439 8800; e reservations@mountcinnamongrenada.com; www.mountcinnamongrenada.com. Luxury boutique hotel located at the southern tip of Grand Anse Beach. Contemporary & colourful, the hotel's design successfully fuses European & Mediterranean chic with the essence of Grenada to produce vibrant & comfortable accommodation. Suites & villas are furnished with sitting rooms, kitchen & b/fast bars, TV, balcony with sea views. Mount Cinnamon is also home to Savvy's Mediterranean & Creole restaurant. Accommodation only. HB weekly supplement available. Min 7-night stay. $$$$$

🏠 **Coyaba Beach Resort** (80 rooms) Grand Anse; ☎ 473 444 4129; f 473 444 4808; e reservations@coyaba.com; www.coyaba.com. Luxury resort hotel with a distinctively ethnic feel, paying homage to the island's first settlers in name, thoughtful design & furnishings. Beautifully airy with tropical gardens, the resort is located right on Grand Anse Beach. Rooms overlook pool or gardens & have en-suite bathroom, AC, TV, ceiling fan, mini-fridge, safe & phone. The Arawakabana Carbet restaurant serves fine local & international cuisine. Massage & beauty services, tennis, swim-up bar, gym & watersports also available. Prices inc tennis, golf at the Grenada Golf Club, non-motorised watersports, croquet, table tennis & shuffleboard. Dbl occupancy $$$$

casual waterfront dining with regular live entertainment. Rooms have AC, TV, ceiling fan, kitchenette, patio or balcony. Facilities include marina, dock & berths, scuba diving, yacht charters, ocean kayaks, Hobie Cats & 2 swimming pools. B/fast inc. $$$–$$$$.

🏠 **Grenada Grand Beach Resort** (240 rooms) Grand Anse; ☎ 473 444 4371; f 473 444 4800; e paradise@grenadagrand.com; www.grenadagrand.com. Enormous resort hotel located on Grand Anse Beach. Rooms & suites have en-suite bathrooms, private balcony or patio with either beach or garden view, AC, TV, phone & internet access. The resort's impressive facilities include the 100m fantasy pool with waterfalls, jacuzzis & sunken bar, & the 20m sunset pool. There is also a private 9-hole par 3 golf course, & there are 2 floodlit tennis courts. The Fantasy Bar & Grill, the Sunset Bar & the Waterfront Restaurant offer drinks & dining. Accommodation only. Packages available. $$$–$$$$

**Flamboyant Hotel & Villas** (63 hotel & villa rooms) Grand Anse; ✆ 473 444 4247; f 473 444 1234; e flambo@spiceisle.com; www.flamboyant.com. Large hotel with room, suite, self-catering studio & villa accommodation located on the southern tip of Grand Anse Beach. All accommodation has en-suite bathroom, AC, TV, phone, private balcony or patio with sea views. Facilities include swimming pool, sun terrace, large restaurant, beachside cabana, sports bar & entertainments. The hotel is home to Dive Grenada, offering a full range of PADI courses as well as regular boat & snorkelling excursions to nearby sites. Accommodation only. Wedding packages available. $$$

**Allamanda Beach Resort** (50 rooms) Grand Anse; ✆ 473 444 0095; f 473 444 0126; e stay@allamandaresort.com; www.allamandaresort.com. Located right on the Grand Anse Beach, the Allamanda is an established resort hotel with 50 1- & 2-bedroom ground- & upper-floor rooms that are equipped with en-suite bathroom, AC, ceiling fan, TV, phone & safe. Some suites also have a whirlpool bath. Wireless internet is also available. In the centre of the resort is the swimming pool & Sapphire Restaurant serving Creole & international dishes to hotel guests & the general public. Amenities & activities include massage, tennis & watersports. Dive packages also available. Accommodation only. $$$

**Best Western – South City Plaza Hotel** (24 standard rooms, 1 presidential suite) Grand Anse; ✆ 473 439 3949; f 473 440 8915; e mail@southcityplaza.com; www.southcityplaza.com. Business-style hotel located on the main highway in Grand Anse above the South City Plaza shopping mall. All rooms have AC, TV, fridge, microwave, coffee-maker & high-speed internet access. Presidential suite also has a lounge, kitchenette, bar & jacuzzi. Continental b/fast inc. $$$

**Grenada Grand View Inn** (76 rooms, 8 1-bedroom apts, 3 2-bedroom apts) Grand Anse; ✆ 473 444 4984; f 473 444 1512; e gvinn@spiceisle.com; www.grenadagrandview.com. Located close to both Grand Anse & Morne Rouge beaches with great sea views. All rooms have AC, ceiling fans, fridge, en-suite bathroom, balconies. Apts have kitchenette. Facilities include Pirates Cove Restaurant Terrace & Bar, serving local & international cuisine. Swimming pool & conference room. Meal plans available. $$

**Monmot Hotel** (20 suites) L'Anse Aux Épines; ✆ 473 439 3408; f 473 444 3407; e monmothotel@spiceisle.com; www.monmothotel.com. Located in L'Anse Aux Épines, close to the beach & bay, this hotel has 20 flexible hotel suites that can easily double-up as self-contained holiday units. Each suite is located around the swimming pool & Garth's Restaurant & Bar which serves Creole & international dishes. Each suite is equipped with en-suite bathroom, AC, TV, phone, refrigerator & cooking facilities, private balcony or patio. Massage, reflexology, tours & activities are available. Price inc b/fast & lunch or dinner. $$

**Siesta Hotel** (37 rooms/apts) Grand Anse; ✆ 473 444 4646; f 473 444 4647; e stay@siestahotel.com; www.siestahotel.com. In pleasant gardens & within walking distance of Grand Anse Beach, the Siesta Hotel has 37 well-appointed rooms, suites & apts that all face the sea. Each room has en-suite bathroom, AC, TV, phone, refrigerator & private veranda or terrace. Swimming pool & Deliciosa Restaurant, serving Creole & international cuisine, enhance the hotel's amenities & pleasant, friendly ambience. Prices seasonal. Accommodation only. $$

## BUDGET HOTELS AND GUESTHOUSES

**Grenada Point Salines Hotel** (22 rooms) Point Salines; ✆ 473 444 4123; f 473 439 0524; e foxinn@spiceisle.com; www.foxinn-grenada.com. Located close to Point Salines International Airport, rooms have AC, TV, fridge, en-suite bathroom. Swimming pool. $$

**Blue Orchid Hotel** (15 rooms) Grand Anse; ✆ 473 444 0999; f 473 444 1846; e blueorchid@spiceisle.com; www.blueorchidhotel.com. Located on the main highway in Grand Anse close to the beach. Basic accommodation with AC, TV, private balcony with sea views. $

**Windward Sands Inn** Grand Anse; ✆ 473 444 4238; e windwardsandsinn@spiceisle.com; www.windwardsandsinn.quickonthenet.com. Sgl & dbl rooms plus SC efficiency apts located near Grand Anse Beach. AC & en-suite bathrooms. $

**Beach Inn** (10 rooms) Grand Anse; ✆ 473 444 4216; e beachinn@spiceisle.com; www.beachinngrenada.com. B&B accommodation located on the Grand Anse main road to the north of the beach. Rooms have en-suite bathroom. There is a shared TV & kitchen area, & access to private jetty. Watersports & fishing trips arranged. $

## UPPER-RANGE AND LUXURY SELF-CATERING APARTMENTS, COTTAGES AND VILLAS

🏠 **Lance Aux Épines House** (7 rooms, 1 tower) L'Anse Aux Épines; ☎ 473 415 1770; f 473 444 3321; e info@lanceauxepineshouse.com; www.lanceauxepineshouse.com. Luxury accommodation in renovated English colonial-style estate house. Gardens, beach, waterfront, dock, infinity swimming pool, jacuzzi. Rooms have en-suite bathrooms, AC, TV, internet, 4-poster beds. Tower is located separately & has 2 en-suite bedrooms. Price inc housekeeping staff. Chef extra. Powerboat & captain also extra. $$$$$

🏠 **Maca Bana Villas** (7 villas) Magazine Beach; ☎/f 473 439 5355; e macabana@spiceisle.com; www.macabana.com. Located above Magazine Beach, Maca Bana's villas are thoughtfully designed around tropical fruits & plant themes. They are spacious, private & luxuriously furnished. All have AC, TV, lounge, bedrooms, en-suite bathrooms, fully equipped modern kitchen, utility room, screened private sun deck with hot tub. $$$$$

🏠 **Ixora Villa** (3 dbl bedrooms) L'Anse Aux Épines; ☎ (UK) +44 121 246 6066; f (UK) +44 121 246 7077; e enquiries@ixoravillagrenada.com; www.ixoravillagrenada.com. Stylishly designed & furnished villa located in Coral Cove. 3 bedrooms, bathrooms, living area, sun terrace, kitchen, swimming pool, gazebo, whirlpool bath, utility room, internet connection, library, private jetty & kayak. $$$$$

🏠 **Môr Gân Villa** (2 bedrooms) L'Anse Aux Épines; ☎ 473 439 2486; f 473 535 1494; e spiceislevillas@spiceisle.com; www.spiceislevillas.com. 2-bedroom villa located in Coral Cove with sea access, jetty, swimming pool, sun deck & mature tropical gardens. Facilities include AC, TV, fully equipped kitchen, living area, large veranda, maid & laundry service. $$$$$

🏠 **Mount Hartman Bay Estate** (estate house 8 rooms, beach house 4 rooms) L'Anse Aux Épines; ☎/f 473 444 4504; e enquiries@mounthartmanbay.com; www.mounthartmanbay.com. Located on a private peninsula on the south coast, with private helipad & jetty, this stunning accommodation consists of estate house & separate beach house. Its original design has accurately been described as a combination of Gaudi meets James Bond. Facilities include swimming pool, sun terrace, private speedboat with captain for cruising & waterskiing, sea scooters, 2 4x4 vehicles, AC, TV, library, in-house gourmet chef, waiting staff & maid service. Prices are seasonal & inc all meals, drinks & facilities. $$$$$

🏠 **Owl Cottage** (2 bedrooms) L'Anse Aux Épines; e smith@owl-cottage.com; www.grenadaexplorer.com/owl. Villa accommodation a short distance from the beach. 2 bedrooms, living area, kitchen, AC, TV, ceiling fans, large balcony, swimming pool, terrace garden. $$$$$

🏠 **Swallow Villa** (3 bedrooms) Grand Anse, L'Anse aux Épines; ☎ 473 439 2486; e spiceislevillas@spiceisle.com; www.spiceislevillas.com. Luxury villa overlooking Prickly Bay with bathroom, living area, kitchen, fully equipped exercise area, AC, TV, computer with internet access, laundry. Outdoors there is a sun terrace, garden & infinity pool. Prices seasonal, quoted per week. $$$$$

🏠 **Villa Amarillo** (4 suites) True Blue; ☎/f 473 439 0858; e annaglean@spiceisle.com; www.grenadaexplorer.com/amarillo. Villa accommodation comprising 4 2-bedroom suites, pool, gazebo & tropical gardens. The villa has AC, TV, ceiling fans, living room, kitchen, laundry room, terrace & verandas. $$$$$

🏠 **Reef View Pavilion Villas** (2 villas) L'Anse Aux Épines; ☎ 473 439 5979; e reefview@spiceisle.com; www.reefviewgrenada.com. Luxury villas located on a hillside, with sea views & private swimming pools. Tradewind pavilion has 3 bedrooms, bathrooms, AC, TV, living area, kitchen, verandas, internet, swimming pool & rooftop pavilion with bar, BBQ & views. Turtleback pavilion is a 1-bedroom suite with similar facilities & also has private swimming pool & rooftop pavilion. $$$$$

## MID-RANGE SELF-CATERING APARTMENTS, COTTAGES AND VILLAS

🏠 **Gardenia Cottage** (3 bedrooms) L'Anse Aux Épines; ☎ 473 439 5297; e email@grenadavilla.co.uk; www.grenadavilla.co.uk. Located in Coral Cove with swimming pool, gardens & beach access. Villa has private bathrooms, living area, kitchen, TV, AC. $$$$

🏠 **Caribbean Breeze** (1 villa, 1 cottage, 2 apts) Grand Anse; ☎ 473 439 0897; f 473 439 3910; e caribbeanbreeze@spiceisle.com; www.caribbeanbreeze.net. The 3-bedroom fully furnished villa overlooks the golf course, has private veranda, living area, AC, TV, private bathrooms. 1-bedroom self-contained cottage has bedroom, shower room, TV, ceiling fans, veranda. 1- & 2-bedroom self-catering apts overlook gardens & golf course & have private bathroom, living area, kitchen, utility room, ceiling fan, TV. All accommodation has access to shared swimming pool. $$$

🏠 **Blue Horizons Garden Resort** (26 1-bedroom suites, 6 studios); Grand Anse; ↘ 473 444 4316; **f** 473 444 2815; **e** blue@spiceisle.com; www.grenadabluehorizons.com. The resort is located within 2.5ha tropical gardens with colourful flowers & many species of local birds. A short walking distance from Grand Anse Beach, Blue Horizon's 26 1-bedroom deluxe suites have AC, TV, fully equipped kitchen, CD player, phone, safe & terrace. The slightly smaller superior studios have king-size bed, kitchen & terrace. La Belle Creole, a popular fine-dining restaurant serving Creole & international cuisine is situated on site. $$$

🏠 **Twelve Degrees North** (8 apts) L'Anse Aux Épines; ↘/**f** 473 444 4580; **e** 12degrsn@spiceisle.com; www.twelvedegreesnorth.com. Located by the beach. Each suite is furnished with en-suite bathroom & private balcony facing the sea. Maid & housekeeping service providing b/fast & lunch on your balcony. Pool, laundry service & non-motorised watersports equipment all included. $$$

🏠 **Jenny's Place** (4 apts) Grand Anse; ↘/**f** 473 439 5186; **e** info@jennysplacegrenada.com; www.jennysplacegrenada.com. Located on the northern end of Grand Anse Beach. 2 ocean-view & 2 garden-view sgl-bedroom SC apts with bathroom, living room, kitchen, TV, AC, ceiling fans, private veranda. B/fast inc. $$$

🏠 **L'Anse Aux Épines Cottages** (11 cottages/apts) L'Anse Aux Épines; ↘ 473 444 4565; **f** 473 444 2802; **e** reservations@laecottages.com; www.laecottages.com. Relaxed & friendly family-run SC resort on the beach. 1-, 2- & 3-bedroom cottages & apts are located in beautifully natural surroundings with lovely beach & sea views. Each

cottage & apt has living room, fully equipped kitchen, AC, phone & internet connectivity. Shared big-screen TV & games room also includes billiards, table tennis. $$$

🏠 **Recoben Apartments** (3 self-contained family apts) Morne Toute; ↘ 473 443 0772; **f** 473 444 5189; **e** recoben@spiceisle.com. Each apt is a fully furnished & equipped unit with 3 bedrooms, making it ideal for families. $$$

🏠 **Spicetree Suites** (2 2-bedroom suites) L'Anse Aux Épines; ↘ 473 439 5979; **e** reefview@spiceisle.com; www.grenadapropertyrentals.com. Holiday suites with bedrooms, bathroom, living area, kitchen, AC, TV & veranda. Outdoor garden & BBQ. $$

🏠 **Coral Cove Cottages & Apartments** (11 cottages & apts) L'Anse Aux Épines; ↘ 473 444 4422; **f** 473 444 4718; **e** coralcv@spiceisle.com; www.coralcovecottages.com. 1- & 2-bedroom cottage apts located in pleasant gardens on the beach with swimming pool, tennis courts & boat jetty. All apts have private bathroom, living area, TV, ceiling fans, kitchen & veranda. $$

🏠 **Sunset Apartment** (2 bedrooms) Fort Jeudy; ↘ 473 536 5234; **e** info@plantationprojects.com; www.plantationprojects.com. Located on the southern tip of Fort Jeudy with orchard & access to small beach. Accommodation comprises 2 bathrooms, living area, fully equipped kitchen, ocean-facing b/fast nook, laundry, wireless internet. Prices on request.

🏠 **GEM Holiday Beach Resort** (18 apt suites) Morne Rouge; ↘ 473 444 4224; **f** 473 444 1189; **e** gem@spiceisle.com; www.gembeachresort.com. SC apt suites located on the beautiful Morne Rouge Beach, a short distance to the southwest of Grand Anse. Each suite has bedroom with en-suite bathroom, fully equipped kitchen, living area, AC, TV, phone & internet access. Ocean-view & garden-view suites. Sur La Mer Restaurant & Fantazia Bar & Nightclub are located here. Wedding packages available. $$

# BUDGET SELF-CATERING APARTMENTS, COTTAGES AND VILLAS

🏠 **Palm Court Apartments** (12 apts) Grand Anse; ↘/**f** 473 444 4453; **e** palmcourt@spiceisle.com; www.grenadaexplorer.com/palmcourt. 1- & 2-bedroom self-contained apts with private bathroom, kitchen, living area, AC, fans, veranda. $

🏠 **Seaview Apartments & Wellness Centre** Grand Anse; ↘ 473 444 3175; **e** seawellgnd@yahoo.com; www.grenadaexplorer.com/seaview. Located at the

northern end of Grand Anse Beach. 1-bedroom apts with bathroom, living area, kitchen, AC, TV, ceiling fans. $

🏠 **Grand Anse Heights** (5 apts) Grand Anse; ↘ 473 439 5334; **e** grandanseheights@spiceisle.com; www.grandanseheights.com. 1-bedroom SC apts with sea views. Private bathroom, AC, ceiling fan, TV, living area, kitchen, veranda. $

🏠 **Roydon's Apartments** (16 apts) Grand Anse; \/f 473 444 4476; e roydons@spiceisle.com; www.roydons.com. Studio plus 1-, 2- & 3-bedroom apts with views of Grand Anse Bay. Apts have private bathroom, AC, TV, ceiling fans, kitchen, verandas. $

🏠 **South Winds Holiday Cottages** (14 1-bedroom apts, 5 2-bedroom cottages) Grand Anse; ✆ 473 444 4310; f 473 444 4404; e southwinds@spiceisle.com; www.southwindsgrenada.com. SC holiday units with bathroom, kitchen, AC, TV, veranda. Maid service provided. $

🏠 **Wave Crest Holiday Apartments** Grand Anse; ✆ 473 444 4116; e wavecrest@spiceisle.com; www.grenadawavecrest.com. Smart & clean 1- & 2-bedroom apts with garden or sea view. All rooms have private bathroom, living area, kitchen, AC, TV. There is also a shared b/fast area. $

🏠 **Bougainvillea Apartments** (21 apts) Grand Anse; ✆ 473 444 4930; f 473 444 3391; e bougainvillea@spiceisle.com; www.grenada-bougainvillea.com. Located close to Grand Anse Beach & local amenities. 1- & 2-bedroom apts are fully furnished, with AC, TV, kitchen, internet access. $

🏠 **Candle Glow Apartments** L'Anse Aux Épines; ✆ 473 439 4916; e candleglow@spiceisle.com; www.candleglowgrenada.com. Modern 1- & 2-bedroom apt complex with AC, TV, living area, private bathroom, kitchenette, balcony or patio. $

🏠 **Caribbean Cottage Club** Grand Anse; \/f 473 444 5676; e info@grenadacottages.com; www.grenadacottages.com. 1- & 2-bedroom wooden cottages in tropical gardens close to the beach. Each has private bathroom, living area, TV, fans, mosquito nets, kitchen, private veranda. $

🏠 **Hideaway Apartments** (3 apts) Grand Anse; \/f 473 444 0011; e hideaway@grenadaexplorer.net; www.grenadaexplorer.com/hideaway. 2-bedroom apts located on the seafront to the north of Grand Anse Beach. Each has bathroom, living area, kitchen, fans & private patio. $

🏠 **Maitland's Apartment** (2 bedrooms) Grand Anse; ✆ 473 439 1926; www.grenadaexplorer.net/maitland. 1- & 2-bedroom SC apts located at the northern end of Grand Anse Beach. Accommodation includes bathroom, living area, kitchen, AC. $

## ✖ WHERE TO EAT AND DRINK

The southwest peninsula is crammed full of great places to eat and drink. From haute cuisine to casual beachside barbecue and beer, the range of dining experiences should have something that matches both your palette and your wallet. Calling ahead, especially for dinner, is always recommended, particularly if you are looking for something seasonal, like lobster or lambie. Sunday lunchtime is usually very busy, especially at the more popular beachside restaurants, so arrive early to get seated. Many restaurants will take a day off on either Sunday or Monday, though hotel restaurants are open every day. Most restaurants and certainly all hotel restaurants will accept credit cards. See page 61 for restaurant price codes.

### CREOLE AND INTERNATIONAL – FINE DINING

✖ **Rhodes'** Calabash Hotel, L'Anse Aux Épines; ✆ 473 444 4334; ⊕ daily. Currently Gary Rhodes's only restaurant outside the UK. Recipes are a delicious fusion of Creole influences & Rhodes's unique style of cooking. Reservations required. $$$

✖ **Laluna** Morne Rouge; ✆ 473 439 0001; ⊕ daily. Award-winning restaurant at the exclusive Laluna boutique hotel. Noted for fine Italian & Creole fusions. Dinner by reservation. $$$

✖ **Oliver's** Spice Island Beach Resort, Grand Anse; ✆ 473 444 4258; ⊕ daily. Gourmet international & Creole dining in very beautiful setting. Reservations recommended. $$$

✖ **Le Phare Bleu** Petite Calivigny; ✆ 473 443 3443; ⊕Tue–Sun. Fine dining aboard a converted lighthouse ship in the new Le Phare Bleu Marina & Resort. Choose from 3 to 7 courses of 'tradewind cuisine'. Dinner reservations recommended. $$$

✖ **Savvy's** Mount Cinnamon, Grand Anse; ✆ 473 437 2889; ⊕ daily. Fine Mediterranean dining with a hint of the Caribbean. Located in the colourful setting of Mount Cinnamon with pool & poolside bar. Dinner reservations recommended. $$$

✖ **The Aquarium** Magazine Beach; ✆ 473 444 1410; ⊕ Tue–Sun. Very popular & well-known restaurant built into the cliffside with wooden decking & direct access to the beach. Highly recommended. The more casual beach bar is a great place for lunch & a drink when taking a swim or soaking up the sun. Live music & BBQ on Sun. $$$

X **The Arawakabana** Coyaba Beach Resort, Grand Anse; ℡ 473 444 4129; ⊕ daily. Haute Caribbean & international cuisine in a beautiful setting. Dinner by reservation. The Carbet Restaurant & Pool Bar, also part of the Coyaba Beach Resort, has à la carte poolside dining & drinks. $$$

X **True Blue Bay Restaurant** True Blue Bay Resort, True Blue; ℡ 473 443 8783; ⊕ daily. Specialising in a combination of Caribbean & Mexican dishes,

served along the waterside. Dinner by reservation. $$$

X **The Beach House Restaurant & Bar** Located off the airport road next to the Rex Grenadian Resort; ℡ 473 444 4455; ⊕ Mon–Sat. Excellent food & service in a beautiful setting alongside Dr Groom's Beach. Highly recommended. Dinner reservations advised especially in the peak season. $$$

X **La Belle Creole** Blue Horizons Garden Resort, Grand Anse; ℡ 473 444 4316; ⊕ daily. Fine international cuisine with a Creole influence in beautiful tropical garden surroundings. Dinner reservations recommended. $$$

## CREOLE AND INTERNATIONAL – CASUAL

X **Sapphire Restaurant & Bar** Allamanda Beach Resort, Grand Anse; ℡ 473 439 3900; ⊕ daily. Specialising in French Creole & international dishes. Reservations recommended. $$

X **Dodgy Dock** True Blue Bay Resort, True Blue; ℡ 473 443 8783; ⊕ daily. Very popular deck & terrace bar beside the water. Casual & relaxed international dining. Jazz on Fri, live music Sat. $$

X **Gath's** Monmot Hotel, L'Anse Aux Épines; ℡ 473 439 3408; ⊕ daily. Poolside dining with a wide selection of Creole & international dishes. Dinner reservations recommended. $$

X **Beachside Terrace** Flamboyant Hotel, Grand Anse; ℡ 473 444 4247; ⊕ daily. Wide selection of local & international cuisine with great views of Grand Anse Beach. $$

X **De Big Fish** True Blue; ℡ 473 439 4401; ⊕ daily. Chicken, ribs, fish, fajitas, shrimp & vegetarian dishes. Located on a deck by the waterside in True Blue Bay, near the coastguard station. $$

X **Deliciosa** Siesta Hotel, Grand Anse; ℡ 473 439 1700; ⊕ daily. Mexican, Creole & international dishes. Seafood, meat, chicken & vegetarian options also available. $$

X **Island View Restaurant** Woburn; ℡ 473 443 2054. Creole & international restaurant & bar on a wooden deck overlooking the very pretty Clarke's Court Bay. $$

X **Kudos Bar & Grill** L'Anse Aux Épines; ℡ 473 444 1250; ⊕ Tue–Sun. Chilled-out restaurant on the main L'Anse Aux Épines road serving a selection of Creole & international dishes. $$

X **Pirate's Cove Terrace Restaurant & Bar** Grenada Grand View Inn, Morne Rouge; ℡ 473 444 2342;

⊕ daily. Local & international cuisine, overlooking the beautiful Morne Rouge Beach. $$

X **Coconut Beach** Grand Anse Beach; ℡ 473 444 4644; ⊕ Wed–Mon. Creole & international dishes served both on & beside the beach. Seafood, steaks, chicken & more. $$

X **The Red Crab** L'Anse Aux Épines; ℡ 473 444 4424; ⊕ Mon–Sat. Relaxed restaurant with a good selection of high-quality international & local dishes. $$

X **Sur La Mer** Gem Holiday Beach Resort, Morne Rouge; ℡ 473 444 4224; ⊕ daily. Beachside cabana restaurant serving Creole, seafood & international dishes. Located alongside the picturesque Morne Rouge Bay. $$

X **Little Dipper Restaurant & Bar** Lower Woburn; ℡ 473 444 5136; ⊕ Tue–Sun. Genuine hidden treasure along the Woburn highway. Cosy, friendly, great local food & wonderful sea views. Highly recommended. $$

X **Bananas** True Blue, St George's; ℡ 473 444 4662; ⊕ daily. Lively restaurant, sports bar & nightclub with casual dining including BBQ, wings, burgers & wood-fired pizza. $$

X **The Pizza Place** & **Tiki Bar & Restaurant** Prickly Bay Marina; ℡ 473 439 5265; ⊕ daily. Very casual waterside dining includes pizzas, burgers, sandwiches, grilled fish & lobster. $$

X **Le Chateau** Le Marquis Mall, Grand Anse; ℡ 473 444 2552; ⊕ daily. Casual restaurant serving a selection of Creole & international dishes including seafood, steak & chicken dishes. $

X **Chef's Castle Restaurant & Bakery** Excel Plaza, Grand Anse; ℡ 473 440 4778; ⊕ Mon–Sat. Burgers, pizzas, salads & local cuisine. $

**VEGETARIAN** The majority of the restaurants described previously have a good selection of vegetarian dining options.

✗ **Rumors Vegetarian Restaurant Bar & Seafood Place** Waterfront, Lower Woburn; ✆ 473 443 5650. Fresh local produce served along the waterfront at Clarke's Court Bay. $$

## ITALIAN

✗ **La Boulangerie** Le Marquis Mall, Grand Anse; ✆ 473 444 1131; ⏲ daily. Covered terrace setting for great Italian pizza & pasta dishes. Also open for b/fasts, serving fresh juices, croissants & pastries. Try the homemade Italian ice cream. $$

✗ **Di Vino** Le Marquis Mall, Grand Anse; ✆ 473 439 7227; ⏲ Mon–Sat. Italian wine bar serving a selection of cold cuts such as prosciutto, salami, bresaola & more. $$

## CHINESE

✗ **Oriental Restaurant** Rex Grenadian Resort, Magazine Beach; ✆ 473 444 3333; ⏲ dinner only on selected days. Located within the Rex Grenadian Resort on the road to the airport, serving a selection of dishes from the east. Call first. $$

✗ **Chopstix** Spiceland Mall, Grand Anse; ✆ 473 444 7849; ⏲ Mon–Sat. Take-away or sit-down Chinese food in the Spiceland Mall. $–$$

## SUSHI

✗ **Carib Sushi** Le Marquis Mall, Grand Anse; ✆ 473 439 5640; ⏲ daily. Fresh local fish, Japanese style. Sushi, sashimi, uramaki, hosomaki & more. $$

## FAST FOOD

✗ **KFC** Grand Anse. Southern fried chicken located next to the Spiceland Mall. $

✗ **Rick's Café** Grand Anse Shopping Centre. Pizza, subs, burgers, hot dogs, etc. $

## BARS AND NIGHTLIFE

☆ **Fantazia** Gem Holiday Beach Resort, Morne Rouge; ✆ 473 444 4288; ⏲ Wed, Fri & Sat. Popular nightclub on Morne Rouge Beach.
♀ **Garfield's Beach Bar** Grand Anse Beach. Located near the Grenada Grand Beach Resort. Small & cosy but a great place for a snack, a cold beer & some relief from the sun.

☆ **The Owl** Flamboyant Hotel & Villas, Grand Anse; ✆ 473 444 4247; ⏲ daily until late. Late bar, music & karaoke. Happy hour 16.00–19.00 then again 23.00–midnight.
♀ **Papa Joe's Sports Bar** Excel Plaza, Grand Anse; ✆ 473 440 4778. Casual sports bar.

## SHOPPING

The shopping malls of the southwest peninsula are designed to cater for a local and international customer base. You will find well-stocked supermarkets, fast-food restaurants, clothes boutiques, craft and souvenir shops, banks and ATMs.

### SHOPPING MALLS

**Excel Plaza** Grand Anse. On the road between Grand Anse & the junction for L'Anse aux Épines & the airport.
**Grand Anse Shopping Centre** Grand Anse. On the main road between St George's & Grand Anse, near the Grenada Grand Beach Resort.
**Le Marquis Mall** (The 'Roundhouses') Grand Anse. Alongside the roundabout junction in Grand Anse, near the beach.
**South City Plaza** Grand Anse. On the main road between St George's & Grand Anse, part of the Best Western Hotel complex.
**Spiceland Mall** Grand Anse. Alongside the beach in Grand Anse, opposite the Coyaba & Allamanda resorts.

## SUPERMARKETS

**The Food Fair** Grand Anse Shopping Mall; ⏲ Mon–Sat

**IGA Real Value Supermarket** Spiceland Mall; ⏲ daily (Sun from 10.00)

## CRAFT AND SOUVENIR SHOPS

**Art & Soul** Spiceland Mall, Grand Anse. Original paintings by Susan Mains & Asher Mains, books. **Imagine** Grand Anse Shopping Centre. Handicrafts, gifts & souvenirs.

**Presents Too** Excel Plaza, Grand Anse. Gifts & books. **Pssst Boutique** Spiceland Mall, Grand Anse. Local & Caribbean arts & crafts.

## EXPLORING THE SOUTHWEST PENINSULA

The southwest peninsula has a number of beautiful beaches, the majority of which are very accessible. Most are located in the north, on the Caribbean side of the peninsula. On the south coast there are a number of pretty bays, marinas and anchorages as well as rugged volcanic headlands. Our journey will begin at Grand Anse and head south and then east around the peninsula until we reach Fort Jeudy.

**GRAND ANSE BEACH** Grand Anse is Grenada's signature beach. Over 3km in length and located some 5km to the south of the capital St George's, it is where you will find a number of the island's premier resorts and luxury hotels. As it consists of fine, white powdery sand with the gentle rollers of an azure Caribbean, it is easy to understand why many of Grenada's visitors are drawn to this spot.

Despite its enormous popularity, it never appears to be too crowded. Towards the northern end, off the Grenada Grand Beach Resort, it is probably at its busiest as the hotel is huge and has a very long beach frontage. Sunloungers and parasols can appear to crowd this small section at times, but there is more than enough room on this beach for everyone. Looking out from Grand Anse across St George's Harbour, you can clearly see the capital, Fort George, the Carenage, and sailing boats and motor cruisers at anchor.

From Jenny's Place at the northern tip to the Flamboyant Hotel at the very southern end, you will find a number of bars and restaurants along Grand Anse Beach, serving up a variety of cold drinks, breakfasts, lunches and dinners. Also, if you are looking for watersports, most dive shops have a presence here, offering a variety of services from scuba-diving lessons, boat diving, boat trips, snorkel hire, kayak and Hobie Cat hire. A number of local vendors pound the beach every day in the hope of selling trinkets and souvenirs, snacks, clothing and even a massage.

If you are not staying at one of Grand Anse's large resort hotels, you must find a public access point. You can get onto the beach in a number of different places including the path next to the Coconut Beach Restaurant and at the end of Camàhogne Park, near the Spiceland Mall.

**MORNE ROUGE BEACH** Morne Rouge is a really beautiful horseshoe-shaped beach and bay located to the southwest of Grand Anse Beach. With powder-white sand, Morne Rouge Beach is very sheltered and so the sea is usually completely flat and perfectly clear. Small almond trees are scattered along the rear of the beach providing welcome shade. Usually very quiet, Morne Rouge is a great escape and perfect for families with small children. Look out for the *Rhum Runner II* boat excursions that arrive in the afternoons bringing cruise-ship tourists during the height of the season when the beach suddenly fills up for a few hours. As with Grand Anse, vendors may approach and ask you if you would like to buy their wares or take a tour. You can also hire beach chairs here if you so wish.

To get to Morne Rouge Beach, follow the main Grand Anse Beach road past the resort hotels and then around the corner and up the hill along the perimeter of the Flamboyant Hotel. Walk or drive over the ridge and straight down the next hill, ignoring the road on the left. Follow the road down to the bottom and around to the left until you reach the entrance of the Gem Holiday Beach Resort. To the right of the gates are some steps leading down to the beach.

**PORTICI BEACH** This beach is quite tricky to reach. It is located below the Laluna luxury hotel to the south of Morne Rouge Bay and Petit Cabrits Point. To get there from Morne Rouge, you must walk around the rear perimeter fencing of Laluna and then follow a path down alongside the resort until you reach the beach. From the main airport road, follow the signs to the Beach House Restaurant, and at a fork in the road, bear right. This road becomes a dead end near some residential houses. A path to the right of a house at the end of the paved road eventually joins up with the track that follows the Laluna perimeter fencing. It is quite an effort to reach this one and, unless you are beach-bagging, you may want to skip it in favour of one of the others.

**DR GROOM'S BEACH** This is a really nice white-sand beach that is located to the south of the hard-to-reach Portici Beach and north of Magazine Beach. From the main airport road simply follow the signs to the Beach House Restaurant. At the gated entrance to the restaurant's car park, you will see a path on the left before you enter. This short path takes you to the beach. The Beach House is ideally placed to make this a great place to soak up the sun and the surf and to follow-up your day with some really excellent dining.

**MAGAZINE BEACH** Also a very pretty white-sand beach, and quite often deserted, Magazine Beach is a little further towards the peninsula's southwestern tip, between the Rex Grenadian Resort and the Aquarium Restaurant. To get there you must head for the airport and follow the road past the terminal building. It will curve to the right, past staff car-parking areas before turning back around again to the left on a road that goes to the La Source resort, Maca Bana and the Aquarium. Before you reach any of these, however, at the apex of the hairpin bend that curves around to the left, there is a wooded area on the right-hand side with a vehicle track next to it. Next to a large house you should spot a paved road heading steeply downhill. This will take you to the beach. It is beautiful and there is a very welcome area of shade beneath a small beachside copse of manchineel and almond trees. At the southern end of Magazine Beach you will find the Aquarium Restaurant which, on Sundays, has a barbecue and live music. Not to be missed!

**PINK GIN BEACH** Pink Gin Beach is to the south of Magazine Beach and is very beautiful. Alongside it is the exclusive La Source resort and the beach is very difficult to access unless you swim or are in a boat.

**L'ANSE AUX ÉPINES BEACH** This beach is located on the western side of the L'Anse Aux Épines peninsula, a little to the north of the Prickly Bay Marina. It is a narrow stretch of white-sand beach and its waters are very calm, making it suitable for families with small children. On the western end of the beach is the Calabash Hotel and on the eastern end is where you will find public access. From the small traffic junction in Grand Anse, head south to L'Anse Aux Épines and look for signs to the Calabash Hotel and Monmoth Hotel near to a small playing field. Access to the beach is just a little further along the main road, beyond the playing field on the right-hand side.

**ALONG THE SOUTH COAST FROM POINT SALINES TO FORT JEUDY** The southwest coast of Grenada comes to an end at **Point Salines**, which is also the location of the international airport. The road to the airport continues a little way beyond it, before coming to the end of the peninsula. It passes several hotels and restaurants along the way, including the very popular Aquarium Restaurant, Maca Bana Villas and the La Source resort. Along the south coast, to the east of the airport, is **True Blue**. This is where you will find St George's University of Medicine and a peninsula separating True Blue Bay and **Prickly Bay**. These pretty bays are very popular anchorages and each have world-class marina facilities. Prickly Bay is located to the west of the **L'Anse Aux Épines** peninsula, the location for a number of resort hotels, villas and self-catering holiday accommodation, as well as some very luxurious homes. L'Anse Aux Épines, meaning 'thorny bay' was perhaps the inspiration for the name Prickly Bay, in reference to the acacia trees that grow in abundance as part of the dry coastal woodland in this region. You will notice that there are several different ways of spelling L'Anse Aux Épines, and very often you will see it written 'Lance aux Épines'. *L'Anse* was the original French spelling and meant 'bay' and over time it has simply become anglicised, hence the variations you see today. Just to make it even more complicated, most people drop the 'aux' when pronouncing the name, so when spoken it simply becomes 'Lance Épines'.

The small bars and eateries of Prickly Bay Marina are very popular with visitors, watersports operators and the sailing community, especially in the evenings at weekends. The marina is located a little beyond the playing field near the Calabash and Monmoth hotels, down a rather steep and narrow road. The Calabash Hotel is where you will find Rhodes', the signature restaurant of the acclaimed British chef. A walk to the end of L'Anse Aux Épines is a pleasant activity, especially after a rather large lunch. You can saunter past and admire the very luxurious houses and the equally salubrious sailing boats of the marina, before reaching the beautifully rugged headland of Prickly Point, with its nice views along the coastline and also of Hog and Calivigny islands (see page 122).

**Glover Island** is located south of the peninsula and was once the home of a whaling station. As early as the mid 19th century, whaling boats were plying the waters of the Caribbean and in the 1920s a station was constructed on Glover Island by Norwegian whalers. The station processed whale oil for export and meat for local consumption. During the second half of the 1920s, the life of Glover Island's whaling station came to a premature end. Through a combination of a decline in whale numbers and new 'factory' boats that could handle the processing themselves, the need for Glover simply disappeared. In 1929, the station was dismantled though the ruins remain.

To the east of L'Anse Aux Épines is the **Mt Hartman National Park**. It is an area of dry coastal woodland on a wide peninsula between Mt Hartman Bay and Clarke's Court Bay. It is also often referred to as the 'Dove Sanctuary' because it is thought to be home to around 20% of the global population of the Grenada dove (*Leptotila wellsi*) and has been designated an Important Bird Area (IBA) by Birdlife International. In 2007, Grenada's government of the day stated that in fact only 30% of the Mt Hartman Estate had been designated a restricted area, paving the way for a large resort development project. This project has caused some alarm amongst environmentalists though both the previously incumbent government and hotel developer have stated that the sanctuary will be preserved and the endangered dove's habitat will not be adversely impacted. Though usually very dry, the national park is a very pretty place, one of quiet solitude and natural beauty.

**Hog Island** is located at the entrance to Woburn Bay and is a popular sailing and day-trip anchorage. **Roger's Bar** has reached almost legendary status within the yachting community and the island's small beaches are very popular places to relax with drinks and a barbecue. A number of tour operators run half- or full-day trips that touch down at Hog Island. Some trips include snorkelling, beach barbecues and fishing for your own lunch. All are fun ways to spend a day in the area (see pages 67 and 70 for operator information).

**Woburn** (both Upper and Lower) is located to the east of the Mt Hartman Estate. Separating Woburn from Mt Hartman is the pretty Woburn Bay (more commonly known as Clarke's Court Bay) where you will see a number of sailing boats resting at anchor or alongside the jetties of the Clarke's Court Bay Marina.

The **Egmont and Petit Calivigny** peninsula is the location of a large residential development called Grand Harbour (*www.grandharbourgrenada.com*) and, when completed, it is clearly going to be very luxurious indeed. From the coastal road to the east of Woburn you will see a sign to **Le Phare Bleu**. Follow this road and at the bottom of the hill go right, over the bridge. The expanse of water you can see, with its margin of dense mangroves, is Egmont Harbour (sometimes also referred to as Petit Calivigny Harbour) and it is very tranquil and quite beautiful. Once over the bridge, follow the road to the left and then straight up and over the hill. Below you is Le Phare Bleu, a lovely complex that includes state-of-the-art marina facilities, self-contained holiday accommodation and restaurants, one of which is located on the refurbished lighthouse boat at the end of the jetty. It is a very pleasant place to relax and where you are made to feel very welcome, whether you are part of the boating fraternity or just a dreamer with a tendency of spending countless hours gazing longingly and bleary-eyed at sailing boats you can't afford.

**Calivigny Island** is located off Petit Calivigny Point and can be very clearly seen from the coastal road in Lower Woburn or from Le Phare Bleu. It is a privately owned island and, though beaches are part of the public domain in Grenada, visitors have consistently reported being made to feel very unwelcome there. To avoid any unpleasantness it is, regrettably, best avoided.

**Fort Jeudy** is also the subject of a development project, though it is already becoming quite an established and very upmarket residential community. It is a long peninsula to the east of Egmont Harbour and has a very pretty coastline with great views. You can get right to the Point of Fort Jeudy by following the paved road and then a track to the rugged coastline (see page 127). There are nice views along the coast to Calivigny Island, Egmont and Adam Island as well as a number of rocky outcrops to the east in the parish of St David.

## WHAT TO DO

If you can tear yourself away from the great food, the cocktails and the beaches, there are some fun activities on offer in the southwest.

**GO SCUBA DIVING** Grenada is developing a reputation for its scuba diving and there are some very nice reefs and a selection of interesting shipwrecks that are definitely worth exploring. If you cannot scuba dive, why not give it a go? All of Grenada's dive operators offer try-dives as well as full certification courses. For those who are already certified, all diving is from a boat and you are guided by a divemaster who usually tows a surface marker buoy. Some operators offer pre-blended enriched air (Nitrox). For information on Grenada's dive sites, see page 74.

**Scuba-diving operators** For a complete list of scuba-diving operators, go to *Chapter 3*, page 77. Most scuba-diving operators offer four boat dives per day – two in the morning and two in the afternoon. They often schedule their dives in advance and post them on notice boards in the dive shop so you can see the sites they plan to visit each day. Remember that operators will require proof of

5

Scuba (often written SCUBA) stands for 'self-contained underwater breathing apparatus'. It is essentially a reference to all the gear you need to be able to explore the underwater environment and still be able to breathe. At first, scuba diving looks and sounds all very complicated, so many people find walking into a dive shop a little daunting. There is no need to worry about any of that. Scuba diving is actually quite straightforward and dive-shop staff will be very happy to explain it to you without any pressure or making you feel silly. It is, after all, in their interest for more people in the world to take up diving.

Scuba equipment consists of a cylinder of compressed air (not oxygen, as many believe), usually made of aluminium, that will last the average recreational diver around 45–60 minutes. The cylinder is attached to a sleeveless jacket (called a BCD, or 'buoyancy control device') that has an air-tight bladder inside that can be inflated just like a life jacket. This keeps you afloat when you are on the surface and helps you to maintain a constant depth when you are underwater. Attached to both BCD and cylinder is a regulator. This is a device that usually has four hoses. One is connected to a gauge that tells you how deep you are and how much air you have left; a second is connected to your BCD so you can inflate it by pressing a button; a third is connected to a mouthpiece through which you breathe; and a fourth is connected to a second mouthpiece which acts as a spare. A dive mask covers your eyes and your nose. This means you breathe through your mouth only, just like snorkelling. Around your waist is a belt with weights on it to help you sink. The number of weights you wear is relative to your own body weight. Finally on your feet you wear a pair of fins (you probably call them 'flippers') that propel you through the water. You do not have to be a great swimmer to go scuba diving. Once you are underwater, you become 'weightless' (or 'neutrally buoyant') thanks to the combination of your body mass, weights on your belt and air in your BCD. You simply use your legs and fins to move around.

The dangers? Well yes, there are some, but they are also very easily avoided. The most important rule of scuba diving is 'never hold your breath', because doing so can mean that the changes in pressure and volume that you experience in an underwater environment would cause you to damage your lungs. This can be fatal. To avoid any injury, just keep breathing. If you go too deep for too long you can get decompression sickness, or 'the bends'. To avoid it, don't go too deep for too long! The change of pressure also affects the air spaces in your ears. To 'equalise' the pressure, you must breathe out against a pinched nose as you descend every metre or so. This should clear it.

Scuba instructors are trained to take you on a try-dive or to teach you a certification course. A try-dive consists of a briefing about the basics, familiarisation with your equipment, and some practical exercises. After that you go diving to around 10m accompanied by your scuba instructor. A standard recreational certification consists of theory, pool exercises and sea, or 'open-water' exercises. A certification course usually takes between three and four days and once it is successfully completed, you can dive anywhere in the world.

certification before they take you. PADI, SSI, NAUI and BSAC are recognised everywhere. Rental equipment is available and scuba cylinders are aluminium rather than steel.

**TAKE A BOAT RIDE** A boat ride could either be a sedate sailing cruise or a wild and exciting speedboat trip. Some excursions include lunch, barbecue and snorkelling.

Usually operators will pick you up from the most convenient place for you, often right off Grand Anse Beach.

**Boat tour and charter operators** For a list of operators see page 68. It is also worth checking with your hotel to ascertain whether they recommend or have working relationships with tour operators or water taxis. Some of the best days out can be had with local water-taxi operators or fishermen who will take you around the coast on their small boats, try to catch some fish with you, and then prepare a makeshift barbecue on a beach somewhere.

**GO KAYAKING OR HOBIE CAT SAILING** Several of the dive shops along Grand Anse Beach offer ocean kayak hire as do many of the resort hotels. You can also hire Hobie Cats and do a little sailing. Usually sea conditions are calm as most of the inshore waters are sheltered. Take care on Grand Anse Beach when entering and exiting the water, however, as the surf can kick up from time to time. Be sure to wear buoyancy jackets and protect yourself from the sun with a combination of T-shirt, hat and sunscreen. It is extremely easy to get sunburned when you are out on the water so be sure to cover up. For a list of operators, see pages 72 and 77.

**GO WHALE- AND DOLPHIN-WATCHING** Grenada's waters have whales and dolphins all year round though the best months for spotting them are between December and April. You are never guaranteed sightings on your trip but success rates are high. Look out for humpback whales (*Megaptera novaengliae*), sperm whales (*Physeter macrocephallus*), Bryde's whales (*Balaenoptera brydei*) pilot whales (*Globicephala melaena*) or pods of dolphins including spinner dolphins (*Stenella longirostris*), bottlenose dolphins (*Tursiops truncatus*), Fraser's dolphins (*Lagenodelphis hosei*) and common dolphins (*Delphinus delphis*). **First Impressions** (↘ 473 440 3678) offers a four-hour whale and dolphin trip aboard a purpose-built power catamaran for around US$65 per person. Their office is located at the Allamanda Beach Resort where you can check to see when trips are scheduled. See page 83 for additional contact information.

**PLAY GOLF** The **Grenada Golf Course & Country Club** is located to the east of Grand Anse, in the Belmont area. It is a nine-hole golf course with nice views of both the Caribbean Sea and the Atlantic Ocean. Club rental, instruction and caddy service are available. Green fees are US$16 for nine holes and US$23 for 18 holes. (*For more information* ↘ *473 444 4128.*) If you are staying at one of the resort hotels at Grand Anse you may find they offer complimentary golf club membership and transportation.

## WALKS AND HIKES

Aside from shopping and looking for a nice place to have lunch, there are not many walking or hiking options in this region. Nevertheless, here are a few suggestions for those interested in stretching their legs beyond the short journey from sun lounger to tiki bar:

**A LEISURELY STROLL ALONG GRAND ANSE BEACH** At 3km in length, a walk along the length of Grand Anse Beach is not only a pleasant way to pass an hour or so, it is also great exercise. Dawn and dusk are nice times to walk the beach, when it is cooler and there is less chance of sun damage. With Jenny's Place, the Coconut Beach Restaurant, Garfield's Beach Bar and the Flamboyant Hotel's Beachside Terrace Restaurant all located *en route*, refreshments are never too far away and always a great incentive to keep going. From one end to the other takes around an hour or so, depending on how many times you can resist jumping into the sea for a bathe or stopping for liquid refreshments along the way. Remember, beer and rum punch are no substitutes for water and, though the reverse may also be true, do be sure to hydrate your body properly.

## A LEISURELY WALK THROUGH L'ANSE AUX ÉPINES TO PRICKLY POINT (*Duration: 1½–2hrs there & back; grade 1; guide: not required; site fee: none*) This is a pleasant, leisurely walk through the well-to-do residential area of L'Anse Aux Épines to the wild and rugged headland of Prickly Point. You will pass some very impressive residences and a marina along the way. Places to eat and drink around here include Gary Rhodes's restaurant at the Calabash Hotel. But be sure you call first!

Start your walk at the small playing field that sits between the Calabash Hotel and the Monmot Hotel in L'Anse Aux Épines. After you pass the L'Anse Aux Épines Cottages resort, you will see a small park with beach access. Take a short diversion down to the shore for a view across the bay and perhaps a dip in the water. Follow the road as it snakes slowly up the hill to the large residential houses and holiday villas. After around 15–20 minutes you will see a sign and a road down to the Prickly Bay Marina. At the time of writing, a renovation and new-construction project was still in development, though there were some very nice sailing boats, a pizzeria and a small bar for refreshments. The design of the apartments is meant to reflect the shape of superyachts, complementing the maritime theme of this area. You may decide to call in at Prickly Bay Marina on the way back for a drink, rather than on the outward leg.

Just keep following the road all the way to the end. Depending on your pace, this will take anywhere from 45 minutes to a little over an hour. Pass the lighthouse residence and walk to the end of the point. You will see a dramatic coastline of volcanic rocks and cliffs with a wild sea smashing against them. It is quite beautiful. You will also have views across Prickly Bay to True Blue.

## A CIRCULAR HIKE THROUGH THE MT HARTMAN NATIONAL PARK (*Duration: 2–2½hrs; grade 2; guide: not required; site fee: none*) Note that at the time of writing work had not yet commenced on a proposed resort development in this area. By the time this book goes to print, it may have started and things could have changed a little.

If, in order to reach the starting point of this walk, you are driving on the main road between Point Salines and Grand Anse, look for a roundabout with one road heading to L'Anse Aux Épines and Grenville. Take this road but do not turn right to L'Anse Aux Épines at the next mini-roundabout; continue straight ahead along the east coast road. After just a few minutes, you will see a large white sign for the Mt Hartman National Park on your right. If you are travelling by bus, take an orange number 2 from the terminal in St George's.

This is a very nice hike through the coastal woodland trails of the Mt Hartman National Park. It can be very dry here, with little shade, so please ensure you have plenty of water, sunscreen and a hat when taking on this hike. Aside from the sun, the hike itself is not very demanding. There are one or two slopes, some rather large cows and sometimes horses to negotiate along the way, but for the most part it is even and fairly easy going.

On the road towards Woburn from Grand Anse there is a sign on the right indicating the Mt Hartman National Park. Next to the sign there is a small road that quickly becomes a rough dirt track as it passes some local residences. This is the start of the hike.

Follow the vehicle track downhill as it passes the houses and then leaves them behind in favour of dry woodland. After around five minutes you will reach a crossroads. Follow the main track straight ahead. After around 15–20 minutes the track curves around to the east. There is some open grassland to the right. Keep your eyes and ears open for the elusive Grenada dove! Moving onwards you will see the rocky peak of Mt Hartman on your left.

You will reach a fork in the trail with a vehicle track to the left and another to the right. Take the right-hand track and follow it as it curves back to the south and begins a gradual climb uphill. At the top of the hill the track curves back around to the east. Soon you will have views of Woburn Bay (also called Clarke's Court Bay) and Hog Island on your right. These views improve as you walk down the hill towards the sea.

At the bottom of the hill the track curves around to the south and then forks. Here you have an option. The track to the right is a little diversion. If you follow it for around ten–15 minutes you will reach a T-junction as the track meets the mangroves of the shore. A little walk to the right will bring you to a small beach. There are three wrecks grounded near the shore but also beautiful views across the bay. This is a nice spot for a dip or a picnic. A little further to the right are two more beaches, though somewhat smaller. The track continues into overgrown scrubland so don't take it any further.

Back at the fork in the trail, the left-hand track is our loop trail. You will shortly reach some open grassland where the trail seems to disappear. Simply walk towards the treeline against the shore and keep going left. At the end of the clearing you will pick up a clear track that runs along the water's edge. There are nice views of Clarke's Court Bay, Hog Island and lots of sailing boats at anchor.

Follow the track as it narrows through trees. Watch your footing, as there is a steep drop to the right. After a short distance you reach the Clarke's Court Bay Marina. It is a nice place to pick up a refreshing drink and admire those boats again!

Follow the main road out of the marina. You will come to a concrete road as it climbs uphill. Once at the top, the path becomes a dirt track again. A couple of minutes after reaching the top of the hill, by some small houses, you will see a wide vehicle track emerging from the left. Take this path and walk back into the woodlands of the park. Should you decide to bail out of the hike, you can continue straight ahead where you will emerge at the main road between Grand Anse and Woburn in around 20 minutes or so.

Continuing the loop hike, follow the vehicle track on the left until it forks. Take the wider left-hand spur, not the narrow one on the right, and continue onwards through the woodland. You will soon reach a place you have been before. On your left is a track that joins the path you are now walking on. That track is the one you took on the outward leg taking you towards the shore. So continue straight ahead and you will be back at the beginning of the hike after another 20 minutes or so. Did you spot any doves, or were they hiding from diggers and building contractors?

**A HIKE TO THE POINT OF FORT JEUDY** (*Duration: 2½–3hrs there & back; grade 2; guide: not required; site fee: none*) To reach the starting point of this hike, take the south coast road past L'Anse Aux Épines, Clarke's Court Bay and Woburn. Before you come to Westerhall you should see a sign on the right-hand side for Fort Jeudy (for some odd reason the development is also referred to as the 'New Westerhall'). By bus take an orange number 2 from the terminal in St George's.

As with many places in Grenada, especially in the south, Fort Jeudy is witnessing changing times. In addition to the beautiful new residential houses that have been and continue to be constructed here, there is also the possibility of a hotel development before too long. Hopefully access to the point will never be restricted. It is an area of natural beauty with marvellous views along Grenada's rugged coastline, as well as to the more sheltered sanctuaries of Egmont and Calivigny.

This hike passes through the residential community of Fort Jeudy until it reaches the point itself. You will pass some extremely luxurious residences on this walk. When you reach Fort Jeudy you will meet a wild, rugged and very beautiful volcanic rock coastline. There are great views along the coast, there is a large sea cave and there is a sea arch which you can pass over. The walk to the point is mostly uphill along a road and vehicle track.

On the road south of Marian there is a sign welcoming you to Fort Jeudy. This is the start of the hike. Follow it uphill until you reach a fork. Take the 'Sunset' road on the right. Walk up through the residential community of Fort Jeudy for around 30–45 minutes or so. There are nice views of Egmont Harbour on your right-hand side.

Once you get to the top of the hill and the end of the houses, continue along the paved road to its conclusion where there is a small roundabout by the very last power pole. A narrow trail continues through the grassy headland towards the end of the point where you will reach rocky volcanic cliffs. It is a lovely place with nature untamed. The semi-submerged rocks out to sea are constantly battered by the waves, as are the cliffs below you. Do not walk too close to the edge – it is slippery and the rock crumbles. Along the cliff you will see a trail that runs to the right. Follow it a short distance until you see a huge cave in the cliffside where the waves roll in. This is also a lovely spot. Take a seat on the grass and enjoy.

On the way back, a little way down the paved road from the point, you will come across another very narrow paved road running down to the right. Take a short walk down there to the end of the road. Once at the end, look for a track on the right. Follow it along the grassy headland. There are great views of the sea again. Continue along the track, ignoring a spur to the right that heads down to the cliff. Pass through some overgrown bushes along the narrow trail until it emerges at an enclosed cove. Well, not quite enclosed. Look more carefully and you will see the waves rushing in through a large stone arch in the cliff beneath your feet. It is truly an amazing natural phenomenon. The trail runs over the top of the arch and follows the grass out to the pointed volcanic headland a little further to the east. Keep an eye on the trail you are walking because once at the point, there are several other tracks running off in various directions. You should reach this beautifully wild spot in about 20 minutes.

Walk back the way you came, around the cliff, up the narrow paved road to the top. Turn right and follow the road back down through the community to the main highway.

# 6

# Gouyave, Grand Étang and the West

It would be wrong to state that by heading north from the elegant resorts and marinas of the southwest peninsula you are heading into the 'real' Grenada. All of Grenada is real; it is simply becoming a more diverse and interesting place. The differences are immediately noticeable. As you head into the interior, you begin to climb, your surroundings are ever greener and buildings become fewer. Forest takes over, steep ridges offer breathtaking and quite toe-curling views, traffic noise abates and nature moves in all around you. Along the west coast, the road twists and turns alongside black-sand beaches, up and around tall cliffs, and through small villages where life is played out along the roadside, in snackettes and rum shops, in the fields, and from colourful wooden fishing boats. Welcome to an unpolished, very beautiful, and quintessentially candid Grenada.

This chapter will start by explaining how to get to this region and it will list a selection of places to stay, eat and drink. It will then explore the area in some detail, travelling north along the west coast from St George's up to the small fishing town of Gouyave. From the west coast we journey inland and discover Grenada's forested interior and the wonderful Grand Étang National Park. Finally, there is a selection of things to do as well as detailed descriptions of the walks and hikes that are possible in this part of mainland Grenada.

## GETTING THERE

If you are driving up to Gouyave from the southwest peninsula you need to head for St George's, drive around the Carenage and pass through the Sendall Tunnel. Continue past the bus terminal on Melville Street until you reach the Queen's Park National Stadium. Just before the stadium there is a tiny roundabout with one road heading north along the coast and a second heading east along the river. Gouyave and the west coast are straight on. If you are travelling by bus to Gouyave from St George's, take a yellow number 5.

To get to Annandale and the Grand Étang National Park and visitor centre by car from the south, you need to follow the same road north from St George's until you arrive at the small roundabout junction before the National Stadium. This time turn right along the river. When you reach the next junction, simply follow the signs. It takes about 30 minutes to get to the Grand Étang National Park from St George's. If you are travelling by bus take a white number 6 from the terminal on Melville Street. For Annandale, take a red number 7.

It is possible to get to the Grand Étang National Park by car from Gouyave. This road is quite a challenge, however, and, at the time of writing, particularly poorly signposted once you make it to the centre of the island. Indeed you could quite easily end up in Grenville if you take the wrong turn. I recommend you take the much easier and well signposted route from the National Stadium north of St George's.

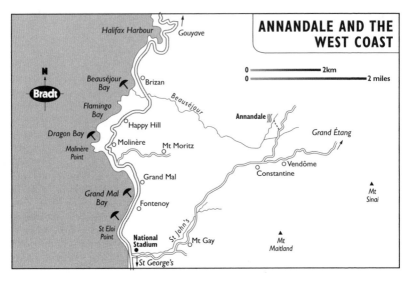

## GETTING AROUND

Buses are a great way to get around this region. They run very frequently along the west coast road as well as through the interior from St George's to the Grand Étang National Park. A hire car will give you that extra flexibility, of course, and if you do not fancy walking from the main road up to the Concord waterfalls, for example, then a hire car is a must as no public buses make this trip. Public buses also do not usually take the route inland from Gouyave via Belvidere to the Grand Étang National Park.

 ## WHERE TO STAY

Once you leave the southwest peninsula, accommodation options are much fewer. Nevertheless there are still some great places to stay.

### MEDIUM-RANGE HOTELS AND GUESTHOUSES

🏠 **Blue Bay Lodge** (10 rooms) Mt Nesbit, Gouyave;
☎ 473 437 0997; e info@bluebaylodge.net;
www.bluebaylodge.net. A perfect location for exploring the west coast, the waterfalls & forested interior of the Grand Étang & Mt St Catherine national parks, & also for enjoying Gouyave's famous Fish Friday. Spacious rooms, nicely furnished in local woods with AC, TV & en-suite bathrooms, enjoy daily maid service & outside terrace. There is a pool, garden, restaurant & bar. Regular weekly events are scheduled, including BBQ & steel pan. Expect a warm & friendly welcome from owner Lisette who will organise tours & excursions for

you & may even show you around some local sites herself. Blue Bay is located in the small community of Mt Nesbit, just a few mins south of Gouyave. B&B basis: $; FB basis: $$
🏠 **Sunset View Restaurant & Beach House** (4 rooms) Grand Mal; ☎ 473 440 5758;
e tropicanainn@spiceisle.com; www.tropicanainn/sunsetview.htm. Partner guesthouse to the Tropicana Inn on the Lagoon in St George's. Rooms have en-suite bathroom, AC, TV & private patio with sea views. Popular bar & restaurant serves local & international cuisine either outside on the deck or in the dining room. $

### MID-RANGE SELF-CATERING APARTMENTS, COTTAGES AND VILLAS

🏠 **Mango Bay Cottages** Woodford Estate;
☎/f 473 444 3829;

e info@mangobaygrenada.com;
www.mangobaygrenada.com. Located near to Black

130

Bay & Concord, very attractive, nicely furnished SC cottages enjoying tropical gardens & sea views.

Cottages have private bathroom, kitchen, ceiling fans & veranda. $$

## BUDGET SELF-CATERING APARTMENTS, COTTAGES AND VILLAS

🏠 **Willie's Court Apartments** St Benoit St, Gouyave; ☎ 473 437 0235. SC accommodation in the heart of Gouyave. Studio apts have 1 bedroom, private bathroom, living area, AC, fans, fully equipped kitchen. $

# ✕ WHERE TO EAT AND DRINK

## CARIBBEAN AND INTERNATIONAL

✕ **Blue Bay Lodge** Mt Nesbit, Gouyave; ☎ 473 437 0997. Authentic, high-quality Grenadian cuisine by reservation. BBQ & live steel pan on Sun nights. $–$$

✕ **Sunset View Restaurant & Beach House** Grand Mal; ☎ 473 440 5758. Popular waterside restaurant & bar with indoor & alfresco dining. Caribbean & international dishes. BBQ on Fri & Sat nights. $–$$

✕ **Kelly's Hot Spot** Lower Depradine St, Gouyave; ☎ 473 444 8322. Popular local eatery with bar. $

✕ **Licks & Bytes** Lower Depradine St, Gouyave. Local dishes & high-speed internet café. $

✕ **LIL Continental Restaurant** Upper Depradine St, L'Anse, Gouyave. Local food & drink. $

✕ **Mo's Delight Restaurant & Mini Bar** Upper Depradine St, L'Anse, Gouyave. Colourfully decorated eatery serving a selection of local food & drink. $

✕ **Paul's Catering & Mini Restaurant** Upper Depradine St, L'Anse, Gouyave; ☎ 473 444 9204. Serving a selection of local & international dishes. $

✕ **Restaurant & Bar** St Peter's St, Gouyave; ☎ 473 444 8526. Imaginatively named eatery serving rotis & a variety of other local cuisine. $

✕ **Spiceisle Restaurant & Bar** Lower Depradine St, Gouyave. Good selection of local food & drink. $

✕ **Step In Delight** Central Depradine St, Gouyave; ☎ 473 437 1270. Local eatery serving a selection of traditional Grenadian & international dishes. $

🍨 **Strictly Local** Cnr St Peter's St & St Dominic St, Gouyave. Delicious homemade ice cream. $

🍨 **Wilson's Snackette** Upper Depradine St, L'Anse, Gouyave. Colourful snackette & roadside bar. $

## SEAFOOD

Fish Friday in Gouyave! See page 141. $–$$

## BARS AND NIGHTLIFE

Look out for the blackboards that hang on poles in the village. They are used to publicise local events, live music and entertainment.

☆ **Caribbean Heights** (known locally as the 'White House') Central Depradine St, Gouyave. Popular on Fri nights.

🍸 **Mama Lee Easy Going Back In Time Refreshment House** St Dominic St, Gouyave. Local bar with a nice atmosphere.

🍸 **Seabreeze Bar** Beachfront, L'Anse, Gouyave. Popular karaoke & drinking venue, especially after Fish Friday.

## EXPLORING THE WEST COAST FROM ST GEORGE'S TO GOUYAVE

Along the coast from St George's to **Molinère** is the sweeping **Grand Mal Bay** with its petroleum storage tanks and oil depot. The area has a very urban and industrial feel, particularly with the outskirts of St George's just a short hop away around St Eloi Point.

**Mt Moritz** is a village located on a hill to the east of Molinère. Today it is an ordinary Grenadian village but it started out as a community of poor white farm labourers who came from Barbados in the latter half of the 19th century. Having

6

Commonly referred to as the Molinère Marine Park or sometimes the Grenada Marine Park or Marine Reserve, this area of protected seascape is found on the west coast between Molinère Point and Flamingo Bay, just 5km north of the capital St George's, or just 15–20 minutes by boat from Grand Anse Beach. This protected area of underwater habitat is home to a variety of hard and soft corals, sea fans and sponges. There is an abundance of colourful schooling reef fish as well as seahorses, grouper, moray eels, turtles and occasional manta and eagle rays. Dive sites that fall within this protected area include Flamingo Bay (6–27m), Happy Valley (6–27m), Dragon Bay (8–28m) and Molinère Reef (18–40m). The **Underwater Sculpture Gallery** is located on the northern edge of Molinère Reef (see page 139). Management of the Molinère Protected Seascape falls under the remit of the Grenada Fisheries though dive and tour operators are trying to collaborate to take a more proactive approach. At the time of writing the area has no site fee nor proper moorings and is being subjected to occasional damage by boats dropping anchors on or around the reef system.

very little need for business or social interaction with anyone outside the area, it essentially became a closed community and stayed that way for almost 100 years. It was not until the 1970s and '80s that things really changed in Mt Moritz with many of its residents migrating overseas and people from surrounding villages beginning to move into the area. The few descendants of those original settlers still living there are affectionately known as Mt Moritz Bajans.

**Beauséjour Bay** is located between **Brizan** and **Happy Hill**. It is a large sandy bay and an outlet for the Beauséjour River that finds its source in the mountainous interior of the Grand Étang National Park, and runs to the sea via the Annandale Waterfall. The area was settled by the French in the mid 17th century and, due to its location at the mouth of one of the island's largest rivers, became a 'beautiful place' for people to live outside of Port Louis (St George's). Inland from the bay is the former Beauséjour Estate, once a 280ha sugar estate that was home to an ice factory in the mid 1900s. Beauséjour was the site of military conflict during the US intervention in 1983.

Just before you reach Beauséjour Bay you pass **Flamingo Bay**, **Dragon Bay** and **Molinère Point**. This area forms part of the **Molinère Protected Seascape** and is very popular with scuba divers and snorkellers thanks to its shallow reef formations that provide a home to lots of colourful fish, hard and soft corals, gorgonians and other interesting marine creatures. The very unique **Underwater Sculpture Gallery** is located just off Molinère Point (see page 139).

**Halifax Harbour** is a pretty bay spoiled by the encroachment of a large and very pungent landfill site on the nearby Perseverance Estate. A tranquil anchorage surrounded by greenery and a narrow stretch of sand, Halifax Harbour is very picturesque indeed, especially with its very own shipwreck grounded on the southern bank. The location of the landfill site has been the subject of controversy as not only does it threaten this natural haven, it is also positioned near to one of the island's endangered Grenada dove habitats. A little to the north of Halifax Harbour are the ruins of the former Woodford Estate, once an Amerindian settlement and then later a thriving sugar estate. In 1778, a coastal battery was constructed here to protect the entrance of Halifax Harbour (then known as Petit Harve).

**Grand Roy** is one of the largest villages between St George's and Gouyave. It sits along each side of the Grand Roy River and is a colourful place with a lively

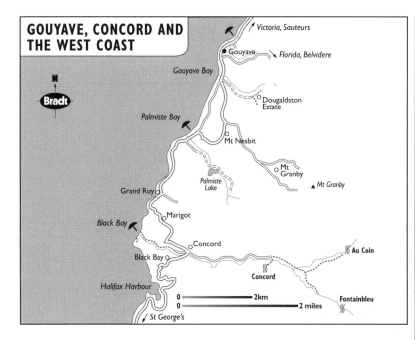

Victoria, Sauteurs

Gouyave

Florida, Belvidere

Gouyave Bay

Dougaldston Estate

Palmiste Bay

Mt Nesbit

Mt Granby

Palmiste Lake

Mt Granby

Grand Roy

Marigot

Black Bay

Concord

Au Coin

Black Bay

Concord

Halifax Harbour

0          2km
0                    2 miles

Fontainbleu

St George's

atmosphere and friendly people. **Black Bay** is located a short distance to the south of Grand Roy and is perched on the hillside of the 37ha Black Bay Estate, an agricultural area that was once the site of a sugar plantation and mill. The estate was purchased in 2006 and is the subject of an investment project which aims to develop an organic farm and luxury resort there. The area still contains the ruins of a waterwheel, machine works and former estate buildings. The bay is quite sheltered and the beach is rich black sand. On Black Bay Point, a small rocky outcrop to the south of the beach is a natural cave which is known locally as **Trou Mais** where, it is believed, Amerindian settlers may once have stored corn and other agricultural produce. (See *Hike to Black Bay*, page 149.)

The road inland from Black Bay runs through the village of **Concord** and along a river valley directly to the first of three waterfalls where it comes to an end. The valley is beautiful, lush and green. Small farms (or 'gardens' as they are referred to locally) mingle with occasional cocoa and nutmeg trees that grow on the hillsides above the sparkling river below. (See *Hike to the Concord Falls*, page 146.)

South of **Mt Nesbit**, a small residential community that was once a fortification during the Fédon Rebellion, the coastal road passes alongside **Palmiste Bay** where there is a narrow sandy beach suitable for picnics and bathing. Running inland from the coast is a rough, narrow road that climbs up the hillside towards **Palmiste Lake**, also known locally as Palmiste Dig. Originally a manmade lake that was created by damming the Great Palmiste River to provide water power to the former Palmiste Estate, it is now a very natural and peaceful sanctuary for wildfowl. (See *Hike to Palmiste Lake*, page 148.)

Located to the north of Mt Nesbit is the community of **Mt Granby**. This village sits at the top end of a valley that leads to the summit of a 680m mountain ridge bearing the same name. Whilst the village itself is a fairly ordinary residential community of board and block houses and the road up to it simply ends at small hillside farms, the valley in which it sits is really very beautiful indeed. Ascending the long narrow road up to the village, you pass through extraordinarily lush greenery covering the steep slopes and ridges of the surrounding hillside. Among the villagers who have lived here for most of their lives there is talk of an old track that runs up and over the ridge across to the settlement of Belvidere, in the shadows of Fédon's Camp. Watch this space.

Just before you arrive in Gouyave you will come to the **Dougaldston Estate** which was established in the mid 18th century and is one of Grenada's oldest working estates. Though originally it was around 300ha in size, over the years it has gradually been getting smaller and smaller as lots are sold off for the construction of new domestic residences. It started out as a sugar estate, and the ruins of the original waterwheel and machine works can still be seen below the Great House which stands at the top of the hill behind. Copper pots lie on the ground all around and the place has a distinct feel of abandonment and decline. Following sugar production, the estate moved into spices, and in particular nutmeg and cocoa. Today the *boucan* still operates, processing cocoa beans and drying them in retractable wooden trays. Visitors may also see local women removing mace from nutmeg crops, ready for processing at the 'Pool' in Gouyave. (See *Visit The Dougaldston Estate*, page 141.)

The small fishing town of **Gouyave** (pronounced *gwav*) is located on the northwest coast of Grenada in the parish of St John, some 20km from the island's capital, St George's. Though the area was no doubt inhabited by early Amerindians, the settlement is thought to have been established in the 1730s by the French who named it Bourg de L'Anse Gouyave. In 1763, when Grenada was under British rule, the village was renamed Charlotte Town, after the wife of reigning monarch King George III. Though both names became interchangeable for many years afterwards, Grenadians now commonly refer to the town as Gouyave and this is how it appears on maps. 'Anse', or L'Anse, is an old French Creole word meaning 'bay'. Anglicised versions of the word are also written as 'L'Ance' or sometimes simply 'Lance'. The northern half of Gouyave is still referred to by locals as the L'Anse (or Lance).

The people of Gouyave and the surrounding parish of St John have traditionally

## FISHERMAN'S BIRTHDAY

The Roman Catholic feast of St Peter is celebrated on 29 June each year. This feast day is very significant to the people of Gouyave and is therefore a time of great celebration. St Peter is the Roman Catholic patron saint of fishermen and, of course, Gouyave is one of the largest fishing communities on the island. In addition to this, Gouyave is also the location of the Diocese of St Peter in Grenada.

On Fisherman's Birthday, Gouyave's villagers, especially those directly associated with fishing, attend a morning church service. Afterwards, the congregation assembles by the numerous colourfully painted fishing boats that are drawn up along the shoreline. Once the priest has completed the formalities of blessing the fishermen's boats and fishing nets, the fun begins. There are fishing-boat races, displays of fish, speeches by visiting dignitaries, a variety of entertainment from comedians and singers, and, naturally, lots of dancing, eating and drinking. The celebrations also include award ceremonies for best catch and fisherman of the year. The event is very entertaining and has survived Hurricane Ivan to complement Fish Friday in cementing Gouyave's position as a premier fishing village. These community events not only promote the village, they help to provide an essential source of income for local people. They are also a great way to let your hair down and just have fun.

> ## CONKIE
>
> Conkie is a traditional food usually made from cornmeal flour, but also sometimes with plantain, pumpkin, cassava or sweet potato. The cornmeal flour is sweetened with sugar, raisins and coconut milk, and then spices are added before the mixture is wrapped in a freshly cut banana leaf. The parcel is then steamed until it is cooked. It is a delicious dish that finds its origins in west Africa. For a great conkie, pay a visit to Mr Moralis Banfield who lives on St Dominic Street in Gouyave (look out for the large chest freezer outside his house – you can't miss it). His homemade conkie is the best.

eked a living from the sea and from the land. This is still the case, though the devastating effects of Hurricane Ivan in 2004 threw the island's agricultural economy into serious decline, a tragic moment in history that is still sadly very evident today. One of the island's three major nutmeg-processing stations is located in Gouyave, the other two being in Grenville and Victoria. The station in Gouyave, commonly referred to as the **Gouyave Nutmeg Pool**, or sometimes simply 'the pool', is the only one of the three that still processes nutmeg and mace for domestic and overseas consumption. (See *Visit the Gouyave Nutmeg Processing Station*, page 142.)

Gouyave's main thoroughfare is named after Jean de Pradines, a French planter of the 1700s. On the southern half of the town the road is called Lower Depradine Street, in the centre of the town it is Central Depradine Street, and in the north of the town, the area known as the L'Anse, the road becomes Upper Depradine Street. It is along this street that the majority of shops, eateries and bars are to be found. Also located on this thoroughfare is the police station, the fire station, the post office, bank and ATM, and the Gouyave Nutmeg Pool. Shops consist primarily of convenience stores, boutiques, salons and hardware stores. The Gouyave fisheries is located on Upper Depradine Street in the L'Anse area.

The main junction in Gouyave is with St Peter's Street which runs from the town into the interior and all the way across to Grenville. St Peter's Street is where you will find St John's Anglican Church (St John the Divine) and the St Rose Modern Secondary School. The church was built in 1846, with some later additions, and was the first permanent Anglican chapel in the parish of St John. Adjoining St Peter's Street is St Dominic Street where you will find both the old and the new Roman Catholic churches. Construction of the original church was started in 1829 on the site of a previous chapel, but was not completed until many years later. Built in the so-called Caribbean Gothic revival style, its octagonal open metal bell tower is unique in Grenada. The church was replaced by a newer, larger one in 1902 and today it stands abandoned and is sadly in a state of ruin. In a side street off St Dominic Street you will find market vendors selling local produce. Together with St Dominic Street, this side street is one of the locations for Gouyave's weekly **Fish Friday**, a popular and celebrated event created, operated and managed by people from the local community. On Friday nights these streets are crammed with stalls selling a wide variety of fresh fish dishes as well as with visitors and locals out to sample the fare and have a nice time. Also on St Dominic Street you will see the new St Peter's Catholic Parish Church, which is a very pretty stone church with high wooden ceilings and pews, large arched windows and blue stained glass projecting an interesting glow onto the whitewashed walls.

The northern end of St Dominic Street emerges on the main thoroughfare of Central Depradine Street. To the north is a colourfully painted bridge over the Little River and into Upper Depradine Street, or the L'Anse. Beyond the bars and

6

Julien Fédon was born the son of Pierre Fédon, a French jeweller who travelled from Bordeaux, France, in 1749 to the Caribbean island of Martinique. His mother was a freed black slave residing in Martinique. The family emigrated to Grenada in the 1750s and, in 1780, Julien married Marie Rose Cavelan who was a 'free coloured', or *mulatto* woman. In 1791, they purchased the 182ha Belvidere Estate in today's parish of St John. The estate had a labour force of around 100 slaves.

When they arrived in Grenada in the 1750s the island was under French rule. In 1763, Grenada was ceded to Britain under the Treaty of Paris, but was recaptured by the French in 1779. In 1783, the island was once again ceded to Britain, this time under the Treaty of Versailles. It was during the next ten years or so that a number of factors influenced the life of Julien Fédon for good. The first factor was the repressive regime of British colonial rule following the island's recapture after the Treaty of Versailles. Despite belonging to the island's largest population group, 'free blacks' and 'free coloureds', many of whom, including Fédon, had become wealthy estate owners, the British denied them the rights, privileges and political freedoms enjoyed by white Protestants. The second most influencing factor on Julien Fédon was the French Revolution of 1789. It proved to be both his inspiration as well as his downfall.

Encouraged by the republican Governor of Martinique, Victor Hugues, Julien Fédon was appointed commandant-general of the French republican forces in Grenada. Inspired by the republican cry of 'liberté, égalité, fraternité', during the early hours of 3 March 1795, Fédon, together with a band of around 100 former slaves and 'free coloureds', led a raid on the settlement of Grenville. They burned and plundered houses, dragged the British inhabitants out into the streets and executed them. At roughly the same time as the attack on Grenville, another detachment of rebels attacked Gouyave. On their return to the mountains, they were joined by large numbers of slaves who had abandoned plantations in the area as well as a third detachment of insurrectionists who had advanced south from Sauteurs. By the following day, almost every Frenchman and a large number of slaves and 'free coloureds' had joined Julien Fédon at his headquarters in Belvidere. The rebellion had begun.

Over the next year, Julien Fédon led the uprising from his camp fortifications in Belvidere. The fighting was widespread and the rebellion of slaves, the burning and

buildings on the western side of the L'Anse is the bay itself. Here you will discover a beach full of colourful fishing boats, people mending nets and making general preparations for the next outing. Together with Gouyave Bay to the south of the village, it is quite common to see fishermen working together along the shore to pull in their seine nets, accompanied by onlookers with bags, hoping to buy supper.

## FROM THE WEST COAST INTO THE INTERIOR

The road from the National Stadium on the northern outskirts of St George's goes to the Grand Étang National Park. It passes through a number of communities before reaching a fork between the villages of **Constantine** and **Vendôme**. The narrow road to the left hugs the side of a very steep cliff before reaching the **Annandale Waterfall**. Because of its accessibility and proximity to the southwest peninsula, this short but pretty waterfall is extremely popular with visitors. It has a deep pool and a very pretty tropical garden. (See *Annandale Waterfall*, page 140.)

Taking the right-hand fork at the Annandale junction leads you up into the heights of the Grand Étang Forest Reserve and Grand Étang National Park. You will notice the temperature becomes a little cooler and the tall banks along the sides plundering of estates and the killing or capture of British planters took place throughout Grenada. Fédon based his camp fortifications high in the mountains above his estate. His lower camp, known as Camp de la liberté, was at the foot of the Montagne du Vauclin (now known as Morne Fédon) and a series of upper fortifications ran from the summit of this mountain across the ridge to Mt Qua Qua. His upper camp also later became known as Camp de la mort, due to the bloody fighting and executions that took place there throughout and towards the end of the campaign.

On 8 April 1796, Fédon lost a brother in a failed and bloody attack on his camp by the British. In revenge he ordered the execution of 48 prisoners at his upper camp, including former governor Ninian Home. Despite the fact that his supporters were running the beleaguered British quite ragged the length and breadth of the island, Fédon failed to make a successful full-scale attack on St George's and historians agree that it is primarily this failure that ultimately led to his defeat. Too many times he resisted the opportunity to attack and allowed the British to regroup and re-strengthen. This failing also caused him to lose the faith and support of his republican commanders in Martinique and Guadeloupe.

On 9 June 1796, a full-scale offensive was launched by the British upon Fédon's encampments at Belvidere. Fédon's headquarters at Camp de la liberté were successfully taken, forcing Fédon and his remaining men to retreat to the heights of the mountain. Next came an attack on the high lookout called Vigie. Fédon's men suffered huge losses during this attack, forcing those who survived to cross the mountainous ridge to his last camp. Realising that they had lost, Fédon and some of his men threw themselves down the steep mountainsides. Those who didn't were either captured or killed.

No-one knows quite what happened to Julien Fédon as his body was never recovered. The most accepted version of events is that somehow he survived his escape from the steep mountain slopes but was drowned in an attempt to sail by small boat to the salvation of his brother in Trinidad. The rebellion lasted 15 months during which time it is estimated that machine works and buildings were destroyed on around 100 estates across the island. Crops for the years 1794 to 1796 were all lost.

of the road are covered with verdant green moss and ferns. As it nears its highest point, the road becomes steep with several hairpin bends. If you are driving, take it slowly and use your horn. Once at the peak, the road descends slightly as it follows the ridge and soon arrives at the national park visitor centre. From here there is access to the Grand Étang Lake plus a number of forest and mountain hikes. (See page 143 for details of hikes in the Grand Étang National Park.) The road beyond the lake descends steeply through St Margaret, Adelphi, and on towards Grenville and the east coast.

**Florida**, **Clozier** and **Belvidere** are rural farming hamlets on or near the inland road that runs from St Peter's Street in Gouyave, along the northern edge of the Grand Étang National Park and on to Grenville. These areas were significant nutmeg producers prior to Hurricane Ivan in 2004 as their high elevation and cool temperatures were ideal for the nutmeg tree to thrive. Nutmegs continue to grow here, along with other crops such as cocoa, peas and beans, but their numbers are much fewer than they used to be and the people of these rural farmlands have to work very hard to make ends meet. From Florida the road climbs to Plaisance Estate (also known as Mt Pleasant), which used to be a major agricultural centre before the storm. The estate continues to operate though it is sadly a faint shadow of its former self. This area is very pretty. It is lush and green, and the narrow and winding country roads are lined with nutmeg trees.

Belvidere is the location of the former Belvidere Estate, once owned by Julien Fédon, leader of the insurrection of 1795. The estate produced coffee, cocoa and spice and became very prominent as one of the island's best producers during the late 1800s. During the early 1900s the estate transitioned to nutmeg cultivation and became one of the largest and most successful nutmeg-producing estates in the world. Recently, as with many once thriving agricultural estates in Grenada, Belvidere suffered at the hands of Hurricane Ivan and the majority of the nutmeg crop was lost to the storm. Local people still cultivate nutmegs, cocoa, vegetables, ground provisions and fruit crops.

**THE GRAND ÉTANG NATIONAL PARK** The Grand Étang National Park was established in 1992. It is a 1,000ha swathe of mountainous forest in the centre of the island and to the northwest of the 1,540ha Grand Étang Forest Reserve that was created as far back as 1906. The name 'Grand Étang' is derived from the French meaning 'large lake', in reference to the 12ha crater lake which sits at an elevation of 530m at the southeastern boundary of the national park. Also located within the Grand Étang National Park are the summits of Mt Qua Qua, Mt Granby and Morne Fédon (also commonly known as Fédon's Camp or simply Fédon). Waterfalls found within the park include the three that comprise the Concord Falls – Concord, Au Coin and Fontainbleu. Located on the southwestern perimeter of the park is the frequently visited Annandale Waterfall. No doubt there are other natural sites waiting to be discovered and named.

The mountainous ridges of the national park are steep and narrow. They are home to a variety of trees including gommier (*Dacryodes excelsa*), a tall gum tree that Amerindians used for making their canoes; mahogany (*Swietenia mahogani*); teak (*Tectonia grandis*); balata (*Manilikara bidentata*); and maruba (*Simaruba amara*), to name just a few. Prior to Hurricane Ivan in 2004, the tall trees of the Grand Étang National Park and the Grand Étang Forest Reserve provided a high forest canopy that in turn created a wet rainforest habitat on these elevated slopes and ridges. Unfortunately the high winds of the hurricane had a devastating effect upon the rainforest habitat, particularly on the windward-facing slopes that were exposed to the full force of the storm. The taller trees were either uprooted or cropped by the wind and the result is that there is no longer a high canopy creating wet rainforest conditions. This in turn means that many of the plants, flowers and creatures which you would normally expect to find in Grenada's rainforest habitat are no longer as prevalent as they once were; in fact some are now quite scarce. Despite the storm, the forest is growing and recovering though it will clearly take a few years.

The forests of Grand Étang are also home to the **mona monkey** (*Cercopithecus mona*) which was probably introduced to the island from Africa during the years of the slave trade. The monkeys used to be a popular visitor attraction though sightings have become fewer in the wake of two hurricanes. Of particular concern is the destruction of the monkeys' habitat and the fact that there appears to be little enforcement of the law ensuring their protection from hunters within the national park's boundaries. Hopefully something will be done about this before the mona monkey goes the way of the agouti (*Dasyprocta leporina*) and is hunted out of existence in Grenada altogether.

Nevertheless, despite natural disaster and a lack of priority on conservation issues, the Grand Étang National Park is still very beautiful and the high mountain ridges offer unsurpassed panoramic views of the island. At the Grand Étang crater lake, there is a visitor centre with a collection of interesting and informative

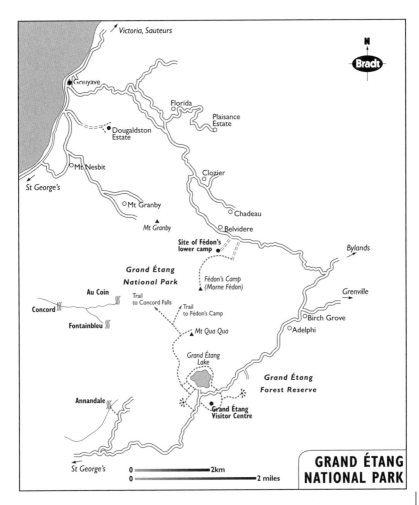

presentations about the geological formation of Grenada's mountainous interior, and about the types of vegetation, habitats and species of wildlife visitors may be fortunate to encounter. Entry to the Grand Étang National Park at the time of writing is US$2 per person and is paid at a booth near the visitor centre and entrance to the lake itself. There are a number of hikes throughout the park though some of the more inaccessible and challenging ones have yet to be properly cleared and repaired following the storms. Some of these trails require local knowledge as well as sharp cutting tools to clear the route. More accessible trails include those to the Concord waterfalls, around the Grand Étang Lake and up to the summit of Mt Qua Qua. Many of the island's tour operators offer excursions and guided hikes to these sites.

## WHAT TO DO

**DISCOVER THE UNDERWATER SCULPTURE GALLERY AT MOLINÈRE** (*www.underwater sculpture.com; scuba-diving & snorkelling tour operators (see page 77) offer excursions here, usually on scheduled days; from US$90 for a 2-tank boat dive or US$30 for a snorkelling trip*)

The park is the unique creation of UK sculptor Jason de Caires Taylor whose works explore the relationship between art and the environment. Over time we are able to observe the natural ecological processes that take place as his sculptures become artificial reefs, therefore transitioning from pieces of art to become more at one with nature. Jason's sculptures are located in fairly shallow, clear waters enabling them to be viewed by scuba divers, snorkellers and people on clear-bottomed boats. The visibility around the Molinère reef system is usually good and surface conditions calm.

*Vicissitudes* is a circle of figures, all holding hands, located at a depth of 5m. The figures are life-size casts of children from different ethnic backgrounds. *Vicissitudes* is a reflection of how children change as a result of and by adapting to their environment. Each of the sculptures physically changes over time according to sea and weather conditions and through the natural growth of corals. The *Un-Still Life*, at a depth of 8m, is a table with cement objects on top, including a vase, a bowl and some fruit. It is a classic still-life image, yet also 'un-still' because it is constantly changing with its environment, especially coral growth. The *Lost Correspondent* is a man sitting at a desk in front of a typewriter. Scattered over the desk are newspaper clippings of articles and news about the political events of Grenada in the 1970s and '80s. *Grace Reef* at a depth of 4m comprises 16 figures of a Grenadian woman, all scattered over a wide area of sand. Each of the figures is positioned facing a different direction, and from time to time some of them become partially, or even completely covered depending on the strength and direction of tide and current. *Sienna* is a character from a story called *A Different Ocean* by Jacob Ross. It is the tale of a young girl who was a gifted free diver and who became exploited in a search for lost treasure. The metal structure of this sculpture allows nutrient-rich water to pass through Sienna providing the ideal habitat for filter feeders to develop and give the figure physical substance over time. *La Diablesse*, or she-devil, lies in deeper water. With her wide-brimmed hat she is a reflection of a Grenadian folklore that finds its roots in Africa. Hidden within the reef, she offers a surprising and awe-inspiring encounter. Other artworks within the sculpture park include *TamCC Project* in 2m, *The Fall From Grace* in 7m and *Arawak Head* in 5m.

## VISIT THE ANNANDALE WATERFALL AND EXPLORE THE TROPICAL GARDENS The
Annandale Waterfall is probably the most frequently visited of all the islands' falls and cascades. This is because it is one of the most accessible and is located just 16km from the capital, St George's. Named after the surrounding estate, this waterfall is around 10m high with a fairly deep pool. It sits on the Beauséjour River and is set against a backdrop of forest and very colourful tropical gardens.

Because it is so frequently visited, it has lost just a little of its natural charm, though it is still very pretty. Access is via a paved footpath leading to a viewing platform. There are plenty of vendors, there is a nearby bar for refreshments, and there are people offering photographs of themselves jumping from the waterfall for a few dollars. Despite a few 'touristy' downsides, the Annandale Waterfall is an accessible site that offers visitors a small taste of the island's natural attractions. It also has a very pretty tropical garden with a well-defined footpath that takes you to the top of the waterfall and then back down to the exit. It is a really nice walk, especially for those who are interested in flowers and plants. Keep a lookout for the resident mona monkey.

*En route* to the waterfall, just before the entrance, and on the opposite side of the road, is a second waterfall which, in the wet season, is often fuller and higher than the main attraction (but don't tell anyone I said that). There is a rough track to this cascading fall from the main road. When visiting the Annandale Waterfall, visitors should bear in mind that it will be very busy during the cruise-ship season so a good time to go is later in the afternoon when the crowds and tour buses have dispersed.

The road to Annandale is north of the capital, St George's. From the southwest, pass around the Carenage and the Sendall Tunnel and turn right along River Road just before the National Stadium. Follow the road to a signposted junction. Tempe is to the right, Grand Étang and Annandale to the left. Continue along this road until you reach Constantine (look out for the Amba Kaila store on your right) and you should come to a fork in the road. At the time of writing there is no signpost here. The road to the right goes to Grand Étang , the fork to the left to Annandale. Follow the narrow road along the cliff for around five to ten minutes until you come to the signposted waterfall. If you are travelling by bus from the terminal in St George's, you need to take a red number 7 that is marked Annandale and Willis.

**ENJOY FISH FRIDAY AT GOUYAVE** Established after Hurricane Ivan in 2004, the Gouyave Fish Friday event is proving to be a huge success. Set up as a local community project with the aim of cementing the identity of Gouyave as a fishing village as well as generating income for the people living in the parish of St John, Fish Friday is now a regular on the Grenada calendar of events. It attracts locals as well as visitors, with many hotels and tour operators running regular Friday night excursions to the town. The atmosphere is lively and extremely friendly, and there is usually live music in the form of steel pan or drumming to accompany your evening out.

Located along a couple of narrow streets in the heart of Gouyave, Fish Friday is essentially two long lines of stalls cooking and selling a wide variety of tasty and fresh seafood dishes. Here you can sample fried, steamed and sauté fish, grilled lobster, fish cakes, fish kebabs, titiri, shrimp and lambie. The smell of cooking, the sizzling of the frying pans, the smoke from the barbecues, the live music and the banter, all combine to generate a fun and fascinating evening. Stroll along the stalls and sample a little of everything. There is always plenty of liquid refreshment to accompany your fish dishes, including beers, local juices and, of course, a wide selection of Grenadian rum.

Fish Friday starts at around 19.00 and runs until around midnight. Often people will move on to other venues including the 'White House' (Caribbean Heights) on Central Depradine Street, and the Seabreeze Bar on the beachfront in the L'Anse.

A number of tour operators run bus excursions to Fish Friday (see page 141). Your hotel may also organise trips for its guests.

**VISIT THE DOUGALDSTON ESTATE** The Dougaldston Estate is one of the oldest functioning estates in the Caribbean. It was established as a sugar estate in the 1700s and continued operating into the 1800s. Though some of the estate has been sold off as residential and agricultural lots, it once ran to around 300ha in total area and produced nutmeg, spices, cocoa and banana. Today most of the original estate buildings and machine works are neglected and sadly lie in ruins. However, a historic, functioning cocoa processing station remains, making the estate well worth a visit. It also boasts the introduction of a number of innovations such as a cocoa bean polisher and a nutmeg oil distillery. Today, the estate still claims to have the last remaining, and still working, cocoa steam drier in Grenada.

Dougaldston Estate is located south of Gouyave along the banks of the Little River. From Gouyave, go south along the coast and turn left over the bridge along the riverbank. At the junction, instead of following the main road to the right, continue straight on along the river beside some banana plants. The road becomes rough and soon reaches the remains of a stone wall marking the entrance to the estate. The path to the left goes to the still functioning cocoa station and the path straight on leads uphill to the ruins of the former estate buildings. These ruins are

6

interesting in terms of their historical context and also worth exploring. They include a stone aqueduct that carried water to the wheel that drove the machinery, the Great House at the summit of the hill, and large copper pots that would have been used as part of the cane juice filtering process as well as for cooking by the estate's enslaved workforce.

The functioning cocoa station is fascinating. The main wooden building, known as the **boucan**, has displays of cocoa and spices. Beneath the *boucan* are large cocoa drying trays that are pushed out manually along iron rails to enable the cocoa to dry naturally in the sun. When the sun goes in or when it rains, the trays are pushed back under the shelter of the building. When the station is processing more cocoa than the trays can handle, there is a movable roof operating along a second set of rails to cover cocoa that is drying on the ground. Near to the *boucan* you can also see the wooden fermentation bins that are used for the first stage of the cocoa process (see page 14 for more information on how cocoa is processed). Inside the *boucan* there are interesting displays of cocoa and other spices produced in Grenada.

At the time of writing, access to the estate is free and you can go there every day. The *boucan* is a place of work as well as one of the island's heritage attractions (⊕ *Mon–Fri & Sat mornings*).

## VISIT THE GOUYAVE NUTMEG PROCESSING STATION (⊕ *08.00–16.00 Mon–Fri; 20min tours US$1 or EC$2.70 pp*) The nutmeg processing station at Gouyave, referred to by local people as 'the pool', is located in the centre of the village on the coastal side of the road, just south of the bridge to L'Anse. Owned by the Grenada Co-operative Nutmeg Association, it is the largest of three nutmeg processing stations in Grenada. It was constructed in 1947 on the site of a former coastal battery that was built by the French in the 1700s to protect this west coast settlement from attack and invasion.

The co-operative was formed in 1952 with the aim of removing the monopoly of nutmeg processing, sales and export from the plantation owners. Farmers who are members of the co-operative agree to sell their produce exclusively through the co-operative. In its heyday Gouyave would process up to 2,700 tonnes of nutmegs for export. The impact of Hurricane Ivan in 2004 devastated the industry, however, and today Gouyave is the only station on the island that continues to process nutmegs for domestic consumption and export. Despite this serious setback, the Gouyave station is a fascinating place, and a visit there provides visitors with an insight into an important aspect of Grenada's agricultural past and its stark economic present. Wooden machine works and huge curing trays, together with men and women engaged in manual sorting, grading and packaging activities, combine to paint a fascinating picture of the island's cultural heritage as well as provide an educational insight into the processing of nutmeg and mace.

The nutmeg station has a gift shop where you can buy nutmegs, spices and a variety of local products and crafts. Several tour operators include a visit to Gouyave Nutmeg Pool and it is also usually part of a cruise-ship shore excursion. If you are travelling independently, please take the time to visit and support the nutmeg workers of Grenada. The tour is definitely worthwhile.

## GO BIRDWATCHING AT PALMISTE LAKE (PALMISTE DIG) Palmiste Lake, locally known also as Palmiste Dig, is a manmade lake located on the hillside above Palmiste Estate and Palmiste Bay. It was constructed by the French owners of the estate to channel water from the Great Palmiste River to turn the waterwheel and run the machine works that would have crushed sugarcane. Today the lake is not used and rarely visited. It provides a sanctuary for a variety of water birds and is therefore an interesting and beautiful site for birdwatchers to visit. Egrets and

herons are commonly observed together with other species of resident and migratory waterfowl. (See *Hike to Palmiste Lake* , page 148, for more information on Palmiste Lake and how to get there.)

## WALKS AND HIKES

At the time of writing a number of the trickier interior hikes are overgrown and quite impassable. If you decide to tackle any of the more challenging trails, be sure to take a local guide with you or go with a tour operator. Many of these hikes follow very narrow, precipitous ridges, there are often spur trails and access may be blocked by fallen trees or landslides in some places. Always exercise caution and ensure you are properly prepared. (See *Walking/hiking operators and guides* in *Chapter 3*, page 82.)

### HIKE AROUND GRAND ÉTANG LAKE (*Duration: 1–1½hrs; grade 2; guide: not required; site fee: US$2 pp*) The Grand Étang is a 12ha crater lake located at an elevation of 530m above sea level at the heart of the Grand Étang National Park. Prior to Hurricane Ivan, the lake's forest habitat included fine specimens of gommier and mahogany trees, several varieties of ferns, heliconia, gingers and many other plant and flower species. This dense forest habitat was home to a number of birds, frogs, lizards, opossum, armadillo, mongoose and the mona monkey. Unfortunately, because the hurricane destroyed the majority of tall trees, the habitat has changed and is currently in a state of flux, still trying to sort itself out. Many of the tallest gommier and mahogany trees are gone and the mona monkey is less frequently sighted. Given time and conservation efforts, this situation will no doubt change for the better. Despite this storm impact the lake is still a natural beauty and the circular hike around it is an enjoyable one.

The trail starts near the Grand Étang visitor centre. Purchase your pass from the ticket booth and then walk down the steep main road away from the building. You will reach a second booth and a sign pointing to the lake. Simply show your pass and walk down. To your left you will see wooden picnic huts with some steps and a wooden handrail running up the side. Walk up the steps and you will reach a sign indicating the start of the lake trail.

This path is easy to follow – you cannot possibly get lost – but the terrain can be a little challenging, especially in the wet season. The first 20 to 30 minutes is a woodland trail, fairly dry and clear. There are some steps and you must manoeuvre yourself around a narrow stretch of tree roots, but it is for the most part straightforward and uncomplicated. The second 20 to 30 minutes is a different challenge altogether. The path is rough and in the wet season extremely swampy. In fact there are some stretches that are very close to impassable. To add to the challenge of making your way through swamp and mud, there are no views of the lake during this stretch. Once you are two-thirds of the way around, you do see the lake again and the path becomes much easier and less muddy. Take time to enjoy the environment, the plants, the birdlife and the peace and quiet of the lake.

This final 20 minutes is easy and rewarding. You will emerge at a concrete dam, which you must cross. From here the track runs up to the main highway. Carefully cross the road and pick up the trail again on the other side. Walk up the steps to the top of the ridge. Once at the top, take a diversion to the left. Follow the trail for five to ten minutes up the hill to a viewing point. There are magnificent panoramas across the forest reserve to the east coast. Back along the trail to the junction, take the trail straight on and up the hill to the Grand Étang visitor centre.

For details of how to get to the Grand Étang visitor centre see *Getting there* on page 129.

## HIKE TO THE SUMMIT OF MT QUA QUA FROM GRAND ÉTANG LAKE (*Duration: 3–4hrs there & back; grade 4; guide: recommended; site fee: US$2 pp*) Mt Qua Qua is located within the Grand Étang National Park. It is part of a long, high ridge that runs from the south side of the lake northwards to Fédon's Camp. The ridge rises to a peak on the northwest side of the lake at a height of 720m, which is Mt Qua Qua.

The trail to Mt Qua Qua is clear and easy to follow. It climbs at a steady gradient to the summit and is actually not that physically demanding. The trickiest part of this hike is the height. The trail runs along the very top of the narrow ridge. There is little tree cover on either side and the drops are extremely precipitous. In some areas, landslides have caused the trail to erode and it is slippery with a few short, but steep scrambles. This hike is not for acrophobia sufferers. The sheer drops on either side of the narrow trail and exposure to the elements make it rather more mentally than physically challenging. The spectacular views on a clear day, however, make this hike well worth the effort.

The trail starts near the Grand Étang visitor centre. Purchase your pass from the ticket booth and then walk down the steep main road away from the centre. You will reach another booth and a sign pointing to the Grand Étang Lake. Show your pass and walk to the lake. You will see wooden picnic huts on your left with some steps and a wooden handrail on the right-hand side of them. Walk all the way up to the top of the steps until you reach a sign for the Qua Qua trail to the right. This is the start of your mountain hike.

Follow the trail straight on past a sign for the lake walk. The route begins a gradual ascent through trees to a narrow ridge. There are amazing views all the way across the Grand Étang National Park to the southwest peninsula and Point Salines. The trail narrows and follows the apex of the ridge, with steep drops to the left and soon also to the right. As the trees become more sparse there are also superb views back across Grand Étang Lake itself. It is interesting to observe the damage to the forest that still remains following the hurricanes. This is particularly evident in the many trees and stumps that have been completely defoliated on the windward-facing slopes above the lake. This face would have experienced the full force of the storm, hence the severity of the deforestation.

Follow the trail downhill for a short distance through some trees and a rather muddy stretch. Once again the track begins its ascent along the narrow ridge and you will soon find yourself exposed to sheer drops on both sides. For a short distance the path turns away from the lake before curving back around again. At this point you can clearly see the route you must take to the summit of Qua Qua which is the highest point of the ridge in front of you.

Take great care scrambling up a stretch of path that has severely eroded. The drops on either side are seriously steep. Once up, take your time for this final stretch of the hike as you continue along the narrow ridge as it curves northwards. The views are now unrestricted all around. If you have a clear day, you should be able to see the west coast and the Concord River Valley, the peak of Fédon's Camp, Grand Étang Lake, the east coast and the southwest peninsula. Make your way along the path to the boulders at the summit and enjoy. It is a wonderful place to be.

### Further trails from Mt Qua Qua
Before Hurricane Ivan it was possible to continue from the Mt Qua Qua trail to Fédon's Camp and also to the Concord waterfalls. Unfortunately, as with many of the more difficult, extreme and exposed hikes, the trails have not been cleared and have also become very overgrown. Passage at the time of writing, without a very knowledgeable guide, is unfortunately not possible. Hopefully this situation will change and the powers that be will be able to do something to improve the condition of these once

popular, challenging and very beautiful hiking trails. Should these trails have been cleared by the time this book goes to print, you should still take a guide with you on these hikes.

For details of how to get to the Grand Étang visitor centre and the trailhead for the Mt Qua Qua hike see *Getting there* on page 129.

## HIKE TO FÉDON'S CAMP FROM BELVIDERE (*Duration: 6–7hrs there & back; grade 5; guide: essential; site fee: none*)

At the time of writing, due to the effects of Hurricane Ivan and subsequent lack of use, the climb up to the mountain summit location of Fédon's Camp is extremely difficult. A local guide with a sharp machete is essential and a good one will also be able to enhance the hike with the historical context of this area. One contact is Justin A Modeste (known as 'Gurry') (✆ 473 437 0997). There is also rather a lot of razor grass towards the summit of this hike. For this reason you should consider wearing long trousers and a long-sleeved top. Take plenty of water, at least two litres, and definitely a change of clothes. You will be tired, hot, thirsty and very muddy by the time you return. The difficulty of this hike should not put off experienced and adventurous hikers. It is a great mountain hike and the views from the top are magnificent on a clear day. Add to this the historical context and the effort of achieving what is probably one of the toughest hikes on the island, and it is extremely rewarding.

From St Peter's Street in Gouyave, the road runs into the interior to the heights of the Grand Étang Forest Reserve. A short distance beyond the small hamlet of Belvidere is a narrow concrete road that runs from the main road sharply up a hill. This road goes up to what was once the location of Fédon's main camp and gaol. The ruins are covered in bush. A little further along the main road is a second narrow concrete road that also heads steeply upwards. The hike begins at this point.

Follow the concrete road to the top of the hill and then alongside farmlands. To your right you may notice the start of a narrow ridge that climbs steadily upwards. This is where the trail began before a series of landslides made passage very difficult. An alternative way of reaching the mountain trail is to follow the concrete road to the banana fields on the far side of the valley. It will curve around past a small wooden shack before it comes to an end. Once there, the ridge you must ascend to find the mountain trail is up to your left. Passage to the foot of the ridge is across the banana field, which is private, so please ask for permission before crossing. Not doing so is not only inconsiderate, it is also trespassing. Local farmers are very friendly and they will usually be happy to help you on your way.

On the far side of the banana field you will arrive at thick bush at the foot of the ridge. You have to make your way to the top where you will find the trail. This is where the guide and his machete come in. (You could also look out for the red ribbons that yours truly tied to trees all the way to the summit of Morne Fédon.) The ascent is difficult through the bush. Fallen trees and dense thickets of bamboo make it hard work. At the top of the ridge, look for the trail. It is there, and it is quite obvious once you find it.

Hopefully you do find it, so follow it up the ridge. Be careful. At the time of writing, the trail was covered in bush, fallen trees and landslides and there were some really tricky stretches – both in terms of finding the route and also in passing through the bush without finding yourself about to walk off the ridge itself. Keep an eye out for those ribbons!

Continue your climb as the ridge rises very steeply to a first peak. The views here are stunning. You can see right across to the east and southeast coast. You may also notice a slight change in temperature as it starts to become cooler. From this first ridge you will descend a little before climbing again. This final ascent is

6

difficult as it passes through dense bush, fallen trees and lots and lots of very aggressive razor grass. You will find yourself crawling on your hands and knees in the mud, under trees, over branches, scrambling up slippery, sodden banks and dropping into unexpected holes in the path. It is a really strenuous challenge and your language may become quite colourful.

At the summit you will see a rough, weather-worn stone memorial commemorating the site of Fédon's Camp. Relax in the circular clearing and enjoy your achievement, plus the awesome views all around.

You will see the beginning of a second trail down the opposite side of the peak. This is the trail that runs from Fédon's Camp to Mt Qua Qua with a spur trail running down to the Concord Valley. Unfortunately at the time of writing these tracks are in really poor shape. They are almost completely overgrown and have suffered severely from landslides and fallen trees. Hopefully this situation will improve, enabling this hike to be extended once again to these two destinations.

**HIKE TO THE CONCORD FALLS** The turn-off for the Concord Falls is very well signposted on the west coast road between Black Bay and Grand Roy – so long as you are approaching from the south. If you are coming from the north, the sign is unfortunately completely obscured! If you are walking from here, follow the road up the valley for around an hour until you reach the first waterfall. If you are driving, it will take around 20 minutes. If you are travelling by bus from St George's take a yellow number 5. Buses do not go all the way up to the waterfalls so you either have to walk or hitch a ride from the coastal road junction.

There are three waterfalls, with rumours of a fourth, that make up the Concord Falls. The falls are very easy to reach from the west coast. They are popular with visitors to Grenada and the first waterfall features on many cruise-ship land excursions and organised bus trips owing to its accessibility. Before Hurricane Ivan the waterfalls could also be reached via a more difficult route from the interior, along a trail from Mt Qua Qua and Fédon's Camp. At the time of writing, these trails are impassable and should not be attempted until they have been cleared and improved.

**Concord – first waterfall (Concord)** (*Duration: 1hr walk from the west coast; grade 1; guide: not required; entrance fee: EC$5 pp*) From the small coastal hamlet of Black Bay which lies to the south of the fishing village of Gouyave, there is a very large sign indicating the Concord Falls. Either walk or drive up the narrow paved road that meanders through the village of Concord, passing alongside the river and then climbing up the hillside through a really beautiful valley before reaching the first waterfall, which you can see as you approach. The drive up takes around 15 to 20 minutes, the walk between 45 minutes and an hour.

The entrance to the first waterfall is through the shop and bar. Follow the signs and pay your entrance fee. Stone steps lead down to the bathing pool. Although the pool is around 6m deep you should think twice about jumping in. There have been fatalities here. If you just cannot resist it, then please jump, rather than dive. The pretty waterfall cascades down a rock face into the pool. From there, the river runs down a second cascade which you can view from the top.

**Concord – second waterfall (Au Coin)** (*Duration: 1½hrs there & back from the first waterfall; grade 2; guide: not required; entrance fee: none*) The hike to the second waterfall (Au Coin) follows the vehicle track beyond the shop and the first waterfall. Walk along the track to a small river and then cross it. The trail narrows and can be a little muddy, though it is flat and easy going as it passes through a small nutmeg plantation. Cross the river again and then climb up over some rocks and a gentle slope. You should be able to see some nice river cascades and small pools. Cross the river again and keep following the clear trail as it widens and an old stone road becomes visible through the grass beneath your feet. On the left you may notice some thick clusters of bamboo plants. From here the path begins another gentle ascent. You will see colourful ginger lilies, nutmeg, cashew and mango trees before the trail levels out and begins a short descent. Cross the river once more and then pass over a stone bridge.

Just after this bridge there is a fork in the trail. Go left. Follow it as it narrows and gets a little rougher, steeper and muddier. Cross the river again. Follow the trail for a very short stretch and then go back down to the river for a final crossing. Climb up the narrow, muddy path past bamboo and clusters of pretty heliconia. Keep climbing. You are now quite high above the river, which should be running down on your left-hand side.

Take it steady down the muddy track to the river. You should be able to see the waterfall ahead of you now. Follow the river, sticking to the right for a while before reaching a large boulder where you have to cross to the left in order to reach the foot of the waterfall. Scramble over a large boulder and some fallen trees to reach the small but very nice pool where you can take a refreshing bathe. The waterfall is a nice one, around 15m high, cascading down a steep cliff face.

## Concord – third waterfall (Fontainbleu) (*Duration: 1½hrs there & back from the first waterfall; grade 3; guide: recommended; entrance fee: none*) The hike to the third waterfall is the most difficult. It is predominantly a river hike and should only be attempted by people of reasonable fitness. The rocks along the river can be slippery, you have to scramble over some tricky cascades and you also have to climb over fallen trees. A guide is recommended though not absolutely essential. The Fontainbleu Waterfall was a popular hike prior to Hurricane Ivan but the trail was damaged and is now overgrown. The river is also strewn with large broken trees and remnants of landslides making certain sections tricky to pass. The waterfall is a cascade of around 15–20m falling into a deep pool and is surrounded by a circular cavern. The river hike is great fun and the waterfall's pool a nice place to bathe.

The hike follows the first half of the trail to the second waterfall, so follow it all the way to the stone bridge. At the fork on the other side, take the trail to the right.

Walk up the ridge towards a small cultivated plot and a wooden shack. Pass to the left of the shack along a somewhat overgrown trail that narrows considerably at points with steep drops down to the river on your right. Keep going but be careful. Grab hold of whatever is fixed to the ground, even if it is just grass, weeds and roots, to avoid sliding. The track descends and reaches a tree where it forks. Straight on goes into the bush and was probably the original trail. The trail to the right goes down to the river. Take this one.

Once at the river simply follow it upstream for around 30 minutes. (By the way, 'upstream' means against the flow of the water.) You will pass some small cascades and fairly shallow pools. It is quite straightforward and, so long as you take your time and watch your footing, it should also be fun and not too challenging. The final ten minutes is tricky however. There are a number of large, fallen trees and further evidence of landslides that have not been cleared since the hurricane. Just imagine the force of nature that brought these trees down and washed them into this river valley. You must climb up over them to get to the waterfall. Be very careful as the wood is rotting and some pieces will move. Take your time and test each log or branch before giving it your full weight.

Once over them, rejoin the river and follow it as it snakes around to the left. You should now be in sight of the waterfall. There is also a small cascade to your right though this may not always be evident in the dry season. Approach the pool with caution as the final track is covered with weeds that conceal holes, rocks and rotting branches. Enjoy the waterfall and a refreshing dip in the pool.

## HIKE TO PALMISTE LAKE (PALMISTE DIG) *(Duration: 1½hrs round trip; grade 2; guide: not required; site fee: none)* Palmiste Lake, often called Palmiste Dig by locals, is a manmade lake that was formed by the construction of a dam across the Great Palmiste River on its course from the hills of Mon Plaisir and Mt Granby down to Palmiste Bay. It is believed the thick stone walls of the dam were built by the French during their occupancy of Grenada during the early 1700s. The water was then channelled a short distance downhill to power a waterwheel, which in turn would drive the cogs and machinery to crush sugarcane. Historical records show that the estate was an 82ha sugar plantation owned by a family called Heritiers Delesnables. During the British occupation of Grenada, the estate increased to 140ha and had a workforce of almost 200 slaves. Today, like many estate buildings, it is in ruins and covered by bush. However, some of it is accessible with care, and it is worth a short diversion.

On the main west coast road between Grand Roy and Gouyave is Palmiste Bay. (If you are travelling by bus from St George's take the yellow number 5 and get off at Palmiste Bay.) Opposite the bay is a paved road that is a little obscured by a steel fence, running past a building marked 'Newlo'. This is the route you must take. The road becomes a rough vehicle track as it winds its way uphill past some new houses and then up through the forest. You should see the old stone walls of the estate ruins after around 20–30 minutes or so. The lake is around 15 minutes further up the track. When arriving at the lake you can see the thick stone wall of the dam on the western edge. The lake itself is serene and beautiful and is a nice place for birdwatching or a picnic.

## HIKE TO MT PLEASANT ESTATE FROM GOUYAVE *(Duration: 3–4hrs round trip; grade 2; guide: not required; site fee: none)* The Mt Pleasant Estate (known locally as 'Plaisance') is located in the hilly forests between the hamlet of Florida and the foothills of Mt St Catherine. Though it still plants and harvests a variety of agricultural produce, it is another example of a business that was severely impacted by Hurricane Ivan in 2004. The walk to the estate buildings is pleasant and not particularly demanding. It passes through some very pretty countryside with lovely views of forest and sea. Do not expect much when you reach the estate itself, however. It is a working estate rather than a visitor attraction and you may be viewed with more than a little curiosity when you arrive. However, the people are friendly and they are more than happy to chat or show you around. The fun of this hike is in the beauty of the countryside along the way rather than the destination itself, though there are great views from the top of the estate.

From Gouyave walk east along St Peter's Street through the village, past the Anglican church and school and follow the paved road alongside the river. After around 20 minutes or so you will reach a junction. A sign indicates Clozier and Grenville to the right. Go straight ahead, around a bend and across a bridge. You should start to see nutmeg trees lining the road. Follow the road for another 20 minutes or so until you reach a second junction. This time take the road to your left. Walk past St John's Christian School and then over a stone and steel bridge.

The road begins to ascend and there are nice views of the valley and the sea to your left. After a further 20 minutes you will reach a T-junction. Go right and follow the road to the heart of Florida village. At the main junction, take the second road on the left – the wider one that goes uphill, not the narrow one that runs sharply downhill. The road becomes broken and transitions to vehicle track. Lined with nutmeg, cocoa, mango and banana the walk is very pleasant, interesting and serene. The track winds its way uphill until it reaches the summit and the estate some 20 minutes later.

Walk past the wooden shack and the farm track on the left and you will reach the main buildings and a small shop. From the ruins of a former concrete building you have great views down the valley to the sea and the coastal village of Maran.

**HIKE TO BLACK BAY** (*Duration: 1½hrs round trip; grade 1 (trou mais 2); guide: recommended; site fee: none*) The hike from the village of Black Bay passes the ruins of a sugar estate as it makes its way to the crescent-shaped bay. The beach itself is rich black sand and very pretty. For the adventurous, there is a climb to a cave known as **trou mais**, meaning 'corn hole', on Black Bay Point, which is thought to be a place Amerindians used as a storeroom for their crops. You will need to bring along a flashlight if you wish to explore it. This area was also the site of a coastal battery built by the French during the 1700s.

In Black Bay village, just south of Grand Roy and directly opposite the sign for the Concord Falls, there is a paved road running down through some houses towards the shore. A short walk of around 15 minutes brings you to the end of the paved road to a grassy vehicle track. The track passes some small gardens growing saffron, bananas, pigeon peas, dasheen (calalou) and more. The trail is also lined with a variety of trees including nutmeg, mango, tamarind and cinnamon. The path follows the river, which is on your right. It can be muddy in places and is strewn with large boulders.

After around five minutes the trail crosses the river over a small concrete bridge and then some rocks. Take care as it can be slippery here. After a short distance you will see the ruined stone walls of the Black Bay Estate buildings. The track forks. To the right are the estate ruins and to the left is the track down to the bay. At the ruins, beneath the creeping undergrowth you will find not only stone walls but also some of the machinery of this former estate, including the waterwheel and the cane crusher which dates back to 1862.

From the ruins of the estate, continue down the track with the river on your left. On your right is another stone wall which used to be part of a *boucan* (drying house) for cocoa production. Pass by an old iron bridge and emerge onto the bay where river meets black sand and sea. The walk from the road down to the beach will take around 30 to 45 minutes.

Fairly sheltered, the beach is also suitable for swimming. You may see fishermen hauling in nets from their colourful wooden boats around the river mouth.

Walk along the beach to the south side (left, if you are facing the sea) and you should find a steep track to the left of an old white cedar tree. This track is steep and the ascent to the top of the point is a tricky scramble through the bush. A guide with local knowledge is a good idea as it is surprisingly easy to get lost here. A challenging 15- to 20-minute scramble will take you to trou mais. Watch out for cow-itch or *pwa gaté* (*Mucuna pruriens* – see page 44) which seems to thrive around here and can cause severe skin irritation. A little to the right, and above the main entrance is a pot-hole that drops down into the cave. Take care not to fall in – it is dark and believed to be some 30m long!

To get to the west coast village of Black Bay by car, follow the coast road from St George's towards Gouyave. If you are travelling by bus from St George's take a yellow number 5 and get off at the Concord Falls sign.

# bluebay lodge

Escape from the pack and discover tailored holidays for independent travellers.

sail snorkel & hike

relax & rest

traditional & modern caribbean cuisine

more information online

Bluebay Lodge is located on a picturesque hillside in the western region of Grenada approaching the traditional fishing village of Gouyave home to fish Fridays. Perfectly located in the centre of the island, so visits to the north, south, and east of Grenada are made simple.

Mount Nesbit, Gouyave, St Johns, Grenada, WI Tel: +001 473 437 0997

# www.bluebaylodge.net

# 7

# Grenville, Grand Étang and the Southeast

From Mardigras to Balthazar, a tall mountain ridge skirts the elevated, densely forested interior of the Grand Étang Forest Reserve. Its numerous steep ridges and deep river valleys fan out towards the south and the east, creating an equally dramatic coastline of volcanic outcrops, beautiful bays and beaches, sheltered natural harbours, coastal woodlands and mangrove swamps. Between mountain and coast there resides a magical cocktail of people who eke a living from the soil, the sea, from handmade crafts, stores and boutiques, from tourism, sailing, and from spices and rum. For the visitor there is a rich variety here, and this area of Grenada is definitely worth exploring.

This chapter will start by explaining how to get to this region and it will list a selection of places to stay, eat and drink. It will then explore the area in some detail. Firstly we will travel from Grenada's interior, eastwards from the forests and waterfalls of the Grand Étang National Park to the small coastal town of Grenville. Once we have arrived in Grenville, we will take a look around. Our final two journeys will take in the southeast where we will explore two options for getting from the southwest peninsula to the east. One route takes us from Westerhall to Grenville along the bays and anchorages of this very beautiful coastline, the other is a picturesque inland route from St Paul's to St David's. Finally in this chapter there is a selection of things to do as well as detailed descriptions of walks and hikes in this region.

## GETTING THERE

To get to Grenville and along the east coast by car from the southwest peninsula, head for L'Anse Aux Épines but, instead of turning right at the small roundabout junction, go straight on towards Woburn. From there just keep the sea to your right all the way to Grenville.

For St Paul's and the inland road to St David's, head for St George's and, at the roundabout near the north end of the Lagoon, take the fork to the right and follow the signs for Richmond Hill. Stay right at the next fork and, when you reach the next major road junction, which is located on a sharp bend, turn right. Follow this road to St Paul's.

If you are travelling by bus, a bright green number 4 will take you from the capital to Vincennes via St Paul's (make sure you see Vincennes written on the front of the bus) and an orange number 2 bus will take you to Grenville along the east coast. From St George's, the white number 6 passes through Grand Étang to Grenville. There are no buses between Vincennes and Thebaide, but it is a really nice walk.

## GETTING AROUND

Buses are a convenient way of travelling between St George's and Grenville and they regularly ply the routes along the east coast as well as via Grand Étang. If you

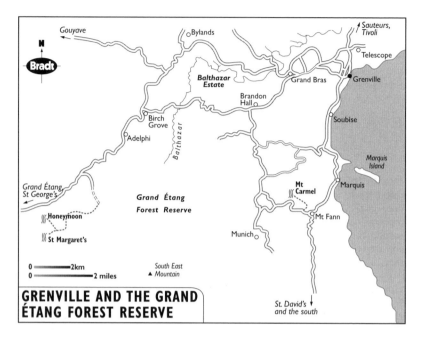

GRENVILLE AND THE GRAND
ÉTANG FOREST RESERVE

wish to get to the region's bays and anchorages, you must either have a hire car or be prepared to walk from the main road (see page 163 for details of some of these walks).

The small town of Grenville has a very simple one-way system. There are essentially three streets running in a north–south direction. The street closest to the sea, Victoria Street, is for traffic heading south. The middle street is for traffic heading north, and the third street, the one farthest from the sea, seems to be for traffic heading in both directions. If you get it wrong, don't worry; absolutely everyone will let you know.

## WHERE TO STAY

Though limited in number, the southeast coast has some lovely places to stay. Many are nestled close to quiet beaches or tranquil coves and anchorages. See page 57 for price codes.

### UPPER-RANGE HOTELS

**La Sagesse Nature Centre** (12 rooms) La Sagesse Beach; ✆/f 473 444 6458;
e lasagesse@spiceisle.com; www.lasagesse.com. Luxurious accommodation in a perfect setting. 5 rooms are in the Old Manor House, which is the former La Sagesse Estate House, 5 more are located within the new resort building, & the final 2 are in a separate cottage. All accommodation is tastefully furnished & just a short walk from the peaceful beach. Room facilities include en-suite bathroom, ceiling fans & verandas. The open-air restaurant has pleasant sea &

beach views & serves local & international dishes. $$$

**Paradise Bay Beach Resort & Spa** (9 villas) La Tante; ✆ 473 405 8888;
e info@paradisebayresort.net; www.paradisebayresort.net. 1-bedroom villa rooms & suites with private bathroom & veranda. Suites have jacuzzi. Facilities include Aloe Vera Restaurant serving local & international food, & beach spa gazebo. Basic & all-inclusive packages available. Contact for details.

## MEDIUM-RANGE HOTELS

⌂ **Cabier Ocean Lodge** (8 rooms) Crochu; ☎ 473 444 6013; e info@cabier.com; www.cabier.com. Extremely pleasant & peaceful Austrian-run hideaway located on a privately owned peninsula alongside the tranquil Cabier Beach. Artistically decorated rooms have private bathroom, & veranda with ocean view. The fresh sea breeze negates the need for AC or fans. Dining is in the open-air terrace restaurant & the Birdcage Bar offers over 35 different rums. Activities include wellness therapies in the hotpot aroma spa, massage, archery & ocean kayaking. Approached by vehicle track so 4x4 is recommended. $$

⌂ **Epping Forest** (2 dbls, 1 family) St Paul's; ☎ 473 440 3333; e eppingforestholidays@hotmail.com; www.grenadaguesthouse.com. Restored plantation house in tropical gardens with swimming pool & forest & mountain views. Peaceful accommodation with a traditional feel; each room has private bathroom, dbl bed, ceiling fan, mosquito net & access to the large shared balcony. No credit cards. $

## BUDGET HOTELS

⌂ **Grenada Rainbow Inn** (15 rooms) Grand Bras; ☎ 473 442 7714; f 473 442 5332; e rainbowinn@spiceisle.com; www.spiceisle.com/rainbowinn. Close to the town of Grenville, accommodation includes private bathroom, AC, TV & some rooms with private balcony. $

⌂ **Sam's Inn** (10 rooms, 3 self-contained apts) Dunfermline; ☎/f 473 442 7853; e samsinn@spiceisle.com; www.samsinn.com. Located close to Grenville & Pearls Airport, rooms have private bathroom, TV, fridge, balcony. Apts have 2 bedrooms, living area, kitchen, TV. $

## UPPER-RANGE APARTMENTS, COTTAGES AND VILLAS

⌂ **Villa Caribella** (3 beds) Westerhall; ☎ 473 443 5319; f 473 443 3971; e macford@spiceisle.com; www.grenadavilla-caribella.com. Luxury villa accommodation with patio, pool & beautiful sea views. Facilities include bedrooms, bathrooms, living area, fully equipped kitchen, laundry, AC, TV, ceiling fans. Housekeeping service available. $$$$$

⌂ **Bel Air Plantation** (5 cottages, 6 villas) St David's Point; ☎ 473 444 6305, US toll free ☎ +1 866 504 3359; f 473 444 6316; e info@belairplantation.com; www.belairplantation.com. Luxurious accommodation located alongside the tranquil St David's Harbour. Cottages have 1 bedroom, villas have 1 or 2. All have private bathrooms, stylishly furnished living areas, fully equipped kitchen, AC, TV, ceiling fans, private verandas. Original artworks decorate each cottage & villa, there is a panoramic lounge, infinity swimming pool, dinghy dock, tropical gardens, spa, gift shop & local & international dining at the Water's Edge Restaurant & Bar. $$$$

⌂ **Villa Heron's Flight** (3 beds) Westerhall Point; ☎ 631 714 4428; f 631 790 5685; e sales@heronsflight.com; www.heronsflight.com. Luxurious home away from home with swimming pool, gazebo, panoramic ocean views, & tropical garden with secluded beach. 3 bedrooms with en-suite bathrooms, AC, TV, ceiling fans, living area, fully equipped kitchen. $$$$

⌂ **Petit Bacaye Villa Hotel & Restaurant** (5 villas) Petit Bacaye; ☎/f 473 443 2902, UK ☎ +44 1794 323227; e hideaways@wellowmead.u-net.com; www.petitbacaye.com. Castaway-style accommodation on the margins of Petit Bacaye Bay. SC villas with private bathroom, inside & outside shower rooms, kitchen, living area, fans, verandas, decks or private gardens. Narrow sandy beach with tranquil waters suitable for swimming. Restaurant & beach bar serving local & international dishes. Aromatherapy & massage available. $$

## MEDIUM-RANGE AND BUDGET APARTMENTS, COTTAGES AND VILLAS

⌂ **Mangi House** (2 rooms) Crochu; ☎ 473 444 6013; e info@mangigrenada.com or info@cabier.com; www.mangigrenada.com. Located on the Crochu Estate overlooking Menere Bay, this open-plan wood & stone atelier home is a tranquil hideaway retreat. Fully equipped kitchen, living area & spacious veranda with ocean views. Approached by vehicle track so 4x4 is recommended. $$

⌂ **Big Sky Lodge** (2 cottages) Crochu; ☎ 473 444 7277; e office@grenada-lodge.org; www.grenada-lodge.org. Basic 1-bedroom cottage accommodation with private bathroom & veranda with sea views. Use of shared kitchen & cooking facilities. Restaurant & bar serves local cuisine. $

🏠 **Grenada Gold Guest Apartments** (2 apts) Westerhall; ☎/f (UK) +44 1293 426832; e info@grenadagold.com; www.grenadagold.com. Family-run 2-bedroom apts. Fully equipped with open-plan kitchen & living area, TV, ceiling fans & access to shared laundry room, patio & swimming pool. $

## ✗ WHERE TO EAT AND DRINK

In addition to the restaurants listed below, look out for some great local cooking at a wide selection of eateries in Grenville and the surrounding area. It is always worth giving these places a try. Their food is usually good and always very reasonably priced.

✗ **La Sagesse Nature Centre** La Sagesse Beach; ☎ 473 444 6458. High-quality local & international lunches & dinners in a very peaceful & beautiful setting overlooking La Sagesse Beach & Bay. Dinner reservations recommended. $$

✗ **Water's Edge Restaurant & Bar** Bel Air Plantation, St David's Point; ☎ 473 444 6305. Enjoy local & international cooking as you look out at the sailing boats of the very peaceful St David's Harbour. Dinner reservations recommended. $$

✗ **Cabier Ocean Lodge** Cabier Beach, Crochu; ☎ 473 444 6013. Caribbean dining on the lovely deck of Cabier's alfresco restaurant. With views of Crochu Harbour, and a cool sea breeze, follow your meal with one of 35 different rums or an Italian coffee. Advance reservations required. $$

✗ **Petit Bacaye Villa Hotel & Restaurant** Petit Bacaye; ☎ 473 443 2902. Home-cooked Caribbean lunches & dinners, with lobster salad a speciality, served in the delightful tropical garden & beach surroundings of Petit Bacaye Bay. Dinner reservations recommended. $$

## FROM THE GRAND ÉTANG NATIONAL PARK TO GRENVILLE

The road from the Grand Étang visitor centre winds tightly downhill to the north and then curves to the east. Along the route there are magnificent views of the forest, mountain ridges and the Atlantic Ocean. From the depths of the forest you emerge in the village of Adelphi and pass colourful board houses, snackettes and bars such as the First & Last Stop Bar, and a number of small banana plantations that line the road and seem to fill all the gaps between the area's residences. The road follows the Great River as it winds its way down to the settlement of Birch Grove. Through Birch Grove the road passes a nutmeg receiving station, concrete and board houses and colourful gardens with ginger lilies and crotons on either side, adding a sharp vibrancy to the greenery all around. Just before you cross over the Great River at Balthazar Estate, a little beyond Birch Grove, you will pass the Guess Club, offering drinks, other refreshments, entertainment and river bathing. River tubing, an increasingly popular activity undertaken by many visitors to the island, especially those who arrive on cruise ships, also takes place at this spot (see page 73 for more information on river tubing). Over the river, the road passes through a cocoa plantation and then back across the river again before arriving at the village of St James. In this small village there are more colourful board houses, a nutmeg receiving station and lively snackettes and bars such as the House of Commons Bar, where you can be sure animated political debates take place throughout the day and well into the evening. From St James the road passes the Spice Café and 3Js Snackette & Bar before entering the east coast's largest population centre, the small town of Grenville.

## EXPLORING GRENVILLE

Grenville was founded by the British and named after George Grenville who was British prime minister between 1763 and 1765. During the French occupation it was renamed La Baye, and despite changing back to Grenville in 1796, La Baye is a name that is still quite commonly used. The town is protected by a long coral reef that stretches the entire length of Grenville Bay and boats must use channel markers for safe passage. Despite these natural hazards there is a thriving fishing community both here and also along the length of the coastline southwards through the villages of Soubise and Marquis.

During the Fédon Rebellion of March 1795 to June 1796, Pilot Hill, to the north of the town centre, was a strategic site that changed hands through bloody fighting on a number of occasions. The British routed the rebels in March 1796 after a joint offensive that included Post Royal Hill to the south.

The Grenville of today is an interesting town, a compact place of noise, hustle and bustle, contrasting starkly with the space and serenity of the surrounding forests, villages and beaches. There are numerous stalls selling fruits, vegetables and spices. Clothes boutiques, barbers' shops, bars, snackettes, food being cooked by the roadside and, yes, even more clothes boutiques seem to crowd every space available on the town's busy streets, giving it the feeling of a subcontinental bazaar. Grenville has quite a sizeable East Indian community, reflected in the people you will see in the area, in some of the food and cooking, and also in the name of a number of the stores and businesses here. Grenada's East Indian community has its ancestry in the indentured labour force that was brought to the island in the mid 19th century as estate owners tried to come to terms with the abolition of slavery and the dearth of an inexpensive workforce. Descendants of these immigrants have gone on to become very successful businesspeople and many still live and prosper in this area.

**Grenville Nutmeg Station** (or 'pool'), is one of three main nutmeg processing stations in Grenada. The station offers guided tours to visitors (see page 160). Today it simply receives nutmegs and prepares them for processing in Gouyave. A tour of the station is well worth it and you will be directly helping people whose livelihoods have suffered following two recent hurricanes.

Victoria Street is Grenville's main thoroughfare, running from north to south along Grenville Bay. At the northern end of the street is the **Grenville Anglican Church** and school. Located behind them, on the waterfront, is the newly built **Grenville fish market**, where you can buy all kinds of fresh fish throughout the day. Also along Victoria Street you will find the Grenville police station, the post office and several banks with ATMs. There are a number of small supermarkets, boutiques, pharmacies and a wide selection of eateries including the **Natural Juice Bar & Restaurant**, located on the first floor of a building near the Anglican church, and **Smoothie Fusion**, also on the first floor of a building on the opposite side of the street selling a curious yet very original combination of soups, salads and smoothies. All the way along the street you will find stalls selling everything from fruits and vegetables, to spices and fast foods. At the southern end of Victoria Street you will find the **Melting Pot Sports Bar & Grill**, a **KFC** and just around the corner on Jubilee Street, **Ru-Dee's Snack Bar**.

The street parallel to Victoria Street where traffic runs in the opposite direction, from south to north, is Sandal Street. It is also lively, noisy and full of interesting eateries, shops and market stalls. Look out for **De Hott Roti Shop**, **Pepper Bar**, a popular watering hole near to the marketplace, **My Place Roti Shop** and **Molly & Son Snackette** selling great fish and chips. Also along Sandal Street is the Grenville Magistrates' Court and at the southern end of the street is the library.

There are a couple of roads bisecting these north–south thoroughfares. This is where you will find numerous market stalls selling fruit and vegetables, spices and clothes. There are also more clothes boutiques, small supermarkets and popular local eateries such as **Hotter Than the Rest Restaurant & Bar** and the **Charles Supermarket & Bar**.

The southeast coast of Grenada juxtaposes pretty rural villages with luxury modern residences. Its terrain is a stimulating combination of wild rocky peninsulas, beautiful bays, sandy beaches and mangrove swamps. Modern marinas and natural anchorages offer sheltered havens for both recreational mariners and traditional fishermen. It is a fun place for explorers and hikers, as well as sailing enthusiasts and sun worshippers. As you travel along the coast from south to north you will clearly see the transition from luxurious and modern, with a distinctly overseas feel, to a more rural, very natural and quintessentially Grenadian domain.

The **Westerhall** peninsula has become an exotic tropical sanctuary that has been designed and constructed exclusively for those who can afford it – the very wealthy. It is a gated community of luxurious residences, beautifully manicured gardens and private boat jetties. The point itself is very pretty and is worth a trip. On the western side is Chemin Bay and the tranquil waters of Calivigny Harbour, and to the east is Westerhall Bay, a beautiful haven for sailing boats and dreamers.

To the north of Westerhall Point is the **Westerhall Estate** where you will find ruins of the former sugar, cocoa and lime estate and rum distillery together with its contemporary counterpart. Guided tours of the estate and distillery are offered for a small fee and are very interesting (see page 162 for more information).

Heading east from Westerhall you will pass **Petit Bacaye**, where there is a narrow beach, mangrove swamp and hotel resort at the bottom of a steep hill. After Petit Bacaye you will see the signs for the Bacolet Bay Resort and Spa development, an award-winning project designed to become a resort that will comprise apartment, villa and cottage accommodation in a 16ha setting of tropical gardens. The resort's facilities will include spa and fitness centre, tennis courts, bars and restaurants. This ambitious project is scheduled to be completed sometime in 2011. The road through the resort development goes on to Little Bacolet Point. It is a narrow rocky outcrop with nice views along the coastline, but unfortunately much spoiled by the dirt and diggers of the resort project together with what appears to be a growing tendency to use the area as a place to dump rubbish. An exploration of this peninsula is probably best left until after 2011, when the dust has settled, so to speak.

Before reaching the village of **Corinth**, look out for **Keith's Runaway Bar** where you can get a great selection of local food and enjoy televised sports events. Further along the road there is a turn-off to St David's Point. The road can be identified by a sign indicating **Megrin**, the site of the very first European settlement in Grenada (see page 167). Just to the east of Corinth is the extremely picturesque **La Sagesse Estate**. On your left-hand side (if you are travelling east) you will see the ruins of the sugar mill, and on the coastal side of the road is a sign for the La Sagesse Nature Centre. This road takes you to the very beautiful La Sagesse Bay (see page 162). Very close to La Sagesse is Marquis Point, another area of luxury residential property development.

## KITE FLYING

On Easter Monday look and listen out for colourful kites filling up the skies around the islands, made from all kinds of materials, with imaginative designs and long flowing tails. Children and adults will find beaches, hills and any other open spaces to launch their creations. A number of kite-flying competitions also take place on this day and if a strange buzzing sound is keeping you awake that night, you will know you must be sleeping within close proximity to a winner.

From La Sagesse, the coastal road begins to climb up towards the village of **St David's**. Set against a lush tropical forest backdrop, St David's Roman Catholic Church is usually the first thing that catches your eye. Standing high above the village and dominating the skyline, it is a captivating picture. Its full title is the Church of the Immaculate Conception and St Joseph, and it was constructed in the second half of the 19th century. Located at a slightly lower elevation and closer to the main road is St David's Anglican Church. Constructed in the first half of the 19th century, this church also has a very prominent position, looking out over the parish's simple dwelling houses, farmlands, sharp mountain ridges and the coastal forests and bays that ultimately meet the wild Atlantic Ocean. Across the road from St David's Anglican Church is a large building housing St David's post office, police station and magistrates' court. Although it is the administrative centre of the parish, St David's is actually a very small village and it seems that the very moment you arrive is also the moment you leave.

As you take your leave of St David's, heading northwards, you will see **Peckish Delights**, serving great value local food and a variety of fresh fruit juices. From here the twisting coastal road passes through **Pomme Rose**, a very pretty village of colourful board and block houses, bars and shops, that are perched high up along the hillside above the coast and the sea. In the middle of Pomme Rose there is a road junction on a sharp bend with a narrow secondary road that runs directly down towards the coast and **La Tante Bay**. It is an expansive bay, often very deserted, with a dark sand beach (see page 166).

From Pomme Rose the road continues to wind its way along the coast until it reaches the village of **Crochu**. At the centre of this village is an area called Café Junction. From here a secondary road passes through the small settlement of Mahot, along a narrow ridge and down to Crochu Point, with the very pretty **Cabier Beach** and bay to the north of the coastal headland (see page 167) and **Crochu Harbour** to the south. Both bays are usually very tranquil and quiet save for an occasional fishing boat either putting out or returning through the light surf. Cabier Beach has white sand, shallow waters and a wooded and grassy fringe that is the perfect location for a picnic. Crochu Point itself is occupied by Cabier Ocean Lodge, a hotel, restaurant and wellness retreat. Just up the road from Crochu is **Rastafari Dynesty** (✆ *473 444 7358;* **e** *rasdynesty@spiceisle.com*), a really nice shop selling authentic African wares including colourful materials, soaps and oils, plus a delightful garden bar selling fresh juices and herbal teas. Drop in and say hello to Ogondola Izack if you can; it will make your day.

From Crochu the road heads north towards **Hope Estate** and Great Bacolet Bay. Hope Estate is being sold as residential lots and so new houses are slowly appearing along this steep grassy headland. **Great Bacolet Bay** has a very accessible crescent-shaped beach with rough, but motorable vehicle tracks running to its northern and southern ends. Look out for the rocky Bacolet Island (sometimes called Hope Island) located a little offshore at the centre of the bay. The beach is very nice, clean and a popular bathing spot with locals. For details on how to walk or drive to Hope Beach at Great Bacolet Bay see page 165.

North of Hope Estate is the village of Mt Fann. Just as you enter this village from the south, on the apex of a bend, you will see a signposted road for Mt Carmel Waterfall. In actual fact, the start of the short waterfall trail is very close to this road junction, hidden between the houses near to the very appropriately named **Waterfall Bar** (see page 163). If you continue inland from here you will find yourself passing near or through a series of small and colourful villages including Munich and Plaisance. This road eventually emerges at a junction with the main interior road between St George's, Grand Étang and Grenville.

Continuing north along the coast from Mt Fann, you arrive at the village of

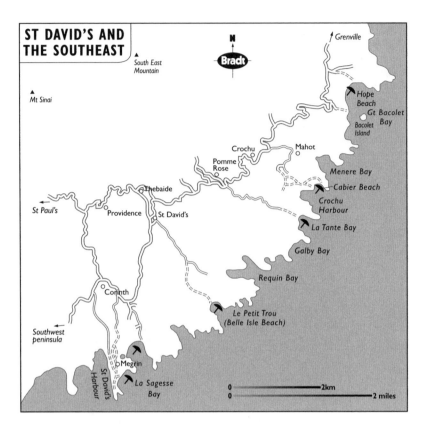

South East
Mountain

N

Brandt

Grenville

Mt Sinai

Hope
Beach

Gt Bacolet
Bacolet Bay
Island

Crochu
Pomme
Rose
Mahot

Thebaide

St Paul's

Providence
St David's

Menere Bay

Cabier Beach

Crochu
Harbour

La Tante Bay

Galby Bay

Requin Bay

Corinth

Le Petit Trou
(Belle Isle Beach)

Southwest
peninsula

Megrin

St David's Harbour

La Sagesse
Bay

0      2km
0      2 miles

**Marquis**. Designated a 'cultural landmark' by the government of Grenada, Marquis is one of the island's oldest European settlements. It was established by the French in the latter half of the 17th century and its full name was Grand Marquis until the British renamed it Grenville when they took over governance of Grenada in 1763. In the early hours of 3 March 1795, Julien Fédon and his followers attacked the town, completely sacking it and killing 11 British settlers. Noted as the start of the Fédon Rebellion, this act began a period of uprising against the British that lasted until June 1796 and brought mayhem to the country (see pages 136 and 137). The result of this initial attack was that Grand Marquis, or Grenville, was abandoned. A little further up the coast, the village of La Baye was itself renamed Grenville at the end of the rebellion. That village became the main settlement on the east coast and still bears the same name today. Marquis is now a village of fishermen and craftspeople. Using the boiled and dried leaves of the screw pine (*Pandanus utilis*), craftsmen and women fashion small spice baskets, mats and hats that are sold around the island and also in the Marquis Craft Centre at the heart of the village along the coastal road.

To the north of Marquis is **Battle Hill**. The shrine of Our Lady of Fatima is a draw for Catholic pilgrims who make their way from the St Andrew's Roman Catholic Church in Grenville to this spot each year. For an area of peace and worship, it has a somewhat inappropriate name. This is because, together with Pilot Hill to the north, it was considered a strategic position during the Fédon Rebellion and several fierce battles were fought here.

Before reaching the town of Grenville, you will pass through the village of

**Soubise**. It seems rather fitting to end a southeast coastal journey that began with the luxury and affluence of Westerhall, with its large residences and private jetties, and arrive further up the coast in Soubise, a village where, all along the narrow shoreline, small wooden houses sit precariously perched upon cinder blocks for when unpredictable, rough Atlantic seas cause flooding, and where brightly coloured wooden fishing boats are hauled out manually after a hard day's work at sea. Soubise and Westerhall are both settlements on the southeast coast of Grenada; both accommodate people whose lives are in some way entwined with the sea, and yet they are a world apart. In many ways, Westerhall and Soubise seem to perfectly portray the contrasts and interesting diversity of the people and lives of contemporary Grenada.

## A PRETTY INLAND ROUTE FROM ST PAUL'S TO ST DAVID'S

Between the villages of St Paul's and St David's there is a narrow, winding road that hugs the steep cliffs and slopes of the mountainous ridge that runs along the southeastern edge of the Grand Étang Forest Reserve. It is a very pretty road, often quite vertiginous and it has spectacular views of forest and coast.

The village of **St Paul's** lies a little to the east of Richmond Hill and its forts. It is a pretty village with a mix of block and wooden houses, a church and police station. It is also the home of **De La Grenade Industries**, producers of nutmeg jams, jellies, syrups and liqueurs. Look out for the original wooden carvings of the **Camàhogne Art Gallery** and the rather stately and curious building known as **'The Tower'**. Built in the 1800s by a British barrister named Renwick and subsequently, it is told, gambled away in a game of cards, it consists of a large family home and a five-storey tower built of granite and brick. It has risen to prominence for its gardens which have been acclaimed by the Royal Horticultural Society for their wide and interesting variety of tropical flowers, trees and shrubs. Now owned by the Slinger family, The Tower's gardens form part of some of Grenada's

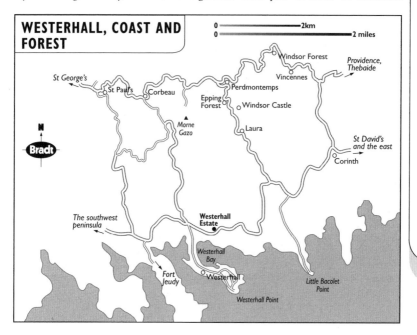

7

horticultural tours (see Sunsation Tours, listed in *Chapter 3*, page 72). As it is a private dwelling, visitors to the area should not simply turn up at The Tower and expect to look around. To the right of the police station in St Paul's there is a small road that goes to the **Bay Gardens**. Here it is possible to simply turn up and take a tour, and if you are interested in tropical flora then the Bay Gardens is definitely worth visiting (see opposite).

From St Paul's the road snakes along the steep slopes through the villages of Corbeau, Mt Pleasant and Mt Rose where there are superb views of St George's and the coast. In Corbeau look out for the **Wildlife Bar** and next to it a narrow road heading towards the pointed summit of Morne Gazo (see page 165). Beyond Corbeau the road continues to the village of **Perdmontemps** where a road junction offers the choice of continuing eastwards through these elevated villages towards St David's, or heading down towards the coast. The road to the south coast passes through the curiously named villages of **Epping Forest** and **Windsor Castle** before reaching **Laura** where you will see signs for the **Laura Herb & Spice Garden** (see opposite). The road to the east continues along the high forested foothills of Mt Sinai, passing through the villages of **Windsor Forest** and **Vincennes**. The views along this stretch of road are quite breathtaking and offer a glimpse of the everyday lives of the people who live in Grenada's rural communities. You will see small farm holdings where subsistence crops are grown on steep slopes and terraces, and the road itself is lined with banana plants, mango, breadfruit and cinnamon trees. Occasionally a pick-up truck will pass along the road with fresh produce, building materials, nutmegs, manure or perhaps fish for sale. Snackettes and convenience stores offer opportunities for people to meet and talk, take a drink, play a game of dominoes or just watch the world passing by. The road from Vincennes meets a junction where the road south goes to Corinth and La Sagesse, and the road east passes through the rural communities of **Providence** and **Thebaide**, before finally arriving at the Roman Catholic church in St David's.

## WHAT TO DO

**VISIT THE GRENVILLE NUTMEG STATION** (*15–20min tour US$1 or EC$2.70 pp*) Grenville Nutmeg Station was one of three major stations on the island that used to process nutmegs. The other two were at Victoria and Gouyave on the west coast. All of this changed with the arrival of consecutive hurricanes in 2004 and 2005. Before the hurricanes, Grenada produced approximately 2,700 tonnes of nutmegs and the Grenville Nutmeg Station employed around 140 people to receive and process them. Today the island produces around 10% of pre-hurricane volumes and the Grenville station, or 'the pool', has had to become a receiving station. At the time of writing its employees only number around ten.

The impact of these hurricanes on the nutmeg industry and upon the lives of ordinary Grenadians has been a silent tragedy, and for some of them it has become too much to bear. Given that it can take up to ten years to grow a productive nutmeg tree, many in the industry have had to figure out alternative ways of earning a living. Local people have been remarkably resolute in the face of disaster and a visit to the nutmeg stations at either Gouyave or Grenville should be on the agenda of everyone visiting Grenada. By taking a short tour, by learning, by listening and by paying the tour fee, you are making a very positive contribution, regardless of how small it may seem to you. It is also fascinating and very enjoyable.

A tour takes around 15 to 20 minutes and takes you through the nutmeg station. You pay the tour fee at the window by the entrance, but you may also want to give your tour guide a little tip at the end. You will see trays of nutmegs and the original wooden machinery that was used to process them (these days they are dried and bagged here before being sent to the Gouyave station for processing and export). It is very interesting, but when your guide vividly describes how animated, noisy and busy it was before 2004, compared with how quiet and relatively empty you see it today, it is also a little sad. Please travel positively and visit Grenada's nutmeg stations. To get to Grenville see the *Getting there* section on page 151. The nutmeg station is located on the most westerly of the three main roads.

**TAKE A TOUR OF THE LAURA HERB & SPICE GARDEN** (*20min tour EC$5 pp*) A little off the beaten track but quite accessible via a newly constructed road, the Laura Herb & Spice Garden is one of the few places in Grenada that is actually well signposted. The easiest way to get there is from the coastal road. A little to the west of the Bacolet Bay Resort and Spa development there is a small roundabout with a road running inland and a sign to St George's. Take this road and after a drive of around five to ten minutes you will see signs to Laura Herb & Spice Garden on the right. Follow these signs for a short distance up a narrow road that curves around the hillside, keeping to the left until you see the signs again. If you are coming from St Paul's, simply follow the winding road through the villages until you reach Perdmontemps. Here you should take a right down a new concrete road. From this road you will see the signs to the gardens.

If you are travelling by bus from St George's, you should take a bright green number 4 and get off at Perdmontemps. You can either walk or hitch a lift from here.

A short guided walk around the Laura Herb & Spice Garden is informative and interesting. You will learn to recognise a number of spices, plants, fruits and herbs as well as discover their medicinal properties and how they are used as natural remedies for sicknesses. The tour is easy-paced and relaxed. If tropical plants and spices are new to you then this little excursion is definitely worth it.

**VISIT THE BAY GARDENS** (*30min tour EC$5 pp*) The Bay Gardens are located very close to the village of St Paul's. From St George's simply follow the signs to St Paul's or Fort Frederick and Richmond Hill. Instead of turning right to Fort Frederick, follow the road as it winds around the steep hillside ridges until you reach St Paul's. Continue along the main road through the village until you come to St Paul's Police Station. There is a narrow road running downhill right next to the station building. If you follow it for a little way, you will see a sign on the right for the Bay Gardens. Follow this road up and then downhill for a short distance until you come to the reception building for the Bay Gardens which will be on your left. By bus, take the bright green number 4 from St George's to St Paul's and get off by the police station. You then have a short walk of around 15 minutes to the Bay Gardens following the directions described above.

If you are interested in gardening and in particular learning about some of the tropical flora you can see in Grenada and the wider Caribbean, then the Bay Gardens are most definitely worth a visit. It is a charming place with a quaint reception and refreshments building, a beautifully natural garden and very friendly and knowledgeable staff to show you around. The gardens are in two halves, on either side of a narrow road running south from the village of St Paul's. They contain a wide variety of plants, trees and flowers including gingers, heliconias, palms, orchids, bromeliads and bamboo. The flowers attract hummingbirds and butterflies to add that extra air of tranquillity and colour. You could easily spend a couple of hours here. Not to be missed.

**TAKE A TOUR OF THE WESTERHALL RUM DISTILLERY** (*20min tour EC$5 pp*) The estate is located on the main coastal road near Westerhall Point. It is well signposted and very easy to find. If you are travelling to Westerhall by bus, take the orange number 2 from St George's.

Sir William Johnstone of Dumfriesshire, Scotland, purchased the Grand Bacaye Estate in the late 1700s and renamed it, presumably after his ancestral home of Westerhall. The estate changed hands a number of times over the coming years. In the 1860s, sugarcane processing began using two waterwheels, two cane mills and two boilers. A manmade canal channelled water from the St Louis River to the wheels which in turn drove the machinery to crush the sugarcane and extract the juice. This juice was then fermented, distilled and turned into rum.

The waterwheels were decommissioned as late as the 1970s and were replaced by a more modern diesel-powered mill. In the 1980s, Morne Delice Sugar Mill was used to crush and boil the cane juice and Westerhall simply carried out the fermentation and distilling processes. Today Westerhall Estate produces five different rums: Westerhall Plantation Rum, Rum Sipper Strong Rum, Westerhall Superb Light, Westerhall Strong Rum and Jack Iron.

In addition to learning about modern blending processes, you will be taken on a tour of the former estate ruins on the hillside behind. The two waterwheels plus an assortment of machine works are on display around the well-tended estate garden.

**EXPLORE LA SAGESSE BEACHES AND MANGROVE SWAMPS** On the coastal road between the villages of Corinth and St David's you will see the ruins of the La Sagesse Estate buildings on the side of the road. Opposite them is a sign for the La Sagesse Nature Centre. Follow the narrow paved road, taking a left where it forks with a vehicle track and pass alongside a cricket and athletics ground. Continue along the road and at the bottom, where it meets with a new concrete road leading uphill to the Marquis development project, follow the old road around to the right until you reach the gates of La Sagesse Nature Centre. If you are driving, park outside. There is a paved path along the right-hand side of the hotel and restaurant that goes to the bay. If you are walking, it will take around 30 minutes from the main coastal road. An orange number 2 bus will take you to the junction for La Sagesse.

At La Sagesse there is a very beautiful crescent-shaped beach and bay. The waters are clear and shallow making it an ideal place for families to have fun and relax. Located at the eastern end of the bay is the La Sagesse Nature Centre, with its luxurious accommodation, and excellent restaurant and bar. At the western end of the beach, just before you reach the rocks, you will see a narrow track. Follow it alongside the mangrove swamps, brackish pool and salt ponds for about five minutes and you will emerge on the other side of the point to a second, somewhat more secluded beach.

If you are interested in birdwatching, then the mangrove swamp, inland pond and coastal forest in this area are home to several varieties of waterfowl as well as birds of prey. (There is also a rumour of a toucan sighting, weirdly enough.) A network of tracks and trails criss-cross their way through the mangroves and coastal woodland, many of which are very overgrown, so please take care not to get lost. For guidance on trails and the varieties of birdlife you may be lucky enough to encounter here, check with the La Sagesse Nature Centre for further details as well as organised nature tours. If you are travelling along the southeast coast of Grenada, then you should definitely try to visit La Sagesse.

**GO RIVER TUBING** Take a 90-minute river-tubing ride along Grenada's Great River through picturesque tropical vegetation. You receive a safety briefing and demonstration before you set off, and you are accompanied by guides all the way.

River tubing is popular with day visitors arriving on cruise ships, so it may be busy at the height of the season. Travellers with back, neck or heart conditions should seek advice before river tubing. Also check minimum age requirements. (See *River-tubing operators* in *Chapter 3*, page 73.)

## WALKS AND HIKES

**HIKE TO MT CARMEL (MARQUIS) WATERFALL** (*Duration: 30mins there & back; grade 2; guide: not required; site fee: EC$5 pp*) Mt Carmel Waterfall is located on the Marquis River, close to the hamlet of Mt Carmel, which is found on the road between Mt Fann and Munich. It is also known as the Marquis Waterfall. The trail is very short and easy to follow. There is one river crossing if you wish to get close up to the waterfall and another if you wish to see a second, much smaller one, along the same river.

The Mt Carmel Waterfall is quite well signposted though the trailhead itself is not obvious. To get there from St George's, follow the coastal road along the southeast coast up towards Grenville. After passing through the village of Crochu the road will wind its way up the coast in a northerly direction until it reaches a junction on a tight bend. To the right is the village of Mt Fann and the road to Grenville, to the left is the trailhead to the Mt Carmel Waterfall. Look for the **Waterfalls Bar** on the junction. If you are travelling by bus from St George's you should take an orange number 2 and get off at this point.

Almost on the junction itself, you will see a number of small snackettes as well as the very appropriately named Waterfalls Bar. There are also likely to be several young men offering their services as guides. They will also ask you for an entrance fee, or 'contribution'. The guides are all local people just trying to earn a living – which they most certainly do when tour buses arrive. Most guides here will not name a price to accompany you down the trail; they will simply ask you to 'pay what you think' at the end. If you decide you would like a guide, you should pay EC$5–10 per person depending on your group size. A 'contribution' or 'entrance fee' should be no more than EC$5 each. Remember, it is a very short trail and not particularly difficult. If your guide enhances the walk by giving you background information and helping you out – rather than just heading off into the distance and leaving you to it – by all means tip a little higher.

Follow a path that runs next to and then around behind the small wooden house that is located next to the snackettes and bar. Once at the rear of the house, the path becomes a trail through the woodland, running alongside the Marquis River. It widens as it goes quite steeply up to the crest of a hill and then down again on the other side. You will see two spurs running off to the right. The first spur is a short track that leads down to a bathing pool. (This is actually the nicest pool on the walk.) The second trail goes down to the river and crosses it to the other side. It is a very shallow crossing over rock, but take care as it can be extremely slippery. You must get your feet wet here. On the other side a short track leads to a second, very small cascading waterfall. Once you have taken a look, head back to the main trail.

Continue along the clear track until you reach the Mt Carmel Waterfall itself. To get close to it, you must cross over the river and clamber over a few boulders. The waterfall is a large cascade caused by the Marquis River tumbling over a huge, flat rock face. The water splashes down onto more rocks and there is a small, though somewhat unappealing, pool to the left.

**HIKE TO THE ST MARGARET'S FALLS** (*Duration: 1½–2hrs there & back; grade 2; guide: recommended; site entrance fee: EC$5 pp*) To reach the starting point of this hike from St George's, follow the interior road to Annandale and Grand Étang. Keep heading towards Grand Étang, which is clearly signposted. The road is very steep as you approach the heights of the forest reserve and it has some sharp hairpin bends, so take care and get full value out of your car horn. Pass the Grand Étang Forest Reserve visitor centre and continue along the main road, which now runs downhill for a short distance. You will see a sign for St Margaret's on the right-hand side. Take this narrow road uphill and you will come to the shop and parking area for the St Margaret's Falls on the right-hand side. If you are travelling to St Margaret's Falls by bus from St George's, you will need to take a white number 6.

This is a moderately easy hike to two very pretty waterfalls with nice, deep and refreshing bathing pools. The trail follows a dirt track which is steep and quite muddy and slippery in places. You must cross a small river to reach the falls right at the end of the trail. The waterfalls are on a river that finds its source in the Grand Étang Lake and which becomes a tributary of the much larger Balthazar or Great River.

Though the trail is, for the most part, very obvious and clear (it is frequently walked by cruise-ship visitors), it is worth taking a guide along to help you out over some of the trickier stretches and to tell you about some of the vegetation you will see along the way. Depending on your group size, a guide's services should be around EC$20–40 in total. If you have not already employed a guide via one of the tour operators who run hiking trips here (see *Chapter 3*, page 82), then one will almost certainly make himself known to you. Whether you hire a guide or not, you should pay your EC$5 per person entrance fee at the shop.

Once you are ready, head out of the parking area and turn right, following the paved path for a short distance. You will see the path curves down to the right and into the valley below. Follow it as it passes through small farms. Along the route you will see bananas, plantain, nutmeg, cocoa and cinnamon. After a fairly easy walk for around ten–15 minutes, you will reach a wooden house. The wide track curves around to the right but the narrow trail to the waterfalls runs along the left-hand side of the hut as you face it. Follow this trail up and over a ridge (there may be someone offering cold drinks or even guide services at this point).

Follow the path sharply down the other side of the ridge. You will have great views on your left across the forest. The path levels out for a short distance as it passes through groves of bamboo before heading downhill once again. Make your way down this quite muddy, rocky and, in some places, fairly steep trail for around 20–30 minutes until the waterfalls come into view. Carefully cross the narrow river to get a closer look and to access the pools.

Before you crossed the river, you may have noticed a narrow trail running uphill into the forest on your right. This is the trail to the Honeymoon Waterfall (see below). To access the upper pool at St Margaret's Falls, simply jump into the lower one and then climb up alongside the cascade. The route back is the same way you came; unfortunately the slippery downhill slopes are replaced by steep uphill ones.

**HIKE TO THE HONEYMOON WATERFALL** (*Duration: 30–45mins there & back from St Margaret's Falls; grade 3; guide: recommended; site entrance fee: EC$5 pp – note, if you have paid to go to St Margaret's Falls, you do not pay again to go to the Honeymoon Waterfall*) This hike runs from St Margaret's Falls up a narrow and steep track to the Honeymoon Waterfall. This small waterfall is very pretty and is located up above St Margaret's Falls on the same stretch of river. The trail is tricky. It is uphill, over rocks and mud and has a couple of narrow river crossings. In order to see the waterfall, you must also climb up a cascade right at the very end of the trail. This part is quite tough.

Just as you reach the St Margaret's Falls you have to cross over a small river. Before you do, look to your right and you should see a narrow trail heading up into the bush. The trail is wet even in the dry season and there are a number of places you must walk over slippery rocks and through areas of shallow water. These stretches can be a little treacherous so take care with your footing. Follow this rocky, muddy and wet trail for around 20 minutes until you reach a large set of rocks on the main river. You should be at a small pool with water cascading into it. Now you must cross the pool (there may still be a fallen tree to help in this rather tricky manoeuvre) and climb up a small rock face. Look for footholds as you walk very carefully up it through the cascading water. Assuming you make it in one piece, follow the rocky river bed for a short distance to some more boulders. Climb up on top of them to see the waterfall, which is just around the corner.

It is a pretty waterfall and has a very nice bathing pool. Take care on the rocks if accessing it. On the way back, take your time going back down the cascade as this is not the place for a twisted ankle or worse. Make your way back down the same route to rejoin the St Margaret's Falls trail.

## HIKE TO THE SUMMIT OF MORNE GAZO

**HIKE TO THE SUMMIT OF MORNE GAZO** (*Duration: 45mins each way; grade 3; guide: not required; site fee: none*) Morne Gazo is located to the east of St Paul's and is a conical peak that has great views of the south and west coasts from its summit. You can actually drive halfway up the peak and then walk the rest of the way, though the latter part of this hike is up a steep dirt track. If you are travelling by bus, take a bright green number 4 and get off just after St Paul's. Between the villages of Corbeau and Perdmontemps look for a petrol station opposite the Wildlife Bar (which is a good place for refreshments on the way back).

There is a narrow road that runs sharply downhill right next to the bar. Follow it for around 20–30 minutes on foot past some houses towards the radio mast, which you should be able to see right ahead of you. The road curves around to the left and turns into a rough vehicle track for a short distance. You will reach a sign for Morne Gazo and see a concrete road on the right-hand side that heads up to the mast. Walk up the very steep road to the mast. If you are in a car, this is as far as you can drive. Even if you just stay here at the mast, you will be able to enjoy really nice views down to the south coast.

To the right, alongside the bush, you should see a narrow trail. Follow it as it winds its way very sharply uphill. Notice how the soil begins to change colour to a darkish red, presumably because of a high iron content. The climb up this slope takes about 15–20 minutes and the last stretch is steep and slippery with little to hold on to, though you may notice that some very thoughtful person has tied a piece of rather disturbingly thin and fraying rope to help! Once you make it to the top you will see a wooden viewing platform that has been erected around a tree. Check the platform and its steps to ensure they will hold your weight before attempting to climb up. The views are panoramic all around. Especially good are the views down to St George's, Grand Anse and the southwest peninsula. Take care if climbing up on to the platform and also take your time going back down the steep track.

## HIKE (OR DRIVE) TO HOPE BEACH AT GREAT BACOLET BAY

**HIKE (OR DRIVE) TO HOPE BEACH AT GREAT BACOLET BAY** (*Duration: 30mins each way; grade 1; guide: not required; site fee: none*) This is a short walk or drive along a paved road then vehicle track to an expansive beach at Great Bacolet Bay. The waters are calm and shallow, making it good for bathing.

On the road midway between Crochu and the Mt Fann/Mt Carmel junction, there is the small community of Hope. If you are travelling by bus, take an orange number 2 from St George's and ask the driver to let you off at Hope Estate. Just to the south of Hope there is a sign on the coastal side of the road pointing to the Hope Development, which is a fairly grand housing project on the former lands of the Hope Estate. Follow the paved road for around 20 minutes, or five minutes by car. On a bend you will see a fork with a rough vehicle track heading downhill to the right. Follow this track a short distance through the forest to the beach itself. The track is easy, a little muddy in places, but not particularly troublesome. If you are in a car, you probably don't have to even engage the four-wheel drive along this short stretch.

It is nice to walk along the beach. Towards the southern end you will come across benches and a picnic area. There is also a vehicle track from here that goes back up to the main road. It takes around 15 minutes on foot.

## HIKE (OR DRIVE) TO BELLE ISLE BEACH AT LE PETIT TROU BAY (*Duration: 1½hrs each way; grade 1; guide: not required; site fee: none*) This hike takes you along a narrow ridge and then down a vehicle track to the very pretty Petit Trou Bay where you will find Belle Isle Beach. This beach is popular with locals, though as it is located close to a large housing development project this may change in the months and years to come. The walk is easy for the most part. The walk is easy for the most part though as you near the beach the track is a little rougher and can be muddy, but it is not too challenging.

If you are travelling by bus, take an orange number 2 from St George's and get off at the village of St David's.

A very short distance to the south of St David's there is a sign on the coastal side of the road that points the way to the Belle Isle & Batou Casse Housing Development.

Follow the clear road along the ridge. There are nice views across the valley to the north and the community of Requin. After around 45 minutes on foot or around 15 minutes by car, you will reach the stone gateposts of the housing development. This looks like it is going to be a gated community at some point in the future. At the time of writing there is free access and, if you feel inclined to do so, there are nice views of the rugged coastline to be had by following the paved road to its conclusion at Requin Point. From the gates, it is around 20–30 minutes on foot or around ten minutes by car to Requin Point.

If you want to head directly to the beach then take the vehicle track that runs to the side of these stone gateposts. This track is rough, grassy, muddy and with one or two large rocks. If driving, you will need to engage four-wheel drive here. The walk down through the pretty forest to the beach takes around 30 minutes. The tranquil waters of this bay are great for bathing. Waves are almost nonexistent and it is shallow, making it a nice place for families to visit.

## HIKE (OR DRIVE) TO LA TANTE BEACH (*Duration: 1hr each way; grade 1; guide: not required; site fee: none*) This hike or drive takes you along a paved road through the community of Pomme Rose (if you are travelling by bus, take an orange number 2 from St George's and get off here) and then down a forest track to La Tante Bay. There is a large area of grassland behind a narrow stretch of dark-sand beach which is a nice place for a picnic. The bay is sheltered to the north and south by La Tante Point and St Pierre Point, making the waters very calm. It is an easy downhill walk or drive.

On the coastal road in the village of Pomme Rose, on a sharp corner next to the Baker's Hut, you will see a sign to Paradise Bay Beach Resort & Spa, which is a cottage resort located on St Pierre Point. Follow a paved road through a residential community for around 20–30 minutes on foot until you reach a narrow stone bridge. Pass over the bridge and continue down the somewhat rough, though still paved vehicle track. Keep going straight down this track for a further 20–30 minutes or so until you emerge at La Tante Bay. On the right is a paved road leading up to the resort which, you will see, has a large wind turbine.

**HIKE (OR DRIVE) TO CABIER BEACH** (*Duration: 1½hrs each way; grade 1; guide: not required; site fee: none*) Crochu Harbour and Cabier Beach are really beautiful and definitely worth visiting. It is a perfect area to relax with a picnic. You can get there on foot or by 4x4 vehicle. There are two beaches and bays that are separated by Crochu Point, a small rocky outcrop that is the location of the Cabier Ocean Lodge. The small beach on the northern side of the point is Cabier Beach and is perhaps the prettier of the two small bays.

To get there, you should start in the village of Crochu on a bend called, and signposted, Café Junction (if you are travelling by bus, take an orange number 2 from St George's and get off here). Painted on a wall is a sign pointing down a narrow road to Cabier. Take this road and follow it through the settlement of Mahot. The road is paved and winds its way downhill along a narrow ridge with board and block houses on either side. You will meet lots of friendly people along the way. There is a turn-off to the left, but ignore it and keep going straight down until you round a bend and come to a T-junction. Turn right, following the sign to Cabier. It should take around 30 minutes on foot to reach this point.

From here on the paved road gives way to a vehicle track. Pass by some more houses and then take care as the track becomes rough and broken as it runs downhill. At the next junction, turn left, continuing to follow the signs to Cabier. At this junction you should see a sign pointing straight on to the Big Sky Lodge. After turning left towards Cabier, head to the next fork, this time ignoring the left-hand spur and continuing straight on. The road is paved for a stretch from here.

At the next fork you will see a concrete road heading sharply uphill on the left and a grassy vehicle track straight ahead. Take the grassy track to the next fork and turn left, again following the sign to Cabier. On your right-hand side, on private land, you will see some of the stone ruins of the former Crochu Estate. Ignore the spur to the right at this point and continue straight on until you reach the brow of a hill. You should arrive at a four-way junction. You need to take the second vehicle track on the left, not the one that goes straight ahead to Cabier, and not the one immediately to the left. Follow this track downhill and around a bend and you should see the sea and beach ahead of you.

## HIKE (OR DRIVE) TO ST DAVID'S POINT AND THE MEGRIN STANDING STONE

(*Duration: 1½–2hrs each way; grade 1; guide: not required; site fee: none*) Megrin is the location of the first European settlement on the island of Grenada. It was a relatively short-lived stay as the settlers found themselves subjected to constant attack and harassment by the Kalinago. It was the combined effort of four Englishmen by the name of Geoffrey, Hail, Lull and Robinson and 199 fellow companions who arrived on three ships that were destined for South America: the *Diana*, the *Penelope* and the *Endeavour*. The sporadic attacks by the island's indigenous Amerindian people made life intolerable for the new arrivals and it was with great relief that they packed up and left the island behind them one year later when a passing ship stopped to see how they were getting along.

Today the location of the settlement is marked by a large standing rock midway along the peninsula that runs from the village of Corinth (if you are travelling by bus from St George's, take an orange number 2 and get off at Corinth) to St David's Point. Unfortunately, like many places of historic or natural interest in Grenada, this one is fast becoming overtaken by the value of the real estate upon which it stands. There are several extremely luxurious homes on this peninsula and lot markings for others can be seen. At the time of writing, it is possible to walk all the way to the tip of St David's Point, though this may change with the development of new residences.

To the south of the La Sagesse Nature Centre, and a little to the north of the village of Corinth, there is a sign on the coastal side of the road pointing to the Megrin Town Project. The rough gravel road runs uphill and then down along the ridge. There are great views of the very pretty St David's Harbour and yachts at anchor on the right. Pass alongside some large residences until you reach a fork. Take the track on the left and follow it down, past some more houses, until you reach the large standing rock symbolising the site of the original Megrin settlement. It takes around 45–60 minutes to reach this point. From the rock, continue downhill until the road becomes a grass track, then concrete for a short distance, followed by a narrow trail through the coastal grasslands. If you are driving, park up at the end of the gravel road and walk from here.

Follow the narrow but clear trail through the grass and some low bushes until you reach the very end of the headland. It takes around 15 minutes on foot from the end of the gravel road to the point. There are great views both to the north and south along the rugged coastline.

On the return journey you may wish to take an alternative trail that ends up in Bacolet, near Corinth (at the time of writing it was too rough to drive). At the end of the gravel road you will see a spur trail that runs along the southern edge of St David's Harbour. If you follow it downhill you will reach the Bel Air Plantation and the Water's Edge Restaurant & Bar. It is a nice place to stop off for some refreshments or a bite to eat. At the end of the bay you will pass Grenada Marine which also has a pleasant beach bar and restaurant. The road becomes paved once it reaches Grenada Marine and then it is about a 30-minute walk back to the main coastal road.

# 8

# Sauteurs, Mt St Catherine and the North

Grenada's north has a wonderful combination of natural beauty and fascinating heritage. You can find yourself deep in the rainforest searching for hidden waterfalls, climbing Grenada's highest mountain or walking on long stretches of beach hoping for a sighting of giant leatherback turtles coming ashore. History reveals itself in the form of Amerindian petroglyphs, the famous 'Carib's Leap', and in plantation estates such as Belmont and the particularly impressive River Antoine where sugarcane is converted to rum in the very same way it was over 200 years ago.

This chapter starts by looking at how you get up to the north from St George's and then how you get around once you are there. Next, there is a short list of places to stay, eat and drink in this area, and after that we take a detailed tour of the region. First of all we head to Sauteurs from the village of Victoria on the northwest coast and, once there, we take a look around mainland Grenada's northernmost town. From Sauteurs we explore the very beautiful Levera Archipelago National Park on the northeast coast before heading south towards Grenville via Lake Antoine. Our final journey in the north is an alternative and very dramatic route that heads south from Sauteurs around the steep ridges and through the densely forested foothills of the Mt St Catherine National Park. The chapter then describes some of the interesting things to see and do in the region and finishes up with some great hiking.

## GETTING THERE

The best way to get to the north from St George's or the southwest peninsula **by car** is to follow the west coast road via Gouyave (see page 129 for details on how to get to Gouyave). It takes about an hour from St George's to Sauteurs. If you are travelling **by bus** then you must take a yellow number 5 marked Sauteurs from the bus terminal in the capital. It is possible to get to the north via the east and also via Grand Étang, but it takes a little longer and it is not as straightforward.

## GETTING AROUND

The most flexible way of getting around the north is by hire car or on foot. Though Grenada's bus system is excellent, there are really only two main bus routes in the north: between St George's and Sauteurs via Gouyave and Victoria (yellow number 5); and between Sauteurs and Grenville via Tivoli and Pearls (pink number 9). If you want to get to the elevated villages of Paraclete and Clabony you will either have to hitch a ride or walk, as buses rarely venture along these narrow and somewhat labyrinthine interior roads.

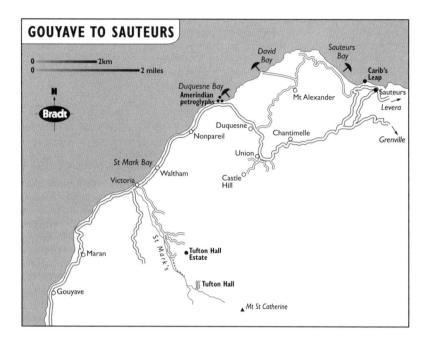

## GOUYAVE TO SAUTEURS

*David Bay*
*Sauteurs Bay*
Carib's Leap
Duquesne Bay
**Amerindian petroglyphs**
Sauteurs
Levera
Mt Alexander
Duquesne
Nonpareil
Chantimelle
Grenville
Union
St Mark Bay
Waltham
Victoria
Castle Hill
Maran
**Tufton Hall Estate**
**Tufton Hall**
Gouyave
Mt St Catherine

0 — 2km
0 — 2 miles

N
Bradt

 **WHERE TO STAY**

See page 57 for accommodation price codes.

### MID-RANGE AND BUDGET HOTELS

 **Barry's Country Retreat** (10 rooms) Castle Hill, La Fortune; ℃ 473 442 0330; f 473 442 0800; e barrysretreat@spiceisle.com; www.barrysretreat.com. Functional rooms with private bathroom, AC, TV. Use of pool & tennis court. Restaurant (see below). ⑤

 **Morne Fendue Plantation House** (13 rooms) Morne Fendue; ℃/f 473 442 9294; e mornefendueplantation@spiceisle.com. Simple,

modern accommodation located in an annex of an 18th-century historic plantation building. Private bathroom, fans & excellent mountain views. ⑤

 **Victoria Hotel** (5 sgl & 5 dbl rooms) Queen St, Victoria; ℃ 473 444 9367; f 473 444 8104. Basic hotel accommodation. Rooms have private bathroom, fan, TV & balcony with sea views. ⑤

### MID-RANGE SELF-CATERING APARTMENTS, COTTAGES AND VILLAS

 **Almost Paradise** Mt Alexander, Sauteurs; ℃/f 473 442 0608; e a.p.grenada@lycos.com; www.almost-paradise-grenada.com. Room & cottage accommodation located on the north coast near Sauteurs. Facilities

include private bathroom, outdoor shower, living area, fans, kitchenette, balcony with hammock, & great views of the Grenadines to the north. Restaurant (see below). English & German spoken. ⑤–⑤⑤

 **WHERE TO EAT AND DRINK**

### CREOLE AND INTERNATIONAL

 **Almost Paradise** Mt Alexander, Sauteurs; ℃ 473 442 0608; ⊕ Thu–Sun. Local & international lunches & dinners in open-air restaurant near Sauteurs with superb views of the Grenadines.

Dinners by reservation only. ⑤⑤
 **Belmont Estate Restaurant** Belmont; ℃ 473 442 9524; ⊕ daily. Serving a range of local & international dishes. Alcohol-free. ⑤⑤

✕ **Helvellyn House** Helvellyn; ☏ 473 442 9252. Garden restaurant serving Creole lunches, by reservation only. $$

✕ **Rivers Restaurant & Bar** River Antoine Estate; ☏ 473 442 7109. Located on the fascinating heritage estate, serving local & international cuisine daily. $$

✕ **Barry's Country Retreat** Castle Hill, La Fortune; ☏ 473 442 0330. Local & international home cooking, by reservation. $$

✕ **Carib's Leap Restaurant & Wine Bar** Sauteurs; ☏ 473 442 1453. Wine bar & restaurant with terrace dining overlooking Sauteurs main street. Serves local & international dishes. $$

✕ **Plantation Bar & Kitchen** Plantation Hse, Morne Fendue; ☏ 473 442 9294; ⊕ daily. Home cooking with marvellous mountain views from the dining terrace. By reservation. $$

✕ **The Heights Café Bar** Mt Alexander, Sauteurs; ☏ 473 442 0843. Local cooking with an international twist. Outdoor relaxed dining with superb views of the Grenadines. Great 'boneless' chicken roti. $$

✕ **Sunset Restaurant & Bar** Sauteurs; ☏ 473 442 9354; ⊕ daily. Local lunches & snacks. $

## A JOURNEY FROM VICTORIA TO SAUTEURS

Once known as Grand Pauvre by the French who established the settlement in 1741, the village of **Victoria** is the main village of the parish of St Mark. It is located on the northwest coast, just a few kilometres from Gouyave. Like Gouyave, Victoria has a tradition of fishing and nutmeg processing, though both have been experiencing a period of decline. The village is located on the beautiful shores of St Mark's Bay, a sweeping coastline of black-sand beach, rocks and, of course, Caribbean Sea.

Victoria is a quiet village with a main street and residential area behind. It has a pretty backdrop of the tall mountain ridges on the western boundary of the Mt St Catherine National Park. Along the main thoroughfare, Queen Street, there are a number of small bars and convenience stores such as **K Bell's Snackette** and **Marshall's Bar**, frequented by locals. Also on Queen Street is the **Victoria Nutmeg Station**. Prior to Hurricane Ivan the Victoria station, together with Gouyave and Grenville, was one of the three main processing plants in Grenada. The Victoria nutmeg station, or 'pool', is now used as a receiving station only. Growers will bring their nutmegs here from their farms, but they will then be taken to the Gouyave Pool for processing.

Queen Street is also home to the Catholic church and the police station. North of the police station is the Anglican church, the post office and the Victoria fish market. On the southern outskirts of the village, just next to the bridge over the St Mark's River is the **Victoria Entertainment Centre** where there is a riverside bar, pool tables and basketball court. On the southern side of the bridge is an adjoining road that heads inland via L'Esperance and Brothers Estate before looping back around to Gouyave. In the centre of town, beside the nutmeg station, is a road that heads inland from Queen Street towards the forests and mountains. This road passes the residential houses of the village as well as the school before winding its way inland along the St Mark's River towards the **Tufton Hall Estate**. Tufton Hall is the site of a proposed development project that has designs on restoring the original plantation house and converting it into an 'eco-spa'. Tufton Hall is also the name given to a waterfall that was once accessible via a riverside trail. The waterfall is a tall, narrow, split cascade that has a lukewarm water stream. Today the trail is unfortunately yet another victim of Hurricane Ivan and subsequent neglect. Nevertheless, a hike along the St Mark's River itself is great fun, though tricky, and still leads to the **Tufton Hall Waterfall** (see page 184).

From Victoria the road runs north along the pretty west coast through the settlements of **Waltham** and **Nonpareil**, a hamlet of colourful board houses and

Visitors to the more rural, less commercial and tourist-oriented areas of Grenada, will encounter small settlements and villages where people live in concrete, block, stone or board houses (sometimes a combination of these). The simplest and most traditional is the board house, also known as the frame house. This style of dwelling stems back to the 1800s when the peasant class and liberated slaves began to replace their cob houses (made from a daub of mud and straw with a thatched roof) with something a little sturdier. Constructed from local woods these board houses were very simple, with a single door, wooden louvre windows, hurricane shutters and a tall pitched roof to provide a degree of protection against wind and rain. Sometimes these little houses were raised on short stilts, depending on their location, to help prevent flooding. The thatched roof was replaced by wooden shingle and some would also have an open veranda. A small garden would surround the house, which was usually a place for growing vegetables, cooking over an open fire, rearing animals, going to the toilet and washing. Although times have changed and hurricanes have wreaked havoc among rural communities and peasant families, the board house remains, though it has evolved a little. These days the shingle roof has usually been replaced by galvanised steel and the louvre windows by glass or a combination of glass and louvre. Many are very brightly painted and decorated with pretty gardens of crotons, bougainvillea and flowering fruit trees. Simple, rustic and sometimes quite stylish, board houses are a traditional characteristic of Grenada's rural villages and suburban settlements.

fishing boats, nestled against the captivating Crayfish Bay. The road between Nonpareil and Duquesne to the north has some excellent views and a very scenic coastline. **Duquesne Bay** is a broad crescent-shaped bay of white sand and brightly painted fishing boats. It is also the location for one of Grenada's **Amerindian petroglyph** sites (see page 182). The name Duquesne comes from a Kalinago village chief known as 'Captain' Duquesne who lived in this area in the mid 1700s and who was very active during the conflicts between the indigenous people and the newly arrived French settlers. Duquesne, together with Waltham and Victoria, was the site of a military fortification constructed by the French during their occupation of the island in the early 1700s. From Duquesne Bay the road turns inland towards the communities of Duquesne, Union and Chantimelle before arriving at Sauteurs. The road is a pretty one, winding through forest and along the banks of the Duquesne River, with vibrant flora and colourfully painted board houses on either side.

From the schoolhouse in Union there is a road that runs uphill towards the settlement of **Castle Hill** on the northern slopes of the St Mark's Mountains. Just below Castle Hill is the small settlement of **Fountain** where there are two natural springs emerging from the mountainside which have been tapped by the residents. A bamboo pipe channels the water into a small enclosed rock pool where, in times of water shortage, local people can come to collect water for bathing. From Fountain there are very nice views across the forest towards Sauteurs on the north coast. The road from Union passes the village of **Chantimelle** before heading downhill towards the coast and Sauteurs. The road passes forested areas as well as residential housing, convenience stores and bars such as **Yvette's Grocery Store and Bar**. Before arriving at Sauteurs there is a road junction. A sign for Leapers' Hill points straight ahead. This is the way to Sauteurs. The road to the right bypasses Sauteurs and runs to Morne Fendue where it joins with the roads heading south to Grenville. Just before you enter Sauteurs you come to an area known as **Marli**. This is the location for one of Grenada's nutmeg receiving stations and also the only one remaining on the island where nutmeg oil processing still takes place.

## SAUTEURS

Sauteurs is mainland Grenada's northernmost community. Its name is derived from the French 'Morne Des Sauteurs' meaning 'Leapers' Hill', the name given to the area following the infamous routing and subsequent suicide of fleeing Kalinago. Rather than surrender to their French pursuers, it is said that around 40 of the embattled Kalinago chose to take their own lives by leaping from a hill to the sea and rocks below. **Leapers' Hill** (also called Carib's Leap) is still remembered in this small town, and a memorial and visitor centre have been erected on the site (see page 182).

Sauteurs is a very small place, consisting of a single main street thoroughfare with residential houses located on the hillside behind. To the west is **Sauteurs Bay**, a beautiful and very expansive bay with a white-sand beach lined with

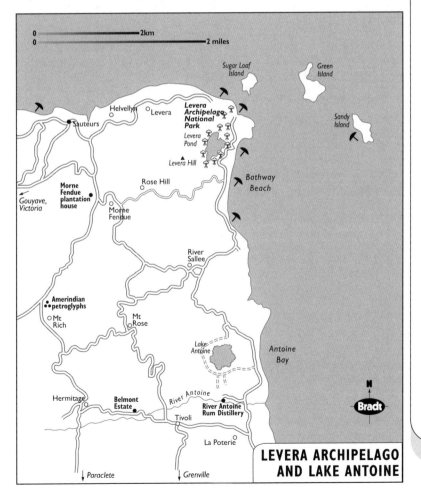

LEVERA ARCHIPELAGO AND LAKE ANTOINE

coconut palms. The beach stretches all the way to Laurant Point, and it is usually very deserted. To the east of Sauteurs are Irvins Bay, the hamlets of Helvellyn and Levera, and then the Levera Archipelago National Park.

Though diminutive, Sauteurs is a pretty coastal town with a vibrant main street where you will find convenience stores, a bank and ATM, fine local eateries such as **Carib's Leap Restaurant & Wine Bar** and **Helen's Eatery & Snack Bar**, the Sauteurs post office and police station, and also bus stops for transportation south along both west and east coasts. The striking St Patrick Roman Catholic Church with its bright red brick stands proud near Leapers' Hill on the west side of the town. The church was built in 1851 on the site of the first Roman Catholic chapel that was erected in the late 17th century by French Capuchin monks. Accessed via steep stone steps the church is bright and airy with a very traditional feel. It is constructed in the Caribbean Gothic revival style, which is typified by the tall, pointed-arch windows and the short, octagonal bell tower. The voices of children from the school yard next door drift in through the large, open arched windows. From the small courtyard in front of the church there are nice views of the town, the hills beyond and of Sauteurs Bay to the west.

Leapers' Hill is well signposted from the main street. Follow a crescent road that loops back to the main thoroughfare on the east of the town and you will pass a residential community of small wood and brick houses as well as some excellent local bars and snackettes such as **Northern Cuisine**, **Patrick's Sports Bar** and **Hayley's Ice Cream Parlour**. Follow the signs through this very friendly community to the gated entrance to Leaper's Hill and the visitor centre. Towards the eastern end of the Sauteurs main street you will find the **St Patrick Anglican Church** with its tall brick bell tower and next to it the Anglican school. Renovation and paintwork disguise the true age of this church. It was actually built in the 1830s and is the oldest surviving church in the parish of St Patrick.

## THE LEVERA ARCHIPELAGO NATIONAL PARK TO LAKE ANTOINE

The **Levera Archipelago National Park** is located at the northeasterly tip of mainland Grenada. Its 182ha encompass marine environment, beach, mangrove forest and swamp and the 9ha freshwater **Levera Pond**. The park was established in 1992, though not officially opened until 1994 when construction of hiking trails, access roads and a visitor centre, funded by the European Union, had been completed. Much has changed since then. The hiking trails are not marked and have become overgrown, and the areas around Levera Pond and Levera Hill are now the subject of a 'world-class luxury eco-resort' development project. In recent times this area has seen a great deal of controversial project development proposals and overseas investment promises. Nevertheless, this latest in what appears on the surface to be a series of stop-start, and rather ill-fated initiatives, seems to be making some progress. Currently the aim is to construct a US$180million resort, which will comprise a boutique hotel, villas, restaurants and outdoor activities including hiking, scuba diving, sport fishing, turtle watching and horseriding. Though the essence of a protected national park appears to have been somewhat sidelined by the intrusion of man and machine into this natural land and seascape, this project at least seems to have an ambition of promoting eco-friendly activities. Watch this space.

On the northern shores of the national park is **Levera Beach**. This is a most beautifully natural white-sand beach with rolling waves and surf. It is also a protected turtle-hatching site where visitors may be fortunate enough to catch a glimpse of giant leatherbacks (*Dermochelys coriacea*), the largest of all living sea turtles, returning to lay their clusters of eggs. The best time for observing this truly amazing sight is during the months from March to October. Levera Beach borders the mangroves and wetlands surrounding the Levera Pond and stretches around to Bedford Point, a rugged volcanic headland that was once the location of a gun battery and small fortification. Offshore, across the protected marine environment of coral reefs and sea grass beds, are three small islands. From west to east, they are Sugar Loaf Island (sometimes called Levera Island), Green Island and Sandy Island.

Beyond Bedford Point and south along the eastern edge of the national park is the magnificent **Bathway Beach**. Of comparable length to the far more commercial and popular Grand Anse Beach on the southwest peninsula, Bathway is quite stunning. Perfect white sand as far as the eye can see, against a grassy headland, with the waves of the Atlantic Ocean rolling in, Bathway Beach is where local people love to come and bathe. So far there are no luxury resort hotels along this beach and no sunbeds for rent. It is still very unspoiled.

Inland is the park's centrepiece, the **Levera Pond**. Hardly visible from its perimeter, the 9ha freshwater pond is surrounded by one of Grenada's largest areas of mangrove forest. The pond attracts a wide variety of migratory and resident waterbirds including the most wonderful scarlet ibis (*Eudocimus ruber*). The best place from which to view and access Levera Pond is from within the grounds of the Levera Eco Resort project. The entrance to this development is just beyond the northern end of Bathway Beach.

Following the main road out of Sauteurs on the eastern side of the town, the road turns towards the south, splitting to forge two alternate routes towards both Grenville and the capital, St George's. Immediately to the south of Sauteurs is the community of **La Fortune** and from here there is a coastal road that runs northeast through Helvellyn and Levera towards the Levera Archipelago National Park. South of La Fortune is **Morne Fendue** where the road forks. The more westerly route skirts the edges of Mt St Catherine National Park and is quite hilly and forested (see *South of Sauteurs and the Mt St Catherine National Park* on page 178), the easterly route is along relatively flatter lands near to the coast (which is the route we are now going to take). Both roads pass through pretty villages and have sites of interest to visitors.

Morne Fendue is located alongside the St Patrick River. It is a residential village with a mixture of modern and traditional board houses. Very near to where the main road forks, there is the **Anglican rectory**, a stone building in a picturesque setting of well-tended lawn, colourful gardens, trees and river. The main road passes the **Morne Fendue Plantation House**, a guesthouse, museum and restaurant with superb views of the surrounding countryside (see page 183).

Continuing south along the main road you will pass the **Pavilion Restaurant & Bar**, the **Central Point** snackette and the **Aroma** bar before reaching a traffic island where the road splits. The road south of the traffic island is the main bus route between Sauteurs and Grenville. It passes through the village of **Mt Rose** which has a quaint church and very traditional and extremely colourful board houses. We are going to head east at the traffic island, however, taking a more circuitous route along the east coast. We will rejoin the main road south at the village of Tivoli.

Taking the road east from the traffic island leads to the village of **River Sallee** where there are roads to both Bathway Beach and Lake Antoine. River Sallee was once a large estate where a waterwheel drove machinery to crush sugarcane. Following emancipation and the subsequent decline of the estates through lack of a labour force, freed slaves began working the land and eventually created a large rural community that is the River Sallee of today. The name of the village is

Yoruba is thought to be one of the world's largest Africa-born religions. Practised by the people of Nigeria, Sierra Leone and Benin, it came to the Americas during the slave trade. As Roman Catholicism was forced upon these captive people, a synergy of beliefs was born that manifests itself in many formats throughout the Caribbean region. These belief systems include Santería, Anago, Oyotunji and Candomblé. All of these entail worship of Orishas, spirits that reflect the many manifestations of one almighty god, Olorun or Olodumare. One popular Orisha is the god of thunder and lightning, Shango. Shango's sacred colours are red and white, his symbol is a double-headed axe and he is the owner of three double-headed drums. He is associated with music, dance and drumming. Ritual ceremonies would usually take place around water and feature drumming, dance, animal sacrifice and spirit possession. Though these beliefs and rituals have been discouraged by the Christian Church they nevertheless survive in small pockets of many countries throughout the modern world, including Grenada.

probably derived from the French, meaning 'salty river', in reference to the highly saline, mineral-rich sulphur springs found in the area. Between the traffic island on the main road south and the village of River Sallee itself, there are a number of small residential houses, some banana fields and then a sign indicating **sulphur springs**. This is one of several areas of residual subterranean volcanic activity in Grenada. Most sites are in the north, and this region around the Chambord Estate near River Sallee is considered the most scientifically interesting. Until fairly recently the springs were also considered the most spiritual by Shango worshippers and Spiritual Baptists who, believing the waters to be sacred or having supernatural powers, would come here on pilgrimages and to perform rituals. Today, however, the springs are actually rather disappointing. Spread over a very small area, the highest concentrations are to be found just a short walk from the road. Follow the sign along a rather muddy track for around five minutes. You will come to an open area of flat rock with the trademark yellow stains of sulphur deposits and sulphur-rich water. The rock contains a number of small, somewhat stagnant-looking pools. In some of them you will see bubbles rising to the surface. All of them are cold and the area is sadly unimpressive.

In the village of River Sallee there is a signposted road junction with routes to Sauteurs, Levera and Lake Antoine. The road to Levera passes residential houses, a church and cemetery and the River Sallee Credit Union. Near the **McKoi Snackette** there are some stone ruins of the old estate, including a windmill tower. The road continues through dry coastal scrub and grassland before reaching **Bathway Beach**. Very popular with local people, this long stretch of white-sand beach is quite beautiful and has so far survived large-scale resort development. If bathing at Bathway Beach, you should exercise caution, as this is the Atlantic Ocean and the surge and undertow are strong and can become even stronger with little or no warning. Along the beach to the north is a picnic area with wooden benches, tables, small bars, and the Levera Archipelago National Park visitor centre which, rather oddly, seems to spend most of its time closed. There is also a well-tended garden and small parkland nearby. It is a beautiful area and can be lively at weekends when locals 'free-up' and enjoy themselves on the beach.

North of Bathway Beach the road leads to the Levera Resort development project. It is from within the grounds of this new resort that visitors will gain the best views and perspectives of the Levera Pond, its birdlife and surrounding mangrove habitat. The road from the Levera Pond becomes a rough vehicle track

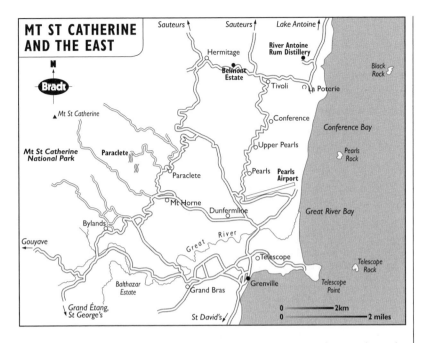

and passes the Bedford Point residential development area before reaching the beautiful Levera Beach.

The road south from River Sallee runs to the villages of La Poterie and Tivoli via **Lake Antoine**. It is a very rural area with a smattering of board houses, small snackettes and bars. The road hugs Antoine Bay and the road to Lake Antoine itself is very clearly signposted. This 6.5ha crater lake is very pretty and supremely peaceful. There is an abundance of birdlife, particularly around the vegetation of the littoral margins. The area around the lake is privately owned and farmed for bananas, pawpaw, watermelon and dasheen. The farmland access tracks are maintained three-quarters of the way around the lake's perimeter and make for a pleasant walk (see page 187 for more information). To the east of the lake is Antoine Bay, a wild and rugged shoreline that takes the full brunt of the rolling Atlantic Ocean waves.

South of Lake Antoine is the **River Antoine Rum Distillery** where visitors can experience the rum-making process almost exactly how it was performed over 200 years ago (see page 180). From River Antoine, the road curves inland at La Poterie and rejoins the main highway at the village of **Tivoli**.

South of Tivoli the road runs toward Grenville through the rural hamlets of **Conference** and **Pearls**. To the east of Conference there is a large coconut plantation before land reaches marshlands and the narrow beach at Conference Bay where the waves of the Atlantic Ocean crash relentlessly onto this very exposed stretch of coastline.

A little to the north of Grenville is **Pearls Airport**. Abandoned since 1984, it is a little surreal. It was built in 1943 when the 153ha Pearls Estate was purchased in preference over Point Salines as the location for the island's first airport. During its construction, Amerindian artefacts were discovered on the site indicating the location of an indigenous settlement. Unfortunately the runway took precedence and the Amerindian site was largely destroyed. The constraints of a small airport and its proximity to high ridges and mountains ultimately resulted in the construction of an alternative, international facility at Point Salines, and Pearls was closed. Today, it is rather an eerie place consisting of skeleton buildings and aircraft wreckage. The runway is used as a road connecting Upper Pearls with Lower Pearls, a place to learn how to drive, and occasionally a motor car-racing venue. From Pearls it is a very short distance to Grenville.

## SOUTH OF SAUTEURS AND THE MT ST CATHERINE NATIONAL PARK

The **Mt St Catherine National Park** is located in Grenada's northern interior, south of Sauteurs and east of Gouyave. This mountainous and forested park covers an area of 580ha and is possibly the least accessible place in the whole of Grenada. The park's terrain is rugged and its hills and mountain ridges are very steep and narrow. Vegetation is montane forest with cloudforest at the highest elevations. Most of the windward-facing ridges were damaged by Hurricane Ivan and the loss of many mature trees has caused considerable disruption to what was formerly a wet rainforest environment. Trees are now more thinly spread and the loss of a high canopy that would once have trapped moisture has created a habitat that is in a state of transition and regeneration. At the centre of the park is **Mt St Catherine** which, at 840m, is the tallest peak in Grenada.

There are a number of secondary roads running inland towards the interior of the park though some are in quite poor condition. Hiking trails are rarely maintained and have become overgrown. The ascent of Mt St Catherine itself should not be attempted without a guide who has local knowledge. This particular hiking challenge is not offered by the majority of tour operators, but it is possible. The best time to attempt it is in the dry season as the mountain's steep ridges are narrow, muddy and extremely slippery in the wet. Paraclete, Bylands and Mt Horne are good villages to ask at for local assistance (see box, *Extreme Hiking in Mt St Catherine National Park*, pages 186 and 187). For anyone just wanting to see the summit from a distance, a 4x4 vehicle can make it to the Cable & Wireless communication masts near the settlement of Blaize, to the northwest of Paraclete (see opposite). The road is paved but extremely steep. The views from the station are spectacular and you can see across the neighbouring peaks to the summit of Mt St Catherine itself.

Immediately to the south of Sauteurs near to the Morne Fendue Plantation House, a less frequently used road cuts a winding path through several pretty villages and picturesque countryside. It follows the St Patrick River southwards, high above its western bank as it passes through the settlements of **Snell Hall** and **Ellie Hall** towards **Mt Rich**. Look out for the Seventh-Day Adventist church, a lovely building of cut stone, perched high above the river.

At a road junction on the edge of Mt Rich, look out for a rather derelict and empty building on the river side of the road. It is below this building on the far bank of the river that you can see the huge boulder that hosts the **Mt Rich Amerindian Petroglyphs** (see page 182).

The road south of Mt Rich passes through a rather dramatic cut in the rock and runs alongside small banana, coconut and nutmeg plantations. The village of **Hermitage** is home to a number of attractions. On the north side of the village before reaching the junction for Peggy's Whim and the village church, you will see a sign for the **slave pen**. The sign asks that you call in advance to visit and it is only polite to do so (☏ *473 442 9277*). You may be granted permission by the owners of the site to pass onto their land and take a look at the ruins of the former **Hermitage Estate Great House** which, though in somewhat poor shape these days, stands proud on a small hill above the village. Walk up the track next to the sign and follow it as it curves around to the left. At the large iron gates, simply

Chocolate comes in many forms and is produced from the seeds of the cacao tree (*Theobroma cacao*), which is native to South America. Theobroma's literal translation is 'food of the gods' and is perhaps a reference to the Aztecs' use of a fermented cacao drink in religious ceremonies, particularly those associated with the goddess of fertility, Xochiquetzal. It was thought to have properties that gave those who drank it – usually warriors, priests and royalty – wisdom and vitality. It is said that Emperor Montezuma drank 50 goblets of liquid chocolate a day.

follow the single track around and into the grounds. Continue along the track to the house itself but do not enter. It is private and, at the time of writing, the building is very unsafe. The 'slave pen' relates to the cellar of the great house where slaves were once brought to be broken and then distributed as workers to the surrounding estates.

A little south of the great house is a sign saying 'Welcome to Hermitage Natural Spring'. A rather muddy and steep track close to the roadside leads to natural freshwater springs emerging from the hills. Below the road, on the opposite side to the sign itself, you can see this spring water emerging from pipes that channel it from its source for use by the people of the village. Close to the centre of Hermitage there is a junction with a steep road running up to the settlement of Peggy's Whim. A short distance up this road is the **Grenada Chocolate Company** (see box, page 181).

The road between the villages of Hermitage and Tivoli passes the **Belmont Estate** where visitors can enjoy a tour of the gardens and the working cocoa-processing plant (see page 181). It is here that organic cocoa is harvested from the grounds of the estate itself and then turned into chocolate by the Grenada Chocolate Company.

Between Hermitage and Grenville, the road passes through the high hillside villages of **Paraclete** and **Mt Horne**. The road is narrow and broken in places. It is very steep with some rather unnerving hairpin bends. The views are quite stunning and the journey equally dramatic as the route snakes its way across the vertiginous ridges and slopes of the foothills of the central mountain range and the Mt St Catherine National Park. From Paraclete and Mt Horne there are steep secondary roads and vehicle tracks that climb sharply up the mountain into the regions of **Blaize** and **Mt Hope**. Both roads offer spectacular views of the interior and Grenada's east coast, but if you are driving, you will definitely need a 4x4 vehicle for safe passage. These routes also offer access to a 'Hidden Grenada' (see pages 186 and 187) where the island's least accessible sites may be explored by the more adventurous.

This region used to have a significant nutmeg crop prior to the destructive force of Hurricane Ivan in 2004. The receiving station at Paraclete has now closed down and nutmeg trees, though present, are noticeably sparse.

From Paraclete and Mt Horne the road swings back down the mountainside towards Dunfermline and Grenville. An alternative route extends the hillside journey to the settlement of **Bylands** where there are further routes into the interior. **Clabony**, located on these high forested slopes is where Grenada's best-known hot springs are located. The network of secondary roads and tracks is very confusing in this area and, although there's a sign once you actually get there, it is best to ask for directions from local people in either Bylands or Clabony. In actual fact the hot springs are very disappointing, especially if you either come from or have visited other countries that are known for their hot springs. There is a pool with rather lukewarm, somewhat unappealing water, surrounded by overgrown bush. Of far more interest in this area are the villages, the farms, the rural life and the people themselves who, despite what must be incredibly hard times after the hurricanes, always seem to be resolute, upbeat and very ready to make new friends. A drive or a hike around these remote villages is highly recommended.

## WHAT TO DO

**VISIT THE RIVER ANTOINE RUM DISTILLERY** (*St Patrick, 2.5km south of Lake Antoine, near La Poterie & Tivoli; 20min guided tour EC$5 pp inc a rum-tasting session*) A visit to the River Antoine Rum Distillery is a must-do for visitors to Grenada. It is an absolutely fascinating glimpse into the past and is certain to enthral anyone interested in the cultural heritage of the region. If you have been hiking and have come across ruins of sugar estates, machine works, waterwheels and cane presses covered in bush and weeds, this experience will bring those discoveries to life.

'Captain' Antoine was a Kalinago chief with whom the French settlers sought peace following the series of conflicts leading to the tragic events at Leaper's Hill in present-day Sauteurs. Chief Antoine's village was located in the northeast and so a number of places still carry that name today, including River Antoine, Antoine Bay and Lake Antoine. Black Rock, a small islet located in the Atlantic directly east of the mouth of the River Antoine, is also recorded as being originally named Islet d'Antoine by the French.

Constructed in 1785, the distillery claims to have been continuously running since that time, making it unique in the Caribbean. The machinery and the processes of rum production employed by the estate go back to the 18th century, to a period of colonial rule and of course to a time of slavery. The huge waterwheel, some 8m high, is powered by water channelled from the river along an aqueduct and over large wooden paddles. The wheel in turn drives the machinery, which includes a huge crusher that is used to extract cane juice. The sugarcane harvested from the 180ha estate is cut and then loaded onto a rickety wooden conveyor that transports it up to the crusher. Workers manhandle the cane, pushing it into the crusher and then reloading it for a second run to ensure all the natural juices have been thoroughly extracted. The residue cane, now pulped and dry, is called *bagasse* and is used as a fertiliser and mulch for the cane field.

The cane juice is filtered through wicker mats and then ladled by hand along a succession of enormous copper bowls which are heated by a fire below. The juice develops its sugar concentration before being ladled into cooling tanks where it is given time to allow fermentation to begin. Once this has happened, the cane juice is channelled into large tanks where it ferments for about a week before being super-heated and distilled.

If you are driving to the River Antoine Rum Distillery, head south **from Sauteurs** towards Grenville and when you reach the Morne Fendue Plantation House turn left at the next junction and pass through the village of Morne Fendue. At a roundabout, turn left to River Sallee and from there follow the signs to Lake Antoine. Pass the lake and continue south along the coastal road until you see the Rivers Restaurant on your right and the entrance to the estate itself. If you are coming **from Grenville and the south**, head north to Tivoli. At the junction by the church turn right and follow the road all the way to the end. Turn left here and follow the road a short distance to the north until you reach the estate, which will be on your left. Few buses pass the River Antoine Rum Distillery so if you are heading there under your own steam you will need to get to Tivoli and either walk or hitch a ride from near the church. From both Sauteurs and Grenville, a pink number 9 bus, marked Tivoli, will take you there.

**VISIT THE BELMONT ESTATE** (*Located between Hermitage & Tivoli;* ⊕ *Sun–Fri; 30min guided tour of the cocoa process EC$5 pp, inc chocolate tasting; alcohol-free restaurant serving local cuisine*) This is a historic estate that dates back to the late 1600s when the first French settlers arrived on the island. The estate was a large coffee and sugar producer before transitioning to nutmegs and cocoa in the 1800s. Today it continues to produce cocoa for domestic consumption as well as for export.

The estate was first owned by a French family by the name of Bernego before being transferred to John Aitcheson of Airdrie, Scotland, when Grenada came under British rule following the Treaty of Paris in 1763. In 1770, the estate was leased to Alexander Campbell, a high-standing colonialist and colleague of Ninian Home, then Governor of Grenada. Both men were executed during the Fédon Rebellion (1795–96). Despite Grenada falling into the hands of the French between 1779 and 1783 the estate stayed in the Aitcheson family before being sold to the Houston family and then in 1944 to the Nyacks of Hermitage. The Nyack family was the first of Indian heritage to own an estate in Grenada and it is still owned by them today.

Described as an 'agri-tourism product', Belmont Estate successfully fuses agriculture, history and culture to produce an interesting business and heritage site that should be part of any visitor's agenda. In addition to tours of the cocoa process, there is a picturesque tropical garden, a museum and there are occasional cultural events such as dancing and drumming. But it is the cocoa that really captures the eye and the imagination. If you arrive on the right day you may be lucky to see local farmers bringing in their 'wet cocoa'. These are buckets of cocoa seeds that have been harvested from ripe cocoa pods. When removed from the pods, the seeds are covered in a thick white pulp. Each bucket is strained for excess liquid and then the contents, pulp and all, are placed into plastic bags which are then weighed. The farmer's pay is based on this weight and if you visit on a 'wet day' you will see lots of farmers in the fermentation shed draining and weighing their cocoa harvest, and receiving payment from the cashiers.

Once the seeds have been paid for they are poured into deep wooden fermentation bins where they 'sweat' and the pulp begins to liquefy. The sweating

## THE GRENADA CHOCOLATE COMPANY

The Grenada Chocolate Company was founded in 1999 by Mott Green. It produces organic dark chocolate from locally grown cocoa using refurbished antique machines. Production is in small batches and only uses organic ingredients. The chocolate bars come in distinctive colourful wrappers and are available in two strengths: 60% cocoa or 71% cocoa. The company also produces cocoa tea.

More of a small house than a Willy Wonka-style chocolate factory, the company uses solar panels to power the machinery and is part of a broader co-operative that includes cocoa farmers. The Organic Cocoa Farmers' Co-operative aims to ensure that both cocoa farmers and chocolate producer share their income evenly as well as trying to promote organic cocoa production. Acclaimed worldwide for its approach and success, the Grenada Chocolate Company has been lauded in the international press and has also received recognition at the World Chocolate Awards.

Chocolate bars can be purchased in stores throughout Grenada as well as from the Belmont Estate. They can also be purchased online via the company's website (*www.grenadachocolate.com*). Unfortunately the company no longer runs tours of its factory and production process. You just can't get the Oompa Loompas these days.

process is important for the taste and quality of the cocoa. It helps to rid the cocoa seeds of too much bitterness and it will last for seven to eight days. The next stage is drying. The seeds are drained of any remaining liquid pulp and then laid out on huge trays to dry naturally in the sun. These trays sit on rails and can be wheeled under cover in inclement weather. Workers will walk through the beans to turn them and allow air to circulate through them. The beans dry for around seven days, depending on the weather, and they are then ready for polishing which helps to prevent mould and also makes the cocoa look more cosmetically appealing. Before modern machinery, cocoa beans were polished in large copper pots by workers 'dancing' through them for hours on end.

Visitors to the Belmont Estate are sure to be captivated by the process that transforms a tree crop to the product many of us love so much.

If you are driving to the Belmont Estate **from Sauteurs**, head south towards Grenville. Just as you are reaching Tivoli, turn right. Belmont Estate is signposted. If you are travelling by bus from Sauteurs take a pink number 9, marked Hermitage and Tivoli. The bus will pass the Belmont Estate. If you are driving **from Grenville**, head north to Tivoli and turn left. Belmont Estate is located on the right-hand side of the road, midway between Tivoli and Hermitage.

## VISIT CARIB'S LEAP/LEAPERS' HILL (*Follow the signs from the main street in Sauteurs; guided tour EC$5 pp*)

In 1652, just two years after settling on the island, the French set about ridding themselves of the indigenous people, the Kalinago. Learning of a planned raid by the Kalinago on the settlement of Fort Louis, they launched a fierce counter-attack. Many Kalinago were killed and they were forced into retreat. A few managed to escape over the mountains to the east while others fled to the north. The story goes that around 40 Kalinago reached the northern coast on a high rocky peninsula and, preferring death to enslavement or cruelty at the hands of their pursuers, they threw themselves down the cliff. The French named this place 'Le Morne des Sauteurs' meaning 'Leapers' Hill' and it is found in the present-day town of Sauteurs.

Leapers' Hill has been developed as a tourist attraction and is definitely worth a visit. The site is informative as well as historic. An exhibition room contains ceramic artefacts, basketware and military paraphernalia. There is also an excellent diorama depicting Kalinago village life based on European historical records and archaeological findings.

Beyond the exhibition room there is a paved path to a covered deck and viewing platform. This is a really nice place to relax, enjoy views of some of the islands to the south, cool off in the refreshing sea breeze, or perhaps even enjoy a picnic. A refreshments building and toilet facilities are located nearby. There is also a shop selling souvenirs and local crafts. Beside the deck there is a small path leading to another viewing platform, this one with a map of the Grenada Grenadines and rocky dependencies to the south.

A tranquil spot with an inglorious legacy, Leapers' Hill is one of very few places remaining in Grenada where an insight into pre-Columbian history can be experienced.

## DISCOVER AMERINDIAN PETROGLYPHS AT DUQUESNE AND MT RICH

Petroglyphs are images that have been etched into rock and are found all around the world, having been created by many different people from a range of historical eras. Grenada's petroglyphs are believed to have been carved by the island's earliest Amerindian settlers and are found at several sites in the north. The best known are those at Duquesne and Mt Rich, although the latter has recently become fairly inaccessible. The elaborate carvings appear to depict figures and faces, perhaps even monkeys which appear in ancient myths, though we can only speculate as to their meaning. Most scholars believe the images relate to gods or mythical figures.

The Mt Rich petroglyphs are carved on a large boulder that now finds itself upturned at the bottom of a deep valley alongside the St Patrick River. You can still see the boulder and make out some carvings from the roadside, but it is a strain. The best and most accessible examples of Grenada's Amerindian petroglyphs are at the southern end of Duquesne Bay. To get there, simply walk on the beach and head left all the way to the rock face at the end. There is also a signpost and track from higher up on the main coastal road. It is definitely worth a short diversion to see these petroglyphs.

Duquesne Bay is located on the west coast road to the north of Victoria, at the point where the road turns inland towards Sauteurs. To get there by bus you can take a yellow number 5, marked Sauteurs.

**GO TURTLE-WATCHING** Each year during the months between March and October, it is possible to see giant leatherback turtles (*Dermochelys coriacea*), the largest of all living sea turtles, return to Grenada to lay their clusters of eggs and then to see those eggs hatching. Some of Grenada's tour operators and conservation groups offer evening turtle-watching expeditions. (See *Levera Archipelago National Park*, page 174, and *Turtle-watching operators* in *Chapter 3*, page 79).

**VISIT HELVELLYN HOUSE AND POTTERY** (\ 473 442 9252; e helvellynhouse@ spiceisle.com; ⊕ 09.00–17.00 Mon–Sat) From Sauteurs it is a relatively short walk to Helvellyn. Head east out of the town and at the first junction you come to in La Fortune, go left. Keep the sea to your left and follow the road for around 15 minutes until you reach Helvellyn, which is signposted on the left-hand side.

Helvellyn House is an old family home with carefully tended gardens and a restaurant that serves traditional Creole lunch from 12.00 to 15.00 (reservations preferred). Located at the top of a hill in the hamlet of Helvellyn to the east of Sauteurs, the gardens have panoramic views of the sea and the Grenadines to the north. Down the hill below the house is the Helvellyn Pottery Workshop & Learning Centre where you can see pottery being made. The potter is from Morocco and his work is excellent. Visitors can see how clay from the local area is combined with clay from Pearls on the east coast, prepared and then turned and shaped on a low wheel that is rotated by the potter's feet, before being glazed and fired in a brick kiln. You can also give it a try yourself if you like. The pottery is quite literally crammed with beautiful pieces that are sold at various outlets throughout Grenada as well as exported abroad.

**VISIT THE MUSEUM AT THE MORNE FENDUE PLANTATION HOUSE** (⊕ daily; US$5 pp) Originally a wooden chattel-style house, then reconstructed in 1908 by George Kent from cut stone and held together with a mortar made from powdered limestone and molasses, the great house at Morne Fendue has a very Scottish feel and is home to an interesting collection of historical artefacts as well as a restaurant and guesthouse. Never really a plantation house itself, the great house was the more convenient location for the management of five estates in the area. On the ground floor there is a museum collection of antique furniture, period costumes, artwork and a display dedicated to former owner, Betty Mascoll, a Grenadian-born lady who served in World War II and subsequently dedicated much of her life to community work as well as being a lifelong member of the International Red Cross. Betty was awarded an MBE and was also the recipient of the Florence Nightingale Award. Upstairs there are five bedrooms and a bathroom, furnished in traditional Victorian style. These rooms are essentially for display purposes only.

Guest accommodation is located in a more modern wing to the side of the building. The well-tended gardens at the rear of the house are very colourful and there are expansive views from the terrace of the Plantation Bar & Kitchen, which serves traditional Caribbean fare.

To get to the Morne Fendue Plantation House **from Sauteurs** head south towards Grenville and you will reach the plantation house just a short distance out of the town. It is before you reach the junction for Morne Fendue village and will be on the right-hand side of the road. If you are travelling on foot then it is about a 20-minute walk out of Sauteurs. Alternatively take a pink number 9 bus.

## WALKS AND HIKES

**A RIVER HIKE TO TUFTON HALL WATERFALL** (*Duration: 3–3½hrs there & back; grade 4; guide: recommended; site fee: none*) This is a beautiful, though technically challenging hike, up the St Mark's River through a picturesque valley between the coastal village of Victoria and the foothills of Mt St Catherine, to a cascading waterfall of around 25m in height. Though quite tall, the waterfall is not particularly spectacular, split into two narrow streams that splash down over the rock face. Despite a lack of drama at the end, the river hike itself is the real adventure and it is great fun. There are several tall river rapids that you must scramble over, as well as landslides and fallen trees – the results of Hurricane Ivan. Along the way there are a number of small but quite deep pools that are excellent for a bathe or just to cool off. This hike is not for the faint-hearted. You must hold your nerve and be bold in your approach as you make your way up the river. Do not attempt this hike in periods of heavy rain as, like any river, it is prone to flash flooding.

The trailhead is inland from the town of Victoria. Take the road that heads up the valley from the nutmeg receiving station in the centre of the town. Follow it past a school and up through the countryside. At the first fork, take the road to the right. Do the same again at the next fork a little higher up. The tarmac road comes to an end near a house and a small facility that collects water from the river. To the right of the house and the steel fence there is a concrete bridge crossing the river. The trail starts on a wide grassy path before the bridge on the left-hand bank.

Follow the wide track along the river until it narrows. It is usually very muddy. Although it can be a little overgrown, the route is obvious. Follow this track for around ten minutes until it arrives at a big rock on the riverbank. You should see two concrete weirs where steel pipes collect river water. Owing to hurricane damage and little use, the track is very bad from this point. Not only is it completely overgrown, it sometimes disappears entirely. So at this point, the best trail becomes the river itself.

Take your time, follow the edges where possible and look ahead to plan your route. You must now follow the river for at least an hour, probably a little longer, depending on your pace. Do not rush, watch your step, and when you must cross the river or climb boulders, be sure of your footing and never, never jump. A slip here will mean a graze or a sprain at the very least, and this is not the kind of place where you want to be looking for medical attention.

The hike upriver is fabulous. You will encounter a series of tall river rapids, deep pools and narrow channels. Take care when climbing over fallen trees. Test them before giving them your weight as they may be loose or rotten. You will have to make your way over some rather serious challenges like this before you get to the end. Keep pushing on until you reach a tall cliff face and the waterfall marking the end of your hike. Look up. You are actually quite close to Mt St Catherine now.

Mountaineers and hikers will tell you that most accidents occur on the way back. So, though filled with exuberance and a sense of achievement, it is important that you maintain your concentration as you make your way back downriver to the concrete weirs, the track and the start of the trail.

To get to Victoria by car from the southwest you must pass through St George's and head along the coast through Gouyave. It will take around 45 minutes. From Victoria it takes around 15 minutes by car and around 45 minutes on foot to reach the trailhead. To get to Victoria by bus, take a yellow number 5, marked Victoria and Sauteurs, from the bus terminal in St George's.

**HIKE (OR DRIVE) FROM DUQUESNE TO SAUTEURS VIA MT ALEXANDER** (*Duration: 2½–3hrs on foot, ½hr by car; grade 1; guide: not required; site fee: none*) This is a really pleasant 'long-way-round' journey from Duquesne to Sauteurs whether on foot or by car, passing through forest and small village communities before reaching the coast. A short detour leads to a 'secret' beach at David Bay where you may encounter local fishermen heading out in their colourfully painted wooden boats over the rolling surf. The journey continues northwards to the coast and emerges at Laurant Point and the beautiful long stretch of white-sand beach at Sauteurs Bay.

Starting in the village of Duquesne (to get there by bus you can take a yellow number 5, marked Sauteurs, and get off a few minutes after heading inland from Duquesne Bay), look for a small sign that says 'Duquesne Roman Catholic Chapel', pointing to a narrow road over a small stone bridge. This is the beginning of the trip. Follow this little road as it winds its way upwards and north through a residential community and past banana fields. The more you ascend towards the village of Mt Alexander the better the views of the surrounding area become. Stick to the main road as it reaches the summit of the ridge. There are very nice views of the sea, the north coast and the Grenadines in the distance from here. Begin your descent through the village of Mt Alexander. The road snakes and crosses a couple of small bridges as it passes a number of traditional board as well as more modern block houses. Keep with the main road until you reach a junction. The main tarmac road continues to the right. To the left is a concrete road and an interesting diversion if you have the time and the energy. Follow the concrete road past more houses and over a colourfully painted bridge. It ends at a rough vehicle track near some board houses. Follow this pretty tree-lined track until you reach a narrow walking trail on the right. Take this trail past some ruins through the trees to a lovely secluded beach. You may encounter fishermen either setting out on or returning from their fishing trips.

When you are ready, head back to the junction. Once back at the beginning of the diversion, follow the tarmac road until it too transitions to concrete and winds its way downhill towards Laurant Point and Sauteurs Bay. If you are about ready for a little refreshment you could take a break at **Almost Paradise** or **The Heights** (this is a bit of a climb to the top of a hill!). Look for their signs on the main road. Once you reach the coast at Sauteurs Bay you should notice tracks down to the beach itself. Look out for the ruins of a **lime kiln** on the western end of the beach. This was once used to make white lime from coral and other marine organisms that was then used as a mortar in buildings as well as a fining to remove impurities during rum production. Further along the road towards Sauteurs you will come across wooden benches and tables where you could stop for a picnic. From this point simply follow the main road as it passes over a couple of painted stone bridges before reaching the village of Sauteurs.

**HIKE FROM SAUTEURS TO LEVERA (AND ON TO BATHWAY BEACH)** (*Duration: 3hrs there & back; grade 1; guide: not required; site fee: none*) Levera Beach can be accessed from either Bathway Beach or along the north coast from Sauteurs. The road from Sauteurs makes for a nice walk. The beach and views are very pretty and you could

Though Hurricane Ivan is clearly responsible for the poor condition of some of the island's hiking trails, the lack of investment (in terms of both time and money) in clearing and maintaining them also means that visitors interested in getting to sites that are off the beaten track have to work that bit harder. Two such places can be found in the Mt St Catherine National Park. They are Mt St Catherine itself and the Paraclete Waterfalls.

Local knowledge and a sharp machete for cutting back overgrown bush are essential on these hikes. In the village of Paraclete on the road between Hermitage and Grenville, you could ask for assistance. Good local contacts are Dwane Thomas (✆ 473 442 6109), Reean Gibson (✆ 473 442 5354), Kirby Thomas (✆ 473 442 5520) and Abijah Abraham (✆ 473 442 6552). Both of the hikes to Mt St Catherine and the Paraclete Waterfalls are great fun though very difficult because of the condition of the routes. Properly developed trails in this region would certainly attract more hikers, and perhaps create some employment in communities that have suffered so much from the loss of their nutmeg crops. I encourage you to help create that demand and opportunity by taking on some of these more difficult, yet very beautiful challenges accompanied by good local guides.

**HIKE TO THE SUMMIT OF MT ST CATHERINE** (*Duration: 4–5hrs there & back; grade 4; guide: essential; site fee: none*) Mt St Catherine is Grenada's tallest peak at 840m. There are several routes to the top but perhaps the most common trail starts in the hills above Blaize, off the narrow and extremely steep single-vehicle road that runs up to some telecommunications masts.

On the northern outskirts of the village of Paraclete on the road between Hermitage and Grenville, a road made of two concrete vehicle tracks runs steeply uphill towards a very appropriately named area called Hope. Probably the steepest road in the whole country, it eventually reaches a very remote telecommunications tower. If the cloud ceiling is high enough, you are rewarded with tremendous views of the forest, the coast and Catherine herself.

call in at Helvellyn House and Pottery along the way. The road is paved for most of the journey but becomes a rough vehicle track as it approaches and descends to Levera Beach.

Head east from Sauteurs and a little way out of the village there is a junction at La Fortune. You may see a stone building called Nora's Place on the corner. Take this small road east and walk through the residential communities of La Fortune, Helvellyn and Levera. You will pass Helvellyn House and Pottery on your left (see page 183). Continue along this road as it winds its way through these communities for around 30 to 45 minutes. Pass by, and perhaps stop to look at, the very unusual and unquestionably original artwork of Doliver Morain that may take you a little by surprise along the roadside. The houses will become fewer and the road will reach the brow of a hill and descend towards the sea. At this point the road turns into a dirt track and you get your first views of the coast and Sugar Loaf Island.

Walk down the hill towards the bottom. The path opens up into a small area of grassy pastureland. You may see cows or even horses grazing. Follow the track as it curves to the right until you reach the beach. The boundary of the Levera Resort development project is ahead of you, so take the little track to your left down on to the beach instead. Enjoy a stroll along the beach, following it around the corner right to the end and the sign stating that the beach is a protected turtle nesting site. From here the wide vehicle track passes along the rugged coastline south of

One route to the top starts a little way down the road from the tower. It runs quite steeply downhill for a stretch and then follows a narrow ridge towards the mountain. From then on it is an uphill scramble all the way, slipping and sliding in the mud, and trying to find a tree or a plant that doesn't uproot in your hand when you grab on to it in blind terror and desperation. Actually it is not that bad, but it is steep, it is muddy and it is extremely strenuous. Be sure to take plenty of water and a good, knowledgeable guide. Pace yourself and cross your fingers for clear weather because the summit is frequently cloaked in cloud. As you can imagine, if it is clear, the views are awesome.

**HIKE TO THE PARACLETE WATERFALLS** (*Duration: 2–3hrs there & back; grade 4; guide: essential; site fee: none*) There are two waterfalls hidden in the densely forested foothills of Mt St Catherine. One waterfall is around 20m tall but becomes a trickle during the dry season; the other is around 15m and is always full with a small pool beneath. The hike to these waterfalls is extremely tough. The track is very steep and always muddy. Your guide will take you uphill from the village along a paved road that soon becomes rough and uneven. If driving, you will need a 4x4 vehicle. It may be better to walk. From the village to the trailhead it will take around 30 minutes on foot or around ten minutes by car. Where the track splits, take the left-hand route and follow it until it narrows to a single path. The trail winds sharply uphill and emerges on a narrow ridge. There are expansive views of the east coast down to Marquis Island and beyond.

The trail passes through a nutmeg plantation that suffered at the hands of Hurricane Ivan. Though there are still many trees, the dense nutmeg forests that were there before the storm and provided an income for local farmers have gone. Follow the path down the side of a very steep ravine. It is really muddy here with few footholds and little to hang on to. Be careful or you could very easily find yourself careering uncontrollably downhill (like I did !).

The descent to the bottom of the narrow valley takes around 30 minutes. It is very wet underfoot and you must walk a short distance upstream before you gain sight of the waterfalls.

Bedford Point, from where there are great views of a 'secret beach'. It also passes the mangroves around the margins of Levera Pond before finally emerging at the northern end of Bathway Beach. If you fancy going this way instead of turning back, it will take about 20 minutes to reach Bathway on foot from Levera.

Levera Beach is a great place for a picnic. It is quiet and stunningly beautiful, particularly with the backdrop of Sugar Loaf, Green and Sandy islands. If you decide to bathe, take care as the sea can be a little choppy, there can be a strong undertow and in some places there are cross-currents which may take you by surprise. However, bathing here is fun and the surrounding coastal environment of the Levera Archipelago National Park is quite beautiful.

**HIKE AROUND THE MARGINS OF LAKE ANTOINE** (*Duration: 1½hrs there & back; grade 1; guide: not required; site fee: none*) Lake Antoine is a 6.5ha crater lake located close to the northeast coast. The land around the lake is privately owned and there was a time when you could walk all the way around in a loop, but unfortunately this was not possible at the time of writing. The path three-quarters of the way around is kept clear thanks to the banana farmers who plant around the lake. Unfortunately there is a stretch where they do not plant or require access and this small arc has become very overgrown with dry, tall scrubland bush. Hopefully, this may change and those interested in walking around this pretty crater lake can do so without having to retrace their steps. Despite this, it is still a very pleasant walk. The lake is beautiful and serene and there is an abundance of wildlife; in particular lots of waterfowl can be observed in and around the arum lilies that crowd the littoral margins.

If you are driving to Lake Antoine, head south from Sauteurs towards Grenville and when you reach the Morne Fendue Plantation House, turn left at the next junction and pass through the village of Morne Fendue. At a roundabout, turn left to River Sallee and from there follow the signs to Lake Antoine. Once you reach the sign, follow it up a short hill where the road ends. There are no bus routes that pass Lake Antoine so if you are heading there under your own steam you will need to get to River Sallee and either walk or hitch a ride from there. A pink number 9 bus, marked River Sallee, will take you there.

As you face the lake, you should take the track on the right, walking around the lake in a counter-clockwise direction. For the first ten minutes or so as you walk along the vehicle track, the view of the lake is obscured by trees. Once you are past these tall trees there are nice views of the lake and its birdlife. The geological formation of the crater itself is also clear to see both in the lake and in its surrounding topography. This track can be a little muddy in the wet season so take care with your footing. You will pass two tracks on your left leading down towards the lake. Both are farmland access tracks. The first one is worth a short ten-minute diversion as it brings you close to the margins of the lake where you will get a better look at the littoral vegetation and birdlife.

As you continue along the main track, you will start to ascend. You will also notice that between you and the lake is an area of dense banana plantation, which skirts the entire western shore. You may also encounter people working this area of farmland.

When you have been walking for around 45 minutes or so you will reach a junction of four paths. One route is a continuation of the vehicle track you are on, another vehicle track goes to the right, and a narrow path disappears into the bush on the left. The path on the left is the remainder of the original circular trail around the lake, the path on the right goes to farmland and the path straight ahead continues for another 20 minutes before emerging on the main coastal road on the south side of Antoine Bay between River Sallee and La Poterie. Unless the circular track has been reopened, you should turn and walk back the way you came once you reach this point.

# 9

# Carriacou and Petite Martinique

It is often said that the islands that make up the Grenadines have far more in common with each other than they do with either St Vincent or Grenada. Whether true or not, there is definitely a sense of independence here, a collective indifference to the affairs of the world beyond their shores, indeed an almost palpable feeling of existing in the only space that really matters. When talking to those who were born here, who live and work here, or who have arrived by sailing boat and, for one reason or another, have found it difficult to leave, you get the distinct impression that if the islands were cut adrift from their respective nations, life would simply carry on as it always has done.

Travellers to Grenada should definitely incorporate both Carriacou and Petite Martinique into their holiday. They are not only picturesque islands, they also have fascinating traditions as well as a strong cultural identity. This chapter begins by describing some of this shared history and heritage in detail. It then looks at each island in turn, describing how to get there, how to get around, where to stay, and where to eat and drink. Each section concludes with details of things to do including a number of wonderful walks and hikes.

## GEOGRAPHY

**CARRIACOU** Carriacou is located at 12°29′N, 61°27′W, some 37km north of Grenada. It is the largest of the Grenada Grenadines with an area of 34km². At its extremes it measures 11.3km by 4.8km.

Carriacou's main town is **Hillsborough**, which is situated on the central west coast on a large bay. It is also the island's administrative centre and currently its main commercial port. This is also where the high-speed Osprey ferry service between Grenada, Carriacou and Petite Martinique arrives and departs. Carriacou's main yacht anchorage is Tyrell Bay, a natural horseshoe-shaped bay on the west coast, and location of the island's second-largest community, Harvey Vale.

Carriacou has an undulating coastline with a number of secluded bays, both white- and black-sand beaches, dramatic cliffs, rugged limestone and lava outcrops, mangrove forests, fossil beds and swamps. A broken ridge runs along the spine of the island with its two highest points being in the north and in the south. High North is 291m and Morne Jaloux (also referred to as Chapeau Carré) is 290m. The interior is partially forested, and partially farmed. Farms tend to be smallholdings that support the needs of families and local communities rather than anything on a larger scale. This subsistence farming produces crops such as pigeon peas, beans, corn, cabbages and a variety of ground provisions. Common fruits grown in Carriacou include pawpaw (papaya), watermelon, grapefruit and pineapple.

Outside of Hillsborough, most communities are small villages that are linked by a simple road system, most of which is paved. In one or two areas, notably along

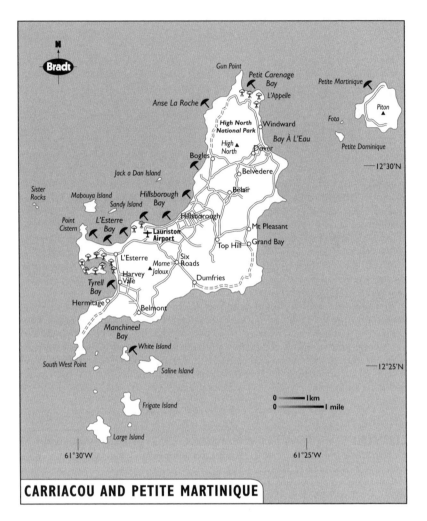

**CARRIACOU AND PETITE MARTINIQUE**

the coast between Mt Pleasant and Limlair, the road is unpaved. At Lauriston Point, between Hillsborough and Tyrell Bay, there is a small airstrip called Lauriston Airport where daily flights operate to and from Grenada.

Carriacou has a number of areas that have been designated national parks, protected seascapes or protected cultural landmarks. At the northern tip is the **High North National Park**, which covers the immediate forested area around High North peak as well as the coastline to the west and to the north. To the west of High North, Anse La Roche is one of the island's prettiest and most secluded bays. To the north is the L'Apelle mangrove forest and bird sanctuary, and beyond it Petit Carenage, a quite beautiful isolated bay and beach. In the centre of Carriacou is the **Belair Forest Reserve**. This area has a protected teak and mahogany forest and is where a well-preserved stone windmill tower can be found. Windmill ruins like this one are scattered all around Carriacou. They were once used as a means of harnessing windpower to run machinery that would crush sugarcane. Unlike Grenada where rivers and waterwheels were used by sugar estates, this has never been an option in Carriacou and Petite

Martinique. Protected seascapes around Carriacou include the mangrove swamps and oyster beds on the northern edge of Tyrell Bay, the reef systems of Mabouya Island and Sandy Island off the west coast, the mangrove swamps off Lauriston Point, and also the very beautiful reefs of Saline Island and White Island off the south coast.

**PETITE MARTINIQUE** Located approximately 5km to the northeast of Carriacou at 12°31′N and 61°23′W, Petite Martinique has an area of just 2km$^2$ and consists of a single peak, called Piton, which rises to 225m. The island's residents mainly live around the western shoreline with the remainder of this island uninhabited.

## CLIMATE

Carriacou and Petite Martinique experience a similar climate to Grenada though here there are no mountains and tropical forests to catch clouds and stimulate rains. The weather is usually dry and there is always a risk of high exposure to the sun. Water shortages can be a problem from time to time, particularly during the dry season (January to June). Most houses have a cistern that uses captured rainfall, which is usually safe to drink, though bottled water is also widely available in shops and restaurants on both islands. Visitors must be sure to prepare themselves for the full force of the sun here. It is for good reason that many people wear hats or try to stay in the shade during the middle of the day when temperatures are highest and the sun is directly overhead.

## HISTORY

The name Carriacou is thought to be derived from the original Amerindian name for the island, Cárou-cárou, whose meaning is 'land of reefs'. Archaeological studies and excavations have found lots of evidence to suggest that Carriacou was inhabited by Amerindians. The majority of finds have been along the coastline, reinforcing the theory that the island's original settlers would have lived primarily off the sea, though may have also undertaken some basic farming. Ceramics and *zemi* stones (see box, below) have also been unearthed. The Carriacou Museum in Hillsborough has a fine display of Amerindian artefacts.

It is thought that European settlers did not arrive on Carriacou and Petite Martinique until the early 18th century. Their coming brought the establishment of estate lands and, with that, slave labour. The estates mainly produced cotton, sugar and limes. At the time the islands would have had a great deal of woodland but the need to grow crops caused a high level of deforestation which in turn

---

### *ZEMI* STONES

Associated with Amerindian spirit worship, *zemis* or *zemi* stones are sculpted objects or idols that are believed to either symbolise or be inherently endowed with a supernatural power. Sometimes carved from wood or conch shell, though usually from stone, *zemis* have been unearthed at archaeological sites throughout the Caribbean and there are records of them even being presented to newly arrived Europeans. A common form of *zemi* is the three-pointed stone version which is believed by some academics to represent the volcanic islands of the Caribbean and their intrinsic nature spirits. You can see examples of these symbolic *zemis* at the Grenada Museum in St George's as well as at the Carriacou Museum in Hillsborough.

resulted in the loss of natural water catchments. Once the cotton and sugar industries fell into decline during the latter half of the 19th century following emancipation, estates were abandoned and former slaves who stayed there found themselves with little land, little water and very little opportunity. Many people left the island in search of a livelihood elsewhere.

As there were so many abandoned settlements, the people of Carriacou and Petite Martinique were able to purchase land quite cheaply from the government and so they began to survive on fishing, boatbuilding, smuggling and subsistence farming. The crops grown then reflect those still grown today, with pigeon peas, corn and ground provisions being the most common. Following the decline of the estates, smuggling became integral to the islands' economies – some say it still is – as islanders felt the squeeze of economic hardship setting in. In latter years the traditional boatbuilding industry also experienced a decline as steel and other modern materials began to replace wood. Many islanders left Carriacou and Petite Martinique to seek employment abroad, particularly in the UK, and those who remained complained bitterly that they were being neglected by mainland Grenada. Indeed the perceived lack of interest and investment in both islands remains a fiercely debated topic even today, though the talk of secession that surfaced in the 1990s appears to have waned.

Lauriston Airport was constructed on Carriacou in 1968 and was upgraded in 1994. It is a small airfield that is capable of accommodating light aircraft only. In 1997, the government appointed a minister for Carriacou and Petite Martinique Affairs who is permanently resident on Carriacou.

## CARRIACOU AND PETITE MARTINIQUE TODAY

Today the islands are very popular with sailing enthusiasts and travellers looking for an interesting destination that is still somewhat off the beaten path. Though some have returned from overseas to retire, many young Carriacouans who have an opportunity to leave and seek their fortune elsewhere will usually take it. Ironically the woodland that was once cut down to grow crops is now once again returning to bush as farming lots and former estate lands outnumber the people willing and able to work them.

Carriacou and Petite Martinique have a very rural feel and the simple life of boatbuilding, fishing under sail and farming has a beguiling allure to those looking for a lifestyle change. As is the case in Grenada, overseas investors are building properties as homes, holiday lets or a combination of both. Communities such as Harvey Vale and Craigston, as well as those with a heritage of European settlers such as Windward, have developed as hideaways for seekers of alternative lifestyles or for those just looking for a little sun, sea, peace and quiet. Carriacou's beautiful white-sand beaches are a draw for day trippers on holiday in Grenada and the annual Carriacou Regatta attracts sailing enthusiasts from all over the world.

### CROMANTIE CUDJOE

According to legend, Cromantie Cudjoe was a slave who fought against the British during the Fédon Rebellion and then escaped by swimming to Carriacou. He has become a symbol of rebellious spirit whose life story is one of myth and speculation. Whatever the truth, he is considered an ancestral spirit of Carriacou and, as he was also an accomplished drummer, a song is usually sung in his honour during Big Drum Dance.

## PEOPLE AND POPULATION

**Carriacou** has a population of around 5,000 and, as in Grenada, English is the official language. The people of Carriacou are officially referred to as Carriacouans but are more commonly known as **Kayacs**. They are a very friendly people with a strong cultural identity that has been shaped in a distinctly different manner from their compatriots on mainland Grenada. They have a strong heritage, which is preserved today in the shape of feasts, music, celebrations, workmanship and folklore. **Petite Martinique** has a population of fewer than 1,000.

## CULTURE

**BOATBUILDING** Both Carriacou and Petite Martinique have a strong maritime history of boatbuilding. In Carriacou this activity is very firmly centred on the community of Windward on the island's northeast coast. In Petite Martinique, you will see boats being built along the shore at Sanchez. Scottish shipbuilders were some of the earliest European settlers in this area and they began establishing a boatbuilding industry on the islands in the 1830s. At first these boats were small wooden sailing boats that were used primarily for fishing, but this soon turned into

### BOAT-LAUNCHING CEREMONY

Word spreads very quickly around Carriacou and Petite Martinique about a forthcoming boat-launching. They are very popular events and can draw quite a crowd. In Carriacou, boat-launchings usually take place in the small coastal hamlet of Windward and on launch day it becomes a hive of activity. Ground provisions, meats and traditional *cou-cou* are prepared in big, heavy pots that are heated over several open fires near the boat-launching area. A makeshift bar materialises and drinks are handed out to both spectators and those helping with the launch itself. The boat that is to be launched stands close to the shoreline, facing the sea. It is held up by wooden props on either side and beneath it there are heavy timber poles that will serve as rollers. A line is attached to the keel and tied to a securing post behind the boat, ensuring that when the wooden supports are removed, the boat does not slide out of control down to the sea.

Occasionally prayers are said and a priest blesses the boat with holy water. Usually the owner will splash rum and water on the ground around his boat. Sometimes rice is also scattered about. Music accompanies the event. From time to time this may be in the form of drumming, but more often is in the shape of traditional sea shanties that are sung by the boat, and are accompanied by guitars and fiddles. Next comes 'cutting down', the process by which the boat is carefully laid on its side on the rollers. In a synchronised effort, the supporting poles are cut, with very sharp axes, at their base. By doing so, each pole gets shorter and shorter and the boat begins to lean over to one side. If this is done properly, the boat comes gently to rest on the heavy wooden rollers ready for the next stage. It is an intense, exciting and very atmospheric activity with both spectators and master boatbuilder yelling out instructions at the tops of their voices.

The finale is the launch itself. With a combination of ropes and sheer brute force, the boat is eased down the rollers towards the sea. Hopefully the boat reaches the water and floats upright in all its majesty. Occasionally, if the tide is a little low, the boat makes it halfway but then sits grounded, somewhat forlornly, waiting for the water to rise. Whatever the outcome, food is enjoyed and drinks flow from dawn until dusk when the revellers finally make their way home again.

Carriacou and Petite Martinique  CULTURE

9

the construction of larger wooden trading schooners and sloops. Though the tradition of boatbuilding still lives on in Windward and on Petite Martinique, during the height of the boatbuilding industry, between the 1830s and the mid 1900s, boats were not only being built in places like Windward, they were being built by master craftsmen all over the island. It is recorded that in 1929 alone a total of 129 trading sloops and schooners were constructed and launched by the boatbuilders of Carriacou. From the mid 1900s it became more and more common for boats to be constructed from steel and, as a result, the traditional wooden boatbuilding industry of Carriacou and Petite Martinique fell into a period of decline. As was common with many former colonies during the 1960s and 1970s, many people left Carriacou and Petite Martinique in search of employment abroad, particularly in England.

Today, many have returned and, thanks to a revival of the craft and the establishment of the annual Carriacou Workboat Regatta, the tradition of boatbuilding is alive and well again. Master boatbuilders and their willing and enthusiastic young apprentices work on the construction of traditional wooden schooners and sloops for all kinds of customers, from both home and abroad. If you are very lucky, your visit to Carriacou and Petite Martinique may coincide with a traditional boat-launching ceremony.

**BIG DRUM DANCE** Big Drum Dance is a cultural celebration that consists of dancing, singing and drumming. It is thought that the west African slaves who were transported to the islands in the 1700s somehow managed to keep their heritage alive through folktales, stories, music and song. Drumming played a significant role among these African tribal people and was very prominent during weddings, feasts, prayer, harvest, birth and death. The Big Drum Dance is a manifestation of the past and is now not only a key feature of Carriacou's cultural legacy, but also very much an integral part of everyday life on the island. Why drumming survived so well in Carriacou and not in Grenada is a puzzle. Perhaps it is because the drums that were made and played by slaves were also routinely taken away from them, or banned, as part of their owners' efforts to crush their spirit and identity.

The drums, collectively known as *lapeau cabrit*, which is Creole for goatskin, were originally made from carved wood, but were later more commonly made from small rum barrels. Traditionally three drums are used. The centre drum, and the most important of the three, is called the **cot drum** and is traditionally made with the skin of a young ewe goat to produce a higher note. A piece of cotton thread with three or four straight pins is attached to the top of the drum to add a unique sound. Always standing upright in the centre of the group, the cot drum is responsible for leading the rhythm and requires a skilled and experienced player. The two drums to each side of the cot drum are known as the **bula drums** and are tilted and played between the knees. The bula drums are traditionally made from the skins of ram goats and are also sometimes known as *babble* or *fule* drums. The singing style of the Big Drum Dance usually follows a traditional call-and-response pattern and songs which, though often sung in Creole, speak of a home in Africa; they lament families that have been separated, and tell of a longing to be free. The dances that accompany the drumming and the singing also originate in Africa though they too have a strong Creole influence, as do the costumes of the dancers themselves. There are dances and songs that are performed to heal sickness, to appease gods, to pray for good harvests, to pray for rain during the planting season, to symbolise the union of a man and woman, or to give thanks for good crops.

If you are fortunate enough to experience a Big Drum Dance during your visit to Carriacou, you will be immediately struck by how much more African, rather than

Ferguson Adams, also known as 'Sugar Adams', was a legendary Big Drum Dance performer. Born in 1890, he is said to have learned to play the cot drum at an early age. By the time he was 60, he had become a famous drummer, dancer and singer. His common-law wife, Mary Fortune, was a very well-known Big Drum singer and together they recorded *Carriacou Calalou*, *Saraca* and *Tombstone Feast*. Often referred to as 'Carriacou's premier music couple', Mary died in 1973 and Ferguson ten years later. They were the inspiration of generations to come and some of today's most noted Big Drum Dance performers were both taught and inspired by the couple.

Creole or Caribbean, the celebration actually is. The music, the singing, the dance and the drums themselves will transport you into the past, to a dark time, when people were plucked from their homes in Africa and brought to these islands where they were forced to spend generations enslaved. It is a very spiritual experience.

**PARANG** *Parang* is a form of Latin American music that is thought to have arrived in Grenada from Trinidad. A typical *parang* music ensemble usually consists of string instruments, drum and percussion which accompany a singer. The song is usually about someone well known, perhaps a politician or a person from the local community, and it tells a funny story, or perhaps a scandal or a rumour about that person. It can be a rather lively and raucous occasion. Grenada's most popular *parang* takes place in Carriacou at Christmas time.

**KALENDA** *Kalenda* is a stick-fighting dance that is thought to have its roots in tribal traditions of west Africa. It is a combination of dance and martial art that became popular at carnival time in the West Indies. Though far less common now, in the main because of its innate danger and risk of serious injury, on occasion it is still possible to see it performed by the *paywo* at the Carriacou Carnival in February. Two contestants square up, each wielding a 1m-long stick which they use to try and either knock their opponent to the ground, or draw blood. The dance (or fight, depending on how you view it) is accompanied by drumming and singing. *Kalenda* is frequently banned because of concerns over its violence and is no longer allowed during the Grenada Carnival in August.

**MAROON FESTIVAL** The Maroon Festival, though occasionally a large annual event, is usually a festivity that is held in villages and communities across Carriacou. Traditionally each 'maroon' was held to give thanks for a bountiful harvest or to pray for one, along with rains, in advance of a forthcoming planting season. Villagers prepare food, commonly referred to as *saraca*, which usually consists of smoked meats, *cou-cou*, rice and peas. At around dusk, the eating and drinking starts and is followed by the traditional 'wetting of the ring' where rum and water are splashed on the ground where the dancing is to take place. By the time the sun has set, the singing begins, accompanied by Big Drum music and traditional dancing which includes the Cromantin dance, the Mandingo dance, the Arada, and the Congo. As it is associated with crops, plantings and harvest, it is commonly said that whenever there is a maroon, 'rain will soon fall'.

If you are planning a stay in Carriacou be sure to ask your hotel if there are any forthcoming village maroon festivals. Often maroons will take place as part of annual village feasts in communities such as Bogles, Mt Pleasant, Grand Bay and Harvey Vale.

Carriacou and Petite Martinique CULTURE

9

**TOMBSTONE FEAST** Perhaps one of the islands' most haunting ceremonies is the Tombstone Feast, which takes place on the first anniversary of a burial. Up to this point there would have been no headstone placed on the grave or tomb of the deceased. Instead it is prepared one year later by a stonemason and then carried in a ceremony to the house where the death took place. Traditionally, the tombstone is placed on a bed and covered with a white sheet. The relatives of the deceased gather together and 'wet the ground' by sprinkling rum and water around it. They then speak to the deceased who, it is believed, is now visiting with them, and they also offer their prayers. The headstone is then taken to the cemetery where it is fitted to the body of the tomb. Sometimes the stone slides into a special opening on the end of the tomb, rather than standing upright upon it. More rum and water are sprinkled around the tomb and sometimes an egg is broken to symbolise a new beginning of welfare and prosperity for the surviving family. The following day there is a feast, or *saraca*, accompanied by dancing, singing and Big Drum.

# CARRIACOU

Carriacou is an island of outstanding natural beauty and rich cultural heritage. As well as stunning white-sand beaches, it has a forest reserve, a bird sanctuary, mangrove forests and oyster beds, pristine coral reefs and a large natural anchorage. The traditions of Big Drum Dance, Maroon Festival and Tombstone Feast are vivid reflections of an African heritage that not only survives but is an integral part of life. Handmade Carriacou sloops are famous throughout the worldwide sailing community and are part of a boatbuilding tradition that was born in Scotland, handed down through generations, and is still very much alive today. You could wander around the hillsides of Carriacou in search of estate and windmill ruins, passing by fields of corn and pigeon peas, perhaps taking time to enjoy some great seafood or the taste of a traditional *cou-cou* along the way.

## GETTING THERE AND AWAY

**By ferry** Osprey Lines (*www.ospreylines.com*) operates a high-speed ferry service between Grenada, Carriacou and Petite Martinique. The ferry arrives and departs from the jetty opposite the fire station on the Carenage in St George's.

The journey to Carriacou takes about 90 minutes, leaving St George's at 09.00 Monday–Saturday and at 08.00 Sunday. A late ferry leaves at 17.30 Monday–Friday and Sunday. Grenada to Carriacou fares are: EC$160 or US$62 adult return and EC$80 or US$31 for an adult one-way ticket; EC$100 or US$38 return, and EC$50 or US$19 for a one-way ticket for children between five and 12 years of age; EC$20 or US$8 return and EC$10 or US$4 for a one-way ticket for children under five years of age.

From Petite Martinique the ferry leaves for Carriacou at 05.30 Tuesday–Friday, and also at 15.00 daily. The ferry leaves Hillsborough for St George's at 06.00 Monday–Saturday, and at 15.30 daily. The ferry does not usually operate on Christmas Day, Boxing Day, New Year's Day or Good Friday.

**By cargo boat and water taxi** An alternative way to travel between Grenada and Carriacou is by cargo boat. This is cheaper but takes longer. Ask one of the boat captains in the Carenage. The other means of transportation between Carriacou and Petite Martinique is by water taxi. You could ask local boat owners on the coast in Dover, Windward or Sanchez for prices.

**GETTING AROUND** The most fun and interesting way to explore Carriacou is on foot and by bus. Combining walking with using local transportation will get you into the heart of this pretty island as well as give you plenty of opportunities to meet and chat with its very friendly residents. Hire car is also a possibility and will certainly suit those who are only on the island for a day or two.

**Car hire** Car hire is available from a number of operators. Hotels and guesthouses either have their own small fleet or can arrange car hire for you. In order to rent a car you must be able to present a driver's licence. Prices are usually anywhere between EC$100 and EC$140 per day (see *Car hire* in *Chapter 2*, page 53). If hiring a car, you should note that the petrol station in Hillsborough is the only one on the island.

**By bus and taxi** In Carriacou most buses also double up as taxis, the difference being the fare and whether you share your transport with others. Buses used to follow a similar system to mainland Grenada, with colours, numbers and designated routes, but this has been abandoned in favour of a more flexible approach. Fixed routes are not as sustainable on this small island, though you will find that some buses do tend to stick with certain roads and destinations. Buses and taxis are small minibuses, the same as on mainland Grenada, and usually have the driver's nickname or motto displayed prominently on the windscreen. Buses and taxi registration plates begin with the letter H and each driver carries an official ID.

Bus fares are very affordable. Most journeys from Hillsborough to anywhere on the island cost around EC$3.50. If you are travelling greater distances than that, then you might expect to pay EC$5 maximum. So long as you don't mind waiting for one, buses are a great way to experience real island life and you are sure to meet some interesting and friendly people on your journey. To catch a bus, just wait by the side of the road, preferably in the shade, and flag one down.

Taxi fares are a little higher. Here are some examples of fares from Hillsborough: Belair EC$20–25; Craigston/Bogles EC$20–25; Dover/Limlair/Bayaleau EC$30–35; Grand Bay EC$30–35; Harvey Vale EC$30–35; L'Esterre EC$25–30; Lauriston Airport EC$15–20; Petit Carenage EC$35–40; Prospect EC$30–35; Windward EC$30–35.

You can also charter a taxi for a Carriacou tour if your time is very limited. Typically a two-and-a-half hour 'full tour' of Carriacou will cost around EC$180–200 and a 75-minute 'half tour' will cost around EC$90–100.

**WHERE TO STAY** Visitors to Carriacou have a number of accommodation options – probably far more than you would expect. Here is a selection of hotels, guesthouses and self-catering accommodation. The list is by no means comprehensive and you should always be sure to check for any price changes before booking. For those interested in renting villas, there are quite a number of properties in the Craigston area that people have built and rent out as holiday homes. A selection are described briefly within the listings below, but www.islandvillas.com has many more. See page 57 for price codes.

## Mid-range and budget hotels and guesthouses

**John's Unique Resort** (12 rooms, 5 apts) Hillsborough; ☎ 473 443 8346; f 473 443 8345; e junique@caribsurf.com. Located close to the main town, rooms have private bathroom, TV, fans or AC, private verandas. Fully equipped apts also have kitchenettes. Restaurant & bar serves local & international cuisine (see *Where to eat and drink*, opposite). Rooms $$, apts $$$

**Green Roof Inn** (5 rooms, 1 cottage) Beauséjour; ☎/f 473 443 6399; e greenroof@caribsurf.com; www.greenroofinn.com. Very nice accommodation with sea views. Each room has private bathroom, fans, mosquito nets & access to shared veranda. The more private cottage is located within the gardens & comes equipped with bathroom, kitchenette, mosquito net, fan & private veranda. Open restaurant with great sea views, serving high-quality international cuisine. Rooms $ inc continental b/fast, cottage $$

**Hotel Laurena** (50 rooms/apts) Hillsborough; ☎ 473 443 8759; www.hotellaurena.com. Large colonial-style hotel located within easy reach of the jetty. A choice of standard guest rooms or self-contained apts, all with private bathroom, veranda, AC, TV & internet. Apts have a kitchenette. Facilities include fitness centre & Ochra Restaurant (see *Where to eat and drink*, opposite). Deluxe suites have jacuzzi tub. Prices seasonal. $–$$

**Carriacou Grand View Hotel** (6 rooms, 7 apts) Beauséjour; ☎ 473 443 6348; e ccougrandview@caribsurf.com; www.carriacougrandview.com. Apt hotel close to Hillsborough. Rooms have private bathroom, TV, AC or fan, balcony. Apt rooms have a kitchenette. The hotel has a swimming pool, restaurant (see *Where to eat and drink*, opposite) & bar & great forest & ocean views. $–$$

**Millie's Guest House** (10 rooms) Hillsborough; ☎ 473 443 6455; f 473 443 8107; e millies@hotmail.com. Located on the edge of town, offers modern rooms & apts with private bathrooms, verandas with sea & forest views & fully equipped SC facilities. Room $, apt $$

**Ade's Dream Apartment Hotel** (23 rooms) Main St, Hillsborough; ☎ 473 443 7317; f 473 443 8436; e adeadea@spiceisle.com; www.adesdream.com. Close to the jetty. 4 studio & economy rooms with private bathroom, kitchenette, TV, AC & veranda. Wireless & hard-wired internet. $

## Luxury self-catering cottages and villas

**Caribbee Country House** (1 villa, 1 cottage) Prospect; ☎ 473 443 7380; e macaws@spiceisle.com; www.themacaws.com. Idyllic villa & cottage accommodation in a private & peaceful setting on the southern edge of the High North Forest Reserve. Sparrow Hawk Villa can sleep up to 5 people, Harmony Cottage sleeps up to 4. Owners have created a bird preserve & breed macaws. Ideal for nature lovers, birdwatchers & people trying to get away from it all. Prices on request.

**Villa Sankofa** (3 bedrooms) Craigston; ☎ 310 472 2343; f 310 472 9612; e villasankofa@gmail.com; www.sankofainternational.com. Featured in regional magazines for its contemporary design, offers luxurious self-contained accommodation with sea views. En-suite bedrooms, mosquito nets, kitchen, ceiling fan, large living area & veranda. Access to secluded beach. $$$$$

## Mid-range self-catering cottages and villas

**Tamarind Cottage** (1 cottage) Belair, Carriacou; ☎ 473 443 8207; e tamarindcottage@grenadines.net; www.islandtrees.com. Self-contained 1-bedroom cottage located in peaceful hillside surroundings with ocean views. The cottage has living area, fully equipped kitchen, bathroom, fans, outdoor shower & patios. Price inc jeep hire & jetty or airport transfers. $$$

**Goyaba** (4 bedrooms) Craigston; ☎ 473 443 8182; e islander@islandvillas.com; www.islandvillas.com/villas/goyaba.htm. 2 shared bathrooms, open-plan living area, kitchen, ceiling fans, veranda & gardens. Easy access to beach. $$$

**Driftwood** (2 bedrooms) Craigston; ☎ 473 443 8182; e islander@islandvillas.com; www.islandvillas.com/villas/drift.htm. 2-bedroom villa on 2 floors with sea views. En-suite bathrooms, mosquito nets, ceiling fans, open-plan living area & kitchen, verandas. $$$

**Yellow Bird** (2 bedrooms) Craigston; ☎ 473 443 8182; e islander@islandvillas.com; www.islandvillas.com/villas/yellow.htm. Compact cottage with sea views includes living area, kitchen, ceiling fans & veranda. $$$

🏠 **Seaclusion Suites** (2 suites) St Louis, L'Esterre; ✆ 473 407 2779; e bob@seaclusionsuites.com; www.seaclusionsuites.com. 2 1-bedroom, fully furnished SC suites with bathroom, kitchen, b/fast bar, & private veranda with great sea views. $$

🏠 **Belair Garden Cottage** (1 cottage) Belair; ✆ 473 443 6221; e belaircottage@spiceisle.com; www.belairgardencottage.com. Located high in Belair near windmill ruins & teak forest, beautifully designed, very private cottage with fully equipped kitchenette, bathroom, outdoor shower & large wooden deck with hammock & great sea views. Homemade breads, cakes & boxed lunches prepared by the owners on request. Complimentary mobile phone & wireless internet. Be warned, a visiting pair of macaws may insist on sharing your b/fast. Highly recommended. $$

🏠 **KIDO Ecological Research Station** Prospect; ✆ 473 443 7936; e kido-ywf@spiceisle.com; www.kido-projects.com. Located alongside the High North National Park, KIDO offers accommodation ideal for ecologists, researchers or students. The villa has 2 bedrooms, bathroom, living area, veranda, reading room. The Pagoda sleeps up to 10 & is ideal for student groups. It has 2 bathrooms & a communal kitchenette. The Octopus has a master bedroom & twin-bed ante room, private bathroom, kitchenette & patio. Meals prepared on request. Ecotours offered. $$

🏠 **Bayaleau Point Cottages** (4 cottages) Windward; ✆/f 473 443 9784; e goldhill@spiceisle.com; www.carriacoucottages.com. Very cosy self-contained wooden cottages with private bathroom facilities, kitchenette, mosquito nets, hammocks, verandas & sea views. Seaside deck offers local & international dinners. *Mostly Harmless* motor launch offers cruising, picnic & snorkelling trips. Prices based on cottage size & season. $–$$

🏠 **Palm Trees** (1 cottage) Craigston; ✆ 473 443 8182; e islander@islandvillas.com; www.islandvillas.com/villas/palmtree.htm. 1-bedroom wooden cottage with nice sea views. Accommodation has master bedroom, mosquito nets, bathroom, kitchen & living areas, spacious verandas. Small bedroom with sgl bed also available. $

🏠 **Bogles Round House** (3 cottages) Bogles, Carriacou; ✆/f 473 443 7841; e info@boglesroundhouse.com; www.boglesroundhouse.com. Rustic cottages located in the village of Bogles to the north of Hillsborough. Self-contained units have bathroom, kitchenette, mosquito net, fan & veranda. Mango & Plum cottages sleep 2 people, Lime Cottage sleeps 3–4. Garden has access to the secluded beach at Sparrow Bay. Award-winning chef, Roxanne Russell, serves great food (see *Where to eat and drink*, below). $

🏠 **Peacehaven Apartments** (2 apts) Hillsborough; ✆ 473 443 8182; e islander@islandvillas.com; www.islandvillas.com/villas/peace.htm. 2 2-bedroom apts on the outskirts of Hillsborough, facing the sea. Apts have ceiling fans, bathroom & kitchenette. $

🏠 **Plantain Dove** (1 apt) Paradise Beach, L'Esterre; ✆ 473 443 7457. Self-contained 2-bedroom apt located on Paradise Beach. Prices on request.

## Budget self-catering apartments, suites and villas

🏠 **Scraper's Bayview Cottages** Tyrell Bay, Carriacou; ✆ 473 443 7403; e scrapersbayview@hotmail.com. Wooden cottages with private bathroom & kitchenette. Scraper's Restaurant is a popular venue for local & international cooking. $

🏠 **Hope's Inn** (6 rooms, 1 apt) Paradise Beach, L'Esterre; ✆ 473 443 7457. Located right on the beautiful beach, 6 upper-floor rooms with shared kitchenettes, bathrooms & balcony, 1 ground-floor self-contained apt with private bathroom, kitchenette & patio. $

✗ **WHERE TO EAT AND DRINK** There are some really good places to eat in Carriacou with a varied selection of both international and Caribbean cooking styles. Most restaurants are open Monday to Saturday, some prefer you to call in advance for dinner.

✗ **Bogles Round House** Bogles; ✆ 473 443 7841; ⏰ Thu–Mon. High-quality local & international cuisine by award-winning chef, Roxanne. Lunch by reservation only, dinner reservations advised. Highly recommended. $$

✗ **Green Roof Inn** Beauséjour; ✆ 473 443 6399; ⏰ daily. Excellent local & international dishes with pleasant surroundings & sea views. Calling ahead is advised. $$

✘ **Ochra Restaurant & Bar** Hotel Laurena, Hillsborough; ☏ 473 443 8759; e andrewsinn@spiceisle.com; ☉ daily. Hotel restaurant serving local & international dishes. $$

✘ **Bayaleau Point Cottages** Windward; ☏ 473 443 9784. Local & international dinners with lovely ocean views, by reservation only. $$

✘ **Carriacou Grand View Hotel** Beauséjour; ☏ 473 443 6348; ☉ daily. Restaurant & piano bar with pool & views, serving local & international dining. $$

✘ **John's Unique Resort** Hillsborough; ☏ 473 443 8346. Hotel restaurant serving local & international food. Call ahead. $$

✘ **Lazy Turtle** Tyrell Bay; ☏ 473 443 8322. Located next to Lumbadive, with great food & views. Pizzas an evening speciality. Great place for drinks, lunch, pizza & good vibes. $$

✘ **Lambie Queen Restaurant & Bar** Tyrell Bay; ☏ 473 443 8162. Popular bar & eatery along the shore, serving local & international dishes. $–$$

✘ **Scraper's Bay View Cottages Restaurant & Bar** Tyrell Bay; ☏ 473 443 7403. Popular eatery serving local & international dishes on the shoreline. $–$$

✘ **Paradise Inn** Paradise Beach; Bar & eatery located right on the beach, serving lunches & dinners. $

✘ **Sandisland Café** Hillsborough; ☏ 473 445 6189; ☉ Mon–Sat. Cosy restaurant tucked away behind gift & souvenir shop, serving local & international dishes. Nice views of Hillsborough Bay & always a warm welcome from Cherril & her staff. $

✘ **Seawave** Hillsborough; ☏ 473 443 7317; ☉ Mon–Sat. Bar & restaurant located opposite Ade's Dream, local & international dishes & sea views. $

✘ **Hardwood Restaurant & Bar** Paradise Beach; ☏ 473 443 6839. Ideally located bar & restaurant serving local dishes & drinks. $

✘ **Off the Hook** Paradise Beach. Bar & grill serving drinks, local cooking & BBQ. Good vibes. $

✘ **Old Rum Shop** Tyrell Bay; ☏ 473 443 7350. Popular local bar & eatery serving home-cooked local food & BBQ. A must-visit. $

♀ **Banana Joe's** Paradise Beach. Tiki bar located on the beach serving welcome refreshments. $

**SHOPPING** Hillsborough is the main place for shopping on Carriacou. It has several convenience stores and small supermarkets, a number of clothing boutiques, souvenir shops and stalls, a pharmacy and a very nice and well-stocked delicatessen. You will also find stalls selling fruit and vegetables as well as a small fish market. From time to time you may see a roadside butcher selling cuts of freshly slaughtered animals. Don't let the blood and the machete put you off… Outside Hillsborough most villages have a store of some kind selling basic food items and essentials. Look out for **Henrietta's Bakery** and **Fidel Productions** in L'Esterre; both are highly recommended and well worth a visit.

**BANKS** Banks open 08.00–14.00 Mondays to Thursdays and 08.00–16.00 on Fridays. Banks are closed Saturdays, Sundays and on public holidays.

$ **First Caribbean National Bank** Main St, Hillsborough; ☏ 473 443 7232

$ **Grenada Cooperative Bank** Main St, Hillsborough; ☏ 473 443 6385

$ **Republic Bank** Main St, Hillsborough; ☏ 473 443 7289

## WHAT TO SEE

**Hillsborough** Carriacou's main town and administrative centre is Hillsborough which is located on the west coast of the island. It is a small, quaint town with one main business street and two quieter roads running parallel behind. With a mixture of Kayacs, visitors and overseas residents, Hillsborough is a charming place where friends meet and greet each other in shops and in the streets, and roadside vendors try to tempt passers-by with fresh fruits and vegetables.

Main Street is where most shops, banks, the police station, post office, customs house and jetty are all located. The jetty is where the Osprey ferry service to and from Grenada and Petite Martinique arrives and departs daily (see page 196 for details of schedules and fares). Outside the jetty gates, to the left as you exit, is the

**post office** (🕐 *08.00–15.00 Mon–Fri*). As the postal service in Carriacou is still not island-wide, you may find that when the mail boat arrives, the post office is rather busy. Opposite the jetty, on the corner of the junction with Church Street, is the **Grenada Board of Tourism** office (🕐 *08-00-16.00 Mon–Sat*), which is located in the Carriacou & Petite Martinique Memorial Centre. The office can provide you with accommodation and transportation advice. It also has brochures, leaflets and a very basic map of the island. (Note that some maps can be a little out of date and still show the old road running south across Lauriston Airport.)

Walking northeast along Main Street (left as you exit the jetty gates), you will pass a number of local snackettes such as **Steamboat Fast Food & Take-away**, **Ann & Sharon's Snack Bar** and **De Matrix Snack Bar**. Also in this direction is the Republic Bank with its Blue Machine ATM. Opposite the Republic Bank is the brightly coloured Digicel shop where you will find Bullen Tours & Travel, a Western Union money transfer desk and an internet café. A little further down the street is the Grenada Cooperative Bank.

Continuing down Main Street there are a number of small gift shops, as well as popular eateries such as the **Sea Wave Restaurant & Bar** and the **Sandisland Café**. Accommodation is available at **Ade's Dream** where there is also a supermarket and car-hire office. At the end of Main Street, as it curves inland away from the sea, there are several colourful snackettes selling refreshments and local food. A little beyond the bend, on the way out of town towards Bogles and Belair, is the Anglican rectory, once the Beauséjour Estate Great House.

Back at the jetty, turning right along Main Street, you will see **Bullen's Super Centre**, a supermarket selling foodstuffs and household goods. Next door to the supermarket is a pharmacy. **Patty's Deli** sells fresh bagels, quiche, cold cuts and a variety of enticing deli items and the **Heat of the Day Restaurant & Bar** offers a shady respite from the sun. An ATM is located at the First Caribbean National Bank which is near to the Carriacou Police Station and Immigration Office.

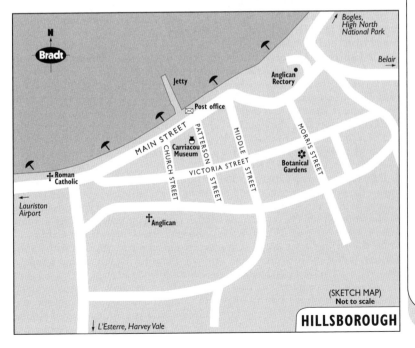

Continuing out of town along Main Street you will pass a couple of guesthouses, more small stores and boutiques and, of course, snackettes, including the **Butterfly Bar** and the **Sea Shell Snack Bar**. Beyond Millie's Apartments & Guest House is **St Patrick's Roman Catholic Church**.

The road running parallel to Main Street is Victoria Street, which is also known as Back Street. It is predominantly an area of small board houses and gardens. At the western end, towards the Roman Catholic church is the **Coconut Bar & Shop** where Yvette hosts occasional live music in the evenings (check it out on Fridays and Saturdays). In the middle of Victoria Street, near the intersection with Church Street, you will find further bars and snackettes including **D Cage** and **Back Inn Snack Bar**. Right down towards the far end of Victoria Street, between the intersections with Middle Street and Morris Street is Hillsborough's **Botanical Gardens**. Rather neglected and a little sad in appearance, the gardens are still worth a visit if you are interested in tropical flora.

Opposite the jetty area, two streets join up with Main Street. They are Church Street and Patterson Street. A short distance along Patterson Street, you will find the **Carriacou Museum** (⊕ *09.30–16.00 Mon–Fri; EC$5 pp*). Established by the Carriacou Historical Society in 1976, the museum is now in its fourth home, a 19th-century cotton ginnery. Small but deceptive, this museum has a very comprehensive collection of Amerindian artefacts, in particular ceramics, that have been unearthed at archaeological sites around the island. There are also very interesting, colourful and informative displays relating to African heritage, European occupation and Carriacou's strong cultural identity, commonly illustrated by the Big Drum and Maroon festivals. Definitely worth a visit.

Along Church Street there are a few stores including **Vibes Records** and **Kim's Plaza Supermarket**. Turning right at the end of Church Street, you will find the **Anglican Church of Christ the King**.

## EXPLORING SOUTHERN CARRIACOU
The road south out of Hillsborough runs along the shoreline of Hillsborough Bay. It is a large, crescent-shaped bay with three outer islands that are both visible and accessible by boat. They are Jack A Dan, Sandy Island and Mabouya Island. The main road veers away from the shore and goes to **Lauriston Airport**. Here the road ends. It used to go across the runway to L'Esterre and Harvey Vale but the increase in both air and road traffic has meant that it is no longer considered safe to have airplanes, vehicles and pedestrians using the runway at the same time. The road to L'Esterre and Harvey Vale now takes a more roundabout route. To get there by vehicle you must take the road from Hillsborough, opposite the Roman Catholic church, head inland a short distance and then turn off on a new road to L'Esterre. Those on foot have a much more fun option of following the beach and a pathway through the coastal mangroves of Lauriston Point to get there (see page 212).

**L'Esterre** is a pretty village of colourful board houses. It is said that this area still retains the influence of France and that some of its inhabitants still speak French Creole. At the centre of the village is L'Esterre Cross, a junction with roads heading to Hillsborough and Harvey Vale and another running through the village towards Point Cistern (see page 213 for details of hiking here). **Uncle Tom's Cabin** and **Over the Bridge** offer simple refreshments and an interesting chat with locals. L'Esterre's primary attraction is the stunning **Paradise Beach** around L'Esterre Bay. The beach is white sand with a fringe of sea almond and grape trees along with the occasional manchineel (see page 44). The water is turquoise and shallow along the shore making it ideal for families with young children. As it is protected, the bay attracts very few waves and little current. With colourfully painted fishing boats and water taxis bobbing sedately offshore, the image is one of serenity and

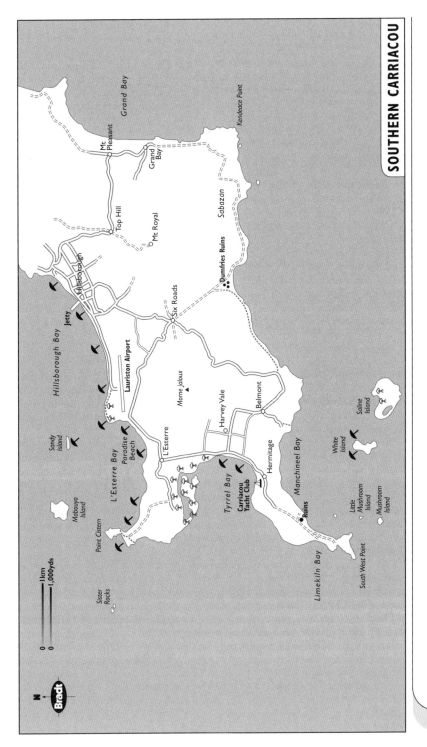

Grand Bay

Kendeace Point

Mt Pleasant

Grand Bay

Top Hill

Mt Royal

Sabazan

**Dumfries Ruins**

Six Roads

Hillsborough

**Jetty**

Hillsborough Bay

**Lauriston Airport**

Sandy Island

Paradise Beach

L'Esterre Bay

L'Esterre

Morne Jaloux

Harvey Vale

Belmont

Point Cistern

Mabouya Island

Hermitage

Tyrrel Bay

**Carriacou Yacht Club**

Manchineel Bay

White Island

Saline Island

Sister Rocks

Limekiln Bay

South West Point

**Ruins**

Little Mushroom Island

Mushroom Island

0 ___ 1km
0 ___ 1,000yds

N

**Bradt**

relaxation. It is an idyllic and peaceful beach, without doubt one of Grenada's best, and it is rarely busy. The trees at the back of the beach offer a degree of shade and there are a number of bars and eateries selling refreshments as well as meals with all the trimmings. Look out for **Paradise Inn, Hope's Inn, Banana Joes, Off the Hook** and the **Hardwood Bar & Snackette**. Water taxis can be chartered at the Hardwood Bar to take you to the outlying islands. **Sandy Island** and its surrounding reef is particularly beautiful and perfect for snorkelling. It has little shade, however, so be prepared and remember that when snorkelling in this climate it is always prudent to do it wearing a T-shirt or a light wetsuit to save the skin on your shoulders and back. Behind the Hardwood Bar along the roadside is **Fidel Productions**, selling a wonderful selection of very unique crafts and original T-shirts. These T-shirts are also available at a selection of outlets on mainland Grenada and there are plans for a shop within the Port Louis Marina development on the Lagoon in St George's.

There is a very long, straight road from L'Esterre Cross to **Harvey Vale**, Carriacou's second-largest settlement, which is located along the shore of **Tyrell Bay**. A natural anchorage, Tyrell Bay and Harvey Vale are said to be home to the 'yachties', the local name given to sailing enthusiasts who have arrived in Carriacou and decided to stay, hang around for a while, or who are just passing through *en route* to their next exotic destination. With sailing boats at anchor, a yacht club and haul-out facility, and a new marina investment project well underway, Tyrell Bay offers a fascinating mix of the old, the new, the local, the international and the downright eccentric. It has a sleepy air, though you feel it is not destined to stay that way for long.

Spread around the bay along the main road are a number of small stores, stalls, bars, snackettes and restaurants. Try one of Natasha and Pumpkin's punches or some delicious oil-down at the **Bay Side Restaurant & Bar**. Other popular eateries and watering holes along the bay front are the **Tyrell Bay Restaurant & Bar**, the **Seaside Fountain**, the **Twilight Restaurant & Bar** and the very popular **Scraper's** and **Lambie Queen Restaurant & Bar**. For evening entertainment check out **Club Indigo** and **After Hours**.

Set back from the bay road, in an area of rather unkempt scrubland that appears to be in the process of development, is a watering hole for cattle and beside it the Harvey Vale Amerindian Well. Unfortunately, the well is a bit of a let-down. The area is very overgrown, particularly with manchineel trees, and, at the time of writing, has the feel of a rather abandoned building plot. The well itself has been recreated in concrete and stone and thus loses a lot of its appeal. However, if you do want to take a look for yourself (the area may have improved between writing and publication, of course), ask for directions and perhaps buy some fruit at the **Jolly Queen** fruit and vegetable stall near Scraper's along the bay.

Harvey Vale itself is primarily residential beyond the bay road. Both Roman Catholic and Anglican churches can be found on the main road heading east, which starts at the junction near Scraper's. Directly to the east is Morne Jaloux and the peak of Chapeau Carré.

South of Tyrell Bay and Harvey Vale is the small community of **Hermitage**. Hugging the cliff side, with a narrow, winding road that passes through colourful residences above the sailing boats and the yard and jetty of the Carriacou Yacht Club, Hermitage has the distinct feel of a remote Cornish fishing village. You may see people working on boats or putting into the yacht club jetty for supplies or a bite to eat at the very popular **Lazy Turtle**, a restaurant that has a reputation for some of the best pizza around. The paved road through Hermitage ends in a vehicle track which continues on to the end of Southwest Point, also known as La Pointe (see page 211 for details of hiking there).

From Harvey Vale, the road inland makes its way to the small hamlet of **Belmont**. Sitting high on a ridge overlooking **Manchineel Bay**, Belmont has excellent views south to the Grenada Grenadines, including White Island and Saline Island. Beyond them you may also be able to make out Frigate Island and Large Island. At a junction on the main road near the Belmont Postal Station is a road heading down to the coast where there is a tiny beach along the bay. Ask at the snackettes located at this junction for information about water taxis offering rides out to **White Island**. They run from the bay at the bottom of the steep road. White Island is beautiful and has an excellent reef for snorkelling.

Continue along the ridge past more snackettes and houses. The road leaves Belmont above Black Bay before heading back inland to the road junction at the aptly named Six Roads. Between Belmont and Six Roads you will pass the **Cowfoot Inn**, a popular spot for a refreshing drink or two and a chat with locals.

South of Six Roads is **Dumfries** where the ruins of a lime factory are located. Though the ruins themselves are very interesting, the road between Six Roads and Dumfries is not a particularly pleasant one, lined on one side by a large vehicle repair yard and on the other by the island's landfill site. Alternative routes to the ruins are via coastal paths from either Belmont or Grand Bay (see page 212 for details of a coastal hike from Belmont). The ruins consist of factory buildings, machinery and a large brick tower. The factory was run by the L Rose and Lime Company which was established in Scotland in the 1860s. The company operated throughout the Caribbean, producing 'Rose's Lime Juice Cordial' and lime marmalade before economic and social circumstances forced it to downsize and withdraw from Grenada in the mid 1900s.

From Dumfries, Great Breteche Bay and Little Breteche Bay are to be found along the wild and windy coast of **Sabazan**, one of the main locations for Amerindian archaeological discoveries on Carriacou. Many of these sites are subject to the harsh conditions along this coast where erosion continuously reshapes the landscape. Northeast of Sabazan and Kendeace Point are the villages of **Grand Bay** and **Mt Pleasant**. These villages, often overlooked because of their somewhat remote location along the centre of the island's windward coast, have a strong sense of community and heritage. Mt Pleasant hosts one of the island's most popular village maroon festivals and the hillside behind it is littered with the remains of stone windmill towers that were once used to drive machine works in the numerous estates that once thrived in this area.

To the south of Hillsborough, midway to Mt Pleasant and Grand Bay, are the communities of **Top Hill** and **Mount Royal**, nestled along the spine of the mountain ridge that runs the length of the island between High North and Morne Jaloux. Mount Royal is where Carriacou's Princess Royal Hospital is located. The hospital has a particularly prominent position along this ridge and the views from its gardens down to Hillsborough Bay are quite breathtaking. You will also find cannons here.

## EXPLORING NORTHERN CARRIACOU

To the northeast of Hillsborough, along the central ridge, is **Belair**. Once a large estate, the small village of Belair is the location of a protected forest containing teak and mahogany trees. Along the edge of this forest is the Belair windmill tower, probably the largest and most prominent of the island's windmill ruins. To the east of Belair, down the windward slopes that were once full of sugar, cotton and lime plantations, is **Limlair**, also once a large estate. On the eastern edge of Limlair, along Jew Bay, is **Tibeau**. In Tibeau there is a cemetery along the sandy shoreline that is slowly being claimed by the sea. Located nearby is **Ningo Well**, a large manmade stone well that would once have been used for storing water for crop irrigation and for cattle. It can be found close to the road, by an old stone bridge (see page 210 for details of a hike from Belair to the Ningo Well).

Between Limlair and the neighbouring village of Dover, you will see a large pond and a wooden cabin, the Big Pond Nature Centre, and home to the Tibeau Limlair Historical Ruins Rehabilitation Project. The centre offers guided walks along the trails around Limlair. Hidden in the undergrowth in the centre of Dover are the ruins of what is thought to be the first church on Carriacou. Unfortunately the ruins are buried deep in bush and, at the time of writing, are extremely tough to reach. Dover has one or two small convenience stores, one of which also houses an internet café. The **Cornerhouse Bar** on the main coastal road is a nice place to stop off for some refreshment and is also where you can ask for information about water taxis offering boat rides, tours and ferry services across to Petite Martinique.

To the north, along the coast from Dover, is the village of **Windward**. This village has a strong heritage of boatbuilding that goes back to the days when Scottish shipbuilders settled in this area. Many of the families still living in Windward have Scottish surnames, and for a while Windward was rather a closed

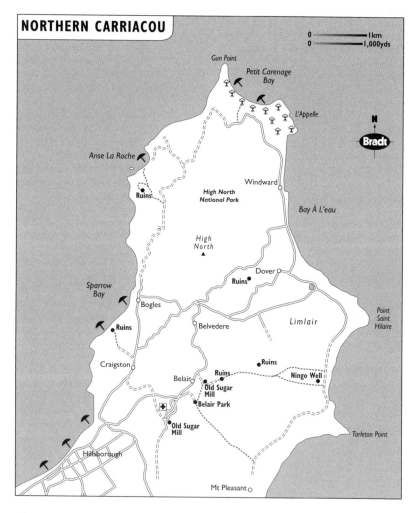

community. In more recent times the original settler families mixed with Kayacs and cultures were shared (see box, *Boat-launching ceremony*, page 193).

The village of Windward itself is very pretty. It has a few small stores and bars, and numerous colourfully painted board houses that are dotted along the road and hillside above the boatyards where, it seems, there is almost always a wooden boat under construction. Customers for these boats sometimes come from very far afield. They are often built to order for overseas enthusiasts or businesses looking for a very traditional, handcrafted boat. Some of the boatbuilders in Windward have been in this business all their years and, thankfully, appear to be passing their skills along to younger apprentices from both Windward and Petite Martinique who are keen to inherit the talents of their seniors.

On the leeward side of the island, just to the north of Hillsborough are the small villages of **Craigston** and **Bogles**. Craigston is the name of an estate where ruins still stand but they are somewhat inaccessible as these lands are private and seem to be being sold off as building lots. Craigston has become very popular with overseas investors who have built holiday homes that they rent out for most of the year. Bogles is a very small village of residential houses and convenience stores. It is also the gateway to the High North National Park. Once through the village of Bogles, the paved road ends and becomes a vehicle track that is the **High North Nature Trail**. This trail runs through the forest along the west coast to the beautiful bay and beach of Anse La Roche and then beyond to the mangrove forest and stunning beach at Petit Carenage Bay in the north (see pages 208 and 209 for details of hiking the High North Nature Trail to these sites).

There are several small islands around Carriacou. North of Hillsborough is the small rocky islet of **Jack A Dan** and to the south of it the very pretty **Sandy Island** which is a favourite picnic and snorkelling spot. You can rent water taxis to Sandy Island from Paradise Beach at the Hardwood Restaurant & Bar. South of Sandy Island is the larger **Mabouya Island**. Off Point Cistern, to the west of L'Esterre are the twin islets of the **Sisters Rocks**. In the south, off Manchineel Bay, there are **Mushroom Island** and **Little Mushroom Island**, **Saline Island**, and **White Island** which is also very popular for picnics, snorkelling and scuba diving. A little further away are **Frigate Island** and **Large Island**. You can get a water taxi to White Island from Belmont or Tyrell Bay. To the north, between Carriacou and Petite Martinique, there is the small rocky islet of **Fota** and the larger rocky island of **Petite Dominique**.

**WHAT TO DO** If you can drag yourself away from Paradise Beach (yes, I know, it is hard) then you may be surprised at just how much there is to do on Carriacou. Be sure to look and listen out for cultural events such as boat-launchings or village maroons during your stay, as they are definitely worth experiencing. There are quite a number of trails criss-crossing the island and the roads have very little traffic, making walking, hiking and biking all great options. The waters are usually calm and clear so boat trips, snorkelling or scuba diving are also pleasant ways to spend your days here.

**Snorkelling or scuba diving** As Carriacou is known as the 'land of reefs' you should definitely plan on dipping your head under the water to take a look around and see what is down there. There are a number of options, depending on your ability, experience and sense of aquatic adventure. If you have never tried snorkelling before, then why not give it a go? If you go to one of the dive operators in Carriacou (see *Carriacou dive sites* and *Carriacou scuba-diving and snorkelling operators* in *Chapter 3*, pages 77 and 79) they are sure to help and advise you, and will offer accompanied snorkelling trips. Snorkelling around White Island, Sandy Island and even Jack A Dan is very good. The reefs are close to the shore and in clear, shallow water. Water taxis or dive operators can take you there. Ask at your hotel for the name of a recommended water taxi. Alternatively go to the Hardwood Restaurant & Bar on Paradise Beach or ask at the stores near the Belmont Postal Station (see also *A boat trip* below). Certified divers will enjoy exploring interesting wrecks and reefs. Those with more experience should definitely try the Sisters and Frigate Island.

**A boat trip** When you are on an island, surrounded by other islands and a rather beautiful azure sea, it seems rather obvious to suggest taking a boat trip. Nevertheless, for those who may not have thought of it there are some interesting options. Local boat owners and fishermen will offer water-taxi services to visitors. Everything is flexible and open to negotiation. You could think about a trip around some of the coastline or outlying islands, an excursion to White Island or Sandy Island where you can do some snorkelling and have a picnic, a fishing trip with a beach barbecue, a ride across to Petite Martinique, or perhaps a trip to somewhere a little further afield such as St Vincent's Tobago Cays, an idyllic desert-island setting for the film *Pirates of the Caribbean*. Boat owners know the waters well and you are sure to have a good time.

Your hotel will probably be able to recommend someone to you as they usually have relationships with boat owners. You could look for water taxis at Windward, by the Cornershop Bar in Dover, and by the postal station in Belmont. **Bayaleau Point Cottages** (☏ *473 443 9784*) offer trips out on their motor launch *Mostly Harmless* and you could also try **Kenroy Noel** (☏ *473 443 8227*) or **Nico Water Taxi** (☏ *473 425 4238* or *473 443 7161*).

**Mountain biking** Carriacou really lends itself to road cycling and mountain biking. Be sure to take a map (or this book) along with you, along with sunscreen and plenty of water. (See *Cycling and mountain-biking operators* in *Chapter 3*, page 70.)

**WALKS AND HIKES** As Carriacou has little tree cover, always make sure you have adequate sun protection in the form of a hat, perhaps a long-sleeve shirt, or sunscreen, and carry plenty of water. There are numerous farm and village tracks criss-crossing the whole of the island. Here is a small selection:

**Hike to Anse La Roche Beach from Bogles** (*Duration: 1½hrs one-way; grade 3; guide: not required; site fee: none*) Anse La Roche Beach is one of Carriacou's finest and this hike takes you from the small coastal village of Bogles, through the High North National Park and then down a steep hillside to the beach itself. There are two routes down to the beach: one is via a narrow woodland trail that goes along the top of, and then steeply down, a grassy hillside; the other is via a wide, bulldozed track, a little further along the High North Nature Trail. The first route is by far the prettier and the one we will take here. The hike through the park is very easy but the descent down the hillside track isn't. In some places there are loose rocks, so it can be slippery underfoot, and it is also quite steep.

Starting at the very informative bulletin board at a road junction in the middle of Bogles, take the paved road north along the coast, keeping the sea to your left and the peak of High North to your right. The road winds sharply around a couple of houses before becoming a wide dirt track. This is the start of the High North Nature Trail. Follow this pretty track through the High North National Park for around 45 minutes. It is a very peaceful walk through coastal woodland where the only sounds you will hear are the waves rolling onto the shore below, birds singing and the occasional rustle of leaves as a disturbed ground lizard runs for cover.

After 30 to 45 minutes look out for a path on the left marked clearly by a boulder sporting a red paint splash. The track is narrow but clearly defined. It passes through some trees and reaches a fork. The path to the left is a little obscure and curls around backwards towards the stone ruins of a house. It is well worth having a look around. Then take the right-hand path down to a second fork. Before taking the trail to the right, take a diversion along the track to the left and then left again at the next fork. You will come to a steep grassy hillside where there are fabulous views down to the bay at Anse La Roche and across the water to Union Island, part of the St Vincent Grenadines. Back at the main fork again, go right and follow a clear trail running along the brow of a hill and then quite steeply downwards. At the next fork go right again through some trees. The path now becomes quite rocky and there are some steps. Follow this trail steeply downhill along a shallow gully. The rocks are quite loose underfoot so be careful along this stretch.

The path forks again but this time it doesn't matter which way you go as both routes meet again on the other side of the trees that are in front of you. The path on the left is perhaps a little clearer. The trail becomes trickier at this point. It is steeper and the stones are loose. Take your time and just keep going straight down the main trail in front of you. Eventually the path will level out as you reach some tall trees. You should be able to see the beach ahead of you now. Just follow the best route through the trees to the bay.

The beach is extremely picturesque though you will probably notice that entry into the sea is quite steep and occasionally the surf is high and strong. You need to be either a strong swimmer or a surfer when sea conditions are like this and the waves are rolling in hard. If you do make it beyond the breakers there are some interesting reef formations and sea caves that are worth exploring if you have brought your snorkelling gear with you. If the sea is not stirring up too much sand, the visibility is usually good enough to see them from the surface. Take care when entering and exiting the water as both undertow and surge can be strong.

There is an alternative route to and from Anse La Roche. At the centre of the beach, near the wooden booth, you should be able to make out a wide path heading inland. This is a vehicle track that winds steeply back up to the High North Nature Trail. It is not a particularly attractive walk in comparison with the trail down the hillside, but you may wish to take it on the return leg. Just follow it through the trees and around to the left. There is a lot of rubble and loose soil underfoot so take it steady. It is also quite steep. At a junction, go right up the hill and keep following the wide track until you reach a gated entrance. There is a track to the side of the gate. You will now be back on the High North Nature Trail. To the right is the trail back to Bogles and the boulder with the red paint splash, to the left the trail to Petit Carenage, the L'Apelle mangrove forest and eventually the boatbuilding village of Windward. It is around 45–60 minutes' walking to both Bogles and Windward from this point.

## Hike to Petit Carenage Beach and L'Apelle mangrove forest from Bogles, Anse La Roche Beach or Windward (*Duration: 1½hrs from Bogles, 45mins from Anse La Roche & Windward; grade 1; guide: not required; site fee: none*) Petit Carenage Beach has to be one of the prettiest on Carriacou. A long stretch of powder-white sand along a crescent-shaped bay with turquoise seas, rolling breakers and the skeleton hull of a shipwreck sitting on the reef at one end make it incredibly picturesque. Add to that the verdancy and tangled roots of the L'Apelle mangrove forest with its plentiful birdlife separating beach from road and you have a very idyllic setting indeed. Despite its apparent remoteness, Petit Carenage is very accessible. You can get there from the High North Nature Trail if you are walking from the west coast

via Anse La Roche, or alternatively you can reach it by walking northwards from the boatbuilding village of Windward on the east coast.

From Bogles, follow the High North Nature Trail to Anse La Roche (see previous hike). From Anse La Roche, continue along the main trail for another 45 minutes or so. You will reach dwelling houses and a paved road. Walk along the paved road past Gun Point and then downhill towards the beach and mangroves which you can see below to your left. Once at the bottom, and past a few houses, look for a couple of wooden signs attached to a tree on your left-hand side. They will read 'Petit Carenage Mangrove' and 'Mangrove Trail' and point to some concrete steps going down below the road. Follow these steps to a very clearly marked trail that is lined on each side with hundreds of sunbleached conch shells.

A ten-minute walk will take you to the beach. Before you get there, you will see a spur trail heading off to the right. This trail continues through the mangrove to the point where the ship is wrecked on the shallow reef. Though nowhere near as picturesque as the main stretch of Petit Carenage Beach, it still makes for an interesting diversion.

As with Anse La Roche, bathing can be tricky at Petit Carenage. The sand shelves steeply, causing large and powerful waves to smash down on the beach from time to time. The undercurrent is also strong. This is not really a bathing beach for families with children.

If you are approaching from Windward, simply keep walking through the village, past the boatyards on your right and then out along the coast. Follow the paved road all the way to the same signs and steps pointing towards the mangroves and the beach. It should take around 45 minutes to walk from Windward to this point.

## Hike to Ningo Well from Belair (Duration: 1½hrs; grade 2; guide: not required; site fee: none) This hike starts in the small, elevated village of Belair and follows a series of grassy tracks down to the windward coast and Jews Bay. Located in this area, known as Tibeau, is the impressive Ningo Well, one of the earliest and largest of the stone wells that were constructed on Carriacou.

If arriving in Belair from Hillsborough, you will reach a junction with a brightly painted bus stop. The road to the left will pass a small playing field before rising again to a crest where there is another junction. The main road to Belvedere is straight ahead and there are rough vehicle tracks to the left and right. The track on the right is the starting point of the hike.

Follow this track for five minutes as it winds around a small peak. To the right you will see a cemetery and the teak and mahogany forest of Belair Park. To the left is the impressive ruin of the stone windmill tower of the Belair Estate. This windmill would have been used for driving machine works to crush sugarcane. Today it is abandoned though has become home to a pair of macaws that were rescued from the Grenada Zoo. The scarlet macaw (Ara macao) is known locally as Antonio, and the blue and gold macaw (Ara ararauna) is known as Ariel. They are semi-tame and are happy to share fruit or crackers with you.

From the windmill tower continue along the track for around five to ten minutes until you reach a three-way junction. Take the trail on the left. After another five minutes or so you will reach another fork. Take the left-hand path once again. Follow the trail as it gradually makes its way downhill. After a further 15–20 minutes, you will come across a viewpoint on the right where you can see the small coastal settlement of Mt Pleasant as well as Petite Martinique out to sea.

Continue down the trail and take a left at the next fork. After that it curves to the left where the views really open up. At the next fork, take the track to the right. You should find yourself walking around the broken walls that once formed the perimeter of the Great House of the 140ha Limlair Estate. Continue walking around until the sea is right in front of you and a path to your left goes up above the ruined walls into the remains of the house itself. Beautiful, large agave plants border the track. Take time to explore the remains of the house that was once the residence of the Munroe family. You will see the house foundations and the shell of the old water cistern.

Continue down the main trail for five minutes or so until you reach a T-junction with a wide vehicle track. Go right at this junction and follow the track down towards the sea. After five minutes or so you will see another, smaller stone windmill tower on your left. The road comes to an open grassy area. Go straight on and follow the somewhat overgrown path downwards. You will reach some farm buildings on your left. Follow the track to the right for another ten minutes or so until you reach the main coastal road.

Turn right when you reach the road and follow it for a short distance. On your left you will see a cemetery that is slowly slipping into the sea. This is Tibeau Cemetery and you will see that some gravestones are right on the beach and are already awash with waves. Located at the southern end of this cemetery is the broken mausoleum of Limlair Estate owner Hugh Monroe and his infant son. The mausoleum dates back to the 1770s.

Continue along the road south of the cemetery for five minutes or so until you reach an opening on the left that goes to the sea, near an old stone bridge. On the bridge there are some markings, including an arrow pointing into the woods. Look to the left of the bridge and you should see a somewhat hidden track running into the trees. Follow it for a short distance, stooping under low branches, until you come upon the very impressive Ningo Well.

Finish up with a 20-minute stroll along the rough coastal road into the settlement of Mt Pleasant for some refreshments at the **Crab Island Wonder** snackette and bar. From Mt Pleasant, you can catch a bus into Hillsborough.

## Hike to southwest point (La Pointe) from Tyrell Bay (Duration: 1½hrs each way; grade 1; guide: not required; site fee: none) This hike starts in Tyrell Bay and follows the road around to the coastal settlement of Hermitage and then beyond, through several livestock farms and past some ruins to the island's southwesterly extreme. Once there you will discover a sandy and remote shoreline at the western tip of Manchineel Bay as well as a remote and isolated bay that is good for snorkelling. Along the way expect to encounter sheep, cattle and lots of goats.

Starting anywhere along the shoreline of Tyrell Bay, head south, away from the marina construction site and mangrove swamp towards the settlement of Hermitage.

The road narrows as it climbs up through Hermitage and past the Carriacou Yacht Club. There are nice views across the bay from over the rooftops of the dwelling houses perched along the hillside. Keep going until the road becomes a wide vehicle track. After around ten minutes down this track you will reach a fork. The track to the left goes down towards Manchineel Bay. Keep going straight ahead (the right-hand fork) and soon you will have fine views of Manchineel Bay, White Island and Saline Island.

Keep going straight, past cattle pens, roaming sheep and goats. On a rise to your left, near a small pond, you may see the ruins of an old estate house. Further along the track, you will come across a second pond on your right. After around 40 minutes or so from the beginning of your hike, you will reach some farm buildings. The track veers around to the right of the building and passes through a wide gate. Once through the gate, continue onwards and the seashore should be close by on your left. After a further ten minutes or so you will reach a fork. Take the longer track to the left and keep following the shoreline until you reach a concrete building. It should take around an hour to reach this point from Tyrell Bay. To the left of the building is a small beach and the waters of Manchineel Bay with views across to White Island and Saline Island with Little Mushroom Island and Mushroom Island in between. To the right of the building there are two tracks. The left track leads to a secluded bay on the northern edge of Southwest Point. The bay is shingle and black sand, the waters are very clear and snorkelling is good around the rocky coastline. The track on the right runs to a desolate grassy area and a ridge. Walk up to the top of the ridge for fine views south to Grenada. Be careful on this ridge as it is clearly eroding.

Walk back the way you came but once you reach the Lazy Turtle in Hermitage, why not stop for refreshments and then complete your walk to Tyrell Bay along the beach?

## Walk to Paradise Beach from Hillsborough (*Duration: 1½hrs each way; grade 1; guide: not required; site fee: none*) Whether you are in Carriacou just for the day or staying longer, a visit to Paradise Beach in L'Esterre Bay is an absolute must. Certainly one of the prettiest beaches on the island, it is within walking distance of town thanks to a track that follows the beach and then meanders through the mangroves of Lauriston Point. It is an easy walk, along both paved road and beach. Be sure to protect yourself from the sun, bring plenty of water and of course swimming gear.

From Main Street in Hillsborough simply walk in a westerly direction out of town (if you are standing outside the exit to the jetty, turn right). Once past the St Patrick Roman Catholic Church and the Carriacou Health Centre, continue along the road. The road is long and straight and follows the sandy beach along the pretty Hillsborough Bay. After around 20 minutes, the road veers to the left. Leave it at this point and walk along the beach.

Follow the beach around the edge of the mangroves, getting your feet a little wet around some of them, until you can quite simply go no further. At this point, a track through the mangroves will open up in front of you. The track is very obvious so if you can't see it you probably haven't walked far enough yet.

Follow the trail as it winds through the coastal mangrove forest around Lauriston Point. Some parts of the trail require you to stoop low beneath branches so watch your head. The trail emerges briefly at a small beach on the tip of the point before re-entering the mangroves again. Keep following it over a dry creek and alongside some brackish water until you finally emerge at the eastern end of L'Esterre Bay. The beautiful Paradise Beach is right in front of you.

## A coastal hike to the Dumfries ruins from Belmont/Tyrell Bay (*Duration: 1½–2hrs each way; grade 2; guide: not required; site fee: none*) This is a hike along the rugged southeast coast of Carriacou to the site of a ruined estate at Dumfries that once processed cotton and lime. The walk begins along a paved road and then heads down across heathland towards the rocky coast. It follows four beaches with a little scrambling over coastal rock formations. The views of Black Bay and along the coastline are quite beautiful and the ruin itself very interesting.

If you are starting from Tyrell Bay, you need to walk to Belmont, which will add an extra 30 minutes to the hike. At the centre of Tyrell Bay, follow the paved road that joins with the coastal road near Scraper's and which passes both the Roman Catholic and Anglican churches on its way inland through Harvey Vale. At the end of this road, turn right at the junction and just keep going. You should reach the Belmont Postal Station and a junction with a number of snackettes after about half an hour or so.

From the Belmont Postal Station, walk through the village, along the paved main road. There are great views to the right across Manchineel Bay to White

Island and Saline Island. Further to the south, you should see the Grenada Grenadines and Grenada itself on the horizon.

The road runs straight for some distance, passing a few snackettes before curving to the left past a house and a large white wall. Keep going straight until you reach the next curve. Right on the apex of the bend, next to a wire fence, is a wide vehicle track heading across the grassland towards the sea. Follow this track. The ground is rutted and a little difficult to walk along, but keep going down towards a small black-sand beach. This is the first of four beaches on this hike.

With the sea to your right all the way, walk along this beach to the end and climb up over the formation. Take your time as this short climb is a little steep. At the top you will cross lots of small rocks as you make your way to the next beach. Follow this beach and at the end climb up over the outcrop to the much larger third beach. On this beach you will pass a dry river mouth. Take care not to walk towards this river mouth as a thin crust disguises a very soft, swampy area that may give you a distinct sinking feeling if you get too close. Keep walking along the water's edge until you come to the end of this beach. It is a steep climb up to the next formation. You may find it easier to pass near some of the bushes on the left. Walk up onto the coastal rock formation with its curious landscape of isolated, sharp volcanic rocks that have been exposed over time as the elements have worn away the sand surrounding them. Pass through the rocks and over this formation to the final, fourth beach.

At the centre of this fourth beach you will see a vehicle track that is used by sand miners. Follow the track inland through a graveyard and past a watering hole for donkeys and other animals. The path curves to the right for a short distance. On your left is a wire fence and you should soon come to an opening. This is the entrance to the historic Dumfries site. Walk through the trees along the path until you come to the ruins and the tall brick chimney. You will see lots of machine works lying around as well as several within the main building itself. Unfortunately, lime processing ended here some time ago and the factory, along with a local community of workers, was consigned to the history books.

Though it is possible to continue on along the vehicle track past the Dumfries site, it is not a pleasant walk as it passes a landfill site further on. It is better to turn back and enjoy the walk along the coast once more.

## Hike to Point Cistern and secluded beaches from L'Esterre/Paradise Beach

(*Duration: 1½hrs each way; grade 2; guide: not required; site fee: none*) This is a relatively easy hike with just a couple of steep hills. It takes you from L'Esterre, or Paradise Beach, all the way around to Cistern Point where there are two fabulous secluded beaches and great views across Hillsborough Bay.

If you are starting from Paradise Beach, walk along the beach until you pass Banana Joe's and Paradise Inn, and arrive at Off the Hook beach bar and grill. To the left of this bar is a vehicle track; follow it for about five minutes to a fork, then turn right. In another five to ten minutes you will reach the main road in L'Esterre opposite a large sign for the Paradise Inn. Turn right and walk along the road for a further five to ten minutes until you reach the junction at L'Esterre Cross. Once there, take the road on the right that goes uphill into the village. Just follow the wonderful smells coming from Henrietta's Bakery. You will pass a couple of snackettes and after ten to 15 minutes the road will curve around to the left. On this bend there is a paved road going downhill and a vehicle track running up alongside a small building with a sign saying Zion Cottage. The track next to the building is the one you must take.

Follow this track as it winds up to the top of the hill. It can be muddy and a little uneven and slippery underfoot so take care. At the top of the hill you will have nice views of Hillsborough Bay, Mabouya Island and Sandy Island, with St Vincent's

Union Island in the distance. Continue past the Seaclusion Suites, always keeping to the main trail. You will come to the crest of a hill and see that the grassy track runs quite steeply downhill towards the point. Once at the bottom you reach a small wooded area. Make your way to the left towards the visible shoreline and continue walking towards the point. You will pick up a narrow path through the grass that heads to the right, around the headland. Follow it until you come to a long, narrow stretch of beach. Look to your right and see how far it stretches. Behind the beach, the track continues towards Cistern Point. Follow it through the trees until you reach a second beach, on the south side of the point. This beach is not as long but it is very pretty, running in a small crescent around a secluded cove. Both bathing and snorkelling are good here.

## PETITE MARTINIQUE

Petite Martinique is a very small, yet pretty island of rugged coastlines, a single peak, sleepy communities, fishermen and boatbuilders. It feels away from it all, a place where life has slowed down and day-to-day living is hard work, but uncomplicated. People just get on with it, plying their handcrafted wooden boats between the islands of the Grenadines, making a living however they can. Visitors to Petite Martinique will discover lovely people and lots of peace and quiet.

### GETTING THERE AND AWAY

**By ferry** Osprey Lines (*www.ospreylines.com*) operates a high-speed ferry service between Carriacou and Petite Martinique. It leaves Carriacou's Hillsborough jetty at 10.30 Monday–Saturday and at 09.30 Sunday. There is also a late ferry leaving at 19.00 Monday–Thursday. The journey to Petite Martinique takes about 30 minutes.

From Petite Martinique the ferry leaves from the jetties at Sanchez to Hillsborough, Carriacou at 05.30 Tuesday–Friday, and also at 15.00 daily. From Carriacou, you can continue on to St George's, Grenada at 06.00 Monday–Saturday, and at 15.30 daily.

Fares between Carriacou and Petite Martinique are: EC$60 or US$24 adult return and EC$30 or US$12 for an adult one-way ticket; EC$30 or US$12 return, and EC$15 or US$6 for a one-way ticket for children between five and 12 years of age; EC$10 or US$4 return and EC$5 or US$2 for a one-way ticket for children under five years of age. The ferry does not usually operate on Christmas Day, Boxing Day, New Year's Day or Good Friday.

**By water taxi** An alternative means of transportation between Carriacou and Petite Martinique is by water taxi. You could ask local boat owners on the coast in Dover, Windward and Sanchez for prices.

### 🏠 WHERE TO STAY

🏠 **Melodies Guest House** (10 rooms) Paradise, Petite Martinique; ✆ 473 443 9052; e melodies@caribsurf.com; www.spiceisle.com/melodies. Located on the shoreline, just a few mins from the jetty, basic but clean upper-floor rooms with private bathroom, 4 with veranda & sea view. Ground-floor restaurant & bar (see *Where to eat and drink*, below). ⑤

### ✖ WHERE TO EAT AND DRINK

Petite Martinique's eateries are open Monday–Saturday and offer a good selection of dishes.

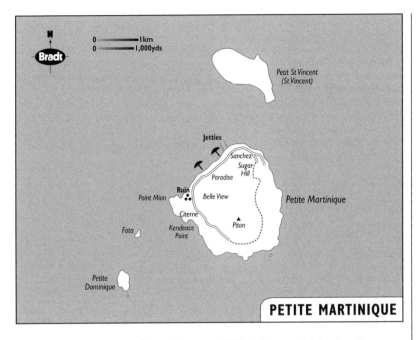

✕ **Palm Beach Restaurant** Paradise; ☎ 473 443 9103. Bar & restaurant next to the beach serving local & international dishes. A great place to hang out while you are waiting for the Osprey. $–$$

✕ **Melodies Restaurant** Melodies Guest House; ☎ 473 443 9052. Located on the beach near to the jetty serving local & international dishes. $

**EXPLORING PETITE MARTINIQUE** When you step off the Osprey ferry you will be on the boat jetty in an area called **Sanchez**. Along the shoreline to your left you will probably see a boat or two in the process of being built, and perhaps the boatbuilders are there working on it, hammering, sawing, measuring or just generally discussing progress on the vessel. It is a poignant and very appropriate introduction to Petite Martinique. Things are a little different here and they tend to revolve around boats.

As you walk off the jetty and down the road you will come to a junction. Welcome to the only main road on the island. To your right is the Thomas Aquinas Roman Catholic School and to your left the Petite Martinique Post Office. Turn right and walk along the main road. You will pass small businesses such as the Mathews shopping centre and the Millennium Connection internet café. On your right-hand side is the **Palm Beach Restaurant & Bar** and, a little further down, **Melodies Guest House Restaurant & Bar**. Along the shoreline of Sanchez there is a narrow strip of white-sand beach where you will see colourful fishing boats resting between trips.

The noise you cannot hear is traffic. As you would expect from an island with a single main road there are not many vehicles. People tend to walk a lot or travel by boat. Some of the young guys like to get about on all-terrain vehicles (ATVs) and you may even see an electric golf cart or two.

At a junction, a narrow road heads uphill on the left to the residential community of **Belle View**. At this junction there are some more small shops, the Petite Martinique Police Station and a couple of snackettes including the **Angel Bar**. Carrying on from the junction you arrive at an area called **Moulin Vent**.

9

Appropriately enough, you should spot the ruins of a windmill tower on the right, perched on the cliff top, overlooking the sea. After Moulin Vent you follow the road as it passes above Mang Bay. To your left is coastal woodland and to your right is the grassy headland of Point Mion with its isolated wooden board houses. Next you come to the community of **Citern** where you will see small plots of pigeon peas growing on the left and a vehicle track heading down to Kendeace Point on your right. The road is now heading in a more southerly direction and you are arriving at the windward coast of this small island. Just offshore is the rugged islet of Petite Dominique and, just in front of it to the right, the smaller rocky pinnacle of Fota. Waves from the Atlantic crash against these islets as well as the increasingly exposed southern coastline of Petite Martinique.

Just beyond Citern the paved road comes to an end and is replaced by a vehicle track. Following this track takes you further around the south and east, circling the conical peak of **Piton** and finally emerging at the elevated northern community of **Sugar Hill** (see below for more information on walking this trail).

Back at Sanchez, to the left of the jetty the paved road is much shorter. Opposite the post office there is a junction with a road heading up to the community of Sugar Hill. The houses in Sugar Hill have super views of Carriacou, Petit St Vincent and the Grenadines. Also at this junction is the **Petite Martinique Roman Catholic Church**. There is a small desalination plant and then nothing but cliff and sea for a stretch before you reach the northern shore and arrive at a residential community where the road comes to an end.

**What to do** There is very little to do on Petite Martinique besides taking a stroll, finding a nice place to eat or drink, or watching the boatbuilders at work on the shore of Sanchez. Local fishermen will offer to take you for a boat ride if you ask them, but the real attraction of Petite Martinique is the simplicity of the island, and the feeling of escape you get when you are there.

**Hike all the way around Petite Martinique** (*Duration: 2hrs; grade 3; guide: not required; site fee: none*) This is a really nice circular hike all the way around the island of Petite Martinique, starting at the jetty where the Osprey high-speed ferry service arrives and departs. The first half of the hike is along a paved road through small communities, the second a more difficult ramble along rough vehicle tracks and narrow coastal trails which are steep in places. Plan conservatively for the hike to take at least two hours so that you arrive back in plenty of time for the departing Osprey ferry if you are just visiting for the day. Also take plenty of water and sun protection along as this island is very exposed and there is very little opportunity for shade along the way.

If you are arriving on the jetty, keep walking straight until you come to the paved road. Turn right and walk past the Thomas Aquinas Roman Catholic School. You will be walking around the island in a counter-clockwise direction.

Keep walking along the paved road, past the communities and landmarks described above. Eventually, once you have passed Citern and Kendeace Point, the paved road comes to an end and a rough but wide vehicle track continues upwards and around the coast. It should have taken you around 30–45 minutes to reach this point from the jetty in Sanchez.

The track is very rocky and quite steep for the first ten minutes or so. Be careful with your footing as a twisted ankle here is not good news. Once at the top of the hill the path becomes a little easier, transitioning from rocks to grass. There are great views of the Atlantic Ocean and the coastal cliffs below.

After another ten–15 minutes the path reaches a wide, expansive clearing where it seems to disappear altogether. You may be welcomed by sheep, goats or cattle when you arrive here. Hugging the trees to your left, walk across the clearing. Open grassland and a ridge are to your right, scrubland trees and the summit of Petite Martinique's Piton immediately to your left. At the end of the clearing you should see a narrow path through the low trees. Follow it to a second clearing, this one much smaller. The narrow trail continues at the end of this clearing and runs steeply uphill to the left. Take your time climbing as the ground may be crumbly and loose under your feet, especially in the dry season. After around five more minutes you will come to a fork. Take the trail on the right and follow it around the ridge of a hill. Take care here as the grass can be slippery underfoot and the path is very narrow. Carefully cross over a small rocky slope and pick up the trail again directly opposite. Follow it uphill until you reach a wire fence. Look to your left and you should see civilisation again. Phew!

Follow the trail downhill alongside the fence and then over a series of tall steps made of volcanic rock. This path is steep so take your time and be careful with your footing. After five to ten minutes you will reach a second fork. Take the path to the left this time and follow it up the side of a hill behind some dwelling houses. You should have great views of Petit St Vincent from here. You soon arrive at the junction with a wide vehicle track. Head left up to the top of the ridge on the left-hand side of a concrete house. Look down and you will see houses, the coastline and the jetty where you started. Follow the vehicle track as it winds its way downhill and then becomes a concrete road. Continue down this road and you will come to the residential area of Sugar Hill and then the Petite Martinique Roman Catholic Church. At the foot of this hill you will emerge on the main coastal road again in the area of Sanchez. The Petite Martinique Post Office is on the corner opposite you. Head left towards the jetty and then follow the signs to the Palm Beach Restaurant & Bar, which is a great place to catch your breath and treat yourself to a well-earned drink whilst you wait for the boat back to Carriacou or the main island of Grenada.

# A VIEW WITH A ROOM...

## LAZY LUXURY & SOULFUL RELAXATION

MACA BANA | ABOVE THE AQUARIUM RESTAURANT
MAGAZINE BEACH | POINT SALINES | GRENADA | W.I.
MACABANA@SPICEISLE.COM | WWW.MACABANA.COM
P +1 473 439 5355 | F +1 473 439 6429

# Appendix I

## ACCOMMODATION AT A GLANCE

Here is an alphabetical reference list of accommodation included in this book. The price code is meant as a basic guide only and you should always check before you book. Also check whether prices quoted to you include taxes and service charges.

**ACCOMMODATION PRICE CODES** Accommodation codes used in this guide are based on the price of a double room for two people per night in the high season (usually November through to April). The symbols and price ranges used are as follows:

| $$$$$ | US$350+ |
| $$$$ | US$250–350 |
| $$$ | US$150–250 |
| $$ | US$100–150 |
| $ | <US$100 |

**ACCOMMODATION TYPE CODE** In the following list, accommodation types are also referred to by a simple code:

| Hotel | H |
| Hotel and self-catering | H/SC |
| Self-catering | SC |

### GRENADA

| Accommodation name | Location | Type | Price code | Page |
|---|---|---|---|---|
| Allamanda Beach Resort | Grand Anse | H | $$$ | 114 |
| Almost Paradise | Mt Alexander, Sauteurs | SC | $-$$ | 170 |
| Barry's Country Retreat | Castle Hill, Sauteurs | H | $ | 170 |
| Beach Inn | Grand Anse | H | $ | 114 |
| Bel Air Plantation | St David's Point | SC | $$$$ | 153 |
| Best Western – South City Plaza Hotel | Grand Anse | H | $$$ | 114 |
| Big Sky Lodge | Crochu | SC | $ | 153 |
| Blue Bay Lodge | Gouyave | H | $-$$ | 130 |
| Blue Horizons Garden Resort | Grand Anse | SC | $$$ | 116 |
| Blue Orchid Hotel | Grand Anse | H | $ | 114 |
| Bougainvillea Apartments | Grand Anse | SC | $ | 117 |
| Cabier Ocean Lodge | Crochu | H | $$ | 153 |
| Calabash Hotel & Villas | L'Anse Aux Épines | H/SC | $$$$$ | 112 |
| Candle Glow Apartments | L'Anse Aux Épines | SC | $ | 117 |

AI

| Accommodation name | Location | Type | Price code | Page |
|---|---|---|---|---|
| Caribbean Breeze | Grand Anse | SC | $$$ | 115 |
| Caribbean Cottage Club | Grand Anse | SC | $ | 117 |
| Coral Cove Cottages & Apartments | L'Anse Aux Épines | SC | $$ | 116 |
| Coyaba Beach Resort | Grand Anse | H | $$$$ | 113 |
| Deyna's City Inn | St George's | H | $$ | 96 |
| Epping Forest | St Paul's | H | $ | 153 |
| Flamboyant Hotel & Villas | Grand Anse | H/SC | $$$ | 114 |
| Gardenia Cottage | L'Anse Aux Épines | SC | $$$$ | 115 |
| GEM Holiday Beach Resort | Morne Rouge | SC | $$ | 116 |
| Grand Anse Heights | Grand Anse | SC | $ | 116 |
| Grenada Grand Beach Resort | Grand Anse | H | $$$-$$$$ | 113 |
| Grenada Gold Guest Apartments | Westerhall | SC | $ | 154 |
| Grenada Grand View Inn | Grand Anse | H/SC | $$ | 114 |
| Grenada Point Salines Hotel | Point Salines | H | $$ | 114 |
| Grenada Rainbow Inn | Grand Bras, Grenville | H | $ | 153 |
| Grenadian (Rex Resorts) | Magazine Beach | H | On request | 113 |
| Hideaway Apartments | Grand Anse | SC | $ | 117 |
| Ixora Villa | L'Anse Aux Épines | SC | $$$$$ | 115 |
| Jenny's Place | Grand Anse | SC | $$$ | 116 |
| Laluna | Morne Rouge | H | $$$$$ | 113 |
| Lance Aux Épines House | L'Anse Aux Épines | SC | $$$$$ | 115 |
| L'Anse Aux Épines Cottages | L'Anse Aux Épines | SC | $$$ | 116 |
| La Sagesse Nature Centre | La Sagesse Beach | H | $$$ | 152 |
| La Source | Pink Gin Beach | H | $$$$$ | 113 |
| Lazy Lagoon | St George's | SC | $ | 96 |
| Lexus Inn | Belmont, St George's | SC | $ | 96 |
| Maca Bana Villas | Magazine Beach | SC | $$$$$ | 115 |
| Maitland's Apartment | Grand Anse | SC | $ | 117 |
| Mangi House | Crochu | SC | $$ | 153 |
| Mango Bay Cottages | Woodford Estate | SC | $$ | 130 |
| Mi Hacienda Boutique Hotel | Belmont, St George's | H/SC | $$$ | 96 |
| Mind & Body Apartments | St George's | SC | $ | 96 |
| Monmot Hotel | L'Anse Aux Épines | H/SC | $$ | 114 |
| Môr Gân Villa | L'Anse Aux Épines | SC | $$$$$ | 115 |
| Morne Fendue Plantation House | Morne Fendue | H | $ | 170 |
| Mount Cinnamon | Grand Anse | H/SC | $$$$$ | 113 |
| Mount Hartman Bay Estate | L'Anse Aux Épines | SC | $$$$$ | 115 |
| Owl Cottage | L'Anse Aux Épines | SC | $$$$$ | 115 |
| Palm Court Apartments | Grand Anse | SC | $ | 116 |
| Paradise Bay Beach Resort & Spa | La Tante | H | On request | 152 |
| Pelican Apartments | Belmont, St George's | SC | $$ | 96 |
| Petit Bacaye Villa Hotel & Restaurant | Petit Bacaye | SC | $$ | 153 |
| Recoben Apartments | Morne Toute | SC | $$$ | 116 |
| Reef View Pavilion Villas | L'Anse Aux Épines | SC | $$$$$ | 115 |
| Roydon's Apartments | Grand Anse | SC | $ | 117 |
| Sam's Inn | Dunfermline, Grenville | H/SC | $ | 153 |

| | | | | |
|---|---|---|---|---|
| Seaview Apartments & Wellness Centre | Grand Anse | SC | $ | 116 |
| Siesta Hotel | Grand Anse | H | $$ | 114 |
| South Winds Holiday Cottages | Grand Anse | SC | $ | 117 |
| Spice Island Beach Resort | Grand Anse | H | $$$$$ | 112 |
| Spicetree Suites | L'Anse Aux Épines | SC | $$ | 116 |
| St Ann's Guest House | St George's | H | $ | 96 |
| Sunset Apartment | Fort Jeudy | SC | On request | 116 |
| Sunset View Restaurant & Beach House | Grand Mal | H | $ | 130 |
| Swallow Villa | Grand Anse | SC | $$$$$ | 115 |
| The Lodge | Richmond Hill, St George's | H | $$$ | 96 |
| Town & Country Guest House | Belmont, St George's | H | $ | 96 |
| Tropicana Inn | St George's | H | $ | 96 |
| True Blue Bay Resort | True Blue | H/SC | $$$-$$$$ | 113 |
| Twelve Degrees North | L'Anse Aux Épines | SC | $$$ | 116 |
| Victoria Hotel | Victoria | H | $ | 170 |
| Villa Amarillo | True Blue | SC | $$$$$ | 115 |
| Villa Caribella | Westerhall | SC | $$$$$ | 153 |
| Villa Heron's Flight | Westerhall | SC | $$$$ | 153 |
| Wave Crest Holiday Apartments | Grand Anse | SC | $ | 117 |
| Willie's Court Apartments | Gouyave | SC | $ | 131 |
| Windward Sands Inn | Grand Anse | H/SC | $ | 114 |

## CARRIACOU AND PETITE MARTINIQUE

| Accommodation name | Location | Type | Price code | Page |
|---|---|---|---|---|
| Ade's Dream Apartment Hotel | Hillsborough | H/SC | $ | 198 |
| Bayaleau Point Cottages | Windward | SC | $-$$ | 199 |
| Belair Garden Cottage | Belair | SC | $$ | 199 |
| Bogles Round House | Bogles | SC | $ | 199 |
| Caribbee Country House | Prospect | SC | On request | 198 |
| Carriacou Grand View Hotel | Beauséjour | H/SC | $-$$ | 198 |
| Driftwood | Craigston | SC | $$$ | 198 |
| Goyaba | Craigston | SC | $$$ | 198 |
| Green Roof Inn | Beauséjour | H/SC | $-$$ | 198 |
| Hope's Inn | L'Esterre | SC | $ | 199 |
| Hotel Laurena | Hillsborough | H/SC | $-$$ | 198 |
| John's Unique Resort | Hillsborough | H/SC | $$-$$$ | 198 |
| KIDO Ecological Research Station | Prospect | SC | $$ | 199 |
| Melodies Guest House | Petite Martinique | H | $ | 215 |
| Millie's Guest House | Hillsborough | SC | $-$$ | 198 |
| Palm Trees | Craigston | SC | $ | 199 |
| Peacehaven Apartments | Hillsborough | SC | $ | 199 |
| Plantain Dove | L'Esterre | SC | On request | 199 |
| Scraper's Bayview Cottages | Tyrell Bay | SC | $ | 199 |
| Seaclusion Suites | St Louis, L'Esterre | SC | $$ | 199 |
| Tamarind Cottage | Belair | SC | $$$ | 198 |
| Villa Sankofa | Craigston | SC | $$$$$ | 198 |
| Yellow Bird | Craigston | SC | $$$ | 198 |

# Appendix 2

## WALKS AND HIKES

This is a quick reference list of all the walks and hikes described in this book. Duration and grade are meant as general guides only and are a reflection of the author's personal experience of the hikes. Though you may decide you do not need a guide to show you the way on many of these walks and hikes, please remember that a good guide will always enhance your walking experience with local knowledge, history, or information about the flora and fauna you may encounter along the way. They will also offer a level of reassurance if you are nervous or not completely sure of the route, and you will be providing income to local people and by extension their communities by employing them. If you would like more information about guides and hiking operators see *Walking and hiking* in *Chapter 3*, page 79, or contact the Grenada Board of Tourism (☎ +1 473 440 2279/2001).

### DIFFICULTY

Grade 1 easy
Grade 2 easy/medium
Grade 3 medium

Grade 4 medium/difficult
Grade 5 difficult

### GRENADA

| Walk or hike description | Duration | Grade | Guide | Page |
|---|---|---|---|---|
| A circular hike through the Mount Hartman National Park | 2–2½hrs total | 2 | Not required | 126 |
| A leisurely walk through L'Anse Aux Épines to Prickly Point | 1½–2hrs there & back | 1 | Not required | 126 |
| A self-guided tour of St George's | 2–3hrs total | 1 | Not required | 106 |
| A stroll along Grand Anse Beach | 1hr each way | 1 | Not required | 125 |
| Hike around the Grand Étang Lake | 1–1½hrs total | 2 | Not required | 143 |
| Hike around the margins of Lake Antoine | 1½hrs there & back | 1 | Not required | 187 |
| Hike from Duquesne to Sauteurs via Mt Alexander | 2½hrs total | 1 | Not required | 185 |
| Hike from Sauteurs to Levera Beach and Bedford Point | 3hrs there & back | 1 | Not required | 185 |
| Hike to Au Coin Waterfall (2nd Concord) from 1st fall | 1½hrs there & back | 2 | Not required | 146 |

| | | | | |
|---|---|---|---|---|
| Hike to Belle Isle Beach at Le Petit Trou Bay | 3hrs there & back | 1 | Not required | 166 |
| Hike to Black Bay and Trou Mais | 1½hrs there & back | 1 | Recommended | 149 |
| Hike to Cabier Beach from Crochu | 3hrs there & back | 1 | Not required | 167 |
| Hike to Fédon's Camp from Belvidere | 6–7hrs there & back | 5 | Essential | 145 |
| Hike to Fontainbleu Waterfall (3rd Concord) from 1st fall | 1½hrs there & back | 3 | Recommended | 147 |
| Hike to Hope Beach at Great Bacolet Bay | 1hr there & back | 1 | Not required | 165 |
| Hike to La Tante Beach | 2hrs there & back | 1 | Not required | 166 |
| Hike to Mount Pleasant Estate from Gouyave | 3–4hrs there & back | 2 | Not required | 148 |
| Hike to Palmiste Lake | 1½hrs there & back | 2 | Not required | 148 |
| Hike to St David's Point and the Megrin Standing Stone | 3½–4hrs there & back | 1 | Not required | 167 |
| Hike to the Concord Waterfall from the west coast road | 1hr each way | 1 | Not required | 146 |
| Hike to the Honeymoon Waterfall from St Margaret's Falls | 45mins there & back | 3 | Recommended | 164 |
| Hike to the Mt Carmel (Marquis) Waterfall | 1hr there & back | 2 | Not required | 163 |
| Hike to the Paraclete Waterfalls | 2–3hrs there & back | 4 | Essential | 187 |
| Hike to the Point of Fort Jeudy | 2½–3hrs there & back | 2 | Not required | 127 |
| Hike to the St Margaret's Falls (Seven Sisters) | 1½–2hrs there & back | 2 | Recommended | 163 |
| Hike to the summit of Morne Gazo from Corbeau | 1½hrs there & back | 3 | Not required | 165 |
| Hike to the summit of Mt St Catherine | 4–5hrs there & back | 4 | Essential | 186 |
| Hike to the summit of Mt Qua Qua | 3–4hrs there & back | 4 | Recommended | 144 |
| Hike upriver to Tufton Hall Waterfall | 3–3½hrs there & back | 4 | Recommended | 184 |

## CARRIACOU AND PETITE MARTINIQUE

| Walk or hike description | Duration | Grade | Guide | Page |
|---|---|---|---|---|
| A coastal walk to Paradise Beach from Hillsborough | 2½–3hrs there & back | 1 | Not required | 212 |
| Hike all the way around Petite Martinique | 2–2½hrs total | 3 | Not required | 216 |
| Hike along the coast from Belmont to the Dumfries ruins | 3½–4hrs there & back | 2 | Not required | 212 |
| Hike to Anse La Roche Beach from Bogles | 1½hrs one-way | 3 | Not required | 208 |
| Hike to Ningo Well from Belair | 1½hrs one-way | 2 | Not required | 210 |

| Walk or hike description | Duration | Grade | Guide | Page |
|---|---|---|---|---|
| Hike to Petit Carenage from Anse a Roche | 45mins one-way | 1 | Not required | 209 |
| Hike to Point Cistern and secluded beaches from L'Esterre | 3hrs there & back | 2 | Not required | 213 |
| Hike to Southwest Point (La Pointe) from Tyrell Bay | 3hrs there & back | 1 | Not required | 211 |

# Appendix 3

## FURTHER INFORMATION

### BOOKS
### Reference

Adkin, Mark *Urgent Fury: The Battle for Grenada* Lexington Books, 1989. ISBN 978-0669207170

Andrews, Alexis *Genesis: Building a Traditional Carriacou Sloop* Indian Creek Books, 2008. ISBN 978-0979011429

Anim-Addo, Joan *Framing the Word* Whiting & Birch, 1996. ISBN 978-1871177916

Anim-Addo, Joan *Touching the Body* Mango Publishing, 2007. ISBN 978-1902294230

Brathwaite, Roger *Grenada: Spice Paradise* Macmillan Caribbean, 2002. ISBN 978-0333801031

Brizan, George *Grenada: Island of Conflict* Macmillan Education, 1998. ISBN 0-333-71023-1

David, Christine *Folklore of Carriacou* Coles Printery, 1985. Privately published.

Douglas, Claude J *The Battle for Grenada's Black Gold* Maryzoon Press, 2004. ISBN 976-8193-39-5

Douglas, Claude J *When the Village was an Extended Family in Grenada* Maryzoon Press, 2003. ISBN 976-8173-48-3

Groome, J R *A Natural History of the Island of Grenada* Caribbean Printers, 1970. Privately published.

Hawthorne, William D *Caribbean Spice Island Plants: Trees, Shrubs and Climbers of Grenada, Carriacou and Petit Martinique: A Picture Gallery with Notes on Identification, Historical and Other Trivia* Oxford Forestry Institute, 2004. ISBN 978-0850741629

Kilgore, Cindy and Moore, Alan *Adventure Guide to Grenada, St Vincent & the Grenadines* Hunter Publishing, 2007. ISBN 978-1588436245

Martin, John Angus *A–Z of Grenada Heritage* Macmillan Caribbean, 2007. ISBN 978-0333792520

McIntosh, Simeon C R *Kelsen in the Grenada Court* Ian Randle Publishers, 2008. ISBN 978-9768167477

Sandford, Gregory and Vigilante, Richard *Grenada: The Untold Story* Madison Books, 1984. ISBN 978-0819143105

Sinclair, Norma *Grenada: Isle of Spice* Macmillan Caribbean, 2002. ISBN 978-0333968062

Steele, Beverley A *Grenada: A History of its People* Macmillan Caribbean, 2002. ISBN 978-0333930533

Wilkinson, Wendy and Lee, Donna *Morgan Freeman and Friends: Caribbean Cooking for a Cause* Rodale Books, 2006. ISBN 978-1594864247

### Fiction

Anim-Addo, Joan *Haunted by History* Mango Publishing, 2004. ISBN 978-1902294032

Buffong, Jean *Snowflakes in the Sun* The Women's Press, 1995. ISBN 978-0704344235

Buffong, Jean *Under the Silk Cotton Tree* The Women's Press, 1992. ISBN 978-0704343177

Buffong, Jean and Payne, Nellie *Jump-Up-And-Kiss-Me* The Women's Press, 1990. ISBN 978-0704342439

Collins, Merle *Angel* The Women's Press Ltd, 1987. ISBN 978-0704340824

Collins, Merle *Because the Dawn Breaks* Karia Press, 1985. ISBN 978-0946918096

Collins, Merle *Lady in a Boat* Peepal Tree Press, 2003. ISBN 978-1900715850

Collins, Merle *Rain Darling* The Women's Press, 1990. ISBN 978-0704342583

Collins, Merle *The Colour of Forgetting* Virago Press,1995. ISBN 978-1853818929

Ross, Jacob *A Way to Catch the Dust* Mango Publishing, 1999. ISBN 978-1902294087

Ross, Jacob *Song for Simone* Mango Publishing, 2004. ISBN 978-1902294063

Wilkins, Verna Allette *Kim's Magic Tree* Tandem Library, 1993. ISBN 978-0613800228

Wilkins, Verna Allette *Toyin Fay* Gareth Stevens Publishing, 1998. ISBN 978-0836820911

## WEBSITES

**www.barnaclegrenada.com** Online newspaper, reviews and commentary

**www.carriacoupetitemartinique.com** General information on Carriacou and Petite Martinique with listings

**www.gogouyave.com** Website dedicated to Gouyave

**www.grenadabroadcast.com** Streaming news, headlines, interviews and editorials

**www.grenadaexplorer.com** General information about Grenada with listings and tips

**www.grenadagrenadines.com** The official site of the Grenada Board of Tourism

**www.grenadaguide.com** General business listings

**www.grenadahotelsinfo.com** Official website of the Grenada Hotel & Tourism Association

**www.grenadavisitorforum.com** Conversations, news, stories and photos about Grenada

**www.thegrenadarevolutiononline.com** Website dedicated to the events of 1983

**www.travelgrenada.com** General information about Grenada with listings

# Index

Page numbers in **bold** indicate major entries; those in *italics* indicate maps. Occasionally (C) has been used when it is necessary to indicate where an entry relates to Carriacou rather than Grenada.

# Bradt Travel Guides

## Africa

| | |
|---|---|
| Africa Overland | £15.99 |
| Algeria | £15.99 |
| Benin | £14.99 |
| Botswana: Okavango, Chobe, Northern Kalahari | £15.99 |
| Burkina Faso | £14.99 |
| Cameroon | £15.99 |
| Canary Islands | £13.95 |
| Cape Verde Islands | £13.99 |
| Congo | £15.99 |
| Eritrea | £15.99 |
| Ethiopia | £15.99 |
| Gabon, São Tomé, Príncipe | £13.95 |
| Gambia, The | £13.99 |
| Ghana | £15.99 |
| Johannesburg | £6.99 |
| Kenya | £14.95 |
| Madagascar | £15.99 |
| Malawi | £13.99 |
| Mali | £13.95 |
| Mauritius, Rodrigues & Réunion | £13.99 |
| Mozambique | £13.99 |
| Namibia | £15.99 |
| Niger | £14.99 |
| Nigeria | £17.99 |
| Rwanda | £14.99 |
| São Tomé & Príncipe | £14.99 |
| Seychelles | £14.99 |
| Sudan | £13.95 |
| Tanzania, Northern | £13.99 |
| Tanzania | £16.99 |
| Uganda | £15.99 |
| Zambia | £17.99 |
| Zanzibar | £12.99 |

## Britain and Europe

| | |
|---|---|
| Albania | £15.99 |
| Armenia, Nagorno Karabagh | £14.99 |
| Azores | £13.99 |
| Baltic Capitals: Tallinn, Riga, Vilnius, Kaliningrad | £12.99 |
| Belarus | £14.99 |
| Belgrade | £6.99 |
| Bosnia & Herzegovina | £13.99 |
| Bratislava | £6.99 |
| Budapest | £8.99 |
| Bulgaria | £13.99 |
| Cork | £6.99 |
| Croatia | £13.99 |

| | |
|---|---|
| Cyprus see North Cyprus | |
| Czech Republic | £13.99 |
| Dresden | £7.99 |
| Dubrovnik | £6.99 |
| Estonia | £13.99 |
| Faroe Islands | £15.99 |
| Georgia | £14.99 |
| Helsinki | £7.99 |
| Hungary | £14.99 |
| Iceland | £14.99 |
| Kiev | £7.95 |
| Kosovo | £14.99 |
| Lapland | £13.99 |
| Latvia | £13.99 |
| Lille | £6.99 |
| Lithuania | £14.99 |
| Ljubljana | £7.99 |
| Luxembourg | £13.99 |
| Macedonia | £14.99 |
| Montenegro | £14.99 |
| North Cyprus | £12.99 |
| Paris, Lille & Brussels | £11.95 |
| Riga | £6.95 |
| River Thames, In the Footsteps of the Famous | £10.95 |
| Serbia | £14.99 |
| Slovakia | £14.99 |
| Slovenia | £13.99 |
| Spitsbergen | £15.99 |
| Switzerland: Rail, Road, Lake | £13.99 |
| Tallinn | £6.99 |
| Transylvania | £14.99 |
| Ukraine | £14.99 |
| Vilnius | £6.99 |
| Zagreb | £6.99 |

## Middle East, Asia and Australasia

| | |
|---|---|
| Borneo | £17.99 |
| China: Yunnan Province | £13.99 |
| Great Wall of China | £13.99 |
| Iran | £14.99 |
| Iraq: Then & Now | £15.99 |
| Kazakhstan | £15.99 |
| Kyrgyzstan | £15.99 |
| Maldives | £13.99 |
| Mongolia | £16.99 |
| North Korea | £14.99 |
| Oman | £13.99 |
| Shangri La | £14.99 |
| Sri Lanka | £13.99 |
| Syria | £14.99 |
| Tibet | £13.99 |

| | |
|---|---|
| Turkmenistan | £14.99 |
| Yemen | £14.99 |

## The Americas and the Caribbean

| | |
|---|---|
| Amazon, The | £14.99 |
| Argentina | £15.99 |
| Bolivia | £14.99 |
| Cayman Islands | £14.99 |
| Chile | £16.95 |
| Chile & Argentina: The Bradt Trekking Guide | £12.95 |
| Colombia | £16.99 |
| Costa Rica | £13.99 |
| Dominica | £14.99 |
| Falkland Islands | £13.95 |
| Guyana | £14.99 |
| Panama | £13.95 |
| Peru & Bolivia: Backpacking & Trekking | £12.95 |
| St Helena | £14.99 |
| USA by Rail | £14.99 |

## Wildlife

| | |
|---|---|
| 100 Animals to See Before They Die | £16.99 |
| Antarctica: Guide to the Wildlife | £14.95 |
| Arctic: Guide to the Wildlife | £15.99 |
| Central & Eastern European Wildlife | £15.99 |
| Chinese Wildlife | £16.99 |
| East African Wildlife | £19.99 |
| Galápagos Wildlife | £15.99 |
| Madagascar Wildlife | £15.99 |
| Peruvian Wildlife | £15.99 |
| Southern African Wildlife | £18.95 |
| Sri Lankan Wildlife | £15.99 |

## Eccentric Guides

| | |
|---|---|
| Eccentric Australia | £12.99 |
| Eccentric Britain | £13.99 |
| Eccentric California | £13.99 |
| Eccentric Cambridge | £6.99 |
| Eccentric Edinburgh | £5.95 |
| Eccentric France | £12.95 |
| Eccentric London | £13.99 |
| Eccentric Oxford | £5.95 |

## Others

| | |
|---|---|
| Your Child Abroad: A Travel Health Guide | £10.95 |
| Something Different for the Weekend | £9.99 |